W.H.G. Kingston

Ron Morton or the Fire Ships

A Story of the Last War

W.H.G. Kingston

Ron Morton or the Fire Ships
A Story of the Last War

ISBN/EAN: 9783337249359

Printed in Europe, USA, Canada, Australia, Japan

Cover: Foto ©ninafisch / pixelio.de

More available books at **www.hansebooks.com**

W.H.G. Kingston

Ron Morton or the Fire Ships
A Story of the Last War

ISBN/EAN: 9783337249359

Printed in Europe, USA, Canada, Australia, Japan

Cover: Foto ©ninafisch / pixelio.de

More available books at **www.hansebooks.com**

RONALD MORTON;

OR,

THE FIRE SHIPS:

A STORY OF THE LAST NAVAL WAR.

BY

W. H. G. KINGSTON,

AUTHOR OF "THE CRUISE OF THE FROLIC,' 'THE BRITISH NAVY,"
"MILICENT COURTENAY," ETC.

London:
GALL AND INGLIS, 25 PATERNOSTER SQUARE;
AND EDINBURGH.

PRINTED
AND BOUND BY
GALL AND INGLIS
LUTTON PLACE
EDINBURGH

AUTHOR'S PREFACE.

THE inhabitants of Shetland have a grievance. It is not that they complain of being badly governed, of being over-taxed, or of being poor, or of their climate, or of the shortness of the days in winter; but they say, with justice, that they are shamefully ill-treated by the map-makers, who place their well-loved little group of islands out of the way in some corner of the map, so that not one person in ten of those tolerably well-informed in geographical matters generally, has a correct notion of their bearing from the other portions of the British Isles. Some years ago, however, I made the discovery that they lie due north of Scotland, Orkney intervening; and as I had a desire to pay them a visit, I took ship and reached Lerwick, their capital, in safety. The kindness I there received will never be erased from my memory. I travelled through all parts of the islands, and visited a number of very interesting scenes. Curious tales were also told me of deeds done in bygone days, when the arm of the law was too short to reach ill-doers at a distance from the centre of government, and when might was looked upon as constituting right in those far-off islands.

One of the strange legends which I then heard has served as the basis of the following tale. For years its gossamer threads have been floating before my eyes, though it is only now that I have caught and woven them into a tangible form, and connected them with events belonging to history rather than fiction.

My aim has been to produce in 'Ronald Morton, or the Fire-ships,' a tale of stirring nautical adventure, and at the same time to introduce characters who may add to its interest, and make it a work which will be taken up with pleasure, and not laid down till the end of a winter's evening.

The present new Edition which the public have called for, shows that the interest in the 'Fire Ships' is still undiminished.

BRENTWOOD.

CONTENTS.

CHAPTER I.
THE SPANISH MAN-OF-WAR OFF SHETLAND.—A CALM.—THE 'ST CECILIA' IN DANGER.—THE PILOT.—BRASSAY SOUND, . **9**

CHAPTER II.
LUNNASTING CASTLE.—THE STRANGER SHIP.—SANDY REDLAND, THE FACTOR.—ARCHY EAGLESHAY.—MISS WARDHILL'S VISITORS.—THE DISAPPEARANCE OF THE HEIR, . . . **21**

CHAPTER III.
LAWRENCE BRINDISTER VISITS THE SPANISH SHIP.—DON HERNAN INVITED TO THE CASTLE.—SURLY GRIND, LAWRENCE'S DOG, . **32**

CHAPTER IV.
HILDA'S FIRST MEETING WITH DON HERNAN.—HILDA ON BOARD THE CORVETTE.—ROLF MORTON PILOTS THE SHIP.—CRUISE IN THE 'ST CECILIA.'—HILDA ACCEPTS DON HERNAN, . . **36**

CHAPTER V.
LAWRENCE'S EXPEDITION.—HILDA'S MARRIAGE IN THE OLD CHAPEL.—A STORM, ... **45**

CHAPTER VI.
ROLF MORTON'S HISTORY.—DON HERNAN AND HILDA IN MORTON'S HOUSE.—MORTON DISPATCHED TO THE CORVETTE, . . . **48**

CHAPTER VII.
DON HERNAN AND HILDA AT THE CASTLE.—THE SPANISH OFFICERS ON SHORE.—DON HERNAN ORDERED TO QUIT SHETLAND, . **56**

CHAPTER VIII.
ROLF MORTON'S EXPEDITION.—WATCHES THE CORVETTE.—HILDA'S MARRIAGE DISCUSSED.—THE STORM.—A SHIP SEEN DRIVING TOWARDS SHORE, ... **68**

CHAPTER IX.
NAVIE GRIND DESCRIBED.—THE WRECK ON SHORE.—THE SHIP DASHED TO PIECES.—THE RESCUED, ... **77**

CHAPTER X.
GUESTS AT THE CASTLE.—THE HEIR OF LUNNASTING.—LAWRENCE BRINDISTER'S CAVE, ... **89**

CONTENTS.

CHAPTER XI.
FATHER MENDEZ IN SPAIN.—THE MARQUIS AND HIS OLD SHIPMATES.—CAPTAIN TACON THE EX-PIRATE, ... 103

CHAPTER XII.
A STRANGE SCHOONER APPEARS OFF LUNNASTING.—THE CASTLE ATTACKED.—THE PIRATES ENTER THE CASTLE.—YOUNG HERNAN CARRIED OFF, ... 117

CHAPTER XIII.
ARRIVAL OF SIR MARCUS.—HILDA AND HER SISTER.—A BRIG OF WAR APPEARS.—EDDA'S MARRIAGE.—ROLF MORTON SAILS ON A LONG VOYAGE, ... 131

CHAPTER XIV.
THE FLEET AT SPITHEAD.—ROLF MORTON'S VISIT TO SHETLAND.—ROLF TAKES RONALD TO SEA.—THE 'THISBE' AND FRENCH FRIGATE.—RONALD MORTON'S FIRST BATTLE.—THE ENEMY STRIKES, ... 143

CHAPTER XV.
MORNING AFTER THE BATTLE.—RONALD PLACED ON QUARTER DECK.—RONALD SENT ON BOARD THE PRIZE.—A SUSPICIOUS SAIL IN SIGHT.—GALLANT DEFENCE OF THE 'THISBE.'—NIGHT CLOSES ON THE COMBAT, ... 161

CHAPTER XVI.
THE 'THISBE'S' CREW PREPARE FOR A FRESH FIGHT, . . . 174

CHAPTER XVII.
THE 'CONCORDE' RECAPTURED BY THE 'ATALANTE.'—THE SHIPS IN A GALE.—THE 'ATALANTE' WRECKED.—RONALD SWIMS ASHORE.—COMMUNICATION ESTABLISHED.—THE ENGLISH SHUT UP IN A TOWER. 180

CHAPTER XVIII.
JOB'S PLAN FOR ESCAPING.—A HINT FROM GERARDIN.—A ROPE BROUGHT IN A BASKET.—DESCENT FROM THE TOWER.—THE GUARD MADE PRISONER.—GET ON BOARD A FISHING-BOAT, . 191

CHAPTER XIX.
A SAIL IN SIGHT.—A GALE COMES ON.—REACH THE FRIGATE.—RONALD REJOINS THE 'THISBE.'—MADE LIEUTENANT, . . 204

CHAPTER XX.
RONALD SECOND LIEUTENANT OF THE 'THISBE.'—A BALL AT CALCUTTA.—RONALD'S GALLANTRY.—A CHALLENGE.—HIS REPLY, ... 215

CONTENTS.

CHAPTER I.
THE SPANISH MAN-OF-WAR OFF SHETLAND.—A CALM.—THE 'ST CECILIA' IN DANGER.—THE PILOT.—BRASSAY SOUND, . **9**

CHAPTER II.
LUNNASTING CASTLE.—THE STRANGER SHIP.—SANDY REDLAND, THE FACTOR.—ARCHY EAGLESHAY.—MISS WARDHILL'S VISITORS.—THE DISAPPEARANCE OF THE HEIR, . . . **21**

CHAPTER III.
LAWRENCE BRINDISTER VISITS THE SPANISH SHIP.—DON HERNAN INVITED TO THE CASTLE.—SURLY GRIND, LAWRENCE'S DOG, . **32**

CHAPTER IV.
HILDA'S FIRST MEETING WITH DON HERNAN.—HILDA ON BOARD THE CORVETTE.—ROLF MORTON PILOTS THE SHIP.—CRUISE IN THE 'ST CECILIA.'—HILDA ACCEPTS DON HERNAN, . . **36**

CHAPTER V.
LAWRENCE'S EXPEDITION.—HILDA'S MARRIAGE IN THE OLD CHAPEL.—A STORM, ... **45**

CHAPTER VI.
ROLF MORTON'S HISTORY.—DON HERNAN AND HILDA IN MORTON'S HOUSE.—MORTON DISPATCHED TO THE CORVETTE, . . **48**

CHAPTER VII.
DON HERNAN AND HILDA AT THE CASTLE.—THE SPANISH OFFICERS ON SHORE.—DON HERNAN ORDERED TO QUIT SHETLAND, . **56**

CHAPTER VIII.
ROLF MORTON'S EXPEDITION.—WATCHES THE CORVETTE.—HILDA'S MARRIAGE DISCUSSED.—THE STORM.—A SHIP SEEN DRIVING TOWARDS SHORE, ... **68**

CHAPTER IX.
NAVIE GRIND DESCRIBED.—THE WRECK ON SHORE.—THE SHIP DASHED TO PIECES.—THE RESCUED, ... **77**

CHAPTER X.
GUESTS AT THE CASTLE.—THE HEIR OF LUNNASTING.—LAWRENCE BRINDISTER'S CAVE, ... **89**

CHAPTER XI.

FATHER MENDEZ IN SPAIN.—THE MARQUIS AND HIS OLD SHIP-MATES.—CAPTAIN TACON THE EX-PIRATE, ... 103

CHAPTER XII.

A STRANGE SCHOONER APPEARS OFF LUNNASTING.—THE CASTLE ATTACKED.—THE PIRATES ENTER THE CASTLE.—YOUNG HERNAN CARRIED OFF, ... 117

CHAPTER XIII.

ARRIVAL OF SIR MARCUS.—HILDA AND HER SISTER.—A BRIG OF WAR APPEARS.—EDDA'S MARRIAGE.—ROLF MORTON SAILS ON A LONG VOYAGE, ... 131

CHAPTER XIV.

THE FLEET AT SPITHEAD.—ROLF MORTON'S VISIT TO SHETLAND.—ROLF TAKES RONALD TO SEA.—THE 'THISBE' AND FRENCH FRIGATE.—RONALD MORTON'S FIRST BATTLE.—THE ENEMY STRIKES, ... 143

CHAPTER XV.

MORNING AFTER THE BATTLE.—RONALD PLACED ON QUARTER DECK.—RONALD SENT ON BOARD THE PRIZE.—A SUSPICIOUS SAIL IN SIGHT.—GALLANT DEFENCE OF THE 'THISBE.'—NIGHT CLOSES ON THE COMBAT, ... 161

CHAPTER XVI.

THE 'THISBE'S' CREW PREPARE FOR A FRESH FIGHT, . . . 174

CHAPTER XVII.

THE 'CONCORDE' RECAPTURED BY THE 'ATALANTE.'—THE SHIPS IN A GALE.—THE 'ATALANTE' WRECKED.—RONALD SWIMS ASHORE.—COMMUNICATION ESTABLISHED.—THE ENGLISH SHUT UP IN A TOWER. 180

CHAPTER XVIII.

JOB'S PLAN FOR ESCAPING.—A HINT FROM GERARDIN.—A ROPE BROUGHT IN A BASKET.—DESCENT FROM THE TOWER.—THE GUARD MADE PRISONER.—GET ON BOARD A FISHING-BOAT, . 191

CHAPTER XIX.

A SAIL IN SIGHT.—A GALE COMES ON.—REACH THE FRIGATE.—RONALD REJOINS THE 'THISBE.'—MADE LIEUTENANT, . . 204

CHAPTER XX.

RONALD SECOND LIEUTENANT OF THE 'THISBE.'—A BALL AT CALCUTTA.—RONALD'S GALLANTRY.—A CHALLENGE.—HIS REPLY, ... 215

CONTENTS.

CHAPTER XXI.

PARTY AT MRS EDMONSTONE'S. — INTRODUCTION TO COLONEL ARMYTAGE. — VISIT TO THE 'OSTERLEY.' — THE 'THISBE' ORDERED TO BOMBAY, ... 229

CHAPTER XXII.

'THISBE' IN SEARCH OF THE 'OSTERLEY.' — A CHASE. — THE 'OSTERLEY' OVERTAKEN. — FOUND IN POSSESSION OF THE FRENCH. — RETAKEN. — THE PASSENGERS NOT ON BOARD. — MORTON PLACED IN COMMAND OF THE 'OSTERLEY.' — THE UNKNOWN ISLAND. — OLD DOULL ACTS AS PILOT, . . . 238

CHAPTER XXIII.

WHAT HAD BEFALLEN THE 'OSTERLEY. — HAD BEEN TAKEN BY THE ENEMY AND CARRIED INTO PORT. — PASSENGERS KEPT PRISONERS ON THE ISLAND, ... 247

CHAPTER XXIV.

THE 'THISBE' APPROACHES THE ISLAND. — OLD DOULL'S REVELATIONS AS TO THE 'OSTERLEY'S' PASSENGERS. — THE FRIGATE PUT UNDER FRENCH COLOURS. — EXPEDITION IN THE BOATS. — ATTACK ON THE FORTS. — 'OSTERLEY'S' PASSENGERS CARRIED OFF, ... 263

CHAPTER XXV.

DIFFICULTY OF NAVIGATION. — AN OLD ENEMY APPEARS. — ENEMY CHASES THE 'OSTERLEY.' — THE 'THISBE' APPEARS, . . 276

CHAPTER XXVI.

RONALD JOINS LORD CLAYMORE'S SHIP. — THE 'PALLAS' AT SEA. — A CHASE. — ENEMY'S FLEET IN SIGHT. — 'PALLAS' CHASED BY ENEMY. — LORD CLAYMORE'S MANŒUVRE. — ESCAPE OF 'PALLAS,' 287

CHAPTER XXVII.

LORD CLAYMORE AND THE FIRE SHIPS. — 'PALLAS' ENGAGES BLACK FRIGATE. — COLONEL ARMYTAGE IN THE PENINSULA, . . 307

CHAPTER XXVIII.

RONALD JOINS THE 'IMPERIOUS.' — CHASE OF A FELUCCA. — THE MARQUIS DE MEDEA. — THE SPANISH PRIEST. — RONALD ASTONISHES THE PRIEST, ... 315

CHAPTER XXIX.

RONALD MEETS HIS FATHER. — OLD DOULL RECOGNISES ROLF MORTON. — MORTON RECOGNISES FATHER MENDEZ. — ROLF MORTON'S DIPLOMACY. — A FORT ATTACKED. — BLUE JACKETS ON SHORE, ... 330

CONTENTS.

CHAPTER XXX.
LORD CLAYMORE ON SHORE.—MORTON AGAIN MEETS EDDA.—RONALD'S NEW FRIEND, DON JOSEF, ... 342

CHAPTER XXXI.
A SPANISH INN.—THE SPANIARDS AROUSED TO ARMS.—RONALD HEADS A GUERILLA BAND.—EDDA RESCUED BY RONALD, . 351

CHAPTER XXXII.
COLONEL ARMYTAGE WOUNDED.—CROSSING THE BAY OF BISCAY.—CHASED DURING A GALE.—THE BRIG DISMASTED.—CAPTURED, 365

CHAPTER XXXIII.
THE 'IMPERIOUS' HOMEWARD BOUND.—THE FIRE-SHIPS ARE PREPARED.—THE FRENCH FLEET IN BASQUE ROADS.—RONALD CONDUCTS A FIRE-SHIP.—GENERAL EXPLOSION OF FIRE-SHIPS, 374

CHAPTER XXXIV.
EDDA IN GERARDIN'S POWER.—THE FRIGATE STEERS FOR ROCHELLE.—CAPTAIN TACON.—PEDRO ALVAREZ AND FATHER MENDEZ.—TACON BETRAYS LORD CLAYMORE'S PLANS, . . . 390

CHAPTER XXXV.
THE FRIGATE ATTEMPTS TO ESCAPE FROM THE FIRE-SHIP.—THE BURNING FRIGATE.—DANGER OF THE PASSENGERS.—ESCAPE FROM THE BURNING SHIP.—ON BOARD THE 'SCORPION.'—LORD CLAYMORE ILL SUPPORTED.—THE 'SCORPION' SENT TO THE NORTH SEA, ... 408

CHAPTER XXXVI.
LUNNASTING CASTLE. — LAWRENCE BRINDISTER. — LAWRENCE'S MYSTERIOUS SAYINGS.—UNPLEASANT ANNOUNCEMENT TO SIR MARCUS.—ARRIVAL OF THE 'SCORPION.'—THE PRIEST'S VISIT TO HILDA, ... 423

CHAPTER XXXVII.
RONALD VISITS LUNNASTING CASTLE. LEGAL VISITORS ARRIVE AT LUNNASTING.—THE RIGHTFUL HEIR DISCOVERED.—THE PRINCE HAS GOT HIS AIN AGAIN, ... 434

CHAPTER XXXVIII.
THE PRIEST GOES IN SEARCH OF HERNAN.—THE 'SCORPION' ENGAGES A FRENCH SHIP.—THE VICTOR'S RETURN, . . 442

"Rushing towards them was a vast fiery mass furiously darting forth flames."—p. 410.

"'Attend to your own duties,' said the priest, in a suppressed tone, 'you will but burn your fingers if you interfere where you have no concern.'"—*p.* 113.

"'If them there to'sels weren't cut by an English sailmaker, I'm ready to pass for a Dutchman for the rest of my born days,' observed Job Truefitt, standing up on the forecastle deck and holding on by the mast."—p. 205.

"Putting spurs to his horse, Ronald, with his small body of companions, darted on, shouting in English and Spanish, 'To the rescue!'"—*p.* 360.

RONALD MORTON.

CHAPTER I.

THE SPANISH MAN-OF-WAR OFF SHETLAND—A CALM—THE 'ST CECILIA' IN DANGER—THE PILOT—BRASSAY SOUND.

'AND! land on the larboard bow!' The cry was uttered in a foreign tongue from the masthead of a corvette of twenty guns, a beautiful long, low, flush-decked craft with dark hull, taunt raking masts, and square yards, which, under all the sails she could carry with a southerly breeze right aft, was gliding rapidly over the now smooth surface of the northern ocean. The haughty flag of old Spain, and the language spoken on board, showed that she belonged to that nation. The crew sat clustered about on the forecastle with their arms folded in a listless, inactive way—some asleep—others smoking cigarillos or playing games of chance between the guns, while a few were disputing on some trivial points with a vehemence which proved the fiery tempers hidden under those calm exteriors. The officers lolled against the bulwarks, sat on the guns, or paced slowly backwards and forwards; but rather more etiquette was kept up on the quarter deck than appeared to be the case among the men forward. The captain walked backwards and forwards with his first lieutenant on the starboard side; they crossed occasionally, and lifted their hands to their eyes to watch the land just sighted as the ship approached and glided by it at the distance of two or three miles. The captain's appearance was in his favour. He was tall and graceful, with the clear olive-complexion, the pointed beard, the thin moustache, and the large pensive eyes, so frequently seen in portraits of high-born Spaniards. Still, though his features were handsome and very intelligent, there was an expression in them not altogether satisfactory. His companion was a short, thick-set man, dark and bearded, with a daring look in his countenance and a firmness in his mouth which might raise a suspicion that in cases of emergency he would be likely to take the command in the place of his superior.

'That land out there should be of some interest to us, Alvarez,' said the captain, pointing to the little conical-shaped islets the ship was passing. 'It was there, so history tells us, that one of the grandees of Spain, the great Duke of Medina Sidonia, was wrecked when he sailed in command of that mighty Armada which would have assuredly crushed the power of England had it not been so completely baffled by the wonderful opposition of the elements. Many of his crew after being saved from the fury of the tempest were cruelly murdered by the barbarous inhabitants, and he and a small remnant only escaped to the main island of Shetland, whither we are bound.'

'Ah! I have heard say that the people in those parts are little better than cannibals,' answered the lieutenant; 'we may as well, at all events, keep our guns run out and double-shotted while we lie here, that we may be prepared for them should they attempt to play us any tricks.'

'Oh! they are tolerably civilized now, I fancy,' answered the captain. 'I myself have some Shetland blood in my veins, so I have been told, though it must be tolerably diluted by this time.'

'You sir! I thought that in your veins flowed none but the

purest of Castilian streams,' answered the lieutenant, with a slight sneer in his tone. It was so slight, however, that his captain did not perceive it. 'How came that about, Don Hernan?'

'I will tell you,' answered the captain: 'an ancestor of mine—in our family tree he appears quite a modern one—commanded one of the ships of the holy Armada. She, like that of the Admiral, was driven north, and ultimately wrecked and totally lost on the land we shall soon make to the northward, called Shetland. He and his crew were kindly treated by the chief of the little island on which they were driven. The crew built a chapel to show their gratitude, and having nearly produced a famine in the district, were conveyed home with honour; while he, to prove his, married the old Udaller's daughter, and thinking it likely that his head might be chopped off as a sacrifice to assuage the rage of our pious monarch Philip, settled on the island, and did not return home till towards the end of a long life. His son, who accompanied him, having recovered his ancestral estates, remained in Spain; but he, when advanced in years, in consequence of being implicated in some political plot, fled the country, and naturally took refuge in that of his mother, where he was cordially welcomed. He was afterwards joined by his son, who, curiously enough, married a Shetland lady, and thus, even in the days of my father, who was his grandson, a constant communication was kept up with our Norse connections. I, also, have more than once heard of them since my father's death, and have determined to become more intimately acquainted with my relatives during this northern voyage of ours. But where are we getting to? What with the strong tide, and the favourable breeze, we positively fly by the land. Send for the chart on deck, Alvarez, and let me have a look at its bearings.'

The first lieutenant beckoned to a midshipman, who soon returned with a large sea-chart, which the captain spread out on the capstan head

'Ah! here we have this small rock—FAIR ISLAND, I see the natives call it—away to the south-west; and that lofty bluff headland, north by west, now shining so white, as if formed of marble, is FITFIEL HEAD, or the *White Mountain*, I see by a note—not an unfit name either; and that high point to the south-east again is Sumburgh Head. What bleak and barren hills appear to the northward again! What a dreadful coast to make during the long nights of winter!' The captain shuddered. 'Unless we find the interior more attractive, I shall wonder how my ancestors could have had so much partiality for such a country.'

'Summer or winter, in stormy weather it is not a coast a seaman would wish to hug too closely,' observed Lieutenant Alvarez; the crews of the ships of our great Armada found that to their cost. However, there appear to be some good roadsteads, where, should bad weather come on, we may be secure.'

'Numbers. See what a curious shape has the mainland, observed the captain, pointing to the chart. 'It is fully twenty leagues long, and yet there does not appear to be a point where it is more than a league across from sea to sea. Those voes run up for a league or more, and make it appear like some huge insect. Then what innumerable islands of all shapes and sizes! The people should be amphibious, who live here, to enable them to visit their neighbours: in a southern clime what a delightful spot it might be! but in this hyperborean region, existence must be a penalty.'

'As to that, my fancy is for a southern clime,' answered the lieutenant, who, by-the-by, did not clearly comprehend all his captain's remarks; 'but I suppose as there are some animals, polar bears and arctic foxes, who delight in snow and frost, so there are human beings who are content to live on in this cheerless region.'

'Not a bad notion, Alvarez,' observed the captain, who continued walking the deck, and talking much in the same strain with his officer. The contrast between the two was very considerable. The captain, Don Hernan Escalante, was a refined, highly-educated man. His knowledge on most matters was extensive, if not profound; he spoke several languages, and among them English, with a fluency few Spaniards attain. Few Spaniards indeed of that day were equally accomplished. His first lieutenant, Pedro Alvarez, was every inch a seaman, and like many seamen despised all who were not so. Again the captain stopped before the chart, and placing his finger on it, observed: 'Here I hope we may anchor to-night, opposite the capital, Lerwick. See, there is a long wide sound marked with good anchorage, called Brassay Sound, formed by the mainland and the island of Brassay. I wonder what sort of a city is Lerwick! It of course has theatres, hotels, billiard-rooms, and balls; these northern people are fond of dancing, I have read. We shall have ample amusement with the fair islanders.'

'The dances will be something like those of the North American Indians, I suspect,' answered the lieutenant, who might have thought that his captain was laughing at him, when he talked of such amusements in a country he believed so barbarous.

The corvette had got close in with Sumburgh Head, when her sails gave several loud flaps against the masts, bulged out, then again collapsed, and she speedily lost all steerage way. The head of the vessel, instead of pointing, as heretofore, towards the north, now began slowly to turn round west, and south, and east, and then, as if some secret power had seized her keel, away she was whirled, now to the westward, and then to the north in the direction of the towering heights of Fitfiel Head.

As the ship lay rocking to and fro under this lofty headland, which they at length arrived at, the sea-birds flew forth in myriads from the ledges and caverns, where, for ages past, in storm and sunshine, in winter and summer, they have roosted undisturbed, wheeling and circling with discordant cries round the stranger, as if to inquire why she had thus come to intrude on their domain. The Spanish seamen, accustomed chiefly to southern climes, gazed with superstitious wonder at the frowning cliff and the screeching birds, and fully believed that those winged denizens of the wild sea-coast were evil spirits sent out by the witches of the country to trick and torment them, and perchance to lead them to destruction.

'Shall we anchor, Alvarez?' asked the captain, anxiously looking around seaward, and then at the frowning height above their heads.

'Anchor!' exclaimed the lieutenant, 'as well anchor in the middle of the Bay of Biscay as in the Roust of Sumburgh with such a current as this, even if the depth would allow. We might get the boats out and tow, and perchance, by gaining time, obtain a breeze to carry us free.'

'By all means do so,' was the answer. The boats were lowered, and their crews were soon lustily tugging at their oars with the head of the corvette to the westward, while long sweeps were got out and run through the ports to impel her yet more rapidly through the water. Suddenly, however, she seemed to be once more seized upon and carried completely out of their control. Her head was to the westward, but she herself was swept away as fast as before to the southward; while so tumbling and breaking was the sea, that it was not without danger of being swamped that the boats were again hoisted in. The crew cast frowning glances towards the shore.

'What are we to do, Alvarez?' asked the captain, not at all liking the condition of his ship.

'Let her drive backwards and forwards till a breeze springs up, I suppose,' answered the lieutenant. 'Should a westerly gale catch us before we again get to the southward of Sumburgh Head, and should we fail to weather some of those ugly-looking points, I doubt much whether St Cecilia herself, after whom our pretty craft is called, could prevent every one of us from sharing the fate which has befallen many a bold seaman before us. However, we'll hope for the best.'

'You do not seem to like the prospects of this northern cruise of ours, Alvarez,' observed the captain. 'You have not been in good humour since we entered the British Channel, and have done nothing but predict disaster.'

'Pardon me, captain,' answered the lieutenant, 'I am not now predicting disaster—though it requires no seer to foretell the fate of the ship, if not of our lives, should certain not unlikely contingencies occur. However, here comes a breeze, I verily believe from the westward too, and if it will but fill our sails for a short half-hour, we may double yon ugly-looking Sumburgh Head, and getting out of the Roust, the tide will carry us along to our anchorage.'

The boats being once more lowered, towed the head of the corvette round to the westward, though all the time several hands were bailing to keep them free of the water, which bubbled and tumbled hissing into them over the sides. The breeze which Pedro Alvarez had observed playing on the surface in the distance, at length filled her sails, and stemming the current, she again got into smooth water and the influence of the tide, making to the northward. The wind also drew round to the southward, and all sails being made, the corvette, with her wide spread of canvas, glided on as smoothly and majestically as before, till the island of Mousa, with its Pictie tower, bore west on her larboard beam. A signal was flying for a pilot, and a long, light boat, pulling six oars, was seen coming off from Fladbister, a town—in reality a little fishing village—on the shore. The heads of her crew were visible a long way off, by the bright hues of their long pendant worsted caps. They wore large sheepskin coats, coming down to the knee over their worsted shirts, and high boots of yellow untanned leather. The corvette was about to shorten sail, but they making signals that that was unnecessary, the boat shot alongside, and two of them sprang on board.

B

'Those fellows would be unpleasant customers if they came as enemies to attack our ship, from the active way in which they leaped up our sides,' observed the captain. 'They would be as difficult to keep out as wild cats.'

One of the two pilots was a man advanced in life, the other was very much younger, and habited in the quaint costume which has been described; his dress, though rough, differed much from the rest, while his easy, unembarrassed manner showed that he was an officer rather than an ordinary seaman. With a brisk step the men came aft, inquiring, as they did so, of the officers if any of them could speak English. They were referred to Don Hernan, who politely returned the salute as they touched their hats to him.

'Well, my men,' said he, 'will you take charge of the ship, and bring her to an anchor in Brassay Sound to-night?'

'That will we, captain, right gladly,' answered the younger of the two, glancing aloft with the eye of a seaman. 'She is as pretty a craft as any one has ever seen in these waters, and well worth taking care of. What is her name? where are you from? and whither are you bound, captain? Pardon me for asking, but it is my duty so to do. They are the questions we always put in these waters.'

'As to that, of course you are perfectly right,' answered the captain. 'Her name is the "St Cecilia," her commander Don Hernan de Escalante, and she carries, as you see, twenty guns. We sailed from Cadiz, and have touched at two or three French ports, and the British port of Plymouth; after visiting Lerwick, we are bound round the north of your island, into the Atlantic again. You see that we have nothing to conceal. The character of this ship is above all suspicion; and you will find, my friend, that you have lost nothing by navigating her in safety wherever we may wish to go.'

'Very likely, captain,' answered the pilot, looking up into the captain's countenance. 'I entertain no doubt about the matter, and if the provost and bailies of Lerwick are satisfied,

I am sure that I shall be: keep her as she goes now for the Bard of Brassay. The tide will shoot her into the sound rapidly enough as we draw near it.'

When in a short time the corvette was off the Bard or Beard of Brassay, as the ragged-looking southern end of that island is called, a turn of the helm to starboard sent the vessel into the Sound, and up she flew with smooth green heights on either side, here and there a few white buildings showing, and numerous rocks visible, till the pilot warned the captain that it was time to shorten sail. At a word the sailors were seen swarming aloft; studding-sails came in as if by magic, royals and top-gallant sails were handed, topsails clewed up, and with her taunt tapering masts and square yards alone, surrounded by the intricate tracery of their rigging, the beautiful fabric glided up to an anchorage off the town of Lerwick.

'Friend, you brought the ship to an anchor in true seaman-like style,' said Captain Don Hernan, touching the young pilot on the shoulder. 'You have not been a simple pilot all your life.'

'No, indeed, captain,' answered the pilot, 'I have been afloat since my earliest days in southern seas, as well as engaged in the Greenland fishery. Lately I have been mate of a whaler, and maybe my next voyage I shall have charge of a ship as master. You have hit the right nail on the head—this is the first summer that I ever spent on shore.'

'Can I trust you, then, to take charge of the ship round the coast?' asked the captain. 'Perhaps, however, you are not well acquainted with that?'

The pilot smiled. 'There is not a point or headland, a rock, or shoal, or island, which I have not as clearly mapped down in my memory, as are the lines on yonder chart, and more correctly, too, I doubt not.'

'That will do—I will trust you,' said Don Hernan. 'What is your name, friend, that I may send for you when you are wanted?'

'Rolf Morton,' was the answer; 'but my home is some way to the northward, on the island of Whalsey. There you have it on your chart. Those who live on it boast that it is the finest of the outlying islands; and well I know that such a castle as we have is not to be found in all Shetland.'

'Ah, it is your native place,' observed the captain. 'You therefore think so highly of it.'

'Not exactly, though I remember no other spot of earth before I put eyes on Whalsey. I was, so I have been told, picked up, when a child, from a wreck at sea; and the men I was with called me Rolf Morton, the name which has stuck to me for want of a better. I know nothing more of my history; but I am prating of myself, and shall weary you, captain.'

'Far from it, friend; I delight in a little romance,' answered the captain. 'How comes it, though, that you remained on shore this summer?—but I need not ask—one of your fair islanders, of whom I have heard so much, was your attraction.'

'Yes, in truth,' said the pilot, laughing; 'she has become my wife, though; and as I could not bring myself to quit her, I bethought me I would try to gain my livelihood by turning pilot. Yours is one of the first ships I have taken charge of. There—I have been frank with you, captain, and told you all my history from beginning to end.'

'And I thank you for it. I saw at a glance that you were above the ordinary style of a pilot. I wanted to find a man like yourself, who would give me the information I require about the country, the habits and customs of the people. I would wish to win their regard. But you have, I suppose, few good families here?'

Don Hernan well knew that the islander's pride would tempt him to launch out in a full description of all the families of consequence in the group, and that he should thus easily obtain, without apparently seeking for it, all the information of that description which he required.

Morton unsuspectingly answered exactly in the tone for which he was prepared.

'Indeed, captain, you are out of your latitude. We have the Edmonstones of Unst, and the Lord Dundas, and the Mouats, and the Ogilvys, and Scott of Scalloway, and Bruces of Sandwick, and also of Symbister; and Spences, and Duncans, and the Nicolson family; baronets of old date, all honourable men, and of ancient lineage; besides many others I have not named, standing equally well in the estimation of the country; and then there is the Lunnasting family of Lunnasting Castle, of which I spoke to you. The owner is Sir Marcus Wardhill, who succeeded to his property by right of his wife, the Lady Margaret Brindister; one of the most ancient of our Shetland families, descended, so it is said, from one of the former chiefs, the Udallers of old. They are very great and important people, at all events when in their own castle, and of course have little communication with a man of my humble rank. Maybe I hear more of them than do others, because my wife's mother was for long the companion of the Lady Margaret, and the nurse to her children. I believe she loved them as her own. Indeed, although but called a nurse in the family, she is nearly akin to the Lady Margaret. But these are matters about which a stranger can have no interest.'

'A stranger might not, but I must not be considered in that light,' answered the captain. 'Strange as it may appear to you, I am connected with that very family of which you are speaking. An ancestress of mine was a Brindister. I must claim relationship with the occupants of Lunnasting. It will, in truth, be pleasant in this remote region to find friends so nearly related to me.'

The reserve which the pilot had hitherto maintained seemed to vanish on hearing the assertion made by Don Hernan.

'I have no doubt, captain, that they would have given you

a warm northern welcome,' he answered. 'But Sir Marcus Wardhill himself, and his second daughter, are in the south, travelling, I have heard, among French and Germans, and it is said that they purpose remaining some time in the big city of London, a place among all my wanderings I have never seen.'

'The Lady Margaret, of whom you speak, and her elder daughter are there, I hope; or is the castle shut up?' asked Don Hernan.

'The Lady Margaret, as we called her, Lady Wardhill, is dead, but her elder daughter, Miss Hilda Wardhill, lives at Lunnasting, and manages the Shetland estates, they say as well as any man would do.'

'Ho, ho! I should like to become acquainted with this talented cousin of mine,' said Don Hernan. 'Is she handsome as well as clever?'

Thus appealed to, Morton replied with even more hesitation than before. 'As to an eye for the look of a ship aloft, or for her build or trim, I'll yield to no man; and maybe I like the faces of some women more than others. This I'll say, sir; it's my belief that there are not many in this world like the Lady Hilda.'

'You have probably heard of the Spanish connection of the family.'

'Yes, once or twice, maybe,' answered Morton; 'my wife's mother often speaks of them. In her father's time they constantly corresponded, and exchanged presents — Shetland shawls and stockings for Spanish silks and brocades. It was said that, during his travels, Sir Marcus thought of visiting his connections in Spain.'

After some further conversation, the captain observed, 'I would pay my respects to the governor or authorities of the town. As you have proved so good a pilot afloat, you shall accompany me as my guide on shore.'

CHAPTER II.

LUNNASTING CASTLE—THE STRANGER SHIP—SANDY REDLAND, THE FACTOR—ARCHY EAGLESHAY—MISS WARDHILL'S VISITORS— THE DISAPPEARANCE OF THE HEIR.

LUNNASTING CASTLE stood on a high rocky promontory, washed by the ocean on the south and east, and by a voe which ran up some way inland on the west. It was a somewhat extensive building; but though of a castellated style of architecture it was not really a fortress further than the naturally inaccessible nature of the ground on which it stood made it so. It stood on the site, and was formed partly of such materials as time had left of an old castle of the earls or ancient Udal lords of Shetland, and had been very much increased in size, and ornamented, as well as rendered a more commodious habitation by the present owner, Sir Marcus Wardhill. The dwelling-house consisted but of two stories, and standing, as it did, elevated some way above the sea, looked lower than it really was. It was surrounded on the north, east, and west, by a high castellated wall, flanked with towers, which, if not capable of keeping out a mortal enemy, served the purpose for which it was built,—to guard the mansion from the assaults of the wintry blasts of the icy ocean. In front, on the south side, that the inhabitants might enjoy the sea view, and that the warm rays of the sun might be admitted, the wall sunk down to the height of a mere ornamental parapet, the round towers at either end giving it some right to claim the title bestowed on it; especially as on the summit of either tower Sir Marcus had mounted a couple of long six-pounders, capable of considerably annoying any hostile vessel of a size at all likely to venture near that part of a coast so full of dangers that no large ship would willingly approach it. The muzzles of some smaller guns appeared through the embrasure of the parapet wall, which was also flanked by a buttress, or rather a circular outwork at either end at the foot of the towers, where pivot guns were placed, so that the one on the west could fire directly up the voe or gulf, and served to flank the western wall. The two principal front towers were connected with the dwelling-house, and had small chambers in them, one above the other, which had been fitted up as sitting-rooms or dormitories.

In a deep window recess, in the highest chamber of the western tower of Lunnasting Castle, sat Miss Wardhill, Sir Marcus Wardhill's eldest child. Although the window matched in appearance the others in that and the opposite tower, which were mere high, narrow, glazed loop-holes, by an ingenious contrivance a huge stone was made to turn on an iron axle, and by pressing a spring, it slid in sufficiently to allow the inmate of the room to gaze out conveniently on the surrounding scene.

Few scenes, to a romantic temperament, could have been more attractive. The subdued twilight of that northern clime reigned over the face of nature, softening and mellowing all objects, but in no way obscuring them. The light was not so bright as that of the day, and yet it partook in no way of the characteristics of night. It was more like the warm light of the dawn of a summer day in the south, just before the sun rises up from below the horizon in refulgent glory. The water near the land was perfectly smooth, though a breeze could be seen rippling the surface in the offing, the ripple being increased probably by the strong current which nearly at all times sets one way or the other round the islands.

Before the castle, on the right, rose the rocky heights and green swelling undulations of the mainland—the Noup of Nesting Kirkbuster, Brough and Moul of Eswick, while the highlands above Lerwick, and the heights of Brassy and Noss, appeared blue and indistinct in the far distance.

To the east, several green islands, or rather islets, known as Grief Skerries, Rumble, Eastling, and other equally euphonious names, ran out of the dark-blue ocean. The last-named being a mile and a half in length, formed with the main island, along the shore of which it ran parallel, and from which it was little more than a quarter of a mile distant, a sound of some extent, where vessels in all but north-easterly winds could ride safely at anchor. Even in these winds the force of the sea was considerably broken by the small island or holm of Isbuster, which lay in the very centre of the northern entrance.

Looking eastward, and north from the towers of Lunnasting, the view extended nearly up the Sound, and commanded the whole island of Eastling, which perhaps obtained its name from lying east of the chief habitation of the lords of the domain, Eastling being a corruption of Eastlying. Such was the view on which Hilda Wardhill was occasionally turning her gaze, though her eyes were more frequently fixed on the pages of a large volume lying open on a dark oak reading desk fixed in the recess, and so placed that the last rays of that precious sunlight which so soon departs in the long winter season of the North, might fall full upon it. The room was of an octagon shape, with dark oak wainscoting and ceiling; the chairs were of a suitable character, mostly with high upright backs, rudely carved, as were some book-shelves, which occupied two of the sides, while a massive table, supported by sea monsters, or at all events by creatures of fish-like form, stood in the centre; another table of similar character stood against the side of the room with writing materials on it, and there was a sofa of antique form, and two large chests of some dark wood, with brass clasps and plates on the lids and sides, so tarnished however by the sea air, as scarcely to be discerned as brass. A second high narrow window, with a lattice, faced towards the west and north, so that persons standing at it could, by leaning forward, look completely up the voo. Thus, from this turret chamber, a view could be obtained on every side, except on that looking inland, or rather over the island.

On one of the eight sides there was, however, a small door in the panelling, which opened on a spiral staircase leading to the very summit of the tower, where, as has been said, a gun was placed, and whence a complete view was obtained over every portion of the island, extending far away over the sea beyond, to the Out Skerries, a rocky group so called; and the distant shores of the large island of Yell. As the roof could only be reached by passing through the chamber below, it was completely private to the fair occupant as long as she chose to close the ingress to her own room.

Seldom has a more beautiful picture been portrayed to the mind's eye of the most imaginative of painters, than that which Hilda Wardhill presented as she sat at the window of her turret chamber, either leaning over the volume which occupied her attention, or gazing out on the calm ocean, her thoughts evidently still engaged in the subject of her studies.

At length she rose, and was about to close the window, when her eye fell on a vast towering mass of white, gliding slowly from the northward down Eastling Sound. She looked more than once, mistrusting her senses, and inclined to believe that it was some phantom of the deep, described in wild romances, often her study, which she beheld, till another glance assured her, as the object drew nearer that it was a large ship, far larger than had ever been known during her recollection to anchor in the Sound. With speed which seemed like magic, the white canvas disappeared, and the tall masts and the yards and the light tracery of the rigging could only dimly be traced against the clear sky.

Whence the stranger had come, or for what object, Hilda

could not tell, but still she had a feeling—how communicated she did not inquire—that the event portended some great change in her own fate. Painful forebodings of evil came crowding like mocking phantoms around her. She tried with the exercise of her own strong will to banish them. In vain she strove—the more they seemed to mock her power. She felt as if she could almost have shrieked out in the agony of her mortal struggle, till her proud spirit quailed and trembled with unwonted fears. Again the clock tolled forth a solitary sound, which vibrated strangely on her overwrought nerves, and seemed more sonorous than usual. She pressed her hand upon her brow, then by an effort she seemed by a single gasp to recover herself, and, closing the window, retired to her sleeping chamber in that part of the house in the immediate neighbourhood of her favourite tower.

At an early hour the lady of the castle was on foot. She at once ascended to the summit of her tower, and gazed eagerly up the Sound, half expecting to find that she had been deceived by her imagination on the previous night, and that the ship she had seen was but a creation of the brain. There, however, floated the beautiful fabric, but there was not the slightest movement or sign of life on board. At all events, it seemed improbable that she would soon move from her present position. At length she descended to her boudoir below, where, as usual, her light and frugal meal was brought to her by her own attendant, Nanny Clousta.

Her meal, at which Nanny stood ready to help her to anything she required, being quickly concluded, Miss Wardhill descended to the large hall on the ground-floor, in the centre of the castle. It was a handsome room, with an arched ceiling of dark oak, supported by pillars round the wall. A long table ran down the centre, at one end of which, on a raised platform or dais, she took her seat. Several tenants of the Lunnasting estate came in to make complaints, to beg for the redress of grievances, to report on the state of the farms, or fisheries, or kelp-collecting; to all of which the lady listened with the most perfect attention, making notes in a book placed before her. Two or three were told to wait till she had seen the factor, that she might hear his reports before deciding on their claims. She looked round as if the audience was over; and inquired why Alexander, or Sandy Redland, as he was called, the factor, did not make his appearance, when an old man, leaning on a stick, hobbled into the hall.

'I come for justice, my lady. Oh, hear me, hear me!' he exclaimed; as if before entering the hall he had worked himself up to address her; 'I am just auld Archy Eagleshay, and as ye ken weel, my leddie, my only son has long gane been awa to sea, and I've been left to struggle on fra ane year to another, till now that I am grown too weak to toil, and the factor, Sandy Redland, comes down upon me, and makes awfu' threats to distrain and turn me out of my sma' holding if I dinna pay; and pay I canna', that is truth, my leddie. Have mercy, have pity, my leddie. Ye love justice whatever else ye love.'

'Justice might induce me to expel you from your holding, if you cannot pay your rent, old man,' said Miss Wardhill, in a cold severe tone. 'However I will listen to what Sandy Redland, the factor, has to say. Ha! here he comes. You are late Mr Redland, in your attendance. What has kept you?'

The man who entered was a tall, thin person, habited in the grey shepherd's plaid of the north. His features were coarse. He possessed a sharp nose, high cheek bones, and small and grey unpleasantly twinkling eyes. He bowed low, and in a voice which was intended to be soft and insinuating, replied—

'It is no fault o' mine when your orders are na implicitly obeyed, Miss Wardhill; but circumstances militate against the best intentions, as may be clear to you oftentimes, I doubt not. I was delayed by having to make inquiries respecting a strange ship, which anchored, it appears, a few hours back, in the

Sound of Eastling, and which, as I opine, is within your leddyship's jurisdiction, I deemed it incumbent on me to ascertain the object of her coming, and the time it might be proposed for her to stay. As she is a foreigner, it struck me that charge might be made for harbour and light dues, and the chances are that it would not be disputed. Ye see, Miss Wardhill, that I have always your honoured father's interests at heart.'

The lady gave a glance towards the factor, which bespoke the most perfect contempt—too cold and confirmed to cause much change in her features.

'And what have you learned respecting this stranger ship?' she asked.

'Nathing, my leddie, nathing,' answered Sandy, shuddering. 'What could I tell but that she might be a pirate or an enemy in disguise, or some ill-doer, and that if I, the factor of Lunnasting, was entrapped on board, I might be retained as a hostage in durance vile, till sic times as a heavy sum might be collected for my ransom.'

A gleam flitted across Miss Wardhill's countenance, as she replied: 'You estimate yourself somewhat highly, factor. Then, in truth, you know nothing of the ship which has anchored in the Sound?'

'Nathing whatever, my leddie,' was the answer. 'But I await the return of Jock Busta's boat which I despatched as soon as I reached Whalsey this morning from the mainland.'

'Bring me the information as soon as you obtain it,' said Miss Wardhill. 'In the meantime let me hear what answer you have to make to a complaint old Archy Eagleshay brings against you.'

The factor gave a variety of reasons for his conduct, to which she listened without replying, and then called up the old man to her end of the table.

'Go home Archy Eagleshay,' she said, in a voice totally different to that in which she had spoken to the factor. 'Rest quiet in your hut. The old and infirm must be sheltered and fed; of that there is no doubt; but let the evil-doer and idle beware. On them I shall have no mercy. Sandy Redland, mark me: I will have no cruelty or oppression—remember that. The instant you receive information respecting the strange ship, let me know through Nanny Clousta.'

There was a cowed look on the countenance of Sandy Redland as he bowed, while his young mistress rose to retire.

Old Archy lifted up his hands, as if about to address her once more, then he turned slowly round. 'Ha, ha!' he muttered; 'if she had yielded to you, cruel factor, I'd have told her all I know, and made e'en her proud spirit tremble; but she's been good and kind to an auld man, and I'll say nothing.'

On leaving the hall, Hilda Wardhill went at once to the turret chamber, and from thence mounted to the platform on the summit of the tower. Her first glance was up the Sound, where lay the stranger ship. The sails were still closely furled; the boats were hoisted up; not a movement of any sort appeared to be taking place. The only object stirring was a small boat, which just then was gliding rapidly close under the headland on which the castle stood. A single rower sat in it, who managed his oars with the skill which long practice gives. He looked up, and seeing Miss Wardhill, flourished his oar as a salute, which she returned with the slightest possible inclination of her head, and then continued pacing up and down, while he pursued his course till he entered the voe, and reached the castle landing-place, where he was hid from view. Miss Wardhill continued her circumscribed walk backwards and forwards across the top of the tower, now stopping to look up the Sound at the ship, now casting her glance round the horizon, speaking frequently to herself, and more than once sighing deeply, as if there was some weight at her heart of which she longed to be relieved.

She had again stopped, and was looking at the beautiful ship in the distance, when she started on hearing herself addressed—

'Good morrow, cousin Hilda,' said the intruder, who had that instant come up from the room below. 'Engaged, as I expected, or you would not be a woman, gazing with curiosity at the strange ship in the Sound, wondering whence she came, and all about her.'

She turned as he spoke, when he lifted a little gold-laced, three-cornered hat from his head, and saluted her with a profound bow, which might have appeared respectful in the extreme, had he not at the same time indulged in a low chuckling laugh, the usual conclusion, it seemed, of most of his sentences. His manner and appearance were peculiar in the extreme: he was broad and large boned, but thin; and a suit of brown cloth, with huge silver buttons, hung loosely about his body; a wide shirt-frill stuck out in front, and his shirt collars reached up to his ears. His gait was shuffling and shambling; he wore knee-breeches and grey homespun stockings, and his shoes, which were ornamented with silver buckles, were far too large for him, and of course, even had he not had the propensity to do so, would have made him shuffle his feet over the ground. His eyes were unusually large, grey, and staring; and his hair, which was already so grey that its original colour could scarcely be perceived, was cut short, and stood up on end, all over his head like the quills of the porcupine; his forehead was somewhat narrow, but his features were neither plain nor coarse; there was, however, a startled, frightened look about them, and an otherwise painful and indescribable expression, which told too plainly that the ruling power of the intellect had been overthrown, and that the living machine could no longer be altogether held responsible for its acts. Such, in appearance, was Lawrence Brindister: had he been of sane mind, he would have been the lord of Lunnasting and the broad acres of several estates, both on the mainland of Shetland and in the north of Scotland; but as he had, long before coming of age, given undoubted signs of being totally incapable of managing his affairs, his claims had been set aside in favour of his cousin, Margaret

Brindister, the next heir, married to Sir Marcus Wardhill. There had been, when Sir Marcus married, three other heirs besides Lawrence, before Margaret Brindister could succeed to the property: the same fever within a few days carried off two of them; and then, and perhaps not till then, a longing desire seized Sir Marcus to obtain the estates. The possessor was an old man—a bachelor. Sir Marcus was not a man —that was well known—who allowed obstacles to stand in his way; in the most unaccountable manner, the next heir, a boy, disappeared: he was supposed, with his nurse, to have fallen over a cliff, or to have been on the beach when a sea came in and swept them both away—either occurrences too likely to happen to allow suspicion justly to rest on any one. A handkerchief of the nurse's, and a plaything of the child's, were found dropped on the road they had taken. Their bodies were searched for in every direction in vain; the old man mourned for the child, of whom he was very fond, and died shortly after. Sir Marcus, too, mourned for the loss of his young kinsman, but instantly commenced a suit which terminated by making poor Lawrence Brindister his ward. There were certain conditions attached, that Lunnasting should be his abode, and that he should be kindly treated and well looked after, and supplied with anything he might in reason require for his amusement: Lawrence himself, so far from opposing, seemed perfectly contented with the arrangement; and while Lady Wardhill, to whom he was much attached, lived, he was always cheerful and good-tempered, though he afterwards exhibited so much extravagance of behaviour that he required to be carefully watched, and his actions more curbed than he liked. He had at first much resented this mode of proceeding with him, but of late years he had become apparently so perfectly harmless, that he was allowed to do exactly as he pleased. Such was the eccentric being who now stood before Miss Wardhill.

'Yes, Lawrence, I have been looking at the ship,' she answered, with so peculiar a calmness, that it appeared to be produced by an effort. 'You have, I conclude, visited her, and can give me some information about the stranger.'

'Ah! that can I, fair cousin,' he answered, with his usual painful chuckle. 'I have been on board the ship, and introduced myself to her captain, and, what is more, invited him to the castle. He has a right to claim our hospitality, for who, think you, is he?—no other than one of those Spanish cousins we have heard often spoken about by her who lies sleeping in yonder churchyard out there—ah's me!—and others. Nurse Bertha will know all about them; we must get her to tell us before he comes: he will be here soon, though. I told him that he must let me go on ahead, to give due notice of his coming, or he would have arrived, and taken you by surprise. He is a gallant-looking knight; a true don of the old school. But I say, Hilda, don't treat him to the scornful glances you cast at me, or he will not like it.'

Miss Wardhill took no notice of the last remark. 'Since you have invited these strangers to the castle, whether they are really our relations or not, we must be prepared to receive them. Go, look for Sandy Redland; he has not left the island yet: he must go round and collect an ample store of provisions, that we may not be looked on as niggards in our hospitality, in this island home of ours. Send Bertha Eswick to me; she knows, better than any other person here, what arrangements should be made to do honour to strangers; it is so long since any one came here, that I cannot hope to remember what preparations are required. Go, Lawrence, and do you remember not to bring discredit on the family by any pranks or strange vagaries you may wish to play.'

CHAPTER III.

LAWRENCE BRINDISTER VISITS THE SPANISH SHIP.—DON HERNAN INVITED TO THE CASTLE.—SURLY GRIND, LAWRENCE'S DOG.

THE accounts which Don Hernan had received from various quarters while on shore at Lerwick about the inhabitants of Lunnasting Castle had excited his curiosity and interest to the highest pitch. Though fully intending to return shortly to Lerwick, he had an object in suddenly leaving Brassay Sound. He also wished to arrive unexpectedly in the neighbourhood of Lunnasting.

Rolf Morton came at his summons; and understanding the 'St Cecilia' was shortly to return to Lerwick, not having reason to suspect fraud of any description, he, without hesitation, took the ship on to Eastling Sound. She had not been long at anchor before Lawrence Brindister—who, as was his custom, had been at an early hour of the morning out fishing—espied her, and very soon made his appearance on board. Lawrence walked about the deck admiring the guns and the carved and gilt work with which the ship was adorned; for it was the custom, especially in the Spanish navy, in those days to ornament ships of war far more profusely than at present. At length Don Hernan came on deck. He observed the skiff alongside; and his eye falling on Lawrence, he very naturally at first took him to be some poor fisherman habited in the cast-off finery of a gentleman. Lawrence, however, guessed who he was from his uniform, and, shuffling along the deck, made him one of his profoundest bows, which Don Hernan returned with one in the same style.

As it had not been impressed on Lawrence's mind that there existed numerous nations speaking different tongues, he at once addressed the Spanish captain in English.

'Your people, good sir, have been very silent: not one has spoken to me since I stepped on board this trim craft of yours; for you have, I conclude, the happiness of being her captain, and you have, I hope, a tongue with which to hold pleasant and profitable converse.'

'I command this ship, and I am able to converse in English,' answered Don Hernan, wondering who his strange visitor could be. 'May I ask in return whom I have the honour of addressing?'

'No less a person than Lawrence Brindister, Lord of Lunnasting Castle and the lands adjacent,' answered Lawrence, drawing himself up—' that is to say, who would be, and should be, and ought to be, had not certain traitorous and vile persons, who shall be nameless, interfered with his just rights, and ousted him from his property. But say not a word about that, most noble stranger. "A guid time is coming—a guid time is coming." "The prince shall have his ain again!"'

Don Hernan at once perceived his visitor's state of mind.

'I had thought that Sir Marcus Wardhill was Lord of Lunnasting, though I am aware that, from times immemorial, it has been held by Brindisters, of whom I conclude you are one,' remarked the captain.

'Ay, there's the rub,' said Lawrence. 'You see, most noble captain, I've a difficulty in steering my craft; I never can keep her in good trim. Sometimes she luffs up, and sometimes she falls off; so as to holding a steady course, I find that out of the question. Ah, now I know all about it. I have come, most noble captain, feeling assured that you are of gentle birth and a man of honour, to invite you and your officers to visit Lunnasting Castle. My cousin and I will do our best to receive you as becomes your rank.'

Don Hernan, who believed that Miss Wardhill had really sent this strange being to invite him to the castle, replied, in suitable terms, that he should have great happiness in paying his respects to her. He also explained his connection with the Brindister family, and begged Lawrence to say that he hoped to visit Lunnasting in the character of a kinsman.

Lawrence was about to step into his boat when he saw Rolf Morton, who, hearing that a boat was alongside, had just come on deck with the intention of going on shore. He and Rolf were always on very good terms; so, when the latter begged for a cast on shore, he gladly undertook to land him wherever he wished.

'Abreast of the ship will suit me, for in half an hour I can be at home,' answered Morton. 'Good-bye, Don Hernan; should the wind shift, I will be on board in a trice; or should you want me, send. We have not so many houses in Whalsey that mine cannot be found without difficulty.'

Saying this, he was following Lawrence into the skiff, when the latter cried out, 'Hold fast! you are stepping on Surly Grind, Morton; he'll not like it, let me tell you. He's apt to treat with scant ceremony those who offend him.'

Morton looked down, and saw, coiled away at the bottom of the skiff, where Lawrence had taught him to lie, a huge black dog, with an unusually ferocious expression of countenance, though from his coat he had evidently much of the Newfoundland breed in him, but his face showed that he had also much of that of the mastiff and bloodhound, probably.

'Lie down, Surly Grind, and treat my visitors with respect,' said Lawrence; and the dog, which had lifted up his head and begun to growl and snarl, crouched down as before.

'Now, take your seat, man, and I'll show you how a true

Shetlander can pull,' said Lawrence, taking his place at the oars and giving several rapid strokes.

'But I deem that I have a right to hail from Shetland also, Master Lawrence,' answered Morton. 'There is no other land owns me, and it is hard for a man to be without a conntry or a home.'

'Ay, true; you have a Shetland look and a Shetland tongue, and I believe that you have a Shetland heart also, Morton. "The prince shall hae his ain again, his ain again!" That's a curious old Scotch song; it's always running in my head. "The prince shall hae his ain again!" Well, but you know, Morton, he didn't get his ain again; so I've heard nurse Bertha say. She's a wise woman, your mother-in-law, and my good cousin, too. Well, well; there are ups and downs in this life. All don't get their ain, that's poz; if they did, another 'd be sitting on George's throne; but that's treason, ye ken; and another 'd be ruling in Wardhill's room, but that's treason, too; so I'd better be holding my tongue, or all the cats I've got in my bag will be jumping out and playing more pranks than either you or I, or Sir Marcus Wardhill to boot, will be able to stay.'

Rolf Morton was too well aware of poor Lawrence's state of mind to listen with much attention to what he said; but his curiosity was sufficiently awakened by some of the remarks he let fall to make him resolve to learn more about the matter from Bertha Eswick as soon as he could meet her.

CHAPTER IV.

HILDA'S FIRST MEETING WITH DON HERNAN.—HILDA ON BOARD THE CORVETTE.—ROLF MORTON PILOTS THE SHIP.—CRUISE IN THE 'ST CECILIA.'—HILDA ACCEPTS DON HERNAN.

THE heiress of Lunnasting was high-minded, unconscious of evil, confident of her own strength and resolution, and utterly ignorant of the world and of its deceits and wickedness. She had for long lived in one of her own creation, which she fancied was like the real world of other mortals. She met Don Hernan Escalante, and at once clothed him with all the attributes and perfections with which a romantic girl could endow the object of her fancy. He, too, at the moment he entered the hall, and found her seated in courtly style to receive him, was struck by her rare and exquisite beauty. He had never seen any being so lovely, and, man of the world as he thought himself, he at once yielded to the influence of that beauty. She herself was scarcely aware of the power she might have exerted over him, but gave herself up to the full enjoyment of the new sensations she experienced.

Hilda occasionally heard from her father and sister, but not very frequently, and their letters contained little more than an outline of their progress, the names of the places they had visited, and the length of their stay at each. Sir Marcus now and then added a few directions as to the management of the estate, but generally wound up by saying, that as he felt sure everything necessary would be done, he would not interfere with any arrangements she might have seen fit to make. Hitherto all had gone well. Hilda had, by a wonderful exertion of resolution, so successfully combated the dreadful malady which, like some monster bird of prey, hung hovering above her, ready to pounce down and dethrone her intellect from its sway, that few, although in constant communication with her, had any suspicion of the real state of the case. Probably at that time only two people in the world had discovered the unstable character of Hilda's mind, and they themselves were the two most opposite in all respects connected with her—her nurse Bertha and her cousin Lawrence; but while the latter had more than once betrayed his knowledge to her, the former had never by word or look allowed her to suspect that she had an idea of the truth.

The Spanish corvette had been nearly a week at anchor in Eastling Sound, and on each day her captain had appeared at Lunnasting, his visits increasing gradually in length as he found them more and more acceptable. Hilda had at first received him in the great hall, into which, as not only the members of the household, but all visitors, had access, their intercourse was too public and restrained to suit the feelings which were springing up in their hearts.

'Lady, the view from the summit of the tower where I first beheld you must be lovely,' said Don Hernan, adding in a lower tone some words which made the colour mantle into Hilda's cheeks. An invitation to visit the tower was the consequence of the remark; but before going there a ramble was taken over the chief part of the castle, to which Don Hernan had not yet been introduced. There was a private entrance to the highest floor of the tower; but as that led through the lady's apartments, they had to descend to mount the more public stair. That was, however, narrow and winding, and somewhat inconvenient; at the foot of it they encountered Lawrence.

'Ah, my brave Don Hernan, so our cousin Hilda is about to show you the secrets of her prison tower,' he exclaimed, in a facetious tone. 'Take care that she does not shut you up, as enchantresses of old were wont to do their captive knights, and never again set you free. However, to prevent such a catastrophe, I'll accompany you. Let me mount first, and show you the way, or you might chance to knock your head against some of the iron-plated gates, which bar the approach to the summit.'

In what direction Don Hernan might just then have wished poor Lawrence, it need not be said. No means of getting rid of him occurred to his mind. Had he been on the top of the tower, he might have felt inclined to throw him over; but as it was, he had to submit to his company with as good a grace as he could command.

'I fear that you may not consider my cousin the best of guides on all occasions; but he can lead the way to the top of our tower as well as a wiser man,' said Hilda, observing the Spaniard's look of anger, and at the same time, from maiden bashfulness, not sorry to have Lawrence as an escort. Up they went, therefore, till they reached Hilda's sitting-room.

'This, you see, Don Hernan, is my fair kinswoman's bower —her boudoir, her retiring-room, or whatever else you like to call it—where she sits brooding in silence, watching the stars and the moon sometimes, ye ken, or reading romances and works on philosophy, metaphysics, astrology, and other subjects far too deep for my poor brain,' said Lawrence, as he entered the apartment.

Don Hernan glanced round with an eye of curiosity and surprise. 'It is indeed a delightful spot for retirement and contemplation,' he remarked, turning to Hilda, as he offered her his hand to assist her up the last step of the stair. 'I would gladly give up my roving life to inhabit it.'

'How strange! for though I love it dearly, I can fancy

nothing so delightful as being able to wander here and there to new and far-off lands,' answered Hilda, smiling.

Don Hernan whispered a few words, which Lawrence could not hear. 'You have now shown me your home on the shore, let me have the opportunity of showing you mine on the water,' he added, taking her hand, with an expression which called forth a deep blush on her cheek; yet her hand was not withdrawn. 'You can, I doubt not, persuade your cousin and good housekeeper to accompany you, and any other escort you may deem advisable. I will send for our pilot, and we will take a short cruise round some of the neighbouring islets.'

Hilda, after a moment's hesitation, consented to the proposal. Lawrence was delighted at the idea of a sail in the big ship.

The summer days of Shetland are few, but they are perfect while they last, and long enough to satisfy the most enthusiastic admirer of out-door amusements. Such was the day Hilda had selected for paying a visit to the corvette. At an early hour the state barge of Lunnasting was in attendance at the landing-place, manned by a sturdy crew of eight of her tenants, whilst Lawrence claimed the privilege of acting as coxswain—a post for which, from his practical knowledge of seamanship, he was perfectly well fitted.

The Spanish captain had wished to send a boat from the corvette, but the offer had been declined, as Hilda knew that it would be considered undignified unless she went in her own. Besides the crew and Lawrence Brindister, her only escort consisted of Bertha Eswick, Nanny Clousta, her own attendant, and her factor, Sandy Redland.

As they got alongside, the crew sprang aloft and manned yards, but instead of cheering they waved their hats above their heads; a salute was at the same moment fired from the guns, and the captain himself descended the side ladder to assist Miss Wardhill on deck. He pressed her hand as he did so, and the glance she gave him showed the pleasure she felt in visiting his ocean home. They said but little, for they already understood each other too well to feel inclined to interchange many words in public. The first lieutenant, Pedro Alvarez, took charge of Bertha Eswick, and one of the junior officers devoted himself to Nanny Clousta, very little caring what was her position in the family. Lawrence, who had constantly been on board the corvette, seemed on intimate terms with every one, while Sandy Redland, the factor, stalked about wondering at the sights he beheld, and not attempting to exchange words with any one. As soon as the last of the party were out of the Lunnasting barge, she was sent back to the castle, with directions to pull off to the ship when a signal should be made; at the same moment the boatswain's shrill whistle was heard, the topsails were let fall, the capstan bars were shipped, and the men tramped round to the sound of fife and fiddle. The wide extending courses next dropped from the brails, the topgallant sails and royals were set, and the ship under all her canvas stood out with the wind on her larboard quarter by the northern passage from Eastling Sound. As she began to move on, Rolf Morton, who had been on the forecastle superintending getting up the anchor, came aft to the wheel to direct her course. He bowed distantly to Hilda, while with affectionate warmth he pressed Bertha Eswick's hand to his lips; Lawrence shook him cordially by his hand, saying as he did so—

'I am glad, cousin, that you have charge of so fine a ship. I hope it will be as profitable as a voyage to Greenland. We are all cousins here, you see, captain—that is to say, all of true Norse blood; and, moreover, are not ashamed of our connections. Here we have Rolf Morton, as pretty a man as you may wish to see, though not Shetland born, as far as we know, married to young Bertha Eswick, daughter to our good cousin Dame Eswick, at present governess, manager, or housekeeper of Lunnasting Castle. Thus, you understand, Rolf Morton is our cousin by marriage; and who would disown him because he is at present but an humble pilot? A finer fellow or a truer seaman does not step, though I say it to his face.'

Morton had not listened to these remarks; but Don Hernan had heard sufficient to understand their tenor, and to make him feel that he was not wrong in placing perfect reliance on his pilot's seamanship and knowledge of the coast. Hilda, who had never before been on board a large ship, was delighted with the sight as she gazed upwards on the towering mass of canvas which seemed to rise into the very blue sky itself; then around on the rich carving and gilt work; on the polished brass, of which several of the guns were formed; on the fresh, bright painting, and the various other embellishments of the ship.

Directed by Morton, the 'St Cecilia' soon glided out through the narrow entrance to the Sound, so close to the black rocks on one side that a good leaper could almost have sprung on shore. The officers turned their eyes now and anon from the rocks, which threatened destruction to their beautiful ship, to the pilot, but his calm, self-confident look assured them that there was no danger, and soon she was rising and falling to the undulations of the open sea, while Whalsey and the other outlying islands blended rapidly into one, and soon could not be distinguished from the main land.

'This is indeed truly enchanting!' exclaimed Hilda. 'Though I have frequently been at sea, it has always been on board some slow-sailing trader or packet, where sights and sounds and associations were all unpleasant together. In a ship like this, how delightful to sail round the world! I should never weary of such a life.'

'Then share it with me, Hilda,' was the natural though unexpected rejoinder of the Spanish captain, spoken in a low voice. 'Oh do not raise hopes and thoughts and aspirations, only to hurl them overboard! We rovers of the sea have but little time to give to wooing. Be mine now and for ever.'

Hilda's countenance betrayed the agitation, doubt, and astonishment which filled her bosom.

'Dearest lady! I would not thus hurriedly press my suit, but any post may bring me orders to leave the coast, never again to return. Your own words betrayed me into uttering a prayer I might not otherwise have ventured so soon to urge; but now it has been made, do not compel me to retract it.'

He stopped a moment to allow his words to take effect. Two or three of his own officers and men only were within hearing, and his calm attitude and manner did not betray the subject of their conversation. Her countenance would have done so to Bertha or Morton, but she turned her head towards the side, apparently watching the ship's course through the water. No one valued her own position more than did Hilda; she had long been taught the importance of keeping her feelings and words under control, from the very reason that she was well aware should she once give them rein they would run wildly off beyond her power. Her thoughts, unhappily, she had never been able to command; and now she found her feelings for this stranger—for stranger he was, though he came in the guise of a kinsman—too powerful for her to conquer. Don Hernan stood gazing into her countenance with as great anxiety, apparently, as if his life hung on her decision. The struggle within her—and a violent one it was—continued till it well-nigh overcame her. She had to hold on to the bulwarks to support herself. Don Hernan began to fear that she would decide against him.

'Speak, Hilda—relieve me from the misery of this suspense!' he exclaimed in a low voice, which could but just reach her ear.

She looked up, and gasped faintly forth—'I am yours, now and for ever.'

Don Hernan poured forth, with all the vehemence of a Spaniard, his expressions of gratitude and joy.

'Happily, there exists no impediment to our immediate

union,' he added. 'I have, as you know, a priest of my own faith on board, and he tells me that there exists on your island a chapel built by some of the seamen of the holy Armada under the direction of my ancestor, and that, although decaying, it is still in a sufficient state of preservation to allow the ceremonies of our religion to be performed in it. Under his directions some of my crew shall be employed, with your permission, in restoring it sufficiently to enable our nuptials to take place there, and your own minister shall afterwards perform the marriage ceremony according to the rites of your church. We will deposit the documents with trustworthy persons, so that no one may afterwards cast discredit on my honour, or utter a word against your fair fame.'

'You have been thoughtfully careful of my interests and happiness, Don Hernan,' answered Hilda. 'I feel that both are safe in your hands.'

It did not occur to her that Don Hernan must have felt tolerably sure of success, to have made all the arrangements of which he spoke.

Calm and collected as the two lovers believed themselves, many eyes on board had been watching their proceedings. Their conversation was interrupted by Rolf Morton coming aft to the captain and inquiring in what direction he would prefer standing.

It was late in the day before the corvette, on her return, approached the Sound. The wind had got round so much to the northward, that Morton determined on taking the corvette into the Sound by the same narrow passage through which she had passed in the morning. Don Hernan consented to his proposal; but when Pedro Alvarez saw the course that was being steered, he showed every disposition to mutiny.

'Because our captain wishes to suit the convenience of a fair lady, and his own pleasure, he will run the risk of casting away our gallant ship. Why not run for Brassy Sound, which is open before us, with a safe entrance?'

These remarks were made to some of his messmates, who were generally ready to assent to his proposals. However, guided by Morton, the corvette stood on, though even Hilda, who had the most perfect confidence in the pilot, as she saw the fierce, foaming waves dashing high up with a loud roar over the rocks to the very summit of the cliffs, could scarcely persuade herself that the ship was not rushing on destruction. The captain stood by the helmsman's side to repeat the pilot's orders. Now nothing but a wall of rocks and foam appeared before them.

'Steady!' cried Morton, 'starboard a little. Steady!' he again cried.

The captain echoed his cry; the passage opened before them; in an instant the ship flew past the rocks; even the oldest sailor breathed more freely when she glided on inside the Sound.

The sails were furled, the anchor was dropped, as she reached the spot from which she had weighed in the morning. The captain insisted on escorting Hilda and her companions on shore.

'In three days, then, at midnight, all will be ready,' he whispered, as he parted from her at the castle landing-place.

CHAPTER V.

LAWRENCE'S EXPEDITION.—HILDA'S MARRIAGE IN THE OLD CHAPEL.—A STORM.

LTHOUGH the sun during the middle of the Shetland summer scarcely ceases to shine, the inhabitants of these isles, like other mortals, require sleep, and take it at the usual time.

Soon after the sea trip Miss Wardhill had taken on board the 'St Cecilia,' Lawrence Brindister was seen one afternoon to descend from his room, booted and spurred, as if for a distant excursion. Hilda, who had her reasons for so doing, watched him anxiously. He stamped about the house, clattering his spurs, and muttering to himself, as was his custom, when anything out of the usual course occupied his mind. At last, going to Surly Grind's kennel, he loosed the dog, and entering his skiff, crossed the voe, as if about to proceed to the mainland.

Hilda breathed more freely when he had gone, but seldom had she appeared so distracted, and little at her ease, as she did till the usual hour of closing the castle gates. The keys were brought to her, as was the custom, by David Cheyne, the old butler, or Major Domo. As he made his bow, he cast a hurried glance at her countenance, and on his way down stairs he shook his head, muttering to himself, 'This foreign gallant will bring no good to the house of Lunnasting—that I see too well; and the sooner the islands are quit of him and his ship—

for all he looks so brave and so bonnie—the better it will be for the young mistress.'

Hilda, instead of retiring to rest, went to her tower; there she remained for some time, pacing up and down the room, now glancing out on the wide ocean, now clasping her hands in a manner expressive of doubt and indecision.

'It is too late to retract,' she exclaimed, at length; 'why should I think of it? What right has my father to complain? He leaves me here without compunction, and am I to await his tardy permission to act, as I have a full right to do, without it? No, that point is settled. Then Bertha suggests that the world will call me unmaidenly, more than indiscreet, and will say that I have been ready to throw myself into the arms of the first stranger I have met; but what care I for this little world of Shetland? I stand on my own rectitude. I shall be far away, and can afford to despise all such insinuations. But the greatest doubt Bertha, in her over-anxious love, has raised up before me, is that regarding Hernan himself. Still I feel sure that he is all that is honourable and noble. He has given me numberless assurances, undoubted, that he is what he represents himself. The proofs he offers are so clear, can I for a moment doubt him? His I have promised to be: his I will be. I should be unworthy of the name of woman were I now to discard him.'

Such was the style of argument with which Hilda Wardhill persuaded herself that she was right in the course she had resolved to adopt.

The marriage was duly solemnized according to the terms of the Roman Catholic Church by Father Mendez. Hilda and Don Hernan signed their names on a parchment placed before them, Bertha and Nanny Clousta signing as witnesses, while Rolf Morton stepped forward and added his name.

Two of Don Hernan's officers, Pedro Alvarez and another, signed their names to the document as witnesses; whilst Lawrence protested against the marriage, as being without the consent or knowledge of Hilda's father, and, therefore, according to Shetland law, invalid. This protest he made with an air of dignity wholly different from his usual manner.

The midnight wedding ceremony at the old chapel terminated in a most terrific hurricane, and the new married couple were compelled to take refuge from the storm in the house of Bertha Morton.

CHAPTER VI.

ROLF MORTON'S HISTORY.—DON HERNAN AND HILDA IN THE MORTON'S HOUSE.—MORTON DISPATCHED TO THE CORVETTE.

ERTHA MORTON had been considered not only one of the prettiest girls in that part of Shetland where she was known, but as good and modest as she was pretty, which is saying much in her favour, where beauty, modesty, and kindness of heart are the characteristics of the people. Her cottage, which was one of the largest in the island, was fitted up with more taste and comfort than was usually found in others, and everything about it bore the marks of competency and good taste. She had but lately married Rolf Morton, who had, a year or two before, been left a small property by his friend and guardian, Captain Andrew Scarsdale. Rolf Morton's own history was somewhat romantic.

Captain Scarsdale, a Shetlander by birth, commanded one of the many Greenland whalers belonging to Hull, Aberdeen, and other northern parts, which touched at Lerwick on their outward and homeward voyages. At length, however, having fallen into ill-health, he was advised to try the effects of a southern clime; and having in his youth made two or three voyages to the South Seas, he was induced to take the command of a South-Sea whaler, which would keep him out three years, or probably more: having no family to bind his affections to England, this was of little consequence.

On his outward voyage, when nearly half way across the Atlantic, he fell in with a raft, on which were three men and a young boy. The men stated that the ship to which they belonged had foundered, and that the boy, whose name they stated was Rolf Morton, belonged to a lady and gentleman among the passengers on board. The rest of the people had perished, and they, with no little exertion, had contrived to save the child.

Captain Scarsdale had, from the first, rather doubted the correctness of their statement, and on his cross-questioning the men separately, his suspicions that there was some mystery in the matter were further confirmed. However, they suspected his object, and he was unable to elicit what he could suppose to be the truth from them. He would have remained altogether in ignorance had not one of them been seized with an illness, and believing himself to be dying, sent for the captain, and made what he asserted to be a full confession of all he knew about the boy.

Captain Scarsdale, who was a cautious man, wrote down all that was told him, and induced the man to sign it. He then instantly sent for the other two men, and telling them what he knew, induced them to confess the truth, and, partly by threats, and partly by persuasions, made them sign the same document. He then carefully locked it up in his chest, and being an upright and kind-hearted man, it was with great satisfaction that he believed he had it in his power to right the wronged.

'Man proposes, God disposes,' is a proverb, day after day proved to be true in the lives of every man. The sick seaman recovered, and he and his comrades, after serving some months on board deserted the ship; and although Captain Scarsdale hunted everywhere, he could gain no further tidings of them.

The child thus strangely found became a fine intelligent

boy, and attached himself warmly to him. His recollections, faint though they were, all tended to corroborate the account the seamen had given. Captain Scarsdale would have sent home the information he had received, and placed the cause of the boy in proper hands; but the men having disappeared, he was afraid to trust the document to a stranger, with the numberless chances of a long sea voyage, against its ever reaching its destination. Unexpected events, however, kept him out in the South Seas far longer than he had anticipated. He did not object to this, for he had the boy as his companion, and he devoted himself to his education. Young Rolf did not show any great talent, but he gave every promise of becoming a fine, manly, true-hearted sailor, and with that his kind patron was amply satisfied.

At length, just as the ship had nearly completed her cargo of sperm oil, and was about to return home, she was overtaken by a hurricane, and driven on shore and lost; the crew were saved, and so was the captain's chest. Most of Captain Scarsdale's hard-earned gains were swallowed up; and the command of another whaler, whose master had died, being offered him, he gladly accepted it, in the hopes that, by remaining out a few years longer, he should be able to retrieve his fortunes; and what was still nearer his heart, of obtaining the means for, as he told his acquaintance, of establishing young Morton's rights. What he considered those rights to be he wisely told no one.

'No, no,' he replied, when asked; 'no one but a fool sounds a trumpet before him to give notice of his approach, that the enemy may be prepared to receive him.'

Rolf Morton had by this time become all that his friend anticipated; but though well-informed for his age, his knowledge of the world and its ways, it must be owned, was not extensive.

The ship was bound to Liverpool, but being dismasted in a terrific gale, she was driven past the entrance to the Channel, and up the west coast of Ireland. Land was made at last on the starboard bow, and hopes were entertained that she might be brought round so as to enter the Irish Channel by the northern passage. Captain Scarsdale himself lay in his hammock, disabled by a falling spar.

Scarcely an hour had passed after the land was seen before the ship struck. It was ascertained that it was on the extreme point of a reef, and the first mate hoped that by lightening the ship she might beat over it. The captain acquiesced, and every article that could be got at was, as soon as possible, committed to the sea.

'Yes, heave away—heave away everything you can lay your hands on, lads!' was the order. 'It will matter but little, I suspect, after all.'

Among other things thrown overboard was the captain's chest; the mate saw it just as it reached the foaming sea, too late to save it. He said nothing to the captain: he believed that the ship herself would be lost, but his prognostications proved wrong; the good ship drove over the bank, weathered out the gale, jury-masts were got up, and she not only got into the Irish Channel, but safe up the Mersey, without any help whatever.

Great was the grief of good Captain Scarsdale, when, on recovering from his hurts, he discovered that his chest and its valuable contents had been hove overboard. As has been said, he was a mild-tempered man, so he did not storm and rage, but as the profits of the voyage had been considerable, he resolved to devote them to establishing the claims of the young foundling. He had never told Rolf Morton what those claims were. He knew that they would only tend to unsettle the mind of the boy, and make him less contented with his lot, should he fail to obtain his rights. Rolf had no more notion, therefore, than the world in general, who he was, and he believed the story which had at first been told by the men, that he was the son of a gentleman and lady who had perished on board a ship which had foundered on its way to South America.

As soon as Captain Scarsdale had settled his affairs in Liverpool, he hastened to Edinburgh, where he had a relative, a writer to the 'Signet.' He laid the boy's case before him.

'My good Andrew, don't waste your money in making the attempt till you have surer grounds to go on than you now have,' was the answer. 'Possession is nine parts of the law. I have no more doubt than you have as to the claims of this boy; but can you prove them without documents or evidence of any sort? Can you expect to overcome a powerful and unscrupulous opponent? You have perfect trust in Providence, Andrew—so have I, lawyer though I am; and be assured that in God's good time justice will be awarded to all parties concerned.'

This was not exactly like legal advice in general; but Andrew Scarsdale at once saw its wisdom, and agreed to abide by it. Proceeding to Aberdeen, he was at once offered the charge of a Greenland whaler. He accepted the offer, taking Rolf Morton with him. He touched at Lerwick both on his outward and homeward voyage. While on shore on the first occasion, he heard that a small property was for sale in the island of Whalsey, nearly the only portion of the whole island which did not belong to the Lunnasting family. He at once authorized the principal legal man in the island to purchase it for him at any cost.

'I have a mind to have it,' he observed; 'remember my ancestors came from Whalsey, and I should like, perchance, to end my latter days there.'

Great was his satisfaction, on his return, to find that the property was his. 'That is well,' he remarked; 'and now, in case of my death, I wish to settle it on my young friend Rolf Morton. You can get the necessary documents drawn up, I hope, before I sail: we seamen learn one piece of wisdom, at all events—the uncertainty of life—however slow we may be to pick up others; and, therefore, when we sail, leave our last will and testament behind us. You'll take care of this for me, and act upon it, should I never return to desire it altered.'

The lawyer promised to see his friend's bequest attended to, but many years passed before he was called on to act in the matter. Not only did Captain Scarsdale come back, but with young Rolf Morton as his companion, he took up his abode for several years, during the winter, in a farm-house which he had considerably improved on his newly purchased property; he claimed relationship, which was fully acknowledged, with the Brindister family, and he and Lawrence, who took also very speedily to Rolf, soon became fast friends. He was invited also to become a frequent guest at Lunnasting Castle, though he showed but little inclination to accept the hospitality of its inmates.

Andrew Scarsdale, however, did not give up the sea. Though possessed of a moderate independence he did not wish to lead an idle life, but every summer he sailed to Greenland in command of a whaler, and most years took Rolf with him: wishing at the same time that his young ward should have the advantages of a liberal education, he sent him for two years to Aberdeen, that he might acquire some knowledge in those branches in which he was himself unable to afford him instruction. Rolf made up by perseverance for what he wanted in talent, and thus, with Captain Scarsdale's help, he obtained not only a necessary knowledge of nautical affairs, but as large an amount of general information as most seafaring men of his position at that time possessed. It might have been better if the good captain, who was now advancing in years, had remained at home; but anxious to increase his means for the sake of the object he had nearest at heart, he took a larger share than before in a whaler, and sailed once more, with Rolf in his company, for Greenland. Eager in the pursuit of the oil-giving whale, he proceeded further north than usual, his ship got nipped in the ice, crushed into a thousand fragments, and Rolf Morton, and six of the crew only escaped with their lives.

Sorrowing deeply for the loss of his kind friend and protector, and caring very little for that of his fortune, Rolf at length returned home to find himself the possessor of the small farm and house on Whalsey, and very little else in the world. He was not in the slightest degree cast down, however; he made another voyage to Greenland as mate, and having been very successful, came home and married young Bertha Eswick, to whom he had before sailing engaged himself.

Bertha Morton, like the rest of her countrywomen, accepted her lot, and notwithstanding the fate to which so many others were subjected, she hoped to enjoy years of happiness with her brave, fine-hearted husband. There was not in all Scotland, just then, a blither or happier woman than Bertha Morton. Her husband had told her that he expected to be at home soon after midnight, and she was sitting up to receive him. As the fury of the storm had not broke till some time after she hoped her husband would be safe on shore, she was not particularly anxious about his safety; still, as time wore on, her keen ear became more and more alive to approaching sounds: at length she heard footsteps. Her husband's voice called to her, and in he rushed with her mother and Nanny Clousta, followed by Don Hernan and Hilda. Her astonishment at seeing them was very great, but without losing time in asking unnecessary questions, she set to work to remedy, as far as she had the power, the effects of the pelting rain to which her guests had been exposed. Fresh fuel was added to the already hot peat fire on the hearth, that the foreign captain and her husband might dry their clothes while she retired with her female visitors, that they might change theirs for such as her own ample wardrobe could supply. Her best Sunday gown well became Hilda, for except in height they differed but little in figure; indeed, dressed as they now were, in the same homely garb, there was a remarkable likeness between them. Nanny soon came back to place certain pots and kettles on the fire to prepare supper, which by the time all the party were ready to partake of it, was placed on the table.

Bertha Eswick's position in the family fully entitled her to sit at table with her mistress, and of course her daughter and son-in-law took their seats at their own table, but nothing could induce Nanny so to intrude herself, and she requested that she might be allowed to carry her plate to a large chest at one side of the room where she might eat her food by herself. Morton and Don Hernan could not help glancing a look at each other, as they observed the similarity of feature, but the tranquil, contented look which those of Bertha wore offered a strong contrast to the agitated unsettled expression of Hilda's. Bertha and her mother did their utmost to tranquillize her mind, and by lively conversation to counteract the effect which the strange scene she had just gone through had produced. The beating of the rain and the roaring and howling of the wind were alone sufficient to baffle all their efforts. The storm continued with unabated fury, and gave every sign of being one of those which last for three or four days.

Hilda having expressed her annoyance at the surmises to which her absence would give rise in the castle, Rolf volunteered to go and inform the household that she had taken refuge in his house, and would return as soon as the weather permitted her to do so, while Don Hernan further commissioned him to proceed on along the shore of the Sound to ascertain that the 'St Cecilia' was in safety, and whether his officers and men had escaped injury, and had returned on board.

'I ought to go myself, Mr Morton, I am well aware of that, but here is my excuse,' he observed, pointing to Hilda: 'my officers are true Spaniards, and will receive it as a valid one.'

'An English officer would consider that his first duty was to look after his ship, whatever else might interfere, and there lies the difference between us,' muttered Morton, as facing the pelting rain and furious wind, he took his departure from his comfortable home.

CHAPTER VII.

DON HERNAN AND HILDA AT THE CASTLE.—THE SPANISH OFFICERS ON SHORE.—DON HERNAN ORDERED TO QUIT SHETLAND.

'O my mind it wad ha' been better for one and a' of us, if Miss Hilda had gone and wed with a true, honest-hearted Shetlander, instead of this new-found foreigner, for all his fine clothes, and fine airs, and silk purse; it's few times I have seen the inside of it.' This was said by old Davie Cheyne to Nanny Clousta, about two weeks after Hilda and her husband had taken up their abode at the castle. 'What Sir Marcus will say about the matter, it makes me tremble to think of. It's my belief he'll be inclined to pull the house down about our ears, or to send us and it flying up into the sky together. I wad ha' thought she might ha' found a young Mouat, or a Gifford, or a Bruce, or Nicolson. There are mony likely lads among them far better than this captain, now; I can no like him better than does Mr Lawrence, and that's a sma' portion indeed.'

'You're too hard, Mr Cheyne, on our new master,' answered Nanny; 'if ye had seen the gold piece he gave me the day we came back to the castle, and the beautiful silver one which he put into my hand only yesterday, with the two pillars on it, ye wad no say a' that against him. No, no, Mr Cheyne, he's a fine gentleman, and a right fit husband for our young mistress.'

For more than a fortnight Don Hernan had not set his foot on board the 'St Cecilia.' Both officers and crew had, however, begun to complain at being left so long in so uninteresting a spot in perfect inactivity; Don Hernan accordingly ordered the ship back to Brassay Sound under charge of Pedro Alvarez.

Strange as it may seem, the news of Don Hernan's marriage with Miss Wardhill had not yet reached Lerwick. There was at no time any very regular intercourse kept up between the islands, and that which was usual had been interrupted by the bad weather.

Rolf Morton, like a wise man, resolved to keep his knowledge of the matter to himself, and to say nothing, while Father Mendez, the only person belonging to the ship who, from being able to speak English, could have communicated it, was not likely to say a word about the matter, unless he had some object in doing so. Bailie Sanderson of Lerwick was a staunch Presbyterian, and a warm hater of Episcopacy and Popery; and it was a sore struggle in his mind how far he was justified in having any dealings with the only representative of the latter power, who had for many a long year ventured to set foot on the soil of Shetland; in vain he tried to make the purser understand him. Stores for the ship of all sorts were wanted, but no arrangements could be made, and at length Father Mendez was called to their councils. The bailie believed himself so fully guarded against any of the doctrines held by the priest, that he had no fear as to any attempts he might make to change his own opinions; but the truth was, that Father Mendez understood him far better than he understood Father Mendez, who, had he thought it worth his while, would not have made his approaches in a mode the bailie was at all likely to discover till the foundations of his fortress had been sapped and undermined. The priest, however, had not the slightest intention of making an attack on the bailie's religious principles, whatever might have been his mission to those northern regions. There were some who did not fail to assert that he had ulterior views; but he made himself generally so very popular, that the greater number considered him a very well-behaved, harmless, kind gentleman, who was ready to smile at all their amusements, even though he might not partake in them, and was conversable and affable with every one.

For nearly three weeks or more the 'St Cecilia' remained at Lerwick, and while her officers were busy gaining golden opinions from the people, they spent a good many golden pieces among them.

'And after a' the real goud is the best thing o' the twa,' as Bailie Sanderson observed. 'The one, unless, maybe, it's the deil's pay, will rest in the purse, or bring something substantial in return, and is muckle like the snow in the spring time; it looks very white and glittering, but quickly vanishes awa.'

At length Rolf Morton arrived from Whalsey with an order from Don Hernan to Pedro Alvarez to carry the ship back to Eastling Sound. The corvette was instantly got under weigh, and tide and wind suiting, she stood back towards Lunnasting Castle. The inhabitants of Lerwick saw her departure with no little astonishment, as not a word had been said to lead them to suppose she was going. Some had their misgivings on certain material points. Bailie Sanderson, especially, was very uncomfortable; he had furnished a large amount of stores —far more than any one else had done; but though he had got in his hands several bills, in the shape of long bits of paper, accepted by Don Diogo Ponti, purser of His most Catholic Majesty's ship, the 'St Cecilia,' and by Don Hernan de Escalante, captain of the said ship, he had received very little hard cash, and several of his friends, when they had looked at those strips of paper, and turned and twisted them about, in a variety of ways, with an expression in their countenances which betokened commiseration, hoped that he might, by the mercy of Providence, get the siller for them, but that it would be next a miracle if he did. In a moment all his airy castles and the delightful profits he had anticipated were scattered to the wind, while no one to whom he applied could afford him the slightest consolation.

The most trying time in Hilda's existence had arrived. She had given her heart to Don Hernan, and she had married him; but she had never dared to reflect on the consequences of her doing so. When at length he told her that the last packet from the south had brought him peremptory orders to proceed on his voyage, the news came on her like a sudden thunder-clap. No longer had she the power of acting, as of yore, according to her own untrammeled will. She had discovered that already. What would he determine? To let him go from her, and leave her alone, were worse than death. When might he return? Would he ever come back? What numberless chances might intervene to prevent him. Yet the thought of leaving the castle, placed under her charge, was naturally revolting to her feelings. Her father had intrusted her with his property. Could she betray that trust without meriting his just censure? Yet had she not already done enough to make him discard her altogether? 'Yes, I have,' she exclaimed, with some degree of bitterness. 'How can I stand the storm of rage, and then the scornful sneers with which he will assail me? Accompany Hernan, I will, come what may of it. If he refuses he shall not leave behind a living bride. Scorn, pity, or anger, would be insufferable, and to all shall I be exposed if I remain.'

To such a resolution it might have been expected that a woman of ardent temperament and untrained mind, like Hilda, would have arrived, whatever course of doubt and hesitation she might have first gone through.

Don Hernan returned with a clouded brow from his first visit to his ship. He found Hilda seated in her turret-chamber. He threw himself on a sofa by her side.

'There has been discontent and well-nigh mutiny among

my people,' he exclaimed in an angry tone. 'I might have known that it would have been so; idleness does not suit the fellows—I must take care that they have no more of it; they will have plenty to do in future. Well, Hilda, our happy days here must now come to an end. They have flitted by faster than I could have expected.' Hilda gazed in his face, trembling to hear what might follow. He spoke calmly: 'Yes, a few short weeks seem not longer than as many hours; and now I fear, dearest, we must part, though it may be but for a short period. I may obtain leave to return with the 'St Cecilia,' or you must travel south by a shorter route through England, and thence on to Spain. I cannot shield you, I fear, from some of the inconveniences to which sailors' wives are exposed.'

'Leave me! Oh, no, no!' exclaimed Hilda, passionately. 'Take me with you. I cannot be parted from you! You tell me you love me: it would be but cruel love to kill me; and I tell you I could not survive our separation. I speak the truth —oh, believe me, Hernan,-I do!'

The Spanish captain looked at her as if he doubted her assertion; but he would indeed have been a sceptic as to the depth of the power of woman's affection had he longer continued to doubt when he saw her beseeching and almost agonized countenance turned on him, waiting for his decision.

'But can you, Hilda, endure all the hardships and dangers we may have to go through?' he asked. 'We may be exposed to furious tempests, and perhaps have to fight more than one battle, before we reach a Spanish port.'

'Yes, yes, I can endure everything you have to suffer,' she answered, taking his hand in one of hers, while she placed the other on his shoulder, and looked up into his face as if she would read his inward soul. 'Why should I fear the tempest when you are on board, or the battle, while I can stand by your side? Take me with you, Hernan. Prove me, and I shall not be found wanting.'

'Hilda, you are a brave woman—you have conquered my resolution. We will go together,' he exclaimed, clasping her to his heart.

The shriek of joy she gave showed the intensity of her anxiety, and how it had been relieved by this announcement.

Still Don Hernan lingered. Was it that he was unwilling to tear himself away from a spot where he had spent some of the brightest moments of his existence? Had he other less ostensible motives for delay?

Hilda's announcement of her intended departure was received in silence by Sandy Redland, the factor, and David Cheyne, the old butler. The former, perhaps, was not ill-content to have the entire management of the estate left in his hands. Nanny Clousta, without hesitation, agreed to accompany her mistress, and thus the only person who really grieved for Hilda's departure was Bertha Eswick. She walked about the castle in a state of bewilderment very different to her usual collected manner, and was continually asking herself if she could not have prevented the result for which she mourned. The only person who seemed totally unconscious that any unusual event was about to occur was Lawrence Brindister. He treated his cousin and Don Hernan with a mock courtesy which was excessively annoying, the more especially as it was utterly impossible to resent it.

The hour of her departure arrived. Hilda had made every preparation for it in her power; still the utter want of propriety in the step she was taking pressed heavily on her spirits. Except her own garments and a few of her books, she took nothing with her. 'It shall not be said that I am spoiling my father's house,' she exclaimed, with some bitterness, as she showed Bertha everything she wished packed up.

Don Hernan's barge was in readiness at the landing-place, where Sandy Redland stood ready to receive the keys. As she left the castle, she looked, as old Davie Cheyne afterwards remarked, 'more like Mary Queen of Scots, or some other great lady, going to execution, than a bride accompanying her husband to his home.' As she was about to step into the boat she took Bertha's hand.

'Dear nurse and cousin,' she whispered, ' you know I loved you more than any other human being, but I dare not show it lest my feelings should run riot with me. Farewell! The future is all obscure and uncertain. I dare not talk of when we may meet again.'

Don Hernan took her hand and helped her into the boat. The word was given to shove off—the oars were dipped into the water—when down from the castle gate rushed Lawrence Brindister, followed closely by Surly Grind.

'Ha! ha!' he exclaimed, in a hoarse, angry voice. 'Fare-thee-well, cousin Hilda—fare-thee-well! though you would leave your kinsman without saying as much to him. And you, Don Hernan, fare-thee-well, too. You think you have wedded with the heiress of Lunnasting. It's a pleasant dream to believe that you will some day be master of those lordly towers. Dream on as you please, but know the truth : " The prince will hae his ain again! the prince will hae his ain again!"'

These words he continued singing at the top of his voice, pointing derisively at the boat as long as she continued in sight.

Don Hernan urged the crew to give way, and with lusty strokes they sent the boat flying through the water, till she was far out of hearing of Lawrence's voice. Hilda sank back in her husband's arms, and hid her eyes while she was passing under the walls of the dwelling she believed that she was leaving for ever. With shouts of welcome the Spanish crew received their captain's bride. Scarcely had she stepped on board than the anchor, which had been hove short, was run up to the bows, the sails were let fall, and, with a light breeze from the westward, the corvette stood out of Eastling Sound.

Rolf Morton was on board as pilot. He bowed to Hilda,

but his duty in attending to the steering of the ship prevented his speaking. As she looked at him, she felt that he was the last link which yet united her with the past, and she almost dreaded the moment that he would have to leave the ship. 'Yet, after all, from what do I sever myself?' she thought. 'From associations only. Begone all such recollections. Let me enjoy the delightful present, and the no less happy future I trust.'

No day could have been more beautiful in any latitude than that on which the 'St Cecilia' sailed from Shetland. The sea was smooth, just broken with a slight ripple, which glittered brightly in the rays of the sun as the ship slipped quickly through it with a gentle breeze abeam. The arrangements, also, which Hilda's husband had made below for her accommodation were perfect. He, too, was kind and courteous in the extreme; and had she been a princess, the officers could not have treated her with greater respect. Over and over again she said to herself, 'I should indeed be ungrateful if I am not happy.'

Having given a good offing to the Out Skerries, so as to avoid the dangers near Feltar, the corvette stood to the northward, it being the intention of the captain to round the northern end of Shetland, and by that course to enter the Atlantic. Rolf Morton's boat was towing astern, and he agreed to remain on board to see the ship clear of the land. The weather was beautiful, the sea was smooth, the wind was light, and there was every prospect of a pleasant commencement of a voyage, as he finally wished her God-speed.

Soon after Rolf Morton had left the corvette, the wind, after veering about for a short time, had got round to the southward, so that she was able to haul up to the southward of west. This appeared a great advantage gained, as it enabled her to keep exactly on her proper course. How shortsighted truly are mortals in discovering what is really to their advantage! The sun sunk in an angry glow of ruddy hue which suffused the whole eastern sky, and cast an ensanguined tint on the foaming crests of the fast-rising waves. Then, as if it had gone to hurry on the storm, there rushed up from the dark bank of clouds numerous detached masses, which flew rapidly across the sky, one chasing the other in their headlong speed.

Don Hernan and his officers saw the storm coming, but they were anxious to get as good an offing as possible before it had time to burst on them, and therefore kept the ship under all the canvas she could carry. On she flew, right into the eye of the rising tempest, so it seemed, though as yet the wind held to the southward. The topgallant masts bent and twisted like wands; still the captain would not allow the sails to be taken in. The wind whistled more and more shrilly through the rigging; each sea that rose seemed to increase in height, and to strike the bows with greater force as the ship, frantically it seemed, forced her onward way, while white driving foam flew in dense masses over her forecastle, and sprinkled with its lighter showers the greater part of the deck. A few stars came out and shone brightly overhead, but they were quickly obscured by the gathering clouds; the darkness increased, till nothing could be seen on either hand but the dark, tumbling seas with their white foaming crests.

Pedro Alvarez had been watching the signs of the weather with anything but a satisfied look. 'We shall have it down upon us, Don Hernan, before long,' he remarked, going up to the captain. 'If it catches us with all this canvas spread, some of our masts will go, I fear.'

'We may hold on yet for some time, I hope,' was the answer. 'I have not forgotten yet the look of that rocky coast.'

'Nor I either; and I therefore would try to keep my sticks to beat it off,' muttered the first lieutenant, as he turned away.

It appeared, however, that he was over-cautious; for some time longer there was no alteration in the weather.

'After all, I am in hopes that the squall will pass over, and by the time we have made good our westing we may get a favourable change of wind,' observed the captain, as the first lieutenant approached him. 'I am going below; call me, should anything occur.'

'You will not have long to wait,' said Pedro Alvarez, bluntly.

He was right. The captain's head was scarcely below the companion hatch, when the ship, which had been heeling over to starboard till the scuppers were under water, righted suddenly, and her sails flapped loudly against the masts.

'Hands aloft, shorten sail!' shouted the first lieutenant, with an energy that made every one start to obey the order. 'Let fly topgallant sheets! Be smart, my men.'

The sails were being quickly handed. The officer had ordered topgallant-yards to be sent down, and topgallant-masts struck, when a vivid flash of forked lightning darted close ahead, across the ship's course, followed by a terrific crash of thunder, which startled all on board. Many thought the electric fluid had struck the ship. The captain sprang on deck. He was just in time to see the ship taken aback by the long-threatening gale, which came down with greater fury from its continued delay. Stern first she drove, the rising seas threatening to engulph her. Pedro Alvarez was shouting out the necessary orders to bring her round, so as once more to get headway on her. But the men were aloft endeavouring to execute the previous order issued to them, and some were obeying one order, some another. In vain Don Hernan endeavoured to aid in restoring order. The object was to reduce the after sails, so that those ahead might have greater influence. All the masts were crowded with the labouring crew; fiercer blew the tempest; there was a crash; wild shrieks, rising high above the howling of the storm, rent the air. The mizen-mast had gone by the board, and falling over the starboard side had carried all those upon it into the boiling ocean.

There was a second crash; the mainyard had gone, and it seemed likely, from the way in which the mainmast bent and quivered that that also would go. In vain many of the poor fellows cast from the mizen-mast struggled for life; their shipmates were too busily occupied to afford them assistance. Some had clung desperately to the rigging, and had managed to regain it, and were endeavouring to haul themselves on board again. Now one succeeded; now another, with a cry of despair, was washed off, as the seas dashed furiously up against the corvette's quarter, threatening to drive in her counter, or to carry away her taffrail.

All the time the butt end of the mizen-mast was striking like a battering-ram against the side of the ship, with every chance of speedily making a hole in it. The main-yard, too, had fallen across the deck, still held by lifts and braces from going overboard, more dangerous in that position than if it had done so. The sudden blast which had caused the destruction was only the first of the tempest. Stronger and stronger it grew. It would be difficult truly to picture the scene of tumult and confusion which the deck of the corvette presented, all the time driving stern first at a fearful rate, now lifted high up by the sea, now rushing downward into the watery gulf, the opposite sea looking as if it would overwhelm her. The officers, with loud shouts, were issuing orders in different parts of the ship; the men, called off from their regular stations, rushing here and there, not knowing which to obey, but still seeing clearly that each order imperatively demanded to be instantly executed. In vain Don Hernan, speaking-trumpet in hand, endeavoured to reduce the confusion into order. At this juncture a flash of lightning revealed a tall figure, with flowing white drapery, standing near the companion-hatch. He shuddered with a superstitious feeling of dread. The next instant he saw that it was his wife; he hurried up to her to entreat her to go below. The darkness concealed the look of astonishment and dismay with which she regarded the scene around her. In a moment Don Hernan was by her side.

'Hilda, my beloved, this is no place for you. Oh, go below, I entreat you, I command you. Any moment your life may be sacrificed.'

'Why should I shun dangers, Hernan, to which you must be exposed?' she exclaimed. 'But what does this mean—what has happened?'

'A mere accident, to which all ships are liable,' he answered. 'There is nothing to fear, if you will remain calmly in your cabin.'

'But shrieks and cries for help reached my ears, and terrific blows,' said Hilda. 'Oh! do not deceive me, Hernan; surely some sad calamity has occurred.'

The captain saw that he could not deceive her, and not till he had explained how matters really stood, could he induce her to return to her cabin. Meantime Pedro Alvarez had succeeded in bracing round the head yards and furling all the after sails. Slowly the ship answered her helm and fell off; but as she did so, two seas in quick succession struck her abeam, dashing across her deck, and carrying away the boats stowed on the boom, and part of the lee bulwarks. Again shrieks for help were heard; but the darkness prevented it being seen from whence they came, though there was too much reason to fear that the same seas which had washed away the boats, had carried off more of their unfortunate shipmates. Once more the ship went ahead, but it was before the wind, and she was flying back towards that iron-bound coast of Shetland, from which all on board had been so eager to escape. Every effort was now made to bring the ship on a wind either to heave her to, or to stand to the northward or southward, so that, should the gale continue, she might weather one end or the other of the islands. After a time it was decided to haul up on the port or larboard tack, as it was believed that she had made but little southing, and was in consequence, nearer the northern than the southern end of Shetland.

On ploughed the 'St Cecilia' through the darkness, and many a heart on board dreaded the sight which daylight would reveal to them.

CHAPTER VIII.

ROLF MORTON'S EXPEDITION.—WATCHES THE CORVETTE.—HILDA'S MARRIAGE DISCUSSED.—THE STORM.—A SHIP SEEN DRIVING TOWARDS SHORE.

AFTER Rolf Morton had left the 'St Cecilia,' and was steering for Yell Sound, he recollected that a long time had passed since he had paid a visit to an old friend, who had been Captain Scarsdale's first mate on several voyages, but who had now retired from sea life, and settled at Hillswick, in the southern part of that peculiarly shaped peninsula of Shetland, called North Maven. There were two ways of getting there. The most speedy was to haul up to the southward at once, and to steer for St Magnus's Bay, so as to round the southern point of North Maven, called Esha Ness; but then, when he wished to return to Whalsey, he would have had to retrace his course along the whole western coast of the peninsula before he could enter Yell Sound. Should the weather continue fine, this would be of little consequence; but in bad weather the voyage would be one of great danger, as standing out as do its lofty cliffs, to brave the whole roll of the Western Ocean, on no part of the coast does the sea break with more terrific fury. The other course was to run up Yell Sound as he had intended; but, instead of passing through it, to land on the southern shore, in one of the many small voes or inlets, to be found there, so that a walk of a mile or so would enable him to reach the house of his friend

Angus Maitland. Before determining what to do, he cast his eye seaward round the horizon. The low bank of clouds he there observed, just rising, as it were, out of the water, made him keep the boat on the course he had before been steering. Before many minutes had passed the increasing wind showed the wisdom of his determination. Away bounded the boat over the rising seas; but no sooner had she entered the Sound than she glided smoothly along over its calm water, and soon reached the point where Morton proposed landing. All the crew, however, had some excuse for visiting Hillswick. Angus Maitland's abode was known for its hospitality, and no one ever came there who did not receive a hearty welcome, and the best accommodation he could afford, suited to their rank and position. The boat was left securely moored in a little voe, where not the fiercest of storms from without could reach her.

Honesty is a characteristic of the Shetlanders, and Morton and his crew knew well that should she by chance be discovered, not a rope-yarn would be taken away. A high heather-covered hill lay between the spot where they landed and Hillswick. Morton stopped when he reached the top, and took a glance along the whole western horizon, which lay open to view. The corvette was already hull down, standing on close-hauled to the southward of west, in which direction the bank of clouds he had before remarked had greatly increased in height and denseness.

'She is making a good offing, and the Spaniards will have reason enough to be glad they have done so,' observed Morton. 'The squall brewing out there will be down upon them before long, hot and strong; but if they heave the ship to at once, it will have blown itself out before they have time to drift back near enough to our coast to come to any harm.'

The men assented to the correctness of Morton's remark. Perhaps they did not as warmly wish for the safety of the corvette as he did. Formerly, probably, they would have prayed that Providence would mercifully drive her back, and wreck her in some convenient spot among the rocks, where, though the crew might be lost, whatever was of value in her might be cast on shore for the benefit of the people.

Angus Maitland spied Morton coming down the hill, and, his portly figure clad in a suit of grey shepherd's plaid, and a stout stick in his hand, he sallied forth to meet him. His greeting was warm and hearty.

'Come along, Rolf—come along, man; now I've got you I'll keep you,' he exclaimed, when Morton had told him how it was he had come to North Maven. 'Your guid wife will spare ye for a day, and she'll guess that you would not pass within hail of our shores without coming to see me.'

Morton, however, urged that Bertha was not aware that he had come round to the west coast; that she would be expecting him, and would be anxious if he did not appear.

'Stay, though,' exclaimed his host. 'There is Sandy M'Nab will be crossing the mainland with his pack, and he will send over a message for you to Whalsey; there will be no lack of opportunities.'

Morton promised to stay away this night, should he be able to send a message to his wife, to the effect that he was doing so. Sandy M'Nab, the packman, was found on the point of starting, with his two half-starved shelties, scarcely the size of ordinary donkeys, but with wonderful strength of limb and power of endurance. He undertook that Morton's note to his wife should be delivered without fail; and this matter being settled, Rolf, in no way loath, accepted his friend's invitation. There was good cheer for all hands, though dried fish, oat-cakes, and whisky formed the staple articles of the feast.

Maitland of course wished to hear all about the extraordinary marriage of the heiress of Lunnasting with the Spanish captain, for strange stories had got about, and, as he observed, it was hard to know what to believe and what to discredit.

'There's nothing so unnatural-like in the proceeding,' observed the old gentleman, after Rolf had given him a true, unvarnished account of the affair. 'He's a handsome gallant, and she's a very fine lassie, there's no denying that; but at the same time, God's blessing does not alight on marriages contracted without the parent's consent; and it's my opinion that Miss Wardhill should have waited till Sir Marcus came home before entering into a contract.'

Rolf hinted that Sir Marcus's whole conduct was not such as to secure the love and obedience of his daughter.

'That may be,' answered Maitland; 'he might not have gained her love, but her obedience still was due to him. He left her, too, in charge of the castle, and now she has fled from her post like a deserter. Poor lassie, I would not be hard on her, though; and I doubt not by this time she is wishing herself on shore again, for the gallant ship she thought so brave must be pitching and rolling pretty heavily by this time.'

The friends were at supper, and while they were discussing their food and this same knotty subject, the loud barking of two Newfoundland dogs which roamed round the premises was heard, answered by the fierce growl of another of the canine race, which seemed to come from some little distance off.

'This is a late time o' night for a visitor to come, but whoever he may be he is welcome,' said Maitland. 'Here's to you, Rolf; we'll just finish this glass, that we may have a fresh brew of toddy for him when he comes.'

Again the deep bark and growl of the stranger's dog was heard.

'There is but one creature in Shetland which barks like that,' observed Morton. 'I should know his voice anywhere; it is Lawrence Brindister's dog, Surly Grind. What can have brought him here?'

'He'll answer for himself, for here he comes,' replied Maitland, looking out of the window, whence the person in question was seen approaching the house, mounted on the smallest and shaggiest of Shetland ponies, and his legs, encased in topboots, almost dragging along the ground, though he managed, by a succession of sudden jerks, to lift them up so as to avoid the numerous inequalities of the way. His odd appearance was increased by his wearing a broad-brimmed hat and feather, and a long-waisted coat, part of an old court-suit. When he came to the door of the house, all he did was to stand upright, and to let his steed pass from under him. He threw the bridle to Surly Grind, who took it in his mouth, and lying down held it fast, the pony agreeing quietly in that novel mode of being tethered. Just as Captain Maitland had risen to receive him, he shuffled into the room, making a bow worthy of a Frenchman of the old school.

'Welcome to Hillswick, Mr Lawrence,' said Captain Maitland; 'it is not often that we have had the pleasure of your company of late. Come, sit down and take your supper; it's a long journey you have made to-day, and the air on the top of Ronas Hill is well calculated to give a man an appetite.'

'Not a bad notion, friend Maitland,' answered poor Lawrence. 'By the same token, too, little Neogle and Surly Grind will be beholden to your hospitality, for it is but a small allowance of food they have had since we left Whalsey this morning. A bone for the dog, and a handful of meal for Neogle, is all I'll ask. The pony will easily pick up enough by himself to finish his supper.'

Captain Maitland gave the necessary orders to an old man who acted as his servant-of-all-work, but Surly Grind would not be induced to let go the bridle, even though a savoury mess besides the bone was placed before his nose, till his master had called to him from the window and released him from his office. The pony, as soon as he had had his basin of brose, and his bridle and saddle were taken off him, trotted off to the plot of greenest grass in the neighbourhood.

'That is a curious name you have given your pony, Mr Lawrence,' observed Maitland, when his guest was comfortably seated at supper. 'It is what would be called in Scotland a water kelpie. Is there anything of the nature of a Trow in your little animal?'

'More, perhaps, than you think of, friend,' answered Lawrence, gravely. 'Neogle can do everything but speak; whatever I tell him he does it immediately. He follows me like my dog; he'll step into my boat and lie down at the bottom of it, as readily as Surly Grind himself, or if I order him to swim astern, he jumps in forthwith; and if I was to take a cruise round the mainland, he would come after me as long as he had strength to swim.'

'He may do all that and not be a trow,' observed Morton, laughing; for he, as well as Captain Maitland, was anxious to prevent Lawrence's thoughts running upon the recent events.

'Right, cousin Morton, right,' answered Lawrence. 'I came honestly by him by purchase, and called him Neogle on account of his strength, and sagacity, and docility. The country people gave the name of the Neogle to a wicked sort of trow, whom they believe lives in the water, and whose great aim is to carry off people to destroy them. On that account he appears in the shape of a pretty pony, bridled and saddled, and all ready for a pleasant gallop across the country. He has a great fancy for carrying off millers. To do this he stops the wheel of the mill. That makes the miller come out of the house to learn what is the matter. On goes the mill once more, and when he looks about he sees the pony. If he is a young miller, and has not heard about the Neogle, or doesn't believe in it, or forgets about it—'Ho, ho!' says he, 'the mill is going on all smooth and pleasantly, so I'll just take a gallop, and be back before it's time to put in more grist.' On that he leaps on the seeming pony, when off goes the trow, fleet as the winds. Away, away he goes. In vain the poor miller tries to throw himself off: a broken leg or an arm would be far, far better than the fate awaiting him. He is though, he finds, glued, as it were, to the saddle. On gallops the Neogle over hill and down, and bog, and loch, and stream, and voe; nothing stops him till the sea is reached, and then across it he flies till he is over the deep water, when down he dives in a mass of flame, with loud shrieks of mocking laughter, and never again is the poor miller heard of.'

'That's a curious notion, Mr Lawrence,' observed Captain Maitland. 'I never heard it before; but do you say the people believe in it?'

'Troth do I; and why should they not?' answered Lawrence, blinking his eyes. 'There are many things which you have seen in your voyages, and which would seem very strange to our people, if you were to tell of them. As to the Neogle, I never saw one that I know of, but I should be very cautious about mounting him if I did.'

The evening was now drawing on, the storm which had for some time been threatening had nearly reached the island; vivid flashes of lightning darted from the sky, and loud thunder claps rolled almost overhead. A sharp neigh was heard, and Lawrence Brindister started up.

'Ah, Neogle is aware of what is coming, and has trotted up to ask for shelter,' he observed, going to the window 'You'll let him have a corner in your stable, captain, I dare say?'

The request was at once complied with, and scarcely was the pony under shelter than down came the storm, the wind blowing furiously, with torrents of rain, while the lightning flashed faster and brighter, and the thunder broke in louder and more crashing peals. The rain kept the party close prisoners in the house till it was time for them to retire to bed. All night the storm raged. At an early hour Lawrence Brindister was on foot, the rain had ceased, but the wind blew as furiously as ever. Lawrence was seen to put on his boots, then hurrying to the stable he mounted Neogle, and followed by Surly Grind, he was trotting off, when Captain Maitland hailed him, and inquired where he was going.

'To Navie Grind, Captain,' was his answer. 'I have a

fancy for watching the sea breaking over those cliffs, as it will be doing this morning, and maybe I shall get a glimpse of the Spanish ship, for she is not so far off our shores as some of you may think, and as those on board would pray they might be.'

'Heaven forbid that the Spaniard, or any other craft, is near our cliffs at this time,' said Morton. 'There are good seamen on board her, and she must have got a good offing before she met the gale.'

'Still, we'll take a stroll across to Navie Grind, and have a look at the Western Ocean,' observed Maitland. 'I love to watch it at all times, in storm or sunshine; but, as my days of romance are over, we'll have breakfast first. Morton, you'll agree to that? Mr Lawrence, you'll join us? The sea will not go down before you have had time to break your fast, nor will, I trust, the Spanish ship heave in sight.'

Notwithstanding, however, all the hospitable old sailor's persuasions, Lawrence would only be persuaded to take a handful of oatcake and a draught of milk; and then away he trotted on Neogle, followed by Surly Grind, towards the west. Morton and their host took their time in discussing a far more substantial breakfast, consisting of salted and dried haddocks, pickled pork, oaten cakes, and other substantial articles of food, sufficient to astonish a southern stomach. The captain then lighted his pipe, inviting Rolf to join him, and they smoked away in that deliberate manner which showed that they considered it a far pleasanter pastime than battling with the fierce gale outside. Captain Maitland at length shook the ashes out of his pipe, and was considering whether he should light another, when Lawrence Brindister's voice was heard from below the window, shouting—

'The spirits of the storm have not failed in their duty; the proud Spaniards will meet with their deserts. I knew it would be so. Hurra! hurra! but I'm off again. I wouldn't miss the sight to be made Earl of Zetland.'

The two friends hurried to the window, and inquired what was the matter.

'Matter!' exclaimed Lawrence. 'Why, that the Spanish corvette is driving ashore, and that ere many minutes are over she and all on board will be hurled to destruction. I would save poor Hilda if I could, in spite of her pride and haughtiness, but that is beyond human power to accomplish.'

'Heaven forbid!' exclaimed Captain Maitland. 'The poor young lady, we must at all events try to save her and those with her.'

'Are you certain, Mr Lawrence, that it is the Spanish ship you have seen?' shouted Morton; but he received no answer, for Lawrence had turned Neogle's head, and was galloping off as hard as the little creature could lay hoof to the ground.

'Whether Spanish or any other ship, we'll try what brave hearts and stout hands can do to help the unfortunates on board her,' said the fine old seaman, Captain Maitland, as he hurried out of the house. 'Here, Sandy Neill, Davie Borthwick,—here, lads!' he shouted, and two stout seafaring-looking men employed on his farm came running up. 'There's a ship ashore, or likely soon to be, and you'll be ready to follow me, not to wreck and to plunder, but to save life, if so we can.'

Both Sandy and Davie agreed to do whatever the captain wished, and Morton's own crew were also quickly collected. Before setting out they provided themselves with such coils of rope and long spars as the captain's store could provide. Morton and his friend, armed with stout sticks and coats buttoned up, followed by their men, set out with the fierce gale blowing in their teeth, on their errand of mercy.

CHAPTER IX.

NAVIE GRIND DESCRIBED.—THE WRECK ON SHORE.—THE SHIP DASHED TO PIECES.—THE RESCUED.

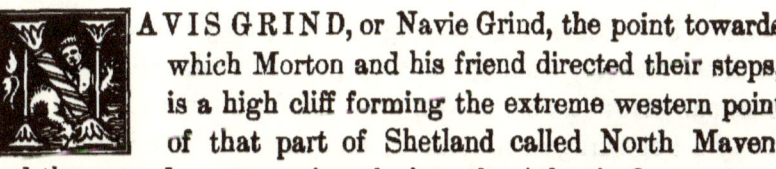AVIS GRIND, or Navie Grind, the point towards which Morton and his friend directed their steps, is a high cliff forming the extreme western point of that part of Shetland called North Maven, and thus stands out prominently into the Atlantic Ocean, some way to the south of Ronas Hill. A short way off from it, due west, like the advanced sentry of an outpost, is the small rocky islet of Ossa Skerry, but this in no way breaks the force of the seas as they rush impetuously onward from far far away across the ocean. It seems, on the contrary, to have the effect of uniting the strength of two seas in one, and of impelling them with double vehemence against the bold cliff which confronts their fury. Solid as is the rock of which the cliff is composed, it has in the course of ages been rent away, quarried out as it were; huge blocks, many of several tons weight, being cast far away inland, while the whole ground, for two or three hundred yards from the edge of the cliff, is strewed with fragments of lesser size, so that the rocks present more the appearance of the ruins of some vast edifice, than, as they really are, masses hove there by the operation of one of nature's most potent agents. At length the sea has worked a deep chasm in the cliff, and each successive storm seems to dig out and force

upward a fresh layer of rock. As the party approached this spot, so wild and desolate at all times, but doubly so now, the seas, dark, towering, and topped with crests of foam, came rolling onward in quick succession, with a fierceness which seemed irresistible, till, meeting the cliff, they rushed upwards in dense masses, making the very ground shake with the concussion. Now a sea, fiercer than its forerunners, would tear away a huge fragment of rock, and throw it into the air as if it had been projected from the mouth of a volcano, or send it rolling along the down, making it dangerous to approach the spot; and, while dense sheets of spray obscured the view seaward, the great body of water was thrown back in a continuous cascade, increasing the tumult of the foaming caldron which raged below.

'It was near this wild place that Lawrence Brindister obtained that strange dog of his,' said Captain Maitland to Morton. 'It was the only living creature washed ashore from the wreck of a large ship—a foreigner, we could not ascertain of what nation. While others were engaged in picking up the treasures they could find, he, at no little risk to his own life, assisted the poor animal, who was sadly battered by the fragments of wreck, and exhausted by swimming to land. The creature looked up into his face, licked his hand, and, from that moment, claimed him as his master, and would follow no one else. See, there he stands; I fear he is to-day in one of his maddest fits.'

The captain pointed, as he spoke, to the top of a high rocky mount which overlooked the sea. Lawrence Brindister, with his two dumb animals by his side, was there seen gesticulating wildly, waving his hand towards the ocean, and shouting apparently with his utmost strength. The roar of the waters, however, as they were hurled against the cliff, added to the howling of the tempest, created a noise so deafening that even the two seamen, accustomed even in the hurricane to make their voices heard, could with difficulty hear each other speak.

Their first glance, as they came in sight of the sea, was in search of the ship of which Lawrence had told them.

'Too true, there she is,' exclaimed Morton, while a sickening feeling came over his heart.

Morton and his friend lifted their glasses to their eyes mechanically, for they could scarcely have expected to have discovered more than their unaided sight would have told them.

'She is the Spanish corvette, there's no doubt about it,' shouted Morton to his companion, who, however, could scarcely hear what else he said, as he added: 'All the poor fellows on board can hope to do is to put off this fatal moment, though I doubt not they have some notion of making Yell Sound; but the sight of Ronas Hill must, if they look at their charts, show them that they cannot fail to drive on shore long before they could reach it.'

'Even now that ship might be saved, or, at all events, the lives of her people, if she had a pilot on board to carry her into Yell Sound,' shouted Captain Maitland. 'What say you, Rolf?'

'That if mortal power could carry a man on board her, I would go,' answered Morton. 'But what boat could live in such a sea as that?'

'If a boat built and manned by human hands can live in this sea, there is one this moment in Hamna Voe as well able to do so as any which floats on water,' answered Maitland. 'Some of her crew may be at their hut even now, though the gale will have given those who live nearest a holiday, and they probably have gone to their houses.'

The voe alluded to was a small but deep one, forming a good harbour on the north side of Navie Grind. High rugged rocks formed the sides, but there was a pathway down them to the water. Towards the inner end there was a piece of level ground, sloping up from the beach; here the fishermen had built a shed, which served them as a dwelling during the fishing season. It was a long, low edifice, composed both of mud and blocks of rock, but chiefly of timber, fragments of wreck cast up on the beach. The doorway was the only aperture, and this served not only for the ingress and egress of the inhabitants, but to admit light, and to allow such part of the smoke from the fire in the centre as ever found its way into the open air to escape; a considerable portion, it appeared clinging to the walls and rafters, which were thoroughly blackened by it, giving it a somewhat gloomy aspect. On one side were piled up masts, and spars, and oars; and sails, and nets, and coils of rope were hung against the walls or on the beams overhead; while, on the other, were a row of bunks or standing bed places, formed out of fragments of wreck-wood. Three or four men, seated on casks or three-legged stools, were busily plying their netting-needles, while several others were fast asleep on the bunks. The pathway, down which Morton and his companions hurried, led close down to the shed. His announcement, as he entered, that there was a ship in sight, partly dismasted, made all hands, the sleepers as well as the workers, spring to their feet. They looked rather blank, however, when Captain Maitland, who entered directly after, added:

'Remember, lads, we must have none of the old customs of the island put in practice, understand that. We want to save the ship if we can, or the lives of those on board. Come, lads, they are fellow-creatures—seamen like ourselves, in distress. Where is the faint-hearted coward who would leave them to perish without lifting a hand to save them. Such a fellow is not to be found among Shetlanders, I hope.'

This appeal had an instant effect. When the men heard that Captain Maitland and Rolf Morton proposed going out in their boat to assist the disabled ship, they agreed to lend her, and to accompany them, the captain undertaking to make good any damage which might accrue, even to the loss of the boat herself.'

The boat, the largest of the class used for fishing on that

coast, pulled twelve oars, and, what with the men belonging to her, and those who had come from Hillswick, as fine a crew as ever manned a boat was collected. The oars and other gear being placed in her, the next thing to be done was to launch her; and while this operation was taking place, Morton and his friend ascended the cliff, to ascertain the position of the corvette, and what prospect there was of getting on board her. As they climbed up the path they observed that the wind had somewhat abated, and this gave them greater hopes of getting to sea. A moment's glance, however, told them, when they reached the top of the cliff, that all hope of saving the ship must be abandoned. Perhaps the Spaniards, mistaking St Magnus's Bay for the entrance of Yell Sound, she had been kept away and then hauled up again; but there she was drifting bodily down towards the terrific headland on which they stood.

Callous and cold-hearted indeed must be the man who can witness with indifference a scene such as that at which the two seamen now gazed—the proud ship, which but the day before had left the shore in such gallant trim, now shattered and crippled, struggling on amid the giant seas which were about, in a few short moments, to hurl her to destruction.

'Nothing can save her, I fear,' cried Morton, his generous heart wrung with sorrow.

'Nothing,' answered his older companion; 'still, by the will of Providence, we may be able to save the lives of some of the people on board; but we must wait and see where she strikes: if we were to attempt to get out to her now we should only involve ourselves in her fate.'

'If she fails to weather Ossa Skerry she will drift right down on Navie Grind, and then Heaven have mercy on their souls, for no human being on board can escape,' said Captain Maitland. 'A few minutes must settle the point.'

'Luff, luff all you can, men,' he exclaimed, as if those on board could hear him. Probably they had caught sight of the terrific sea breaking over the cliffs, and still hoped to weather the little island under their lee bow.

All this time Lawrence Brindister kept his post, with his pony and dog by his side, waving his arms towards the ship, and apparently shouting out as before.

'She will weather the Skerry even now,' cried Morton, but at that instant a squall—one of the last blasts of the tempest—struck her. Over went her mainmast, her head fell off from the sea, on she flew amid showers of foam, and in another minute she was hid to view by the rocky island before them. In vain they hoped against hope to see her appear on the other side. Her fate was indeed sealed. There was only one spot where even in moderate weather a landing could be without difficulty effected on Ossa Skerry. Still Morton and his friend resolved to attempt it. There was not a moment to be lost, already, probably, numbers of the hapless crew were being swept to destruction. They hurried down the cliff, sprang on board the boat, and shoved off. Morton steered; with rapid strokes they pulled down the remainder of the voe; even there heavy waves rolled in and showed the crew the sort of sea with which they would have to contend when they got outside. Few but Shetlanders would have attempted to face such a sea, and the finest of boats alone could have lived in it. They reached the mouth of the voe; their passage through the mouth was the first danger they had to encounter; a huge sea came thundering in.

'Back off all,' cried Morton; and instead of forcing the boat onward, she slowly receded before the wave, which broke in a loud crash directly before her, the foam flying over her bows and deluging her fore and aft. 'Now, lads, give way,' shouted Morton again, and before the next sea broke, the boat had got into deep water. They now encountered the full force of the gale; and none but a boat admirably manned, as was theirs, could have made headway against it, nor could she have escaped being instantly swamped, unless steered with the greatest caution and judgment. Now she rose on the top of a sea surrounded with foam, now she plunged down into the trough, and those standing on the rocks, at the mouth of the voe, feared more than once that she had sunk for ever. Again she rose on the side of the opposite sea; the summit was reached; but once more she disappeared beyond it. At times it seemed as if scarcely any way was made, but still the bold seamen persevered; the lives of some of their fellow-creatures depended on their exertions—how many it was impossible to say, till they had ascertained where the ship had gone on shore. They knew that in all probability in a few minutes, even should the ship hold together, numbers must be swept off from the decks.

Morton's object was to get sufficiently out to sea to ascertain the position of the ship. The rapid diminution of the strength of the wind enabled him to do this with greater ease than had at first appeared possible; still the sea came rolling in as fiercely as before, and rendered the greatest caution necessary to prevent the boat being swamped. At last they got sufficiently to the westward to look along the outer side of Ossa Skerry. No ship was to be seen. Had she foundered, or was it possible that in so short a time she had so completely gone to pieces that not a particle of the wreck was to be seen? If so, not a soul on board could have escaped.

'Poor girl!' thought Morton; 'it will break the heart of Bertha Eswick to hear of it; and my wife, too—it will make her very sad.'

'We will pull out a little further, Rolf,' said Captain Maitland. 'There is a little bay, or bight, nearly at the south-east of the rock—if the ship by chance drove in there we should not see her from hence.'

'Give way, lads!' shouted Morton, with hope revived by his friend's remark.

In a short time they opened the little bay of which Captain Maitland spoke. There lay the ship almost broadside on with the shore, her stern apparently under an overhanging cliff, while her bow, over which the sea made a clean breach, seemed to hang on a rock, and was thus prevented from being driven further in. Her masts and bowsprit were gone by the board: and from the force with which the sea was breaking over her, it seemed scarcely possible that she could herself keep much longer together. An attempt to approach her from the seaside would have proved the destruction of the boat. The only chance of rendering assistance was to land on the east side of the island. Hitherto the boat's head had been kept directly towards the seas as they came rolling in. It was far more dangerous work crossing them as they had now to do, to reach the inner side of the island. Often Morton and his friend watched the foaming masses of water, as they came roaring towards them, with no little anxiety; but by pulling round to face the larger ones, and by then rapidly giving way, the boat at length got under the lee of the islet. To obtain footing on the slippery rock was a work of considerable difficulty, and still greater was it to climb to the summit and to convey them the ropes and spars which they had brought with them. Some of the men remained to take care of the boat, for that alone was not an easy task, as had she been carried away by the sea, the whole party might have been starved before assistance could have come to them. The remainder proceeded, as rapidly as they could, across the island. With more anxiety than they had often felt, Morton and the captain hurried towards the edge of the cliff. Before even reaching it the appearance which the foaming water presented, even some way from the shore, told them too plainly the destruction which had already occurred; while the fearful shrieks, which even through the roar of the angry waters came up from below, warned them that every instant fresh victims were being added to those who had already fallen a sacrifice to the tempest.

Among fragments of masts, and spars, and planks, and

other parts of the ship, were seen the forms of numerous human beings, some yet struggling, but struggling in vain, for life; others floating helplessly among the pieces of wreck, or clinging to them with a convulsive clutch, while many, already lifeless, were tossed to and fro in the boiling caldron, happier than those who were seen every now and then, as they were swept off, to throw up their arms, and then, with a fearful shriek of despair, to sink from sight.

On gaining the edge of the cliff, Morton and Captain Maitland threw themselves on the ground and looked over. The fore part of the vessel had already been knocked to pieces. A few men still clung to part of the bulwarks in the waist; but the sea was making a clean breach over it, and one by one they were torn from their treacherous hold and carried off by the waves. The only part of the wreck which yet afforded a precarious shelter was the poop. The mainmast, in falling, had been washed across it, and the end jamming against the cliff, it formed a breakwater, within which a group of people yet stood, almost paralysed with terror and despair, for the precipitous cliff above them afforded not the slightest prospect of escape, while the violent shaking of the wreck, and the rapid advances of the waves, showed them that in a few minutes even that uncertain foothold would be carried from beneath them.

Morton and his friend beckoned to their companions to bring on the ropes. It was the work of a few seconds to uncoil them and to make one end fast to the spars they had brought. These they fixed in the ground, two of them holding on at the same time to the upper part of the spars.

Not till all the preparations were made did Morton shout to those below to let them know that aid was at hand. In the centre of the group was a female form – that it was Hilda there could be little doubt. The rope was lowered with a pair of slings at the end of it. How anxiously did those both above and below watch its descent! The end dropped some way from the stern of the ship; it seemed a question whether it was within reach of those whose existence depended on clutching it. A seaman sprang towards it as it swung backwards and forwards in the gale, but he missed his aim, and fell headlong into the seething water, which soon silenced his death shriek. Another, an officer apparently, made the attempt; he had secured a line round his body, he clutched the rope and dragged it inboard. Even at that moment Spanish gallantry was maintained; no undue haste was shown by any to secure their own lives. The first care of the men was to secure Hilda in the slings; this was speedily done, but it was soon seen that if she was hauled up by herself she would run great risk of being thrown against the side of the cliff and severely injured. The officer who had hauled in the rope accordingly secured himself to it, and made a sign to those above to hoist away. The fearful rocking of the ship made them do this with all the speed of which they were capable. At any moment the ship might go to pieces; Morton stood nearest the edge. At length the head of Pedro Alvarez appeared, and while with one arm he kept the end of the rope from dashing against the cliff, with the other he supported the almost inanimate form of Hilda Wardhill. She was speedily released from the rope, which was again lowered, while Captain Maitland and one of the men carried her to a hollow in the downs, which afforded some shelter from the wind. The brave lieutenant made signs that he was going to descend again, but Morton, who saw that it would be useless, refused to allow him. The rope was lowered; 'Haul away!' he shouted, and in a little time the priest, Father Mendez, appeared. He was unloosed also, more dead than alive; the rope was lowered, but scarcely had it reached the deck when a raging sea came roaring up—fearful shrieks were heard—the mast was torn away from its hold in the rock—a rush was made at the rope; one man grasped it, but others in their haste dragged him off, and the next instant the remainder of the wreck which hung together was dashed into numberless fragments, while all who had clung to it were hurled amidst them, one after the other rapidly disappearing beneath the foaming waters.

Morton and the Shetlanders looked anxiously over the cliff. It was too evident that not another human being had escaped from the wreck of the 'St Cecilia.'

'There goes the brave ship, and there go my gallant captain and worthy comrades,' cried Pedro Alvarez, wringing his hands and pulling away at his moustachios in the excess of his grief, as he looked over the cliff and watched the utter destruction of the corvette. The priest, when he had sufficiently recovered to understand what had occurred, knelt down, and those who watched him supposed, as he lifted up his hands over the ocean, that he was uttering prayers for the souls of his departing shipmates. Meantime Captain Maitland was kneeling by the almost inanimate form of Hilda, and endeavouring by every means which his experience could suggest to restore her to consciousness. At length he was joined by Father Mendez. 'Let her continue thus, kind sir,' he said. 'It is better that she should not be aware of the calamity which has overtaken her.'

Morton also, followed by the Spanish lieutenant, came up. 'We can render no further assistance to the crew of the unfortunate ship,' he observed; 'not another person who was on board her remains alive but those we have here.'

With the most gentle care poor Hilda was conveyed to the boat, which pulled back towards Hamna Voe.

The priest shuddered as he saw the seas from which he had so lately escaped come rolling up on the boat's quarter, but his compressed lips showed that he was resolved not to give way to his feelings in words. Sea followed sea in quick succession, and Morton's utmost care was required to save the boat from being swamped. All breathed more freely when the entrance of the voe was safely reached. As they pulled up it, Morton heard some shouts. On raising his head, he saw Lawrence

Brindister standing on a height overlooking the voe. He was whirling his arms wildly about as before, and peering down to ascertain who was in the boat. When he discovered a female, he apparently guessed that she was his cousin Hilda; and striking little Neogle, he turned the pony's head, and rode off as fast as the creature could gallop. The boat continued her course to the head of the voe.

A rough litter being formed, Hilda was conveyed to Captain Maitland's house; but as she continued plunged in a state of stupor, Father Mendez advised that she should at once be taken to her home. His advice seemed so judicious, that Morton offered to carry her there in his boat. Captain Maitland also expressed a wish to be of the party, and the next morning, accompanied by Pedro Alvarez and Father Mendez, they embarked for Lunnasting. The only person who appeared on the landing-place was Lawrence Brindister. He stood, hat in hand, with a mocking expression on his countenance, and he was beginning to address the party when his eye fell on Hilda. Her appearance seemed to touch his heart, for he said nothing, but, turning round, walked slowly back before them to the castle.

It is needless to describe the dismay and astonishment which poor Hilda's return excited in the establishment. Lawrence had evidently in no way warned them of what had occurred. Bertha Eswick had need of all her self-possession and presence of mind to perform her duty. It was many days before Hilda returned to a state of consciousness! In the meantime, Father Mendez took up his abode in the castle; and, from the way in which Pedro Alvarez settled himself in his apartment, it looked as if he also intended to be a permanent guest at Lunnasting.

CHAPTER X.

GUESTS AT THE CASTLE.—THE HEIR OF LUNNASTING.—LAWRENCE BRINDISTER'S CAVE.

FOR a long time after Hilda's return to Lunnasting, Bertha Eswick feared that the mind of her young mistress had gone for ever. All the aid which medical skill could afford appeared to be of no avail; the only person who had in the slightest degree the power of arousing her sufficiently to speak was Father Mendez—the means he employed no one could discover. He would sit with her in a turret chamber for hours together; and after several weeks had passed, she was heard talking fluently and rapidly with him; but as soon as she entered the hall, where she took her seat as usual, she relapsed into the most perfect silence. When, however, the priest addressed her, she answered him readily, though briefly, but seemed to be totally unconscious of the presence of any one else. The condition of the unfortunate lady was a sufficient reason for Father Mendez remaining at Lunnasting; indeed, he remarked that he should consider himself guilty of the greatest cruelty should he take his departure till the return of her father and sister. There was no one besides Hilda of sufficient authority in the castle to request him to go, so he remained on. No news had been received of Sir Marcus Wardhill and his daughter, and it was supposed that they were entirely ignorant of the strange occurrences which had taken place. Pedro Alvarez likewise continued to live on at the castle; when he had learned enough English to express himself, he offered several excellent reasons for remaining. In the first place, he said that Don Hernan had confided his wife to his charge, as with a prescience of what was to occur, just before the shipwreck; and that at that awful moment he had vowed to devote himself to her interests as long as his life should last. He also frankly confessed that he had no means of returning home; he had written to Spain for a remittance, as well as to announce the loss of the corvette, and till his cash arrived he could not go away, even if he wished to do so. Father Mendez also stated that it was the wish of his late captain's widow that the lieutenant should continue a guest at the castle, as long as he found it convenient to remain.

Pedro Alvarez and Lawrence after a time became very great friends. They boated, and fished, and shot together; and Lawrence assisted him very much in learning English. When, however, the days grew shorter, and the nights longer and colder, he shrugged his shoulders, and complained that the time was very dull. He had, however, by his frank, open, and unpretending manners, and quiet habits, won very much upon the good opinion of Bertha Eswick, who declared that she would far rather have his society at the castle than that of Father Mendez, whose ways and notions she could by no means understand, although she owned that he spoke far better English, and that no fault could be found with the courtesy and gentleness of his manners. Neither of them gave any trouble. Father Mendez especially was satisfied with the simplest fare. Plain water formed his beverage, eggs and fish his principal food. Pedro Alvarez preferred as great a variety as he could get, and several times descended to the kitchen to instruct Moggie Druster, the cook, in the art of concocting dishes in the Spanish fashion, of which oil (and of that there was an ample supply in Shetland) formed one of the chief ingredients. He was made perfectly happy too with a package of tobacco, which Rolf Morton obtained for him from Lerwick, and which he employed his leisure moments in converting into cigarettes. Lawrence Brindister also still further added to his satisfaction, by putting into his hands five goodly volumes, on opening which he found to be Spanish; travels, histories, and a romance—subjects exactly suited to the worthy Pedro's tastes. They were strangely battered, and stained as with salt water. How he had obtained them Lawrence would not say. The priest saw the books, but turned away from them with a disdainful glance, as if he could take no interest in subjects of a character so trivial. The contrast between the two strangers was very great. Pedro Alvarez was in figure more like an English sailor than a Spaniard. He was somewhat short, and broad-shouldered, and stout, with a frank, open, and ruddy, though sunburnt countenance; his large black sparkling eyes, beaming with good humour, spoke of the southern clime which gave him birth, as did his black curling moustache, and hair of the same hue. Father Mendez, on the other hand, was thin in the extreme, with sallow complexion, and sharp features, but his countenance showed that he possessed a peculiarly intelligent and acute intellect. It could not be said that there was anything unpleasing in the expression of his features; it was rather the total want of expression which they mechanically assumed when he was conversing, or when he was aware that he was observed, of which any one would complain. It was not a stolid look which he put on, but rather that of a person totally unconscious of what was passing around; indeed, so perfect was the composure of every muscle of his face, that it looked completely like a mask with a pair of bright eyes gleaming through it. Though he kept those eyes perfectly fixed, he had not succeeded in obscuring at pleasure their brightness. Nothing could surpass the subdued gentleness of the tone of voice in which he generally spoke, though he could at will raise it in a way to astonish his hearers.

The long winter of Shetland was passing slowly by, without any events of interest occurring in the neighbourhood of Lunnasting; the time was drawing on when it would be necessary for Rolf Morton to go south to look out for a ship, unless he would altogether give up his profession and chance of promotion; but he was naturally unwilling to leave home till his wife had made him a father, which she expected in a very short time to do. It was also generally understood that the unhappy Hilda would shortly become a mother, and already a very general feeling of compassion was expressed for the poor little fatherless babe which was about to be born. How would the poor lady get through her trials? Was she likely to live? If the child lived, would it be the heir of Lunnasting? Or should its father have been heir to estates, and a title in Spain, as it had been said he was, would it succeed instead of him?

These and numerous other questions of a similar character were asked over and over again, but were never satisfactorily answered. Letters had been received from Sir Marcus, but he fixed no time for his return home, and it was very evident from the tenor of his remarks that he believed everything was going on in his castle as he had left it. He might possibly have been rather astonished had he heard what had occurred. The truth was, that neither had his factor Sandy Redland, nor any one else, ventured to write to him, and very naturally Hilda had not done so; Sandy was a man who liked to live a peaceable life, and to have matters his own way, and he knew very well that, should Sir Marcus be hurried back, not only would all peace and quiet be banished from Lunnasting, but he would most certainly for the future have nothing whatever his own way. It is possible that Sir Marcus was not the only head of a family who might have cause to be astonished at the doings of his household during his absence. At length a packet of letters arrived from Spain. It contained some for Don Hernan, as well as for other deceased officers of the 'St Cecilia;' one was for Pedro Alvarez, and several were addressed to Father Mendez, who likewise took possession of all the rest. The lieutenant read his despatch with a great deal of interest.

'And so our poor captain would have been a marquis,' he exclaimed to himself, 'the Marquis de Medea, and owner of those magnificent estates. Well, truly he had something to live for, and yet he was cut off—while I who have not a peço beyond my pay, and little enough of that, have been allowed to remain in existence. I cannot understand these matters—it is very strange; still, I will not forget my vow. I promised that poor fellow to look after his widow, and if she has a son, I will, to the best of my humble power, see that his interests are not neglected. Now I wonder what information Father Mendez has received. He must have heard that Don Hernan, had he lived, would have succeeded to this title and these estates. The letters to the captain, which he has opened, cannot fail of speaking of the matter. Probably they are written expressly to give the information. I wonder, now, whether the father will say anything about it. Well, he does not love me, and I do not trust him, and I will watch him narrowly, and see if I cannot be as close as he can. Bah! if all men would be honest it would save a great deal of trouble. If Donna Hilda's child should be a girl there will be very little for me to do in the affair; she cannot, I suspect, inherit either the title or estates. If the child is a boy he will be the rightful heir, there is no doubt about that; but then he will find a mortal enemy in Don Hernan's cousin, Don Anibal Villavicencio, who will stir heaven and earth to keep the boy out of his rights; the moment he hears of Don Hernan's death he will take possession of the property and assume the title. I must find out what tack Father Mendez is sailing on. Is he in the interest of the living marquis, or of the unborn baby? He is never happy unless he is playing some deep game or other. I suspect that he is waiting to see how things turn out. At all events, though he beats me hollow in an argument, I'll try whether in a good cause I cannot outmanœuvre him. He does not want for money, that I know. He has his belt stuffed full of gold pieces even now, so the want of means to go away does not keep him here. Why he does not offer some to me to get me away I do not know. Probably he looks on me as a rough, untutored sailor, and despises me too much to dread my interference with his plans. Perhaps he intends to buy me over, and to make use of me to aid him. He knows himself pretty well, and thinks all men are likewise rogues. He will be rather astonished if he finds that he has been outwitted by a straightforward, honest sailor.'

At length the event for some time looked for, both at the castle and the cottage, occurred. Bertha Morton presented her husband with a fine boy, and scarcely had the young gentleman—Ronald Morton he was to be called—given notice of his arrival in the world by a lusty fit of crying, and had been exhibited in due form to his father, than the wise woman who attended on such occasions was now moving in hot haste to the castle of Lunnasting, to afford her aid to Donna Hilda, who was, it is said, in sore pain and distress. Alas! she had no fond husband to cheer and console her; no one to whom she could show with pride and joy the little creature about to be born into the world. Bertha Eswick had expressed her hopes that the child would be a girl. A lassie, she observed, would be a comfort and a companion to the poor lady, who would herself be able to instruct her, and would ever keep her by her side; whereas a boy must be sent away to school, and would then have to go into the world, where he would again see little or nothing of his poor mother.

Father Mendez and Pedro Alvarez were walking up and down, but not together, on the sunny side of the court-yard. It was the only spot, they declared, in the whole island where they could be sheltered from the biting keenness of the wind, and feel any of the warmth to which they were accustomed in their own country. Both were anxious to hear whether a son or daughter was born to the lady of the mansion. Pedro Alvarez was certainly the least anxious.

While the two foreigners were thus engaged, Moggie Druster, the cook, put her head out of a window and shouted—

'It's a braw laddie, sirs—a fine strapping bairn. It's like to do weel, and so is it's mother, poor lady.'

'A what do you say it is, Mistress Moggie?' asked Father Mendez.

'A braw laddie; a big bouncing boy, ye would ca' him in English,' answered Moggie, with a slight touch of scorn in her tone.

'A boy!' exclaimed the priest and the lieutenant almost at the same moment.

The priest took several rapid turns up and down the courtyard with compressed lips and knitted brow, but said nothing.

'And how goes the poor lady?' inquired Pedro Alvarez. 'And good Mistress Moggie,' he continued, going up to her and whispering, 'tell her that her husband's warmest friend is ready and at hand to assist and comfort her, as far as he has the power.'

'Ay, that will I, Mr Pedro; ye are a kind-hearted gentleman, that ye are,' answered Moggie, whose heart the honest lieutenant had completely won, in return for the culinary instruction he had afforded her.

Poor Bertha Eswick was nearly worn to death from hurrying between her daughter's cottage and the castle, though her young mistress required, and certainly obtained, by far the greatest share of her care. Healthy, however, as Bertha Morton had always appeared, soon after the birth of her child she caught a cold, and this produced an illness which made her mother and husband very anxious about her, and it became too evident, before long, to the anxious eyes of affection, that she held her life on a most precarious tenure. Hilda, on the contrary, seemed completely restored to health, both of body and mind. She had now a deeply interesting object in existence, and all her thoughts and attention were devoted to her infant.

Lawrence Brindister did not return to the castle till late in the day on which Hilda's child was born. He received the announcement with a look of incredulity on his countenance.

' And so you tell me that an heir to Lunnasting is born,' he exclaimed to Bertha Eswick, whom he met as she was hurrying down for the first time from her mistress's chamber. Ha, ha, ha! how many heirs to Lunnasting are there, think ye? Never mind, good Bertha, " The prince will hae his ain again! The prince will hae his ain again!" Who is the prince, think ye, Bertha? Ye little ken, but I do; the fool knows more than the wise man, or the wise woman either ha, ha, ha!'

These remarks sorely puzzled Bertha Eswick, and made her think a great deal; she knew Lawrence Brindister thoroughly, and seldom failed to distinguish between the mere hallucinations which occasionally took possession of his mind, and the ideas which originated from facts. ' If Marcus Wardhill is not the rightful possessor of Lunnasting, who can be the owner?' she asked herself, over and over again.

Several weeks passed by, and young Don Hernan, for so Hilda's new-born babe was called, gave every promise of being a remarkably healthy and robust child. Father Mendez seemed deeply interested in it, and took every opportunity of watching its progress, and examining it to ascertain that it was a thoroughly well-made healthy child.

At length the father gave notice that he was going to Lerwick: he went, and some of the household declared that they breathed far more freely than they had done for a very long time. Pedro Alvarez walked about with a more self-confident air than usual, and Lawrence sang and laughed and rattled away as had been his custom in former days; even Hilda looked as if she had been relieved of an incubus which had depressed her spirits. She said nothing; she did not even mention the name of Father Mendez, but if by chance she heard it, she gave a slight shudder, while the frown which grew on her brow showed that whatever the influence he had gained over her, it was not of a nature to which she willingly submitted. He had announced that he should not be absent more than three or four days; but more than a week elapsed and he did not return. As no one wished him back, this caused more surprise than regret. Ten days, then a fortnight, passed by, and the priest did not appear. At last Pedro Alvarez whispered his suspicions to Lawrence Brindister that the reverend father had played them a slippery trick, and left Shetland altogether; this idea was found to be correct, when Sandy M'Nab, the pedlar and great newsmonger of the district, paid his next visit to Whalsey. A foreigner who, though somewhat disguised, was recognized as the Spanish priest, Father Mendez, had been observed going on board a ship bound for the south, and he had not since then been seen in Lerwick. The lieutenant was more than usually agitated when he heard this. 'There is some mischief brewing,' he observed, the first moment he found Lawrence alone. 'You and I must try to fathom it, if we can. You can be secret, Mr Lawrence, and with such a man as that cunning priest to contend with, we need all the caution we can exercise.

'Mum's the word with me,' answered Lawrence, looking very sagacious; I love not the priest more than you do, for I believe he would not scruple to stick a dagger in the back of his brother if that brother stood in the way of any object he wished to attain. What he aims at I do not know : whether or not he wishes to advance the interests of Hilda's child, is what I want to discover.'

Pedro shook his head. 'Not he, Mr Lawrence,' he answered: 'he cares not for the fatherless or the widow. I have watched him narrowly : his aim was to get Donna Hilda completely under his thumb, so that he might rule her and her child. While he thought that there was a prospect of success he remained on here, but when he at length discovered that he had totally failed, or that he could not depend for an instant on maintaining his influence, he at once altered his whole plan. You must understand that when we left Spain there were three persons in existence who would by law succeed to the title and estates of the Marquis of Medea before Don Hernan de Escalante. He often told me that he himself never expected to inherit the property, and that he must find some other means of improving his fortunes. It is my belief, however, that Father Mendez, by some of the wonderful means at his disposal, knew that these three persons would die before our return, and that he accompanied us for the very purpose of obtaining an influence over Don Hernan, that his order might thus benefit by the wealth which would be at his disposal. He knew Don Hernan sufficiently to believe that he should obtain that influence, and he probably would have succeeded. Now, however, he is playing another game; he can have no sure hold over a person of so uncertain a mind as Donna Hilda, and he has now returned to Spain that he may be able to make his bargain with Don Anibal Villavicencio, who has already succeeded to the property. Just consider the immense influence he will have over him when he is able to prove that there is an heir alive, who, if produced, will turn him out of the estates and title. What do you say to the question, Mr Lawrence? Do you think I am right in my suspicions?'

'Ay, that I do, most sagacious mariner,' answered Lawrence, who had really comprehended the tenor of these remarks; they were of course made in much more broken English than has been used. 'The priest may be an honest priest, as he is undoubtedly a most polite gentleman; and his ways may be good ways, in his own sight, though they are not my ways; but that he is not labouring for the good of the poor little fatherless child up there, I am clearly of opinion.'

'So far we are agreed, my friend,' said the lieutenant; 'but when the boy succeeds his grandfather, and becomes the owner of the property, he will be able with his own right arm, or rather with his well-filled purse, which is better than a strong arm to him, to establish his rights to his Spanish estates and proper rank.'

'Ah, there a fool may by chance know more than a wise man, friend Pedro,' observed Lawrence, rubbing the side of his nose with his forefinger. 'Come along with me, most worthy lieutenant, and I will show you matters which will astonish you.'

Pedro Alvarez accepted the invitation, and the two oddly-matched friends set out together, towards the east end of the island. Lawrence turned several times to observe if they were watched, and then continued his course across heathery moorland, and valley, and swamp, as rapidly as before.

'I know this spot, surely,' observed Pedro Alvarez; 'it is where the Catholic chapel stands.'

'The same, friend mariner,' answered Lawrence; 'but we have nothing to do with the chapel just now: keep close at my heels, or rather step exactly where I step, or you may chance to have a tumble to the bottom of the cliff, with a broken neck as the consequence.'

Lawrence, as he spoke, reached the brow of the cliff; he slid over it, and dropped himself down on a narrow ledge which appeared to afford scarcely room for his feet to rest. He went on, leaning against the side of the cliff for a short distance, and then let himself down in the same manner that he had before done. The Spanish officer at first hesitated to follow, but a laugh from Lawrence made him ashamed of himself, and when he reached the first ledge, he perceived that there were rings let into the rock, and of the same colour, which made the operation less difficult than it had at first appeared. Three or four ledges were thus reached in succession, and then there was a very narrow winding path cut in the face of the cliff which led down to the very edge of the water. Before, however, Lawrence reached the bottom, he turned off along another ledge, when Pedro entirely lost sight of him.

Following in the same direction, however, he found himself in front of a cave; the entrance was so small, that at a distance it could scarcely be perceived, but on looking in he saw that it expanded into a chamber of considerable dimensions.

'Come in, friend mariner, and survey my marine abode,' exclaimed Lawrence from within.

A few rough steps enabled him to enter, and he discovered that the cave was not only large, but that it contained a bed and table, some stools and several chests, and casks, and bales, besides sails and coils of rope, and spars, and pieces of wreck; indeed, it had somewhat the appearance of a marine store, so various were the articles collected in it.

As he entered he was saluted by a low, fierce growl, and he saw in rather unpleasant proximity to his legs the savage jaws of Surly Grind, wide expanded in readiness to seize him. A word, however, from his master, sent him growling back to his couch at the further end of the cave.

'Never fear the dog; he is the guardian genius of the place, and is in duty bound to defend it against the approach of animated visitors,' said Lawrence. 'But sit down, worthy mariner, and feel that you are in the abode of a friend; eatables we do not require, but I keep a store of some of the luxuries of life of which I know you will not refuse to partake.'

Saying this, he produced some pipes and tobacco, and a bottle of Schiedam, a case of which, he told his guest, had come on shore near his cave. Pedro partook of the latter very moderately, but he gladly replenished his own tobacco-pouch, as his own supply of the fragrant weed was running short. Lawrence then led him to the mouth of the cave.

'Mark the appearance of that line of broken water out there, which with its whirlpools and eddies comes sweeping round from the north and strikes the base of this point. Every object which once gets within its power is driven against this point. All these things which you see arranged round here have reached me in that way. What tales of shipwreck do they tell! Often, too, I fancy the waifs cast up come from far distant shores; strange, also, the water which rushes round the base of this rock is quite warm at times, and I could believe that it still retains the heat imparted to it by the sun of a southern clime. But all these things are useless to you, you will say, and so it may be; but these are the chests, and the bales, and the casks which Surly Grind and I, between us, have hauled on shore. That reminds me I promised to show you the contents of one of the chests; and here—' (he opened a remarkably massive and well-made oaken sea-chest; the lid fitted so well, that although it had evidently been in the water for some time, none had found an entrance; Lawrence had contrived to force it open; lifting the lid, he took from it a tin case, and out of the case produced a document which he put into his companion's hand) 'Read that, and tell me what you think,' he said; and while Pedro opened the paper, and slowly perused it, he fixed his eyes earnestly on his countenance.

The Spaniard read on very slowly, and not without great difficulty.

'It is in English,' he said at length. 'I cannot pretend to understand it all, but from what I do comprehend, I see that if I could fulfil my promise to my dead shipmate and captain, and see justice done to his widow and child, I have greater reason than ever for hurrying back to Spain to try and counteract the schemes of Father Mendez, and to oppose the Marquis Don Anibal Villavicencio, who will of course stir heaven and earth to maintain his position.'

'I thought as much,' said Lawrence; 'you see that his friend here may have very little power to assist him in asserting his rights. Give me back the paper. I keep all my valuables in this cavern; there is no place so safe, for there is little chance of fire, and still less likely are thieves to break in and steal.'

Lawrence pointed to several other chests, but he seemed in no way disposed to exhibit any more of his treasures, whatever they were. The lieutenant, indeed, proposed returning forthwith to the castle. Lawrence having charged Surly Grind to keep strict watch and ward over his storehouse, they set off to return by the same way they had come.

Not long after this Pedro received the long-looked-for remittance from Spain, and prepared for his departure from Shetland. When he went to pay his adieus to Hilda, he dropped on one knee, and taking her hand, respectfully pressed it to his lips, while he silently repeated his oath, to exert himself to the utmost in the cause of her and her child. Accompanied by Lawrence, he then set off for Lerwick, whence he immediately embarked on board a vessel bound for London. He was much regretted by all the inhabitants of Lunnasting, but more especially by Hilda, who, although not aware of the extent of his devotion to her cause, felt that she had lost one of the few friends on whom she could depend for counsel and assistance.

CHAPTER XI.

FATHER MENDEZ IN SPAIN.—THE MARQUIS AND HIS OLD SHIPMATES.—CAPTAIN TACON THE EX-PIRATE.

ATHER MENDEZ, on reaching Lerwick, found a vessel about to sail for Leith. He might probably have taken a courteous farewell of the inhabitants of Lunnasting, had he not wished to steal a march on Pedro Alvarez. He had discovered that the worthy lieutenant suspected his designs, and would, if he had the power, counteract them; he therefore resolved to deprive him, forthwith, of that power. The Inquisition, that admirable institution for the destruction of heresy, existed in full force in those days in Spain, and the father well knew that if he could induce its officials to lay hands on his rival that he would give him no further trouble. The father reached Leith in safety, and thence was able to proceed on, without loss of time, direct to Cadiz. Not far off from that fair city was the magnificent mansion of the Marquis de Medea. The father, on landing, did not at once hasten to visit his relations and friends, to receive their congratulations on his escape; nor did he even go to pay his respects to the superior of his order, but, without a moment's loss of time, he hurried off to the residence of the marquis. He introduced himself without much ceremony The marquis could not at first believe the unwelcome news he brought.

'I have no object in deceiving you, most noble marquis,' answered the priest, with a calm, unruffled brow. 'I have ample proofs of the truth of my statements, and should I bring them forward you could no longer keep possession of this beautiful mansion, of yonder fertile fields, of the time-honoured title you hold. But do not be alarmed; far be it from me to wish to dispossess you; the real heir is the son of a heretic woman, and will be brought up as a heretic; and I feel that I shall but be supporting the cause of our Holy Mother Church by saying nothing about this matter, and by maintaining you in possession of your property; you, who will, I doubt not, prove yourself one of her most devoted and zealous sons.'

The marquis was a person with a narrow forehead, small grey eyes, and that peculiar expression of countenance which the vice of indulged avarice seems generally to produce. Though his lips denoted sensuality, their total want of firmness showed the astute Father Mendez that he would be easily moulded to his will. The marquis was perfectly well aware of the way in which the church was at times apt to bleed those whom she designated her most devoted sons, and he winced at the thoughts of having to part with the large portion of his newly-acquired wealth which would be required.

'I know not what you mean, father,' he answered. 'I have always been a devoted son of Holy Mother Church, and shall ever be ready to pay those dues which she can rightly demand.'

The priest fixed his eyes sternly on him.

'It will be as well, Don Anibal, that we come to a right understanding on the matter,' he remarked, in a low firm tone. 'Remember, I have the power of depriving you of every silver piece of the wealth you enjoy; of stripping you of your title and estates, and reducing you to the state of poverty from which you have sprung; that is what I have the power of doing. The heir—the real owner of this superb mansion, of these broad lands—is a fine healthy child; a word from me would bring him over, and put him, or his proper guardians, in possession of them. Now, if I refrain from doing this, I am in duty bound to demand a sufficient recompense, not for myself —far be it from me to claim any earthly reward, for my labours are for the benefit of our Holy Mother Church, whose devoted servant I am. Here you will see I know the exact value of your property, and its rental. This paper contains my terms: if you agree to them, well and good—if not, you know the consequences. I leave you for half an hour to consider over the matter, while I go and pay my respects to the marchioness; she is a wise woman and a faithful daughter of the church. I doubt not how she will decide.'

Now Father Mendez was excessively clever and acute, but Don Anibal Villavicencio's cunning had been sharpened in the school of adversity. He looked up with an innocent expression of countenance, and asked—

'How do I know that the child you speak of is in existence? Pardon me for putting so rude a question, father. Where is he to be found? Give me particulars which will enable me to judge whether I am making a fair bargain with you.'

The father smiled at Don Anibal's frankness; he was in no way offended at the doubt cast on his veracity; he liked people to be open with him; it gave him, he thought, more power over them. He knew that the marquis could have no interest in bringing the child from Shetland, and as that island was a long way off, he was not likely to set off there to verify the accounts he might give. He might, therefore, have told him any story he pleased. In this instance, however, as it answered his purpose to speak the truth, seeing that the truth would have more influence with Don Anibal than any tale he could invent, he told him all that had occurred, and gave him a full description of Lunnasting, and its position. The marquis had learnt to conceal his thoughts as well as the priest; he assumed a dull and indifferent air as Father Mendez continued his account.

'I see the justice of your remark, father, and rest assured that I will do my duty,' he answered, with a twirl of his moustache and a stiff bow of the head. The child is heir, you tell me, to a good property in this far-off island of Shetland, of which till now I never heard; he may well be content with that; indeed it is clear that he would be out of his element as the possessor of an estate like this; besides, as you wisely remark, he will be brought up as an heretic. Yes, father, my conscience is at rest; I feel that I am doing what must be well-pleasing to the church, and you assuredly shall receive the reward you demand.'

'His conscience!—I wonder of what that is composed,' muttered the priest, and then added aloud, 'You have not yet decided with regard to the paper I put into your hands, Don Anibal.'

'Well, do as you propose,' answered the marquis. 'I hope that you have not been too hard on me, though.'

The priest gave a searching glance at the marquis, and without speaking, left the room. Don Anibal's countenance did not wear a particularly pleasant expression as his eyes followed the priest.

'I'll be even with you,' he muttered, as he ground his teeth and shook his clenched fist towards the door at which the priest had retired. 'What! Does he think I am fool enough to pay him the enormous sum he demands? He has given me the key to the means of settling the matter in a cheaper way than that. I must, however, in the meantime, keep my plans secret as the grave, or he will manage to counteract them.'

At the end of the time Father Mendez had fixed, he returned, and was highly pleased with the ready acquiescence with which the marquis agreed to his proposals. He then, with a conscience at rest, hastened on to his convent to report his arrival, and to give an account of his proceedings. The marquis waited till he had assured himself that he had without doubt left the neighbourhood, and then set out for Cadiz. He had a mansion in that city where he took up his abode. He had been in his youth at sea, and had still a number of seafaring acquaintance. They were not all of them amongst the most respectable orders of society; perhaps they were the better suited to carry out the object he had in view. He was a cunning man if not a wise one, and knew that he was more likely to succeed by doing things deliberately than in a hurry. He began to frequent places where he was likely to fall in with his old nautical associates, and when he met them he seemed to take great interest in their welfare, and made many inquiries as to their late adventures and mode of life.

War had just broken out between England and France, and all the other nations of Europe were in consequence arming, both afloat and on shore, not knowing when they might be drawn into the vortex of strife.

In all the ports of Spain, and at Cadiz especially, not only at the royal, but at the mercantile dockyards, vessels were being fitted out and armed ready to take a part in the contest. People of all descriptions, many who had long been wanderers on the face of the globe, were collected there with the hope of getting employment on board the numerous privateers fitting out, caring nothing which side they espoused, provided an abundance of prize-money was to be obtained. Among these worthies the marquis found several old acquaintances. He did not fail in the course of conversation to make inquiries about other former shipmates. He invited them to his house, and treated them with unexpected liberality. One and all declared that he was well worthy of the exalted rank to which he had attained. He was seated one day alone, not having yet found the description of man of whom he was in search, when a stranger was announced.

'He is a seafaring man,' said the servant, 'but he declines to give his name, as he says your excellency is not acquainted with it.'

'Let him come in—perhaps he may have business with me,' said the marquis; and a tall, thin, swarthy personage, with a large pair of moustaches which totally concealed his mouth, entered the room. He probably was about fifty years old, but he had as much the appearance of a soldier as of a sailor about him; he seated himself in a chair, and immediately said: 'Your very obedient servant, most noble marquis. I understand that you are in search of a trustworthy man to undertake some work or other for you.'

'I—I never said any such thing,' exclaimed the marquis, somewhat confused.

'Your excellency may not have said it, but the tenor of your conduct shows me what you require. You would not trouble yourself with the company of all the people you have lately invited to your house unless you required something from them. Come, be frank; I have guessed rightly, have I not?'

'Before I answer that question I must know whom I address,' answered the marquis, trying to look very wise.

'As to that, my name is not unknown to fame,' replied the stranger in a careless tone. 'I am Don Josef Tacon, or Captain Tacon, as I am generally called; we have met before now in the days of our youth; in the West Indies; on the coast of Africa; you remember me, perhaps. You recollect how we boarded the Dutchman, and how we relieved the Mynheers of their cash and cargo, and provisions and water; and you haven't forgotten the English West Indiaman we captured and sent to the bottom with all her crew when they threatened to send one of their cruizers after us. These and other little similar incidents have not escaped your memory, most noble marquis.'

Don Anibal winced not a little while the pirate—for such he avowed himself to be—was speaking; but he notwithstanding held out his hand and hailed him as an old shipmate.

'My memory is as good as you suppose, my friend,' he

remarked; 'but we will not dwell on those matters. There are some things a man would gladly forget if he could. However, there is an affair in which an intelligent fellow like you would be useful, if you will undertake it.'

'Name your price, Don Anibal, and I will tell you if I can undertake it,' answered Captain Tacon; 'my fortunes are somewhat at a low ebb, and I am ready to engage in any enterprise which promises sufficient remuneration.'

'You were always a reasonable man. What do you say to two thousand dollars? It would be worth a little exertion to gain that,' observed the marquis.

'Tell me what you require to be done, and I will then give you a direct answer,' said the pirate.

The marquis thought for some time before he replied. 'I must swear you to secrecy in the first place, and in the next, that you will decide, when I have put before you the outline of the work required, without obliging me to descend to particulars.'

'Depend on me, marquis,' exclaimed the pirate. 'As I see a crucifix at the other end of the room, I will take the oath; and now hasten on with your sketch; I am a man of action, and will speedily decide.'

'Listen, then,' said Don Anibal. 'You can, I doubt not, obtain command of one of the numerous vessels fitting out as privateers; I will use my influence. I can speak to your character for bravery, enterprise, sagacity—you understand me: you must use every exertion to find a craft. I know your talents—you will not fail.'

Captain Tacon smiled grimly at the compliments the marquis paid him. 'But the enterprise, the work you require of me, most noble marquis?' he said, with a slight gesture of impatience.

'I am coming to that, my friend,' was the answer. 'It lies in a nutshell: in a northern region there exists a child, of whose person, for certain reasons, unnecessary now to state, I wish to obtain possession. He lives in a mansion capable of defence; you may possibly, therefore, have to use force, but that of course will only make the work more agreeable to you. On your bringing me satisfactory assurance that you have disposed of the child as I may direct, the reward shall be yours. In the meantime, this purse, as soon as you decide, I will present to you. It is but an earnest of my liberal intentions.

The exhibition of the gold was a bright thought of Don Anibal's. As the taste of blood whets the appetite of the wild beast, so did the glittering bait the avarice of the pirate.

'Give me the purse,' he exclaimed, eagerly stretching out his hands; 'I will take the oath.'

'Take the oath, and you shall have the purse,' answered the marquis, smiling blandly. 'No mental reservations, though; I do not forget your antecedents, my old comrade.'

Captain Tacon gave a hoarse laugh, and twirling his moustachios, while his countenance wore the expression of a person about to swallow a nauseous draught, he walked across the room towards the crucifix. The marquis followed, with a self-satisfied look, as if he had achieved a victory. It is not necessary to repeat the oath taken by the pirate, or to describe the final arrangements entered into between the two worthies.

In a few days Captain Tacon again made his appearance, habited in a handsome nautical costume, with a huge cocked hat, and a richly-mounted sword by his side, and announced that he had become the captain of the privateer schooner 'San Nicolas.' 'Never did you set eyes on a finer craft, most noble marquis,' he exclaimed; 'she will fly like the wind, and swim like a wild-fowl. She carries eight guns, and an unlimited supply of small arms, with a bold crew of sixty men, villains every one! There is no deed of violence they will not dare or do; and now we are ready to sail when we receive your final orders.'

'I knew that I could trust you in the selection of your followers,' said the marquis, quietly. 'Here are your orders;

you will open them when at sea, and see that you carry them out in the spirit as well as in the letter. You will, of course, be well provided with flags. It may be convenient, at times, to sail under some other flag than that of Spain.'

Don Tacon smiled. 'I have some little experience in those matters,' he answered, 'trust me.'

That evening the 'San Nicolas' privateer was seen standing out of the harbour and steering to the northward. It was announced that she had sailed on a cruise, and would before long return.

It must not be supposed that all these arrangements took place with the rapidity with which they have been described. The Spaniards love dearly to do everything with deliberation; the summer had ended, and the winter had come and gone, before the events just narrated took place.

Two or three days after the 'San Nicolas' had sailed, it became generally known that Lieutenant Pedro Alvarez, the only surviving officer of the unfortunate 'St Cecilia,' had arrived at Cadiz. Such was the case—Pedro had obtained a passage on board an English man-of-war. When some sixty leagues to the north of Cadiz, she had fallen in with a suspicious-looking craft, which hoisted Spanish colours. An officer was sent to board her, and Lieutenant Alvarez was requested to go as interpreter. The stranger proved to be the privateer schooner 'San Nicolas,' and in her captain he recognized an old acquaintance. The last time they had met, it had been under somewhat unpleasant circumstances for Captain Tacon, who had almost got his head into a halter, and but narrowly slipped it out again. The worthy lieutenant very naturally suspected, from his knowledge of Don Josef's previous history, that he was not engaged in any very creditable undertaking. He at once suspected that he was not sailing on a simple privateering voyage, but of course he failed to ascertain the truth. The more questions he asked, the more mysterious and important his quondam acquaintance became. The result of his conversation was, that he resolved, as soon as he arrived at Cadiz, to make all the inquiries in his power about Captain Tacon, and the 'San Nicolas.' Pedro Alvarez was a blunt sailor, but he had a very considerable amount of sagacity. Before long, he discovered that his quondam acquaintance had been known to pay frequent visits to the Marquis de Medea, who was also known to have had some correspondence with the owners of the 'San Nicolas.' More than this Pedro could not discover; but it was sufficient to make him suspect that the schooner's voyage was in some way connected with the affairs of the marquis himself. He was not however a man to do things by halves, so he continued to work on in the hope that he might at last ferret out the truth. However, he had not much time for this occupation; for having reported himself to the naval authorities, he was forthwith promoted, and appointed to the command of a brig-of-war. His great aim, however, before he sailed, was to place in proper train with the legal authorities the claims of young Hernan Escalante to the title and estates now held by Don Anibal de Villavicencio. He was aware that possession is nine-tenths of the law, and that he must expect to have a very tough battle to fight.

'Never fear for the consequences,' said he to his legal adviser. 'I have neither wife nor child, nor any one depending on me, and as long as I have a silver piece belonging to me, I will expend it in claiming the rights of that poor child.'

Having just given expression to this virtuous resolution as he was leaving the lawyer's door, he found himself standing face to face with Father Mendez.

The priest looked narrowly at the house. He recollected that a well-known lawyer lived there. What could the rough lieutenant want with him? He jumped at a conclusion, which was not far from the truth; still his countenance wore its usual calm and inexpressive look.

'Ha! my old shipmate! I did not expect to see you so

soon in our own well-beloved native land,' he exclaimed. 'These are stirring times, and you did well to return: you will not be long on shore, however, I conclude?'

'Not long enough to lose my sea legs or sea manners,' answered Pedro, bluntly.

'Have you another appointment yet, my friend?' asked the priest.

'My superiors think me too useful to allow me to remain long unemployed,' replied Pedro.

'That is well: take the advice of a friend, and attend to your own duties,' said the priest, in a suppressed tone, sinking at last to a whisper; 'you will but burn your fingers if you interfere where you have no concern.'

'Thank you for your hint, most astute priest. Then you guess what I am about,' thought Pedro, but he did not speak aloud. He only tried to look totally unconscious of what Father Mendez could possibly mean. He did not succeed as well as he wished or fancied that he had done, and the father saw that it would be necessary to watch him very narrowly, to counteract any scheme he might attempt to carry into execution.

The lieutenant, meantime, fancied that he had outwitted the priest, and continued with the greatest energy to prosecute the work he had commenced.

Father Mendez was not long in discovering this, and with fully equal resolution took steps to put a stop to his proceedings. He also prided himself on performing whatever he undertook in the most effectual manner. He saw that Pedro might cause him a great deal of trouble and inconvenience. There were two ways which suggested themselves of disposing of him: he might inform the marquis of his proceedings, who would, without the slightest scruple, probably get him assasinated; but the bravo's dagger was not always sure, and if the marquis knew that he was dead he might be tempted to assume more independence than would be convenient. He had another plan, which could not possibly fail.

Pedro Alvarez, as do most captains, lived on shore while his ship was fitting out. He continued to do so after she was ready for sea, and while he was waiting for orders. He had made every preparation for sailing, and was ready to trip his anchor at a moment's notice. At last his despatches arrived. He was paying his last visit to the shore, when, as he was sitting in the room of his lodging glancing over a few accounts which remained unpaid, a stranger was announced. Captain Alvarez rose to receive him, and requested to know the object of his visit. As he did so, he recognized a person of whom he had caught a glimpse more than once, watching him as he left the house.

'No matter who I am,' said the stranger; 'I but obey the orders of my superiors, and I am directed to desire you to attend at the office of the Holy Inquisition, there to answer certain accusations which have been brought against you. This, it is hoped, you can at once easily and completely do, and that you will therefore not hesitate to accompany me. A carriage waits for us at the end of the street. You can arrange the matters about which you are now occupied on your return. I am directed to accompany you, and as the council is now sitting there is no time to be lost.'

'Do you expect to catch a weasel asleep?' thought Pedro, at least an equivalent Spanish proverb occurred to him. Pedro was conscious that he had at times expressed himself, in coffee-houses and taverns, in a way not over complimentary, either to the priests or the Inquisition itself; and he felt very sure that no explanations he could give would prove satisfactory to the Inquisitional council. The bold determined look he gave the officer was such as that worthy officer was little accustomed to receive from the trembling wretches on whom he served his summonses.

'You have performed your duty, my friend, and now go back to those who sent you, and inform them that you have delivered your message, but that my avocations prevent me from acceding to their demands.'

The official looked wonderfully astonished, and, without saying another word, drew a pistol from his bosom, and clapping it to the seaman's head, told him that he must enforce obedience.

'Must you, friend?' exclaimed Pedro, by a sudden movement of his arm striking up the pistol; 'then I must resist by force.'

The official pulled the trigger, but the weapon had not often been used, and the powder flashed in the pan. He was about to draw another, but Pedro's quick eye saw the man's purpose. His own sword lay on the table. He seized it with one hand, while with the other he grasped the barrel of the pistol about to be turned towards him. At that instant the official's foot slipped, and, as he fell heavily forward, the point of the sword entered his throat and pierced through to the spine. Pedro caught him as he fell, but the wound was mortal, and in another minute he was dead.

Pedro Alvarez was as bold and brave a seaman as ever stepped; but he knew full well that killing an official of the Inquisition in the execution of his duty, would make the country too hot for him. The instinct of self-preservation was as strong with him as with most men. He considered how he could avoid the consequences of his act. There was a large cupboard in the room. He dragged the body in, and locking the door put the key in his pocket. The wound had not bled much, and he was able to get rid of the traces without much difficulty. It just then occurred to him that the owners of the house would get into trouble when the body should be discovered; so he wrote on a piece of paper—'This man attempted to kill me, and in self-defence, I, against my wish, slew him.—Pedro Alvarez;' and, opening the door of the cupboard, pinned it on the stranger's coat. He then put all the papers belonging to him into his pocket, and deliberately walked down to the quays. His boat was waiting for him. His heart beat much more regularly than it had done for the last half hour, as he sprang on board and shoved off. His crew gave way, and he soon stepped the deck of his beautiful little brig, the 'Veloz.' The next instant the boats were hoisted in, the anchor was weighed, the topsails were let fall and sheeted home, and the brig, with a fine breeze from the southward, stood out of the harbour. Every sail the brig could carry was pressed on her. The officers and crew were delighted with the way she flew through the water. Her captain turned his spyglass very often towards the town: he made out, at last, a boat pulling off rapidly towards the brig, and shortly afterwards his signal mid-shipman reported that one of the ships-of-war in the harbour was telegraphing to them.

'You must be mistaken, boy; it cannot be intended for us shut up your book, we are beyond signalling distance,' he answered. 'And so farewell to lovely Spain—for ever, perhaps,' he thought to himself. 'It will take more years than I am likely to live to make those wretches forget or forgive the death of their official. From henceforth I am a banished man. For myself I care not; but for poor young Hernan—who is to advocate his cause? Well, I fear for this time the spirit of evil and his imps have got the upper hand of honest folk.'

CHAPTER XII.

A STRANGE SCHOONER APPEARS OFF LUNNASTING.—THE CASTLE ATTACKED.—THE PIRATES ENTER THE CASTLE.—YOUNG HERNAN CARRIED OFF.

HE winds whistled round the towers of Lunnasting, and the wild waves, as they were wont, washed the base of the rock on which it stood, and time sped on without any material change taking place among its inhabitants. Hilda spent the greater portion of the day in her turret chamber, gazing out—when not engaged in nursing her child—on the wide-spread ocean, and thinking of him who slept beneath its surface. Her infant, however, was her constant and only source of interest.

The little fatherless infant grew and flourished, and gave every promise of becoming a strong healthy boy. Meantime the health of Bertha Morton became week after week worse and worse, and her mother began to fear, too justly, that her days on earth were numbered. Rolf had been compelled to make a voyage to Greenland, as first mate of a ship; and he came back only in time to have his little boy put into his arms and to receive the last breath of the wife he so fond'y loved. At Hilda's special invitation the young Ronald was carried up to castle that his grandmother might have the entire charge of him.

' He will make a good playmate for my little Hernan, dear Bertha,' observed Hilda; so you see he will amply repay me for any advantage he may obtain by the arrangement. I trust the boys may be friends through life. They are of kindred blood, and Morton is a person in manners and conduct far above the position he holds. From his appearance it has more than once occurred to me that he must be of gentle blood. He that is gone, who saw a good deal of him, several times made the same remark.'

'He was brought up by a good, kind, Christian man, and it is on that account, rather than on account of his birth, that he possesses the qualities of which you so kindly speak, my dear mistress,' answered Bertha.

Hilda made no reply; affliction had not taught her to adopt the principles which guided Bertha's conduct.

The brief daylight hours of the northern winter had once more begun to increase, when Hilda received a letter from her father, announcing his intention of returning to Lunnasting in the early part of the summer, with Edda. He also spoke of her sister's engagement to a Colonel Armytage, remarking that the marriage would soon take place.

It is scarcely possible to describe the varied, but chiefly painful feelings which this information created in Hilda's bosom. Her father had hitherto remained ignorant of her conduct, and she felt that he would be very justly incensed when he heard of it. Still she was too proud and self-willed to meditate for an instant asking his pardon, or seeking for reconciliation, and her whole thoughts were occupied in considering how she could best meet the storm of indignation and anger which she expected to burst on her. For Edda, however, she had as warm an affection as it was in her nature to feel for anybody so totally different as her sister and she were to each other. She could scarcely help despising Edda for her gentleness and her kind and affectionate disposition, as well as for the implicit obedience she yielded to their father's often imperious commands.

'I pray heaven the gentleman our sweet Miss Edda is going to marry is worthy of her—good, and generous, and kind—or it will break her heart,' said nurse Bertha, as they were talking over the subject together.

'It takes a good deal to break a Wardhill's heart, or mine would have gone long ago,' answered Hilda, with a sigh so deep and sad that it made Bertha's sicken as she heard it.

Lawrence Brindister was as little pleased as any one with the report of Sir Marcus Wardhill's intended return. Poor Lawrence had that instinctive dread of his guardian which a cat or a dog has of the person who takes every occasion of giving them a kick or a buffet when they meet. He felt that he was unjustly and tyrannically treated, yet he had no means of breaking away from his thraldom. Sir Marcus had a very simple plan for keeping him within bounds; he never intrusted him with money; and as poor Lawrence was known to be of unsound mind, nobody was found willing to lend him their gold to supply his wants, as none of it was ever likely to be repaid.

Pending the expected arrival of her father, Hilda was seated as usual at her turret window; now gazing at her infant, who was sleeping on a pile of cushions at her feet; now casting a glance across the ocean, over which the sun, now declining towards the west, was casting a rich glow, when her eye was attracted by the white sails of a vessel which, lighted up by his beams, shone like driven snow. There was a light wind from the south-east, before which the vessel under all sail was standing in towards the land. Hilda, who from having lived all her life near the sea was well acquainted with the rigs of vessels, recognised the one now approaching as a schooner, and from her wide spread of canvas she judged that she was a large one.

On stood the stranger, directly towards Whalsey. At first, from the bold way in which she approached, Hilda thought that she must have a pilot on board, but as she drew in with the channel between the south end of Eastling and the little island known as Grief Skerry, she hauled her wind, and then went about and hove-to, with her head off shore.

'What can possibly be her errand here?' said Hilda to herself. 'Can my father be on board her? But no, he would have stood on, and brought the vessel to an anchor.'

The family retired to rest at the usual hour of ten o'clock, and probably not long after that were wrapped in sound sleep. Not so poor Hilda. The mistress of the mansion slept far less than any of those who obeyed her orders. She invariably retired long after the household were in bed, rose early, and probably seldom obtained more than an hour's continuous sleep. On this evening her child had been somewhat fretful, and Bertha insisted on carrying the little fellow off to sleep in her room with her grandson, Ronald Morton. Hilda had reluctantly consented to the arrangement, and frequently awoke with a start of terror on missing her little companion from her side. At length she had fallen into a comparatively sound sleep, when she was suddenly awakened by a loud, crashing sound. She started up. The noise brought to her recollection, with painful clearness, the moment when the 'St Cecilia' struck on the rocks of Ossa Skerry. She thought she must have been dreaming, but again the sound was renewed. She felt confident that it was caused by heavy blows dealt against a small postern gate which led out on the front terrace overhanging the sea. From the noise, Hilda suspected that this had already partly given way, and she feared that the assailants, whoever they were, would already have gained an entrance before she could summon any of the servants to resist them. Besides Lawrence, it was not likely that there were more than five or six men in the house. The bell belonging to her room led only to the chambers of the women, and she feared that when they awoke, they would do little more for the defence of the castle than scream; nor had she much confidence in the valour of old David Cheyne, the butler. Still she herself felt no overwhelming alarm. Throwing some garments round her, she hurried to the hall, where a bell rope communicated with the servants' room. She pulled it violently, and then hastened on to call Lawrence. She had little confidence, however, in the way he might behave; still, she had no reason to doubt his courage, and knew that if he comprehended what was required, he was likely to be of as much value as any other man. He had fire-arms, and so had all the servants, and she hoped, if there was time for them to collect, to give the assailants a warm reception. The door, it was evident, had resisted the first attack made on it, for again there came a succession of thundering blows, which echoed through the castle, and must have aroused the soundest sleepers. Hilda took a turn up and down the hall to relieve her impatience. She felt inclined herself to go to the gate to ascertain how far it had resisted the attacks made on it, but she reflected that this would be folly, because, should she be seized by the enemy, it would make all further resistance useless. Every moment her impatience increased.

'What! are the men turned cowards?' she exclaimed, when she found that no one appeared; 'are they skulking in bed, afraid to encounter the unexpected foe? Oh! that I were a man, to be able to fight as brave men do! I thought better things of Lawrence. If they would but come, we might yet drive back these marauders. It shall never be said that the castle of Lunnasting was given up without a desperate struggle.'

Again she rang such a peal, that Davie Cheyne must have been aroused, had he been twice as sound asleep as he had ever been before. It produced its effect, and with startled looks, his hair on end, with his night-cap in one hand and his coat in the other, the old butler rushed into the hall, followed by the other serving-men, and some farm labourers who slept in the castle.

'Oh my lady!—oh Miss Hilda! Oh—I beg pardon, Madame Escalante—what is the matter? What is going to happen?'

'That you, lazy-bones, have been snoring in bed, while the

castle is being attacked by a band of robbers or privateers; and that, unless you stir yourselves to defend it, you may all be murdered as you deserve. Quick!—get your arms, and try to defend the place. Where is Mr Lawrence? Is he as cowardly as the rest of you?'

'No, cousin Hilda, he is not,' said Lawrence, who entered at that moment with a musket in one hand, a sword in the other, and a brace of pistols in his belt. 'I have been to take a look at the besiegers. They are taking breath to make a fresh attack, and it's my opinion that we take them on the flank, and if we work our guns well, we shall be able to shoot them down before one of them can return to their boats.'

'Excellent, Lawrence,' exclaimed Hilda, pleased with his unexpected sagacity and promptness. 'Place the men as you think best. What could induce an enemy to attack this place, it is difficult to say, unless from its apparent strength they suppose it contains large stores of plate and jewels. However, I trust to your courage and conduct to disappoint them.'

While Hilda was speaking, some of the men were loading their firelocks; others found that they had forgot their ammunition, and ran back to get it; and Davie Cheyne was putting on his coat and arranging his garments in a seemly manner, and stuffing a night-cap into his pouch, he armed himself with a huge blunderbuss, which, with its ammunition pouches, hung over the mantelpiece.

'Give me a musket!' cried Hilda. 'Where there are not enough men, women must fight. I would sooner lose my life than allow these marauders to enter the castle.'

Hilda was speaking while Davie Cheyne was getting down the fire-arm and handing it to her. Not another moment was then lost, and the party, led by Lawrence, were hastening to the eastern tower which commanded the gate, when several of the women rushed with loud shrieks into the hall, exclaiming that the robbers were breaking into the castle, and that they were all going to be murdered.

'Silence, wenches!' cried Hilda, indignantly. 'When I show signs of fear it is time for you to be afraid. Those who have the nerve to load the guns come with me; the rest go and remain with Bertha Eswick and the children. She will shame you, I doubt not, by her coolness.'

Two of the damsels alone were influenced by this address, and followed their mistress, while the rest, every now and then giving way to a shriek, ran up stairs as fast as they could go, to the nursery, where, surrounding Bertha, who was sitting up with the children, they said the mistress had sent them, and pulling away at her, entreated her to tell them what was going to happen.

'Girls, girls; it is something very dreadful, I doubt not,' she answered, solemnly. 'But shrieking and crying will not ward off the danger. Let us rather silently pray to Him who can alone save us, for protection and the safety of those we best love.'

The girls were silent for a short time, but Bertha's address did not seem to have much effect on them; and the sound of a volley of musketry, which was soon afterwards heard again, set them off shrieking louder than before.

The effects of the volley did not appear to have much availed the defenders of the castle, for, almost before it had ceased, the thundering blows on the gate were renewed with greater violence than before, and the crashing noise which followed showed that it was yielding to them. There were, as Bertha well knew, two small gates, one within the other. The first had, as she suspected, given way to the attack the assailants had first made, the crushing sound of which had awakened her as it had Hilda. The second gate was the one against which they were now directing their efforts. Lawrence had not been aware of this, and he fancied that it was the outer gate alone which had to be defended. On reaching the first storey of the tower, and on looking from the window which commanded the space before this outer gate, he saw a large group of armed men, apparently prepared for attacking it.

'There are the enemy! Have no parley with them! Fire, boys!' he exclaimed, setting the example by discharging his musket. The rest fired likewise, and apparently several of the enemy were hit; but, instead of taking to flight, they fired in return, and several of the Lunnasting party might have been hit had they not speedily retired from the window. In the chamber below, however, there were several loopholes, and in these they forthwith assembled, and commenced firing away as before. Hilda had not used her musket; but she in no way felt inclined to shrink from the contest, and her presence wonderfully animated the rest. They soon, however, discovered that the first of their defences had been taken, and that they were not in the slightest degree impeding the progress of the attacking party, who, in spite of the repeated volleys with which their comrades were saluted, continued to batter away at the door with an evident determination to succeed. At the same time the door was a very solid one, and resisted all their efforts. Several of those outside had been wounded. One or two had been seen to fall. This encouraged Lawrence and his followers.

'Could you not make a sally and drive them off?' at length exclaimed Hilda, as the blows on the door became louder and more reiterated. 'If you rushed out suddenly they would not know how many men were following, and might take to flight.'

'They know well enough how many men are inside these walls, or they would not have dared to attack us, my lady,' observed Davie Cheyne. 'With your permission, my lady, we'll fight on till the powder is gone, with the thick stone between us, but there is na use in venturing our lives against six times our number without some such aid.'

The firing on both sides now became very warm till two of the servants were hit, and a bullet passed through the sleeve of Lawrence's coat. On discovering this Hilda despatched one of the girls for bandages, while she endeavoured to staunch the blood of the man who was most hurt with her handkerchief.

'Thank ye, ma'am—thank ye, my lady,' said the poor fellow, looking up at her with an expression of gratitude in his countenance; 'it will not be much harm done, and if ye will let me I'll be at them again.'

The girl was absent nearly a minute, and, as she appeared, in a voice of terror she exclaimed, 'the gate is giving way, and they will be into the castle in a moment!'

The courage of Hilda and her two attendants formed a great contrast to the behaviour of the women who had taken refuge with Bertha. The more constant the firing the louder they shrieked; and, as the sound of the blows on the gate reached them they clung to her gown, entreating her to tell them what to do. At last there came a crash louder than any that had preceded it, followed immediately by shouts and cries, and the report of fire-arms, evidently inside the castle, and the cries and shrieks increased, and then there was the heavy tramp of men's feet, some hurrying along the passages, others ascending the stairs.

'Oh, they are coming here—they are coming here!' cried one of the servant girls. 'We shall all be murdered,' and the castle will be burnt. Oh, Mistress Bertha, where shall we run to?—where shall we hide?'

'Close the doors, girls,' said Bertha, calmly. 'Perhaps they will not come here.'

The sound of the footsteps drew nearer and nearer. One room after the other was entered, and at last that next to the nursery. A moment afterwards the nursery door was violently shaken. Bertha made a sign to the women to keep silence, but in vain: as a heavy blow was struck against the door, one of them shrieked out. Some words in a strange language were spoken by men with gruff voices, and the next instant the door was burst open, and a dozen or more armed men, fierce looking fellows, rushed into the room. The girls fled to the extreme corner, but the pirates—for that they were desperadoes of that description, there seemed no doubt—took at first but little notice of them, turning all their attention to Bertha and the two children. A tall sinewy fellow, with long moustachios, stalked up to her, and, before she was aware of what he was about, snatched one of the children from her, and scrutinizing its countenance returned it to her, and then seized the other, which he examined still more minutely. He seemed sorely puzzled, and pulled away furiously at his moustachios, while he talked and gesticulated to his companions.

They then commenced an examination of the children, and were so absorbed in the matter, that the serving girls were able to make their escape from the room, while poor Bertha was left alone with the savage-looking band of strangers. However, the matter was soon decided. The tall man, who seemed to be the captain, attempted to snatch the one he had first seized from poor Bertha's grasp. In vain she struggled, and entreated him to let it go. Both the little fellows shrieked out with terror, as, hugging them in her arms, she endeavoured to escape from him; but, tearing the child from her, he held it up to his companions, and seemed to be asking them certain questions. They nodded in return; and while two of them held back poor Bertha, who was struggling to regain the child, he threw a cloak over it, and, calling to his followers, hurried down stairs. Bertha attempted to follow, in the hopes of regaining the child, but, overcome with terror and agitation, she sunk exhausted on the ground. The marauders took their way to the postern gate, by which they had entered the castle. Near it was a room, at the door of which a number of their companions were standing, guarding the defenders of the castle, whom they had overpowered. Leaving them there, he passed on, and, getting over the terrace parapet wall, he descended the cliff with his burden towards the boat which lay at the foot of it, and to which the men who had been wounded had been already conveyed. The little boy was all the time shrieking out most lustily, and desiring to be taken back to his mammá. Placing the child in the boat, with strict charges to one of the men who were in her not to let it out of his arms, he climbed the cliff again with the agility of a cat, and rejoined his comrades. He addressed them in Spanish.

'My men,' he observed, 'we have thus far fulfilled our engagement. Now let us recompense ourselves in case the promised reward should not be forthcoming.'

His proposal seemed to meet with the warm approval of all the party. It was necessary, however, to leave some of them to guard the prisoners, at which those who were to be left grumbled much. 'No matter,' he observed; 'three of you will do, and if any of the prisoners attempt to escape, shoot them. It is the quickest way of disposing of those sort of people.'

Bertha had lain thus for some time, still grasping the little child, and in spite of his piteous cries, unconscious of his presence, when she was aroused by her mistress's voice exclaiming—

'Bertha, Bertha! where is my boy?—where is Hernan?'

'Your boy, Hilda! is he not here?' answered Bertha, scarcely yet fully aroused. 'Is he not here—here in my arms?'

'Here?—no! Where is he? who has him? Give him to me!' exclaimed Hilda, in a tone which showed the agony of her terror.

'Oh! was it not a dream? Where is he, do you ask? What has happened? Those men—they bore him away,' said Bertha, trying to rouse herself.

'My boy gone? You gave him to them instead of your own,' cried Hilda. 'Oh! woman—woman! Did you not know how precious he was to me? And you let them take him! You should have died rather than allow them to tear him from you.'

'You wrong me, dear mistress,' answered Bertha. 'They

chose yours—they had come on purpose to get him, for they rejected mine. But have they gone? Let us follow them: a mother's tears may induce them to give him back.'

'And I have lost all this time!' cried Hilda, putting her hand to her brow, and moving from the room.

When the pirates forced their way into the castle, the defenders were separated; Davie Cheyne, with the two serving girls, hurrying off their mistress in one direction, while Lawrence and the men bravely opposed them for some minutes, till they were completely overpowered, and compelled to submit to the enemy.

Having provided for their prisoners, the captain of the pirates and his men set off to engage in the pleasant occupation of ransacking the castle. From room to room they went, injuring nothing, and breaking nothing, except the locks of drawers, cabinets, chests, and cupboards. These, as the keys were not forthcoming, they burst open to examine their contents. They worked away briskly, but in no undue hurry. They knew that the operation in which they were engaged should not be done slowly, in case of interruption; at the same time at present, they had no reason to expect any interference with their performances. They were most of them evidently practised hands, for they were choice in their selections, and took only the more valuable articles. Plate, jewels, and ornaments were quickly transferred to their pockets, or to bags with which they had come prepared; but, with the exception of a few clothes, to which some of them took a fancy, and a collection of eatables from the housekeeper's store-room, nothing else was carried off.

These matters being arranged, the captain ordered a retreat to be sounded. It was time, for daylight was already coming on, and they could not tell what assistance might be sent to the inhabitants of the castle, as they knew that the sound of their firing must have given notice to the neighbouring population that something unusual was going on. With some derisive expressions, the meaning of which Lawrence alone, of those who heard them, could understand, they left the party in the room, simply turning the key on them, and took their way to their boats. Just as they were shoving off through the twilight, a figure was seen standing on the edge of the cliff, stretching forth her arms, and shrieking out—

'My child—my child! Bring back my boy! Take him not away!'

In vain she cried, and those fierce men, cruel and callous as they were, had not the barbarity to mock her. Without uttering a word, they pulled rapidly from the shore. Giving vent to her feelings in cries, she uttered shriek after shriek, and would have thrown herself into the water, in her eagerness to follow them, had not Davie Cheyne come behind her, and, seizing her in his arms, drawn her back from the edge of the precipice. She broke from him, and was again rushing forward, when Lawrence and a servant, who burst out of the room where they had been locked in, ran forward and surrounded her. When they saw the boats, two of them, who had secured some muskets which the pirates had overlooked, threatened to fire on them; but as they levelled their pieces the captain held up the child, and three or four bullets whizzing above their heads, showed them that they would gain nothing by warlike proceedings. Some of the men—and so did Lawrence—proposed manning Sir Marcus's barge, and going in pursuit of the enemy; but the proposal was wisely overruled by Davie Cheyne. 'How could they expect, with a single boat, and with but few men ill-armed, to capture two boats full of well-armed men, perfectly practised in warfare, and who had already shown their superiority?'

The argument was unanswerable, and the proposal was withdrawn. It was, meantime, with the greatest difficulty that Hilda was held back from the edge of the cliff.

'My child! my child!' she continued crying out. 'Oh, bring me back my child!'

The sound of her voice could no longer reach those she addressed. Away pulled the boat towards the schooner in the offing; and as all hope of recovering her soon vanished, she again sunk senseless into the arms of those surrounding her.

When daylight increased, a schooner, which hoisted French colours, was seen standing away to the eastward; but whence she had come, and where she went to, no one connected with Lunnasting was ever able to discover.

CHAPTER XIII.

ARRIVAL OF SIR MARCUS.—HILDA AND HER SISTER.—A BRIG OF WAR APPEARS.—EDDA'S MARRIAGE.—ROLF MORTON SAILS ON A LONG VOYAGE.

FOR many days after the loss of her child, Hilda remained in a state of such utter prostration, that Bertha, who would allow no one but herself to watch her, often dreaded that her mind would go altogether.

'Perhaps she would be happier thus unconscious of past griefs, or of the dreary future in store for her,' Bertha frequently repeated to herself; but Hilda was not thus to be spared the trials and sorrows sent to purify and correct her nature. Not only did she become fully aware of all that had taken place, but she was made fully alive to events daily occurring, and was able to contemplate what the future might bring forth. On what account her son was carried off, she could form no conjecture, but she always cherished the hope of seeing him again. This hope occupied her thoughts by day and her dreams by night, and appeared to be the chief means of her restoration to comparative health. At first she could not bear the sight of her child's playmate, Ronald Morton; but one day she suddenly desired Bertha to bring him to her, and after gazing at him for some moments, she covered him with kisses, and from that moment could scarcely bear him out of her sight. At first the child cried, and evidently regarded her with dread;

but Bertha soothed him, and persuaded him to go back to her; and Hilda, by gentle caresses, which seemed totally foreign to her nature, soon won him over completely, so that he quickly learned to look on her as really his mother. His father had sailed, at the commencement of the year, for Greenland, and there was no probability of his returning till the autumn.

In spite of the exciting incidents which had occurred, matters at Lunnasting returned very much to their usual condition. Even poor Lawrence Brindister, who had behaved with courage and a considerable amount of judgment when the castle was attacked, very speedily again became the half-witted creature he generally appeared, and once more resumed his eccentric habits and behaviour.

Sir Marcus had before this again put off the time for his return home; but at length a large cutter—a Leith smack—was seen standing towards the castle. She dropped her anchor at the entrance of Lunnasting Voe, and a boat containing a lady and gentleman immediately put off from her, and pulled for the landing-place. Hilda soon recognized her father and sister. As she saw them, she felt every nerve in her system trembling with agitation. Bertha entreated her to be calm, and at last, by a violent effort, she gained sufficient command over herself to hurry down to the landing-place to meet them. Her father met her with his usual polite, but cold and indifferent manner; but Edda herself, blooming with life and health, looked deeply concerned when she saw her altered appearance, for physical suffering and mental anxiety had made sad havoc with those features. Sir Marcus had now to learn, for the first time, of the piratical attack which had been made on his castle, and of the severe loss he had suffered. Every one was anxious to screen Hilda; and probably, had it not been necessary to account to him for the disappearance of so many articles of property, even that event would not have been told him. Of all others, he was allowed to remain perfectly ignorant.

Thus, strange as it may appear, he heard nothing of the circumstances of the visit of the 'St Cecilia,' of Hilda's marriage with Don Hernan, or of the birth of her child. All he heard was, that a foreign ship-of-war had anchored in the Sound, and that, shortly after, she had been wrecked on the west coast of the mainland; so sure are those who attempt to rule their dependents with severity or injustice, to be deceived or misled by them.

Humbled, softened, and weighed down with grief, Hilda could not long keep her secret from her sister; and Edda heard, with amazement and sorrow, all the strange events which had occurred at Lunnasting during her absence. Once having broken through the ice of reserve which had so long existed, the two sisters were on far more affectionate terms than they had ever before been.

Edda did not utter a word of blame. She well knew how little trained Hilda had ever been to bear it, but she gave her sympathy, and treated her with all the tenderness and affection of a loving sister.

Meantime, Sir Marcus Wardhill, who was not a man to suffer an injury without attempting to obtain redress, was sending memorial after memorial to the government in England, to complain of the attack made on his castle, and was also instituting every inquiry to ascertain to what nation the people belonged who had been guilty of the act. All he could learn with regard to the latter point was, that on the day following that on which it occurred, a pilot boat and several fishing vessels had fallen in with a large schooner of a very rakish appearance, under French colours, steering a course apparently with the intention of running between Shetland and Orkney, into the Atlantic.

In the course, however, of his inquiries, information which he little expected came out, and which could not fail to raise his suspicions as to his daughter's discretion. He was, as has been seen, a man wise in the ways of the world, and not at all liable to give way to sudden bursts of temper, great as might be the provocation. Instead, therefore, of rushing into his daughter's room, and accusing her of her misconduct, he kept his counsel, and said nothing whatever on the subject. It might have occurred to him that he should have been wiser had he remained at home, and looked more narrowly after his establishment. He found that he had been deceived—of that there could be no doubt. Information which he naturally expected would have been given to him had been withheld. He knew that this being the case, he was not likely to force it out of his dependents. He went on, therefore, quietly making inquiries, now of one, now of the other, and though he did not gain the whole truth, he ascertained enough to assure him that it would be wiser not to push his inquiries much further. Had he become aware of the exact state of the case, he would have undoubtedly been far more satisfied than he was; but cunning men are often caught in their own snares, and miss the mark at which they are aiming.

It was remarked that, after a time, he took far more interest in little Ronald Morton than he had at first done, and seemed not at all surprised at finding the child so constantly with his daughter. He even made some attempts to play with it, but they were not very successful, and the little fellow invariably made his escape from him as soon as he could.

The time fixed for Edda's marriage had now arrived, and Colonel Armytage was daily expected. Sir Marcus mentioning this to Hilda, remarked, 'You will let that child remain with Bertha Eswick while Armytage is here. I do not object to your petting him, but it is fit that you should pay all the attention in your power to your intended brother-in-law.'

There might have been far more order and regularity in the castle after the master's return, but everybody felt an uncomfortable sensation of oppression whenever he was present. The only sun which shed any light through the surrounding atmosphere was his daughter Edda. Full of life and animation, nothing could quell her spirits, and in most cases she had only to appear to dispel the gloom.

Poor Lawrence, even more than any one else, felt the weight of his guardian's presence whenever he was compelled to remain at home; but he had the resource—of which he never failed to avail himself when the weather allowed him— of going out in his boat, of wandering about the island on Neogle, with Surly Grind, or of visiting his cavern. Sir Marcus had gained that influence over him which a man of strong mind usually obtains over one of weak intellect, and he was thus often able to make him say the very things which he purposely intended to keep secret. Still Lawrence did not tell him the whole truth, and often thus misled him more than if he had not said a word on the subject. Often, too, he would startle him as he walked away by breaking out, as if unconsciously, with 'The prince will hae his ain again! The prince will hae his ain again!'

'What do you mean by that, Lawrence?' exclaimed the baronet, one day, with greater agitation than he usually exhibited.

'The meaning, coz?' said Lawrence, turning round and looking at him hard. 'The true meaning is this: that the king of the land will some day come back, and put his own crown of gold on his head, in spite of the rebels and all the cunning men who try to keep him from it.'

A very uncomfortable sensation crept round the baronet's heart.

Poor Lawrence went his way, rejoicing under the belief that he had frightened the stern, dignified baronet out of his wits. He little understood the tough materials of which his cousin's mind was composed, or dreamed of the injury the hints he had thrown out would induce him to work against those he might suppose stood in his way. At present it was Sir Marcus's wish to keep everything as smooth and pleasant at Lunnasting, that he might be able to give an agreeable welcome to his intended son-in-law.

Colonel Armytage had written word that he had engaged the same cutter which had carried Sir Marcus and his daughter to Shetland. It was very natural, therefore, that Edda should very frequently have her eye at a large telescope Sir Marcus had brought with him, and which he had placed in Hilda's room at the top of the tower. One day, as she was looking through the glass, she exclaimed suddenly to her sister, 'Oh Hilda, Hilda, there is the cutter at last!'

Hilda looked, but her more practised eye told her that it was no cutter, but a square-rigged vessel, which, with a fair breeze, under all sail, was approaching the island. She was sorry to disappoint Edda, and for sometime she did not tell her of her mistake. She herself went several times to the glass, and was convinced, from the squareness of the vessel's yards and the whiteness of her canvas, that she was a man-of-war. Painful feelings crowded to her heart, for the vessel approaching reminded her strongly of the 'St Cecilia:' she stood on boldly, as if those on board were well acquainted with the coast, and in a short time Hilda ascertained, without doubt, that she was a brig-of-war. Poor Edda, with a sigh, discovered that she had been mistaken.

The brig-of-war stood on towards Lunnasting till she neared the south end of Eastling Island, when, as she hauled her wind to stand up the Sound, Hilda saw with a thrill that the flag of Spain was flying from her peak. She brought to, at the very spot at which the 'St Cecilia' had anchored. Before her sails were furled a boat was lowered, and pulled towards the castle. Hilda watched it through the telescope, and, as it passed under the walls, she recognized, in the officer who sat in the stern-sheets, the first-lieutenant of the 'St Cecilia,' Pedro Alvarez. Though eager to learn what cause had brought him to Lunnasting, she was afraid of going down to meet him, lest it should excite suspicion in her father's mind. Trembling with agitation, she sat still, waiting for his appearance, with the hope, though it was full of doubt, that he might bring her tidings of her son.

Meantime, Lawrence Brindister had espied him, and hurrying to the landing-place, welcomed him cordially. 'But I say, old friend,' he continued, holding his finger to his nose, 'the cat has come back, and the mice mustn't play any more; you understand—mum's the word; don't talk of anything that has occurred: let old Grimalkin find out what he can; I delight in teasing him.'

Although the worthy Pedro did not comprehend all Lawrence said, he understood that he was not to allude to past events in the presence of the lord of the castle. Lawrence hurried him on, talking in his usual rambling way, so that before he had time to make any inquiries, he found himself in the presence of Sir Marcus Wardhill. The baronet received him with all due courtesy, and he was invited to stop and dine at the castle—an invitation he at once accepted. Hilda had no opportunity of seeing him till they met before dinner. It was not even then, without great exertion, that she obtained sufficient self-command to speak to him with ordinary calmness.

During the meal little Ronald Morton toddled into the room, having escaped from the arms of his nurse. Captain Alvarez gave an inquiring glance at the child, and at first looked puzzled, and then well satisfied. Hilda was able to converse with him in Spanish, and with his broken English and French he managed to make himself very agreeable to Sir Marcus and Edda; Sir Marcus, indeed, begged that when he could live on shore that he would make his castle his home; he declined, on the plea that he must sail, probably the next day, for the southward.

The attack on the castle had been spoken of, but not a word had been said of the child having been carried off.

Hitherto Hilda had been unable to talk to the Spanish captain alone; fortunately, at length, Sir Marcus left the room; Ronald was sitting playing on the ground near them.

'He is truly a noble child, though his complexion shows

more of his northern than his southern blood,' observed the captain.

'That child!—oh, you are mistaken!' exclaimed Hilda, 'Have you not heard that my own Hernan was carried off?' And she told him all that had occurred.

'The atrocious scoundrel!' exclaimed Pedro Alvarez; 'I feared it would be so, and for your sake, lady, and for that of my late brave captain, I will pursue them round the world, and recover the boy.'

Hilda looked at him with an expression of the deepest gratitude:—

'I was certain that you had come either to bring me notice of my lost one, or that you would aid me in discovering him,' she exclaimed, taking his hand. 'I trust to you, Captain Alvarez, and I am sure that you will not deceive me.'

The captain assured her that he would be faithful to his promise, and explained all he knew of the plot which had been formed to carry off her son, to prevent him from inheriting his title and property.

'But cannot we punish the treacherous marquis and kinsman?' she exclaimed. 'Cannot we compel him to tell us where my child has been carried to? Has the law no power in your country?'

'None, lady, in this matter,' answered Pedro. 'I myself am an outlaw; I can never return as a free man to Spain. I have been guilty of a crime so heinous in the eyes of the law, that should the officers of my own ship discover it, they would be compelled to carry me there in chains. My dread, therefore, is lest we should fall in with any Spanish ship, from which they may learn what has occurred.' He then briefly told her how he had killed the officer of the Inquisition who had tried to apprehend him.

'But the priest, Father Mendez; surely he can aid us?' said Hilda.

'Unless you can show him that by his aiding you he can

advance the object for which alone he lives, he will stir neither hand nor foot in the cause,' answered the Spanish captain. 'Besides, I am certain that he believes the child still safe in the castle.'

'Then, Captain Alvarez, I must place all my hope on you,' exclaimed Hilda.

'Place it on the justice of heaven, lady,' he replied, solemnly.

Hilda made no reply, but her beautiful features wore an expression of the deepest, the most hopeless distress.

Pedro Alvarez having obtained from Lawrence, and others, every particular about the attack on the castle, as well as a description of the child, and even the appearance of the men who carried him off, returned on board his brig, and the next day sailed for the southward.

His coming had thrown Hilda into a painful state of agitation. She had not recovered from it when the smack with Colonel Armytage on board anchored before the castle. Edda's joyous countenance formed a great contrast to her melancholy look. Sir Marcus met her, as she was preparing to receive her future brother-in-law, and harshly ordered her to appear more cheerful.

'Those lachrymose features of yours will raise suspicions in his mind which may induce him to make disagreeable inquiries,' he said, in an angry tone. 'I know his disposition, and fully believe that, should he discover anything to displease him, he is capable of breaking off the match altogether. Should he do so, remember, Hilda, you will be answerable for the consequences.'

'Can you intrust my sister's happiness with such a man?' asked Hilda.

'I am the best judge on that point,' was the answer.

Colonel Armytage soon came on shore, attended by two servants. He was decidedly handsome and gentlemanly, and though at times his manner was somewhat haughty and reserved, he was often so courteous and agreeable, that he quickly regained his place in the good graces of those with whom he associated. Hilda, indeed, soon forgot her father's remarks, and felt perfectly satisfied as to the prospect of her sister's happiness.

Colonel Armytage was accompanied by two friends, brother officers. Their presence made the castle far more lively than it had wont to be for many a long year; but all their sallies could not dispel the melancholy which Hilda could not hide even from them. Sir Marcus very narrowly watched Lawrence, who had become intimate with them; but whether or not he had told them of any of the occurrences which had lately taken place, he could not ascertain. It was a relief to him when, the day of the wedding having arrived, the castle was filled with the families of sufficient distinction to be invited to it. Hilda could not but feel that they generally regarded her with looks of curiosity, and, at the same time, of compassion, excessively annoying to her feelings. Often as she approached a group she found them whispering, and she observed that their manner was constrained, and that they either became silent, or had evidently abruptly commenced a fresh subject of conversation.

Nothing, however, occurred to interrupt the marriage ceremony. How different did it appear to the unhappy Hilda to that by which she had been united to Don Hernan!

It was not till Colonel Armytage was about to take his departure, with his bride, for the south, that on taking his leave of his father-in-law, he showed that he was aware of what had taken place. He drew himself up haughtily as he remarked—

'My love and esteem for your daughter, and a sense of honour, compelled me to fulfil my engagement with her; but I must ever regard with feelings of distrust and contempt the man who would conceal from me matters of which I ought to have been informed. We shall probably seldom, perhaps we shall never, meet again—our doing so can produce little mutual satisfaction.'

Sir Marcus looked confused, and could make no answer, and in silence he handed his daughter into the boat which was to convey them on board their vessel. His feelings were not soothed by hearing Lawrence give a loud laugh, and sing—as he hopped and skipped up the causeway—

'The prince will hae his ain again! The prince will hae his ain again!'

The summer passed away, and business compelled Sir Marcus to visit Scotland. During his absence Rolf Morton returned to Shetland. How different was his home to what it had been! Its chief ornament, its only attraction was gone. He frequently came up to the castle to see his child; but he was soon convinced that he could not, as usual, spend the winter at home, and he determined to go to Leith to seek for the command of some ship sailing to southern latitudes.

A few days before he took his departure Sir Marcus returned to Lunnasting. They met, and the baronet eyed him with so sinister an expression that an uncomfortable sensation crept over the heart of the bold seaman, and he felt that he was in the presence of one who would do him an injury if he had the power.

Bidding farewell, however, to Bertha Eswick and his boy, he sailed for Leith, believing that for this time, however, he had escaped the malice of his enemy. He was mistaken. He had not been at Leith many days before he had the offer made him of the command of a fine ship bound round Cape Horn. The preliminary arrangements were soon made, but the usual papers were not yet signed. As he walked through the streets of Leith he more than once observed a man, who, he felt certain, was dodging his steps, and whom he observed watching him as he entered his lodgings. The matter, however, did not make much impression on him. He was on his way to the owner's office to conclude the arrangements for his taking command, when, as he was passing along the quays, he was accosted by the individual he had remarked following him, and who now asked him if his name was Rolf Morton.

'That is my name,' he answered.

'Then you are the very man I want to see,' was the reply. 'Come along under this archway.'

Morton unsuspectingly followed his guide, but no sooner had he reached the arch, than a body of seamen rushed out of a door close at hand. He was wondering where they were going, when he found himself surrounded by them, and dragged off to a boat lying at a jetty not far off.

He was in the hands of a press-gang. He had no power of making any resistance. He was forced into the boat, which pulled away to a ship-of-war at anchor in the Forth. He explained that he was virtually master of a merchantman, and that the owners would suffer loss should he be detained. He was ordered to exhibit his protection. He had none. His remonstrances were unheeded. He found that with his will, or against his will, he must serve his Majesty. Many other men had been brought on board in the same way that he had been.

'It matters little, if a man does his duty, in what condition of life he is placed; he may be equally happy in one as the other,' he said to himself; 'I shall have fewer cares and responsibilities as a man-of-war's man, than as a master of a ship. Why should I sigh and moan thus over my lot? What can't be cured must be endured. Yes, sir, I'll serve his Majesty, and serve him well, I hope,' he exclaimed aloud, turning to the officer who was examining the pressed men.

Rolf Morton kept his word. He was soon known as one of the best men in the ship, and he had not been long on board before he was raised to the rank of a first-class petty officer. He saw much service in various parts of the world. Wherever work was to be done he was foremost in doing it. Had he been younger, he would probably have been placed on the quarter-deck: but he was unambitious, and contented with his lot, though he, at last, was made a warrant officer, and ultimately became boatswain of a dashing frigate, under as gallant a captain as ever took a ship into action.

CHAPTER XIV.

THE FLEET AT SPITHEAD.—ROLF MORTON'S VISIT TO SHETLAND.—
ROLF TAKES RONALD TO SEA.—THE 'THISBE' AND FRENCH
FRIGATE.—RONALD MORTON'S FIRST BATTLE.—THE ENEMY
STRIKES.

ONE of the most beautiful sights on the ocean, to the eye of a sailor, is the spectacle presented by a large fleet, when the signal for weighing is seen flying from the flag-ship. The boatswain's whistle sends its shrill sounds along each deck; the capstan bars are shipped, the merry pipe strikes up, with sturdy tramp round go the men—others of the crew swarm upon the yards, the broad folds of canvas are let fall, and, as if by magic, those vast machines, lately so immovable, now looking like tall pyramids of snow, begin noiselessly to glide over the blue surface of the water.

Such was the sight witnessed by numerous spectators, both on the Isle of Wight shore and that of Portsmouth, when early in the year 1794 one of England's noble fleets sailed from Spithead. A fine breeze from the northward enabled the ships to be well out round St Helen's, when hauling their tacks aboard they stood down channel under all sail. In the centre were the heavy line-of-battle ships, exhibiting a dense mass of shining canvas; while scattered around on either side were the lighter frigates, like skirmishers on the field of battle feeling the way for the main body of the army. Among the fastest, the finest, and most dashing of the latter craft, was the thirty-eight gun frigate 'Thisbe.'

She had only lately been put in commission, and her captain, officers, and crew, were mostly strangers to each other. Captain Courtney, who commanded her, had the reputation of being brave and enterprising, but his present crew had yet to learn what he was made of.

The day was closing; the fleet had made good progress down channel, and the 'Thisbe' was one of the southernmost look-out frigates; the crew were enjoying a short relaxation from their duties, which were pretty severe, for when a ship first gets to sea there is much to be done to put her in order, to encounter an enemy or a gale.

The captain and two of his lieutenants walked the weather-side of the quarter-deck, while the other gun-room officers and some of the midshipmen, paced the lee side. Captain Courtney's appearance was much in his favour; though his firm mouth and the general expression of his features showed that he was accustomed to command, the pleasant smile occasionally playing over his countenance relieved them from too great sternness.

The first lieutenant, Mr Strickland, looked like his chief, the perfect officer and gentleman, while the second, well known in the service as Tom Calder, was more of the rough-and-ready school.

Tom was broad-shouldered and short, with an open countenance, and a complexion which once had been fair, but was now burnt nearly to a bright copper, but neither winds nor sun had been able to change the rich golden tint of his hair, which clustered in thick curls under his hat, which hat he managed to stick on the very back of his head; whether cocked hat, or tarpaulin, or sou'-wester, he wore it the same; it was a puzzle, though, to say how it kept there. But to see Tom as he was, was to catch him at work, with knife and marlin-spike, secured by rope-yarns round his neck, his hands showing intimate acquaintance with the tar bucket, while not a job was there to be done which he could not show the best way of doing.

Tom Calder, as was said of him, was the man to get work out of a crew, and where he led others were ever ready to follow. Altogether, he was evidently cut out for a good working first lieutenant, and there seemed every prospect of his becoming one. He had entered the service at the hawse-hole, and worked his way up, by his steadiness and gallantry, to the quarter-deck, a position to which he was well calculated to do credit.

On the forecastle the three warrant officers sauntered slowly up and down, stretching their limbs after their day's work was over.

They were accompanied by a fine intelligent-looking boy, apparently of about fifteen, who was attentively listening to their conversation. The likeness which the boy bore to one of them, made it pretty evident that they were father and son.

The boatswain was Rolf Morton. When once pressed into the navy, by the management of Sir Marcus Wardhill, he had, from want of the energy required to take steps to leave it, remained in the service till a warrant had been almost forced on him. Just before the 'Thisbe' was commissioned he had paid a visit to Shetland; he had found his boy Ronald grown and improved beyond his most sanguine expectations. The Lady Hilda, as she was still called, had devoted herself to his education, and treated him as her son; and in the more important matters which she unhappily was unable to teach him, Bertha Eswick had afforded him instruction. But Ronald had another instructor, though an eccentric one, in Lawrence Brindister. Not a more daring or expert boatman, a finer swimmer, or a better shot of his age, or much above his age, was to be found in all Shetland.

Poor Hilda had never heard from Pedro Alvarez, nor had she received tidings of her son, though, hopeless as it might seem, she lived on in the expectation of one day recovering him. Both she and Bertha had so earnestly entreated Rolf to leave Ronald in Shetland, that he would have done so, had he not received a warning, not to be neglected, from Lawrence Brindister, to be off and to take his boy with him.

He had often suspected that Sir Marcus Wardhill was his enemy, and now he learned from Lawrence, that he was the enemy of his son also, and would work him ill if he had him in his power.

'Then I will take him out of his power,' observed Rolf; and before the next morning he was away to Lerwick. Sir Marcus sent a fast rowing boat after him, but when she reached the capital of Shetland, Rolf and his son had already taken their departure. Sir Marcus Wardhill was reaping where he had sown.

From his younger and best-loved daughter he had long been almost totally estranged. Colonel Armytage had for years held no direct communication with him, while Edda's letters were very brief, and she, having become the mother of a daughter, offered this as an excuse for not paying a visit to the north.

It was not till now that Hilda revealed to him the whole history of her marriage and the loss of her boy. His rage knew no bounds when he discovered that no certificate of this marriage was forthcoming. But one witness, who was forthcoming, survived—Bertha Eswick: she, however, had been in a declining state for some time, and but a few days had passed after Rolf and Ronald had quitted Lunnasting before she expired, leaving Hilda more solitary and miserable than ever.

Ronald Morton had commenced his life at sea with the greatest zest, and although he had a few difficulties to contend with, and not a few older boys to fight, he invariably came off victorious, and was altogether a general favourite. Rolf devotedly loved his son, and though not ambitious for himself, his great desire was to see Ronald on the quarter-deck, and rising in his profession: he certainly looked as if it were more his proper place than was the forecastle where he now was.

'Father,' he said, turning his beaming countenance, 'I do long to be in a battle. Are we likely soon to fall in with an enemy?'

'No hurry for that, boy,' answered the boatswain, who had been in many a desperate fight, and knew what fighting was; 'we shall fall in with one before long, depend on that.'

'I hope so, indeed,' exclaimed Ronald; 'those Frenchmen who have cut off their king's head deserve to be thrashed round and round the globe till not a man of them remains alive.'

This sentiment was warmly applauded both by the gunner and carpenter.

'I don't say as how I 'zactly hates the Frenchmen,' observed Mr Rammage, the gunner; 'but it's my opinion that the sea is not big enough for both of us, and the sooner we drives them off it, the sooner we shall be friends again.'

Ronald had not long to wait before he saw, though chiefly at a distance, one of the most important of England's naval battles. The 'Thisbe' formed one of Lord Howe's fleet, when he gained the glorious victory of the 1st of June which taught the Frenchmen, by a lesson often to be repeated, that they must expect defeat whenever they might venture to contend with England's navy on the ocean.

As the 'Thisbe' was employed as a look-out frigate, she took but little part in the action. What she did do, far from damping Ronald's ardour, only made him the more eager to fight again. He had not long to wait. The 'Thisbe,' with the rest of the fleet, returned to Spithead to receive the marks of honour the sovereign and the nation showered on the heads of the gallant chiefs, who had led their ships to victory; but before long she was again on a cruise down channel. Rounding Ushant, she steered to the southward, boldly standing along the French coast, and making what the French probably considered a very impertinent examination of their forts and harbours.

She approached the place to be examined during the night, and at early dawn the required information having been obtained, she was again standing off shore, under all sail, before any of the enemy's ships could get under weigh to pursue her. She proceeded as far south as Rochelle.

Looking one morning into the harbour of that place, a frigate was discovered in the outer roads, apparently ready for sea.

'She seems about our size; if we could draw her out, we might take her,' observed Captain Courtney to his first lieutenant, Mr Strickland.

'No doubt about it, sir,' was the answer; 'she is, however, I suspect, rather larger, but so much the better. There is little honour in capturing a Frenchman of one's own size. That we are of course expected to do. We should be thankful when we fall in with an antagonist of superior strength.'

'You are right, Strickland,' exclaimed the captain, warmly. 'Back the maintopsail and fire a gun towards her. The signal of defiance will be understood, and if her captain has a spark of courage, he'll come out and meet us.'

With colours flying, the British frigate lay-to off the Frenchman's port. While thus defying the enemy a large schooner was seen standing along shore and apparently making for the harbour.

'We'll take her before their very noses, and if that does not rouse them, I do not know what will,' observed the captain, as he gave the orders to make sail in chase.

The schooner, little expecting to be snapped up by an enemy in the very sight of port, endeavoured in vain to escape. The 'Thisbe,' like an eagle towards its prey, flew after her, and in a short time she was a prize.

Taking out the prisoners and putting a prize crew on board, Captain Courtney stood back, with the schooner in tow, towards the mouth of the harbour; then again firing another shot of defiance, he bore away to the westward.

'The Frenchmen will bear a great deal, but they will not bear that,' observed Morton to his son. 'Before this time tomorrow we shall either be inside that harbour, feeling very much ashamed of ourselves—and I don't think that is likely to happen—or we shall have that frigate in there for our prize, and be standing away with her for old England.'

The 'Thisbe' had got some eight miles or so away from the land, when the French frigate was seen under sail and standing towards her. Captain Courtney was anxious to draw the enemy as far from the coast as possible, lest, when the hoped-for result of the action should become known, notice might be sent of the event to other ports to the northward, and a superior force despatched to capture him. He accordingly hove-to occasionally, and then stood on to entice the enemy after him.

When the evening closed in, the Frenchman was in sight about two leagues off, coming up astern. The 'Thisbe,' now casting off the prize, stood towards her. At this time there was no other sail in sight, with the exception of a small boat, apparently a fishing boat, which kept as close as she could to the 'Thisbe,' possibly to watch what was going to take place.

Captain Courtney's object was, of course, to obtain the weather gauge; and in consequence of having to manoeuvre to obtain it, it was not till past midnight that the two ships got within range of each other's guns. Not a man of the 'Thisbe's' crew had turned in. The drum beat to quarters. The men flew to their stations with pistols in their belts and cutlasses by their sides, eager to begin the fight.

The 'Thisbe' was on the starboard tack, when the enemy, on the larboard tack, slowly glided past her to windward, looking like some dark phantom stalking over the surface of the deep.

Ronald, who stood on the forecastle with his father, watched her with intense eagerness. Presently a sheet of flame burst from her side, followed by the loud thunder of the guns and the whizzing of shot. A few came near the English frigate, but none struck her.

'Return the compliment, my lads. Give it them!' exclaimed Captain Courtney.

The crew, with a cheer, obeyed the order, the flashes of their guns throwing a ruddy glow on the bulwarks and the figures of the crew, as stern and grim they stood at their quarters.

'Hands about ship!' was the next order issued; and the 'Thisbe,' tacking in the wake of her opponent, stood after her.

'Father,' asked Ronald, as he stood by Morton's side on the forecastle, 'will the Frenchman try to escape us?'

'No fear of that, he would not have come out at first if he had intended to play us that trick,' was the answer. 'He has made one slight mistake, though; he fancies that he is going to take us; and it's my firm belief that we are going to take him.'

'I hope so, father,' answered Ronald. 'I would sooner die than be taken by a Frenchman.'

'That is the right spirit, my boy,' exclaimed Rolf, warmly. 'But little fear of what will happen—our captain is not a man to throw away a chance of victory.'

While they were speaking, the 'Thisbe' was rapidly coming up with the enemy; and as her guns could be brought to bear they were fired in quick succession—the French frigate returning them with right good will, though as her shot flew high, the 'Thisbe's' masts and spars suffered more than her hull, and few of her men had hitherto been hit.

Morton looked anxiously aloft. 'It will be a bad job if they go,' he muttered to himself. He then sent Ronald aft to ascertain the condition of the main and mizenmast, which he believed had been struck.

His son soon returned with a very bad report. The masts were already badly wounded.

AN ENGAGEMENT AT SEA.

Soon after this the 'Thisbe' got within musket-shot of the starboard quarter of her opponent; and the marines opened their fire, while the firing of the great guns became warmer than ever.

Captain Courtney had never, for a moment, taken his eye off the French ship, that he might watch for the least indication of any manœuvre she might be about to perform. Suddenly he exclaimed, 'Up with the helm!—square away the after yards!'

Quickly the manœuvre was executed, though only just in time to prevent the enemy who wore the instant before, from crossing the 'Thisbe's' bows, and pouring in a raking fire. The two frigates now ran on before the wind, closely engaged, broadside to broadside. Fast came the round shot, crashing on board. Splinters from the torn bulwarks were flying about, from aloft some rattling blocks and shattered spars; while showers of bullets were raining down death and wounds in every direction.

Ronald Morton felt his spirits rise to an unnatural pitch as the fight grew hotter and hotter. Not the remotest thought of death, not a shadow of fear crossed his mind. Others were struck down, but those missiles of destruction were not for him. Others might be hit, but he bore a charmed life.

There is something far more terrific and trying to the nerves in a night action than in one fought by day. The dark, mysterious form of the enemy, the flashes of the guns, the irregular glare, the dim light of the fighting lanterns, the cries and groans of the wounded, the uncertainty as to who is hit or what damage has been done, all combine to produce an effect which the most desperate fight by day can scarcely exhibit.

The crew of the 'Thisbe' could see that their shot was producing great effect on their antagonist. Her masts still stood, but several of her spars were shot away, and her rigging appeared a mass of wreck. The English frigate was also much injured aloft, but her masts were still standing.

By this time the 'Thisbe' had shot ahead of her antagonist. 'Starboard the helm!' exclaimed Captain Courtney. 'Cease firing, my lads! Be ready to give her a raking broadside as we cross her hawse.'

The frigate luffed up into the wind; and, as she did so, her larboard guns were discharged in quick succession into the bows of the Frenchman; but amid the roar of the guns a loud crash was heard, and the mizenmast, unable to bear the additional strain on it, went by the board, but falling to starboard, did not impede the working of the guns. As the crew were running from under it, the tall mainmast was seen to totter, and with all its yards and sails, over it went on the same side. With a groan the boatswain saw what had occurred. He feared, too, that the enemy might escape, as her masts were still standing; but as the 'Thisbe's' mainmast went, the French frigate ran stern on to her, on her larboard quarter, her bowsprit passing directly across her deck over the capstan.

'She is our own if we can but keep her,' exclaimed the boatswain; and, followed by Ronald, he hurried aft, calling to some of his mates to assist him.

The officers and crew had enough to do at that moment, for the Frenchmen trusting to their number, which appeared to be very great, were swarming on the forecastle, and rushing along the bowsprit with the intention of boarding the 'Thisbe.'

'Boarders! repel boarders!' shouted the captain, setting the example in attacking the first Frenchmen who presented themselves as they sprang forward.

Now the clash of steel, the sharp report of pistols, intermingled with the roar of the great guns—those on the quarter and main-decks still continuing to pour a destructive fire into the enemy's starboard bow as they could be brought to bear— the Frenchmen, from the position in which their ship was placed, being only able to reply with musketry. Their critical position made them rush on and on again with the greatest frenzy, but each time they were driven back with heavy loss, many of them falling overboard from off the bowsprit, or being cut down by the British seamen. Meantime Rolf Morton and his followers were busily engaged in lashing the enemy's bowsprit to their capstan with such ropes as they could lay hands on. Captain Courtney looked round, and saw how they were engaged.

'Admirably done, Mr Morton,' he cried out. 'Keep her there, and we will give a good account of the Frenchmen in her.'

At that moment the enemy, with loud shouts and *sacrés* and other oaths, came rushing forward in greater numbers than before, intending to drop down on the 'Thisbe's' deck, and hoping to overwhelm her crew by their numbers. Again they felt the effect of British cutlasses. Desperately as they fought, they were once more driven back with diminished numbers to the ship. In vain the Frenchmen endeavoured to free their ship from the position in which they had placed her. The 'Thisbe' stood on, towing them after her. Scarcely one of their guns could be brought to bear, but the marines, however, kept up a hot and destructive fire of musketry on the deck of the frigate, from the tops as well as from some of her quarter-deck guns which had been run in midships fore and aft. Though the darkness prevented their taking good aim, no sooner was it known that the bowsprit was being made fast to the capstan of the English frigate, than the whole of their fire was turned in that direction. The lashings were not yet completed. Showers of bullets fell around the brave men engaged in the work. Several had fallen. The boatswain did not think of himself, but he dreaded lest his son should be hit. He was considering on what message he should send him to another part of the ship, when he felt a sharp blow, his fingers relaxed from the rope he was grasping, and he fell to the deck. He had the feeling that he had received his death wound. Ronald saw what had happened, and in an instant was on his knees supporting his father's head.

What thought he then of the fierce contest raging? What did he care who gained the victory? All his feelings were concentrated on his father. Was he mortally wounded, or would he recover? He entreated some of the men to carry him below, but they were at that moment too much occupied to attend to him. Rolf recovered slightly.

'No, no, boy; let me remain here,' he said in a firm voice. 'All hands have work enough to do; I am but hit in the leg, and if they would set me on my feet again I could still be of use.'

But Ronald did not heed him, and continued imploring the men to carry the boatswain below. Just then the lashings were torn away, and the French frigate floated clear of the 'Thisbe.' Cries of disappointment escaped from the English crew, but they redoubled their efforts to cripple their opponent, so as once more to get hold of her. Meantime several of the men, being now at liberty, offered to take the boatswain below, but he desired to be left on deck.

'I'll see the fight out, lads,' he answered. 'Help me up, some of you, and pass this handkerchief round the limb. Cheer up, Ronald, I'm not so badly hurt as you fancy, boy.'

'Hurra, lads! here she comes again; we'll have her fast this time,' shouted the captain at this juncture.

The 'Thisbe,' deprived of her after-sail, paid off before the wind, and thus the French frigate ran directly into her, on the starboard quarter, the enemy's bowsprit hanging over the stump of her mainmast. The opportunity of securing the French ship was not lost, though her crew attempted to rush on board, as before, to prevent the operation.

While the captain and most of the superior officers who had escaped wounds or death were engaged in repelling them, Rolf caused himself to be brought nearer to the mainmast, that he might superintend the crew in lashing the bowsprit to it.

This time they took care that it should not again break

away; and now the 'Thisbe,' running directly off before the wind, dragged the Frenchman after her.

The fight had been hot before, but it became hotter still. Again and again the Frenchmen endeavoured to cut away those second lashings, but the English marines kept up so hot a fire, that each time the attempt was frustrated. Still the enemy showed no signs of yielding. Something must be done. Wounded as he was, Morton dragged himself up to where the captain was standing.

'I beg your pardon, Captain Courtney, but if we could get a couple of guns run out abaft on the main-deck, we could silence that fellow pretty quickly,' he said, touching his hat with all due formality.

It was somewhat out of rule for the boatswain to offer his advice unasked to the captain, but under the circumstances the irregularity was easily overlooked by such a man as Captain Courtney.

'You are right, Mr Morton,' he answered; 'send the carpenter and his crew aft, Mr Calder,' to the second lieutenant. 'Get the two after guns on the main-deck ready to run out astern as soon as we have some ports made for them.'

Having given this order, the captain descended to the main-deck.

Mr Gimbol, the carpenter, soon made his appearance there from below, where he had been going his rounds through the wings, to stop any shot-holes which might have been made between wind and water.

With axes and saws he and his crew set to work, but the upper transom beam resisted all their efforts.

'We must blow out some ports,' exclaimed the captain. 'Send the firemen here.'

A gang of men with buckets were quickly on the spot. The guns were pointed aft. 'Fire!' cried the captain. The two guns went off together, and as the suffocating smoke blew off, two holes with jagged edges were seen in the stern, but flames were bursting out around them. These, however, the firemen with their buckets quickly extinguished, and the guns, being again loaded, opened their fire through them on the deck of the Frenchman. The effect produced from this unexpected quarter was terrific. Fore and aft the shot flew crashing between the decks, seldom failing to find some victims, and oftentimes carrying off the heads of half-a-dozen men, as they stood at their guns, in its course from one end of the ship to the other. Never were guns more rapidly worked than were those two twelve-pounders on board the 'Thisbe.' The captain stood by, encouraging the men.

Rolf Morton went about, badly wounded as he was, to ascertain where his services were most required. Ronald followed his father, dreading every moment to see him fall from the effects of his first wound, or to find that he was again hit. Once more they returned to the upper deck. Their numbers were falling, wounds were being received, and havoc was being made aloft and on every side. The masts of the French ship were still standing, but from the shrieks and cries which proceeded from her decks, there seemed little doubt that she was suffering even more than the 'Thisbe.' Ronald kept watching the enemy.

'See, father!—see!' he exclaimed. 'Down, down they come!'

He pointed at the Frenchman's foremast. It bent on one side, the few ropes which held it gave way, and crash it came down over the side. The mainmast stood, but the mizenmast in an instant afterwards followed the foremast, preventing the crew from working the greater number of the guns. However, with those still unencumbered they continued to fire away with the greatest desperation. The English seamen fought on with the same determined courage as at first. They had made up their minds that they would take the enemy, and there was not a man on board who would have given in till they had done so, or till the ship sunk under them. Half-an-hour passed away. It seemed surprising that either ship could float with the pounding they gave each other, or that any human beings could survive on their decks amid the storm of shot and bullets rushing across them. At length a loud cheer burst from the throats of the English seamen, the Frenchman's last remaining mast was seen to lean over, and down it came with a tremendous crash, crushing many in its fall, and completely preventing the crew from working any of their guns.

'They will give in now, father, to a certainty,' exclaimed Ronald.

'Not so sure, boy; see, they are going to make a desperate attempt to revenge themselves.'

'Here they come!' he answered, and then the cry arose from the English ship of, 'Boarders! repel boarders!'

Once more the Frenchmen came on with the most determined courage. Captain Courtney and some of his officers and men who were aft threw themselves before the enemy, to stem the torrent which threatened to pour down on the 'Thisbe's' decks; but with such fury and desperation did the Frenchmen come on, that many of the English were driven back, and there seemed no little probability that the former would gain their object. Rolf Morton, on perceiving this, and forgetting his wound, seized a cutlass, and calling on all the men at hand, followed by Ronald, sprang aft to the aid of his captain. His assistance did not come a moment too soon. Captain Courtney was brought to his knee, and a French officer, who had led the boarders, was on the point of cutting him down, when Ronald sprang to his side, and thrusting his cutlass before him, saved him from the blow intended for his head. Ronald would have had to pay dearly for his gallantry, had not Rolf cut the Frenchman down at the moment he was making, in return, a fierce stroke at his son.

More of the English crew, led by their officers, now came hurrying aft, and the Frenchmen, disheartened by the loss of their leader, again retreated to their ship, leaving eight or ten of their number dead or dying behind them. Still no one cried for quarter; and though not a gun was discharged, the marines and small-arm men kept up as hot a fire as before.

All this time the 'Thisbe's' two after-guns on the main-deck kept thundering away at them, fearfully diminishing their numbers. And thus the fight continued: they made, however, no signal of yielding.

The Frenchmen had scarcely retreated from their daring attempt to board the frigate, when the lashings which secured their bowsprit to her began to give way. The boatswain had, however, got a hawser ready ranged along the deck, and this, in spite of the fire kept up at them, he, with his mates and others of the crew, secured to the gammoning of the Frenchmen's bowsprit.

'Now the lashings may go as soon as they like!' he exclaimed, almost breathless with the exertion; 'the Frenchmen will gain little by the change.'

So it proved: the enemy's ship, when the lashings gave way, dropped astern a few fathoms, and there she hung, towed onwards, as before, by the 'Thisbe,' whose crew were thus enabled to rake her decks with more deadly effect. Still the battle raged as at first.

At length some voices were heard from the bowsprit of the French frigate.

'Quarter! quarter! was the cry. 'We have struck! we yield!'

'Cease firing, my lads!' shouted the captain; we have won the night!'

The order was obeyed. For an instant there was a perfect silence, a contrast to the uproar which had so long continued; even the wounded restrained the expression of their sufferings; and then there burst forth one of those hearty cheers, which few but English seamen can give, and which they so well know how to give with effect. And now many of the brave fellows who had hitherto worked away at their guns without flinching, sank down with fatigue.

Rolf Morton even then would not go below.

'I'll stay on deck and see the enemy secured, and get the ship put to rights a little,' he answered; 'I am only just showing my boy how I wish him to behave. While there is duty to do, and a man has strength to do it, he should not shrink from it, whatever it may cost him.'

Ronald listened to what his father was saying.

'That's it, father; I'll try and stick to that,' he observed, looking up in his father's face.

It was now necessary to board the French ship to take possession of her, but how that was to be accomplished was the question, for not a boat that could swim remained on board either of the combatants.

The second lieutenant—one of the few officers unwounded —volunteered to work his way along the hawser, and a midshipman and several of the men offered to accompany him; Ronald begged leave to go also.

In those days, strange as it may seem, many seamen could not swim.

The boarding-party commenced their somewhat hazardous passage from one ship to the other. The 'Thisbe' had but slight way on her; the hawser was consequently somewhat slack, and the weight of the people on it brought it down into the water. The lieutenant and several of the men clung on, but the midshipman was by some means or other washed off. Unable to swim, he cried out loudly for help, but no one could afford it, till Ronald let go his own hold of the rope, and swam towards him. Of course to regain the hawser was hopeless, and it was equally difficult to swim back to the 'Thisbe.' Ronald had practised swimming from his childhood, and was as much at home in the water as on shore. He struck out with one hand while he supported the young midshipman with the other. His first fear was that the French ship would run them down, but a few strokes carried him and his charge clear of that danger. He next attempted to get alongside her. He looked up, and saw her dark hull rising up above him. There were plenty of ropes hanging overboard; he found one that appeared secure above; he put it into the midshipman's hands.

'There, Mr Glover,' he exclaimed; we shall be the first on the enemy's deck after all.'

He was not long in finding another rope for himself, and to the surprise of the Frenchmen they found two stranger boys standing on their quarter-deck.

'Have you come to take possession?' asked a lieutenant in tolerable English. What! are all your superior officers killed?'

Oh, no, monsieur,' answered the midshipman; they will be on board presently; but we are somewhat lighter craft, so made quicker work of it.'

The second lieutenant of the 'Thisbe' and his companions soon made their appearance, having clambered in over the bows; and the French frigate, which was found to be the 'Concorde'—one of the largest class in the French navy—was formally taken possession of.

CHAPTER XV.

MORNING AFTER THE BATTLE.—RONALD PLACED ON QUARTER DECK.—RONALD SENT ON BOARD THE PRIZE.—A SUSPICIOUS SAIL IN SIGHT.—GALLANT DEFENCE OF THE 'THISBE.'—NIGHT CLOSES ON THE FIGHT.

AS the bright cheerful light of morning broke on the world of waters, there lay the two frigates, which, when the sun went down, looked so gallant and so trim—now shorn of their beauty, shattered and blackened wrecks.

The foremast of the 'Thisbe' was alone standing, while all the masts of the French frigate, with their sails, and yards, and rigging, hung in masses of wreck and confusion over her sides. The decks covered with blood and gore, and the shattered remnants of mortality, presented a horrible and disgusting scene; while the broken bulwarks, the decks ploughed up, the wheel shot away, and the ruined condition of every part of the ship, showed the desperate nature of the conflict, and told of the bravery of the gallant French crew who had endured so much before they had consented to yield.

On board the 'Thisbe' the carpenters were busily employed in patching up some of the boats, so that the prisoners might be removed from the prize, while the rest of the crew were engaged in clearing away the wreck of the masts, and in preparing to make sail on the ship.

Ronald was in attendance on his father in his cabin. The boatswain had been more hurt than he supposed; but he did his utmost to conceal his suffering from his son.

The shout was heard: 'All hands on the quarter-deck!'

The captain was about to address the crew.

Rolf Morton tried to rise, but he soon found that he could not. 'Go, Ronald, and hear what the captain has to say. It will be something pleasant, I doubt not,' he said, pressing his boy's hand. 'Come and tell me when you are dismissed.'

Ronald sprang up the hatchway. The men were mustering aft. The captain and all the officers stood on the quarter-deck —not as usual, in those bright and shining uniforms, but in the dress in which they had fought, most of them still bearing about their persons the marks of the battle.

'My lads, I have called you aft to thank you for the gallant way in which you have fought this ship, and captured an enemy with more men, more guns, and of larger tonnage than ourselves,' he began. 'I do from my heart thank you; and our king and countrymen will thank you, and you may well be proud of what you have done. I wish that I could reward you as you deserve; but when all have done their duty it is difficult to pick out any for especial notice. Still there is one man who much helped us in capturing the enemy. That is the boatswain. He caught, and kept him, by lashing his bowsprit to our mainmast, and by his advice we blew open the stern ports which so mainly contributed to our success. His son, too, saved my life, and afterwards saved the life of Mr Glover, and was, with him, the first on board the prize. The boatswain will, I hope, receive his reward hereafter; but as I have the means of showing my appreciation of his son's gallantry, I gladly do so at once: I have therefore rated him as a midshipman on board this ship. I am sure that no one will think that I have done more for him than he deserves. Come aft, Mr Ronald Morton, and receive the welcome of your new messmates.'

Ronald came forward almost with a bound, though perfectly unconscious that he was moving more rapidly than usual. The wish of his heart was accomplished. His countenance beamed with satisfaction, and he frankly put out his hand towards the midshipmen and the other members of their berth. They all in turns took it and shook it warmly; but none grasped it more heartily than did young Glover.

'I must thank you for myself, Morton,' he exclaimed, in a tone which showed that he spoke from his heart. 'If it had not been for you I should have been among the missing, to a certainty.'

Morton's own heart was too full to answer. Numberless emotions were working in his bosom. He felt a proud satisfaction at having obtained the rank for which he was conscious he was fitted; he sincerely rejoiced at having been the means of saving his captain from a severe wound, if not from death; and scarcely less so at having prevented Glover from being drowned. All these feelings kept him silent: but his silence was understood; and perhaps no one felt more pleased at seeing him on the quarter-deck than did Captain Courtney himself.

'Now back to your duty, my lads,' he exclaimed; 'we have plenty of work before us.'

Three hearty cheers burst unpremeditatedly from the throats of the crew—and then in high spirits they separated to their respective duties. The work was accomplished, as the captain knew it would be, all the better for this little interruption.

Ronald hurried below. He wanted to be the first to tell his father of his good fortune, as he called it.

Rolf Morton was less surprised than he expected. 'I was certain it would be so some day, if your life was spared,' he observed. 'And now, my boy, that your foot is on the first ratline, mount upwards by your own exertions. Be thankful to others who help you, but trust to yourself for success.'

Ronald had got his father to select a little fellow called Bobby Doull, as his boy, whom he had, when he first came on board, taken under his protection.

Bobby had been sent to sea from a workhouse. If not an orphan he was in the condition of one; for his father, who was a seaman, had deserted him, and had not, since he was an infant, been heard of. Ronald had, at first, frequently to do battle in his cause; but he at length taught the other boys to respect him, and to let Bobby alone.

Bobby did his best to repay the kindness he had received, by his constant attention to the wants of the wounded boatswain.

Ronald had now to mess with the midshipmen. One of his first duties was to visit the prize, as soon as the boats had been got ready to transfer the prisoners to the 'Thisbe.'

Glover had insisted on lending him a uniform, jacket, and dirk, till he could obtain a suit of his own.

Ronald did not hesitate about accepting the offer; and, as Doull told the boatswain, he looked every inch a midshipman.

Very little had been done when Ronald returned to the prize towards getting her into order; and as he looked fore and aft along the decks, it seemed scarcely possible that she could ever be put in a condition at sea, to make sail, so as to reach a British port in safety. Some of her crew were already mustered on deck, but others were keeping below. He was accordingly directed to take a party of men round the decks to send them up. As he passed it, he looked into the midshipman's berth, where a boy, whose life he had probably been the means of preserving at the time of boarding, still lay.

The French midshipman recognised him immediately. 'Ah! come in, my friend!' he exclaimed, in broken English: 'I want to recompense you for what you did for me: but—they told me that you were a ship's boy, and now I see that you are of the same rank as myself.'

'I was a ship's boy when I found you under the masts, but now I am a midshipman,' answered Ronald. 'But tell me your name—I shall be glad to help you in any way I can.'

'My name—ah—they call me Alfonse Gerardin,' answered the French midshipman. I am obliged to you for your kindness. A prisoner is little able to requite it. Perhaps I may some day—as I should wish to do.'

'I have done nothing to deserve even thanks,' said Ronald. 'But I must not stay. I will come and see you again as soon as I can.'

Mr Strickland, the first lieutenant of the 'Thisbe,' being badly wounded, Mr Calder, the second, was directed to take charge of the prize.

Robert Rawson, an old master's mate, was ordered to go as his second in command, with Glover and Morton as midshipmen, and a master's assistant called Twigg.

Ronald wished to have remained to look after his father; but Rolf would not hear of it.

'You'll be better in another ship, away from me, boy,' he remarked. 'The doctor and Bobby Doull will look after me. I shall return to my duty in a few days—never fear!'

The peculiar talents of the prize-master of the 'Concorde,' honest Tom Calder, were now brought into full play. Head and hand were busily employed from morning till night, and neither grew weary. Where the hardest work was to be done, there Tom's cheery voice was heard and his helping hand was to be found, and before the two, difficulties, at first deemed insurmountable, vanished like magic.

Tom had naturally a strong fellow feeling for Ronald. He remembered his own annoyances under similar circumstances, and he fancied that Ronald would have to undergo the same. He had, hitherto, scarcely spoken to Ronald, but no sooner did he take the command of the 'Concorde,' than he singled him out to superintend any work requiring more than usual care and judgment.

Ronald in no way disappointed him; everybody, indeed, on board the prize, worked well, and with a will, and in a wonderfully short space of time jury-masts were rigged, and sails were ready for hoisting.

It was evening; the two frigates lay within a few hundred fathoms of each other: the 'Thisbe,' from having her foremasts standing, had a far wider range of vision than her prize.

'The "Thisbe" is signalling us, sir,' said Morton to Mr Calder.

'Get the signal-book, and see what she is saying,' was the answer.

The meaning of the signals was soon ascertained.

'A sail in the south-west,' Morton read; 'An enemy—Prepare for action.'

'That's just like him,' exclaimed Mr Calder; 'if the stranger was a seventy-four he would prepare to fight her. It is to be hoped, though, that she is only another frigate, and then, in spite of the loss of our masts, we may be able to give a good account of her.'

Ronald was ready enough to fight, but could not help thinking that they just then had had enough of it, and therefore hoped that the stranger might prove a friend.

Some time must elapse before the point could be ascertained, and during the interval every effort was made to get sail on the two ships, not for the purpose of flying, but to enable them the better to manœuvre, should fighting be the order of the day.

At length Ronald went below to snatch a mouthful of food, and took the opportunity of paying a visit to the wounded midshipman, Alfonse Gerardin. He had been placed in the gun-room with the rest of the French officers; he lifted up his head as Ronald entered the cabin.

After returning the salutation, he remained silent, and then he exclaimed, somewhat bitterly, 'Ah, how different are our lots! you have gained a victory, have come out of the battle unhurt, and have been placed on the first step of the ladder, up which you may climb to the highest—while here I lie, a prisoner badly wounded, and, alas! have just discovered that I have lost the only friend I had in the world.'

'Oh, you are mistaken; I am sure that I have many, and so would you if you proved them,' said Ronald, in a cheerful tone. 'You are wounded and ill; when you recover you will be in better spirits; but tell me, who is the friend whose loss you mourn?'

'He was the second lieutenant of this ship, and he was killed early in the action with you,' answered young Gerardin, with a sigh. 'He was a brave man. I loved him as a son loves his father, and for long I thought he was my father. Only just before we were going into action did he tell me that I should find all the particulars about myself in a box, in a house where we lived when we were on shore, near Brest. I thought at first that he was jesting, and asked no questions, and it was only after he was killed that I believed he spoke the truth. Poor dear Pierre Gerardin! you were always kind and good to me, and I shall never see you again.'

The young foreigner gave way to his grief with a vehemence which somewhat astonished Ronald, accustomed to the more phlegmatic temperaments of the north. He tried to comfort him, but in vain, and when the surgeon came he intimated to Ronald that he had better leave him, as talking to a stranger seemed to agitate him in an extraordinary degree.

'He seems very sorry for the loss of his guardian, but he is an odd fellow, and I don't quite like the look of his countenance,' said Ronald to himself, as he left the cabin.

As soon as he reached the deck he looked out to ascertain what progress the stranger had made. Her courses were already seen from the deck, appearing above the horizon. The work on board the two frigates was going forward as energetically as ever. Still there was yet much to be done before they could be put in good fighting order. The 'Thisbe' was by far the most advanced of the two, still the bravest on board would rather have avoided than sought a fight just then. On came the stranger.

'Well, Morton, just say what you think of her?' said Dicky

Glover, handing a telescope to Ronald; 'there's a mighty Frenchified look about those topsails.'

'I have not much experience in the matter,' answered Ronald, modestly; 'but she looks very like the "Concorde," as she appeared when standing out toward us.'

'That's what Mr Calder and the rest think,' observed Glover. 'Well, we are ready for the fellow whoever he may be; and for my part, I'd sooner blow our prize up into the sky than let her be taken from us; wouldn't you, Morton?'

Ronald was not quite so sure of that, and he suspected that Dicky himself, if put to the test, might change his mind.

The stranger in a short time drew near enough to see the signals which the 'Thisbe' began to make. Her answers were watched for with intense interest on board both ships. Mr Calder had his signal-book open on deck.

'There goes up the stranger's bunting,' he exclaimed; 'now we shall see what he has got to say for himself.' Again and again his glass was at his eye: at length he shut it up with a loud slap.

'I thought as much,' he added; 'he's a Frenchman; but he will find the "Concorde" a tough morsel if he attempts to swallow her, after she has belonged to us.'

Captain Courtney arrived before long at the same conclusion, and ordered the prize to stand to the northward, under all the sail she could carry.

Tom Calder received the order with a very bad grace. 'I thought that he would at least have let us stop to help him to fight it out,' he muttered to himself as he put his hand to his mouth to issue the necessary orders to his scanty crew.

Sail was made on the prize, while the 'Thisbe' hauled up her courses, and stood slowly after her to draw the enemy more away from the land before the commencement of their expected contest.

Mr Calder felt that he had no right to question his commander's judgment; he could not help seeing, also, that could he effect his escape, he might possibly fall in with another British cruiser, and send her to the 'Thisbe's' assistance.

Even with more intense interest than at first, the approach of the stranger was watched from the deck of the 'Concorde.'

The prize had got a mile from the 'Thisbe' when the French surgeon made his appearance on deck, to enjoy a mouthful of fresh air, after his fatiguing duties below. His eager glance, and the sudden lighting up of his eye, showed that he fully comprehended the state of affairs.

Among the many accomplishments Ronald had obtained at Lunnasting was a certain amount of French. He could not speak fluently, but he could understand what was said. He could not help asking the surgeon what he thought about the stranger coming up from the southward.

'That she is one of the fastest frigates belonging to our navy,' was the answer. 'We were expecting her here about this time; you have no chance of escaping her. We were to have cruised together; perhaps we shall do so now.'

'Ask him what sort of a man is her captain,' said Mr Calder, who saw Ronald talking to the surgeon.

Ronald put the question.

'There are two opinions,' said the surgeon, making a face. 'He would be a coward who would refuse to attack our late antagonist in the condition to which we have reduced her.'

'All right,' observed Mr Calder, when he heard the remark; 'if there are two opinions about a man's courage it is seldom that the favourable one is the right; we shall see, though.'

In accordance with his orders, though much against his inclination, Lieutenant Calder stood away from the scene of the approaching combat.

A flash and a puff of smoke was seen, and soon afterwards a low thundering noise boomed along the waters. The French frigate had fired her first shot at the 'Thisbe.'

'I hope it did not hit her!' exclaimed Morton. 'Oh, how I wish we were there to help her!'

The same sentiment was expressed by all on board.

It seemed probable that the first shot did hit, for the Frenchman now luffed up and fired his broadside at the 'Thisbe.' She waited till he bore away again, and then returned the compliment.

For a few minutes the firing ceased. Probably neither of the combatants had committed as much damage to each other as they expected, and were not desirous of throwing away their shots.

Ronald thought all the time of his father, and the danger to which he was exposed, for considering the comparatively defenceless state of the 'Thisbe' he could not help dreading the result.

The breeze increased, and the 'Concorde' got further and further from the scene of contest. Again the firing commenced. All hands knocked off work to watch the progress of the fight. The officers forgot even to recall them to their duty. The French surgeon and several of the wounded prisoners crawled up on deck to watch it also.

'There they go at it! Well done, "Thisbe"!' exclaimed Tom Calder. 'Never saw a more rapidly delivered broadside. If she had all her spars she wouldn't be long in taking that ship, too. Not certain that she won't do it now. Hurra! there's one of the Frenchman's spars shot away.'

'Hurra for the "Thisbe"!' shouted the crew. 'She's the girl to win the day. Hurra! hurra!'

'Not so sure of that,' muttered Rawson, an old mate, who seldom saw things in a pleasant light. No wonder, for he had seen numbers who had come to sea long after him promoted over his head, and were now commanders and post captains, while he remained almost without hope in a subordinate position. He was pretty certain to be senior of the mess in whatever ship he sailed, and that was his only consolation, as it gave him some little authority, and full licence to growl to his heart's content.

The firing became hotter than ever, though at the distance the 'Concorde' was now from the two combatants it was difficult to observe the changes of the fight. Still all the glasses were kept in that direction.

'There! there! I said it would be so!' exclaimed Rawson, still keeping his eye at the glass.

'What has happened?' inquired Ronald, eagerly.

'Why, the Frenchmen have shot away the "Thisbe's" foretopmast, as far as I can make out—her jury-masts, too,' answered Rawson. 'The "Thisbe's" done for, I'm afraid.'

'What's that you say, Rawson?' exclaimed Lieutenant Calder. 'Done for! not she; she's not done firing, at all events.'

Rawson said no more; still it was very evident that the 'Thisbe' was again almost a complete wreck, while the Frenchman had her rigging comparatively uninjured. The firing on both sides began to decrease. Evening was now drawing on, the wind was increasing, and dark clouds were coming up from the westward. For several minutes not a shot had been heard. Flashes there were, but they were from the clouds, and heaven's artillery now rattled through the sky. The combatants could now scarcely be discerned in the distance.

'The "Thisbe" has struck,' cried Rawson. 'I said it would be so. I knew I should never have such luck as to take a prize like this, and to keep our ship.'

'I don't believe it,' exclaimed Mr Calder. 'Captain Courtney would never have given in to the Frenchman without a harder tussle for it.'

'Perhaps Captain Courtney has been killed,' croaked out poor Rawson, who was very bitter at the prospect of losing his long-looked-for promotion, which he would have obtained as soon as the prize was carried into port. Tom Calder, too, had every reason to wish to escape the enemy, with the same object in view, and he was not a man to throw a chance away.

The wind was fair, and the coming darkness and the rising gale would favour their escape. He now clapped on every inch of canvas which could possibly be set, and did his utmost to keep up the spirits of his crew, rating Mr Rawson soundly for his expressing his forebodings of ill.

The wind increased, and howled through the rigging; the seas came roaring and hissing up alongside, as the frigate, driven onward by the gale, went surging through the foaming water.

Thus on she went for some time.

'If we had but our masts the enemy would have a hard job to come up with us,' observed Dicky Glover to Ronald. 'As it is, I doubt whether she'll find us, after all.'

The two midshipmen were standing aft, looking over the taffrail.

'I wish that I thought we should escape her,' answered Ronald; 'but I say—look!—look!—what's that out there?'

At that moment there was a break in the clouds, and through it a gleam of light fell on the lofty sails of a ship coming up within gunshot astern.

'The French frigate! I knew it would be so,' said the rough voice of old Rawson.

There could be little doubt that he was right. The stranger was supposed by the French officers on board to be the 'Atalante,' a frigate of the same size as the 'Concorde.' What hope then that the latter could successfully resist her? Not many men besides Tom Calder would have had any hope of escaping.

'Never cry out till you are caught,' was his motto on similar occasions.

'That vessel astern has not yet made us out,' he observed to Rawson. 'Though should she prove to be the 'Atalante,' perhaps we may still escape her, or she may be a friend after all.'

'Not likely that last, sir,' said Rawson, 'but whether friend or foe, here she comes! She has made us out clearly enough, too, that I'll be sworn.'

For a short time the clouds had closed in, and the stranger was hidden from view, but they again breaking, she was seen like some huge dark monster, towering up towards the sky, surging onwards on the starboard quarter of the 'Concorde.'

'We shall soon see now, sir, what she is,' observed Rawson to his superior.

The bright flash of a gun, and an eighteen-pound shot, which came crashing into the side of the prize left that point very little in doubt.

'Man the starboard guns!' cried Mr Calder. 'We'll show the Frenchmen that though we have lost our wings we have still got our beaks.'

With a hearty cheer—though, from the paucity of their numbers, not a very loud one—the men went to the guns.

Could they beat off the enemy? They would try, at all events. Rawson in a moment forgot his forebodings, and was all life and courage. The enemy was seen to be shortening sail, so as not to pass the 'Concorde.'

'Fire!' cried Lieutenant Calder. The men obeyed with alacrity, but scarcely had the shot left the mouths of the guns than the enemy replied with a crashing broadside, which shot away several of the stays of the jurymasts, knocked over three or four of the crew, and reduced the frigate almost to the state of wreck in which she had been found when captured.

Rawson was the only officer wounded, but still he cheered on the crew.

'We'll not give in lads! Old England for ever!' he exclaimed, putting his right hand to a gun-tackle, and hauling away. The other arm had been hit.

In vain were all the efforts of those gallant men.

'Here she comes!' was the cry. 'Boarders! repel boarders!'

The enemy gave a sheer to port, and with a loud crash ran alongside the 'Concorde.' Grappling-irons were hove aboard her and the next instant the Frenchmen, in overpowering numbers, rushed like a torrent along her decks.

CHAPTER XVI.

THE 'THISBE'S' CREW PREPARE FOR A FRESH FIGHT.

THE chief anxiety of Captain Courtney when he ascertained that the approaching ship was an enemy, was to secure the escape of the prize.

She would indeed have been of very little use to the 'Thisbe' in repelling an attack, as the French frigate from having all her canvas would have been able to manœuvre so as to engage each of them singly.

'There she goes, and I'll engage Tom Calder's heart is heavier than any one's aboard here at having to run away!' exclaimed Captain Courtney—'Good luck go with him. We'll try and keep the enemy engaged, and wing him, if we can. You'll do your best, I know, my lads.'

A cheerful shout was the answer to this appeal, the last part of which was addressed to the crew.

The men were now seen fastening their handkerchiefs round their heads, tightening their waistbands, most of them having thrown off their jackets and shirts, standing at their guns with their brawny arms and shoulders bare, like pictures of Hercules prepared for battle; not a countenance that did not exhibit a cheerful alacrity for the battle.

As the captain took a walk round the decks, he felt assured that what men could do they would to maintain the honour of old England's flag.

Many bore marks of their recent combat, and several still pale from loss of blood, had insisted on rising from their hammocks and going to their guns. Among them stood the boatswain, Rolf Morton; the captain shook his head at him.

'What! you could not trust us to fight the ship without you, Mr Morton?' he said, in a kind tone of reproof. 'I must let you stay now you are on deck, but I would rather you were snug in your berth.'

'While I've breath for my pipe, and legs to stand on, I'd rather be here, Captain Courtney, thank you, sir,' answered Rolf. 'I would lose an arm rather than let our prize be retaken.'

'So would I, Mr Morton, and we will do our best to help her escape,' said the captain, and he passed on.

With like kind words of encouragement both to officers and men, the captain passed along the guns; not a man of the crew who would not have dropped at their quarters, or gone down with the ship, rather than yield as long as their brave chief bade them fight on.

By the time Captain Courtney regained his post on the quarter-deck, the enemy had got within gun-shot, and commenced firing with her longer pieces at the 'Thisbe,' but the shot fell wide.

'The enemy's gunners want practice,' observed the captain to the third lieutenant, who was doing duty as first, though he himself was severely wounded. We'll reserve our fire till they get a little nearer, and then give it them with a will. They probably expect that we shall haul down our colours after we have satisfied the calls of honour with a few shots.'

'They don't know of whom they have got hold then,' answered Mr Trenane, the lieutenant. In a light wind they might have had too much the advantage of us, but with this breeze, the loss of our masts will matter less, I hope.'

The enemy was now coming up rapidly on the 'Thisbe's' quarter. A shot from her bow chasers whistled through the latter's rigging; several others followed as the guns could be brought to bear.

On she came.

The 'Thisbe' had not fired.

'Down with the helm and give it them, my lads!' suddenly shouted the captain.

The English frigate luffed up, and poured her whole broadside into the bows of the approaching enemy. The Frenchman put down his helm and returned the compliment, and now the two ships stood on for some time exchanging broadsides as rapidly as they could. At length a shot struck the 'Thisbe's' fore-topmast; it had been wounded in the previous engagement. Down it came with a crash, but so eagerly were the crew engaged that few discovered what had happened.

The master with a few hands flew aloft, and quickly cut away the wreck; the crew redoubled their efforts. Still the uninjured condition of the enemy's rigging gave her an important advantage; her shot came crashing on board the 'Thisbe.'

Whatever Captain Courtney might have thought, he appeared as cheerful and confident as ever. His courage kept up that of the crew. The enemy was frequently hulled. Now one spar was shot away; now another; his fire slackened. The British crew cheered lustily. That hearty cheer must have been heard along the Frenchman's decks. It showed him that though his enemy was almost dismantled, the courage of the people was as undaunted as ever.

'We may not take him, but we may prevent his taking us,' observed Morton, as he moved among the crew.

Just then the Frenchman's bow was seen to move up closer to the wind; his tacks were hauled aboard, the breeze was freshening, and away he stood on a bowline under all the sail he could set, leaving the astonished crew of the British ship rubbing their eyes and wondering what he was about. They, however, did not cease sending their shot after him, as a parting compliment.

'She has but hauled off to repair damages,' observed the third lieutenant to the captain.

'Not so sure of that, Trenane,' answered Captain Courtney; 'probably her captain and other superior officers have been killed or wounded, and the rest suspect that we should prove too tough a morsel for them to digest.'

Captain Courtney seemed to be right in his conjectures; the French frigate stood on.

All hands were instantly set to work to repair damages, to be ready for her in case she should return. Many an eye cast an anxious glance in the direction in which she was steering. The brave crew would have welcomed her back, but they wished to be ready first to receive her.

Again she was observed to alter her course.

'She is coming back!' was the cry. 'Hurra, lads, we'll give it her if she does.'

They watched her eagerly. She was steering to the northward under all sail. There could be little doubt that she was in pursuit of the 'Concorde.' More energetically than ever the crew worked away, in the hopes of being in a condition to go to the aid of their consort; but every instant the wind was increasing, the sea was getting up, and their task became more difficult. Dark clouds were gathering in the western horizon. It was evident that a gale was brewing, and there were appearances that it would be a severe one. The safety of the ship demanded all the care of the officers and the redoubled exertions of the men. The guns were secured, the shot holes stopped, the rigging knotted and spliced as strongly as time would allow; everything moveable below was lashed, and the ship's head was brought to the wind to meet the expected blast. Had she had sea room she might have scudded, but, with the land under her lee, that was out of the question. As a brave man girds himself for an inevitable and deadly contest, so was the gallant ship prepared for the desperate conflict with the elements.

The British crew had not prepared unnecessarily to meet the gale, although delayed; down it came at length upon them with even greater fury than was expected. More than once it seemed as if the masts and rigging would give way, and that the frigate would be driven helplessly before its fury. Had a sail gone, had a rope given way, she might have been hurried to destruction; but careful hands had secured the rigging, every rope held, and there she lay nobly breasting the storm. Still she drifted to the eastward, and, should the gale continue long, she after all could not escape destruction.

As the morning approached, the wind blew harder and harder. Daylight exhibited no sign of its abating. All that day it continued, its fury in no way decreased. The weary crew began to faint with their exertions, but the officers went among them, and with cheering words reanimated their spirits. The carpenter had often sounded the well. He now reported that the ship had sprung a leak; the pumps must be manned; the demand on the energies of the crew was increased. Still they worked cheerfully. Even some of the wounded insisted on coming up to take their spell at the pumps.

Night again came on, but not for a moment during the whole course of it did Captain Courtney leave the deck. Often and often did he look out astern. He had good reason for so doing. The order was given to range the cables. It might be necessary to anchor, to make, at all events, the attempt to bring up the ship before she was driven on the enemy's shores.

The morning returned at last, and away to the leeward, amid the thick driving spray, and through the pale cold cheerless light, a line of coast rose above the tumbling waters. Calm, as if no storm was raging, Captain Courtney walked the deck, his eye now turned astern—now at the rigging of his ship. He sent Mr Trenane forward to see that the anchors were ready for letting go. The lieutenant reported all ready.

'Then we have done all that men can do to save the ship, and to Providence we must trust the rest,' observed the captain.

Few words were exchanged by any on board, the crew were at their stations, ready to perform any duty required of them; those told off to labour at the pumps were working manfully; and thus they would have continued till the noble ship had struck on the rocks, or gone down beneath the waves.

Hours passed by. Slowly but certainly she drove stern on towards the land. The captain after a time was seen to look frequently over the side, and to watch the land more earnestly. His countenance brightened.

'There is hope for us yet,' he observed to Mr Trenane; 'the wind is dropping.'

Such was the case. Rapidly the gale abated, the ship no longer laboured as before, the leak was easily kept under, the sea quickly went down, the wind got round to the southward, and by nightfall the 'Thisbe,' under all sail, was steering a course for England.

CHAPTER XVII.

THE 'CONCORDE' RECAPTURED BY THE 'ATALANTE'.—THE SHIPS IN A GALE.—THE 'ATALANTE' WRECKED.—RONALD SWIMS ASHORE.—COMMUNICATION ESTABLISHED.—THE ENGLISH SHUT UP IN A TOWER.

N vain Lieutenant Calder and the prize crew of the 'Concorde' attempted to resist the onslaught of the enemy. Several were killed, others were wounded, and they soon found themselves completely overpowered. No time was lost in conveying them on board the ship which had captured them, which proved to be the 'Atalante,' a consort of their hard-won prize. Most of the wounded French prisoners were removed likewise, that they might be under the care of the chief surgeon of the ship, and among them was Alfonse Gerardin. He had somewhat recovered his strength and spirits, and now that he found himself no longer a prisoner, he talked away freely as well with the young Frenchmen of his own rank as with the English midshipmen.

When the transfer of prisoners had been accomplished, the 'Atalante' took the 'Concorde' in tow and made sail, but the wind increasing, the hawser broke, and both ships had to look out for their safety independently of each other.

In consequence of the comparatively small number of the English prisoners they were not very strictly guarded, and the officers were allowed to go about the decks by themselves.

The gale increased during the night, and when early in the morning Ronald Morton went on deck, he found the French ship scudding before it under bare poles.

There was a good deal of confusion on board; the crew were labouring at the pumps, but in anything but an energetic manner; some would suddenly knock off, and halloa and bawl at their shipmates to come and help them, but it was often long before their places were taken. On looking aloft he saw, too, that the masts were wounded in several places, and though the ship was placed in much greater peril by the way she had been knocked about, it was with no little satisfaction that he observed the battering she had received from the 'Thisbe's' and 'Concorde's' guns. Before long he encountered Mr Calder, whose eyes were engaged as his had been.

'What do you think, sir, of the state of affairs?' he asked.

'That they are as bad, Morton, as well can be,' was the answer. 'Neither captain nor officers know what they are about, and it will be a miracle if they do not cast the ship away.'

'Of course they will,' observed Rawson, who had just then joined them; 'I said from the first that we should have no good luck, and what I said has come true.'

'But other chaps among us said that we should have good luck,' remarked Twigg, the master's assistant, who was always fond of putting Rawson in the wrong. 'Now, you see, old fellow, it was just heads or tails—even, you'll understand—and as ill-luck would have it, you happened to win.'

'It's the only thing I ever did win, then,' answered poor Rawson, in a melancholy tone.

'Well, well, Rawson, the next time you prophesy ill, we'll all pray that you may prove a false prophet,' observed Mr Calder. 'But, my lads, it may before long be of very little consequence to most of us who is right and who is wrong; unless these Frenchmen are steering for some shelter, and know the coast perfectly, they will run us hard and fast on it before the world is many hours older.'

Ronald on this said he would go and learn what he could from young Gerardin, who would probably be able to ascertain what the Frenchmen proposed doing.

Ronald found his way to the sick-bay, where Alfonse was in his cot, able to sit up and talk without difficulty.

'What we are going to do, you demand?' he answered. 'Why, let the ship drive and go to destruction, for what I can tell; all on board seem to have lost their wits, from the captain downwards. They would pitch me out of the ship if they heard my remarks, so do not repeat them.'

When Ronald returned on deck he found things in no way mended. The French crew appeared to be obeying their officers very slowly and unwillingly; indeed, the ship was already in a state of semi-mutiny. The officers, too, seemed to be issuing contradictory orders. Ronald saw them examining a chart, but it was evident from their gestures that they differed very much in opinion as to the course which should be steered. No decision was arrived at, and the ship drove onwards towards the coast of Finisterre.

There were harbours and shelter there in abundance; but judgment and good pilotage was required to take advantage of them, and these qualities were wanting on board the 'Atalante.'

The English officers stood grouped together, affording a strong contrast to their French captors. Mr Calder was cool and collected as ever.

'If the Frenchmen won't let us try and save the ship, we must do our best to save our lives,' he remarked. 'Remember, in the first place, let us all hold together and help each other. We may make a harbour and run no risk of losing our lives, or we may drive on the rocks and have a desperate struggle for them, but in either case, prisoners we shall remain, only in the last we shall have a better chance of making our escape in the end—let us keep that in view, whatever happens. Now, lads! there is the land; it won't be long before we become more nearly acquainted with it.'

Rawson, Morton, and the rest promised implicitly to follow Mr Calder's directions. It was agreed that the instant the ship struck, Morton and Twigg should hasten down to release their own men below, and to tell them what had been resolved on. There was little doubt, even in the expected extremity, that they would willingly follow Mr Calder's directions.

'In ten minutes we shall know our fate,' said Mr Calder, calmly watching the shore, towards which the helpless ship was rapidly driving.

It consisted of a sandy beach, the ground rising a little beyond it, with here and there a low building, and in the centre a ruined mill, or fort, or watchtower—it was difficult to say what.

The sandy beach might have offered some prospect that their lives would be preserved, but in front of it rose among the foaming breakers a line of dark rocks, and no break was perceived in them through which the ship might force her way.

'Few of those on board this ill-fated craft will see another day,' observed Rawson, as he eyed the threatening coast. But he no longer spoke in a desponding tone; the moment of action was at hand, and such a prospect always roused him up.

'There's a fresh hand at the bellows, to help us along to our fate,' he added. 'Well, let it do its worst; Jack Rawson won't flinch as long as he has a head on his shoulders.'

Morton was what is called constitutionally brave, and the calmness of his companions increased his courage. His friend, Dicky Glover, looked at him with admiration; Morton's bearing gave him confidence. If one who, so short a time before, was a ship's boy, was so cool and brave, of course he who was born a gentleman, and had long been a midshipman, ought to exhibit even more calmness and resolution. So in reality, at this trying moment, Glover appeared as much the hero as did Morton.

Mr Calder noted both of the lads, and his heart warmed with pride as he marked the courage of his young countrymen, though he grieved at the too great probability of their being cut off.

The greater number of the Frenchmen were all this time agitated in the greatest degree, each man following his own devices; the officers having lost all shadow of control. Some had hurried below to put on their best clothes, or to secure what valuables they possessed; others had broken into the spirit-room, and with cans and bottles in their hands, came reeling on deck, insisting on their officers drinking with them. Some were dancing furiously; others were singing at the top of their voices, but except a very few, no one was preparing for the inevitable catastrophe. More than half were below when it came.

'Secure that coil of rope, and hold on for your lives!' shouted Mr Calder.

The ship struck, the foremast instantly went by the board; the seas furiously dashed up the frigate's sides, and washed through her ports and over her deck. Each time she was struck, she shivered as if about to be wrenched asunder.

Numbers of the hapless crew were washed away. Men and officers shared the same fate; some were seen for a time struggling between the beach and the ship, but the cruel seas as they rushed back, carried them off, and hurled them among the dark rocks, where life was speedily crushed and washed out of them.

Ronald, Glover, and Twigg, as directed, had instantly the ship struck, hurried below to release their countrymen. The seamen, knowing what had happened, were making desperate efforts to get out of the hold in which they had been battened down. A capstan bar, which Morton and his companions found outside, enabled them to accomplish their object. The English seamen rushed upon deck, for the terrific sounds which reached their ears, and the fierce concussions the ship was receiving, warned that no time was to be lost, if they would preserve their lives.

Morton was hurrying up with the rest, when he recollected the wounded midshipman, Alfonse Gerardin.

'His countrymen won't help him, of that I am pretty certain, and I cannot leave the poor fellow to perish,' he exclaimed to Glover, who was near him.

'I'll help you, whatever you do,' answered Dicky Glover, who was as ready to do a good deed as a mischievous one, if it was suggested to him.

'So will I, Mr Morton,' said a seaman who had kept by the two midshipmen from the moment he had got his liberty, and had moreover possessed himself of the capstan bar, to serve him as a trusty weapon in case of need.

'Thank you, friend Truefitt,' said Morton: 'come along.'

Ronald was well pleased to get such an ally as honest Job Truefitt, for there was not among the crew of the 'Thisbe' a better seaman or a more trustworthy, betterhearted fellow.

While the rest were rushing on deck, Ronald and his companions made their way along the deck to the sick-bay. Many of the wounded were calling on their shipmates to come to their assistance, and uttering imprecations fierce and terrible, when they found that they called in vain.

Gerardin was attempting to get up, but his strength failed him, and he lay back, his countenance betokening a proud resignation to his own fate, and scorn at the terror of the wretches who surrounded him.

'What!' he exclaimed, when he saw Morton and Glover with Job Truefitt, 'have you Englishmen found time, amid all this confusion, to come and look after a wounded wretch like me; an enemy too—who has been taught with his utmost strength to hate the English?'

'We Englishmen have been taught to help our enemies in distress, mounseer,' observed Job Truefitt, as, without waiting a moment to ask leave, he lifted the wounded lad on his shoulders. 'There's no time for palavering. Come along, sirs.'

The midshipmen sprang on, helping Job to support his burden, and they soon reached the upper-deck, when the scene of horror and confusion was indescribable! Not without difficulty, and in great danger of being washed off, they made their way to the after part of the quarter-deck, where Mr Calder, with the other Englishmen, were assembled.

The ship had driven with her larboard side to the shore, and as she heeled over they were partly sheltered from the force of the seas, which dashed in arches of foam high above her.

The English lieutenant and his party had made fast a cask to the end of the line they had secured, and were endeavouring to float it towards the shore, where three or four people stood ready to receive it. In vain they tried. Several times the cask got almost within their reach, and was carried back again with the reflux of the wave. Morton, however, observed to his satisfaction, that just at that part there were no rocks, and that the seas rushed on without any break till they reached the beach.

'If I could but do it,' thought Morton to himself. 'I have swam through some tolerably heavy seas on the Shetland coast.'

He at once made the proposal to Mr Calder.

'Impossible!' was the answer. 'You would be drowned, my boy, to a certainty.'

'But I could do it, and whether I'm drowned or not, it matters little,' exclaimed Job Truefitt. 'Here, who'll take charge of this here young Frenchman?'

Rawson offered also to make the attempt, but he was known not to be a good swimmer.

A thundering crash was heard. It was the fall of the remainder of the foremast, and the breaking up of the fore part of the ship. It was a strong hint to the English party to hasten whatever they might undertake.

'You'll let me go, Mr Calder?' said Morton again.

He and Job Truefitt had secured some light line to the cask, which had just been hauled up. It was again lowered, and the lieutenant nodded his head, but his countenance was very sad, as if he had little hopes of the success of the expedition. The instant his permission was gained, Ronald and Job slid down the side of the ship, and were quickly borne on with the cask towards the shore. They both struck out bravely, and soon reached the cask. They had little at first to do, except to keep themselves afloat. All those who anxiously watched them, knew that the trial would come as they neared the beach, and got within the power of the under suck of the receding waves. At first they merely accompanied the cask, and supporting themselves by it, husbanded their strength.

'They will be lost to a certainty, I know,' observed Rawson. 'If they don't succeed, I don't know who will. I never saw a finer swimmer than that man Truefitt.'

'Oh, I hope they will! I hope they will be saved!' cried Glover, in an agony of terror for Morton, who had inspired him with the sincerest affection.

'There they go! bravely they swim!' cried Mr Calder. 'They are ahead of the cask—they dart forward—the undertow has got them. No!—they are struggling desperately with it—they don't lose ground—on they go!—No!'

There was a cry that the sea had carried them back, but the next moment their heads appeared on the top of a foaming sea, and on it rushed towards the beach.

Now was the critical moment. Their shipmates on board the wreck held their breath as they watched their progress. One was seen to rise up on the beach from out of a sheet of foam, and to hurry upwards; but there was only one. He did not stop a moment. Down he dashed again. He had a grasp of a rope, though the other end of which was held by the people on the shore.

Without hesitation, he plunged once more into the seething

waters; he did not again appear—there was a cry of despair —all thought he was lost—but no—the next instant he was seen, and this time with a companion, and aided by the people, who were on the watch for them, they both together hurried up the beach, and the cask, with the line, was hauled up after them.

The great object was accomplished; a communication was secured with the shore. The passage, however, was still full of danger.

More line was procured. A traveller and slings were fitted, and Rawson volunteered to lead the way. Should he succeed, the passage would be somewhat less dangerous.

The people on shore now tightened the rope. He took a supply of line with which to haul the next person on shore. A shout from the English seamen proclaimed that he was successful.

It was now according to rule, under such circumstances, the privilege of the youngest to proceed. Dicky Glover was ordered into the slings.

'If I must go, may I take the young Frenchman?' he asked. 'I know Morton would wish it.'

'Yes, be sharp,' answered Mr Calder, assisting himself to secure them both. Away they went on their perilous passage. It was near sun-down when the ship struck. It was now rapidly getting dark. What a night of horrors was there for those who were compelled to spend it on board the wreck.

When Dicky Glover had nearly reached the shore, the surf almost tore young Gerardin from the slings, and the hold he had of him. Almost hopelessly he struggled. In another instant they both would have been carried away, when Glover saw some one making his way through the foaming water towards him. A friendly hand grasped his, and in another minute he and his charge were hauled up out of the power of the sea.

Ronald Morton, with a rope round his waist, had been the

means of rescuing him and Gerardin from death. Dicky began to thank him.

'Only obeying orders—helping each other,' answered Ronald. 'But lend a hand, Glover, we have plenty to do.'

Morton and his companions became very anxious for the fate of their gallant superior. Had the frigate been his own ship, he would have been the last to leave the wreck; but now, having seen his own people on shore, he would have no hesitation in coming.

Ronald applied to Gerardin, but he could get no information from his confused countrymen as to what had become of the English lieutenant. The Englishmen, notwithstanding this, continued to assist energetically in hauling the people on shore. Each time a man reached the beach, they hailed him, hoping to find that he was their officer.

Suddenly, as they were hauling in on the line made fast to the traveller, the main line became slack: alas! all communication with the ill-fated ship was cut off.

'Haul on it, lads!' shouted Rawson and Morton in concert.

'It is heavy; there is some one on it,' cried the men. 'Steady, lads, steady.'

Gradually they hauled in the line. The life of one more fellow-creature might be saved. They hauled away. Yes, a man was there! was he still alive, though?

They hailed as he neared them. An English voice answered, 'All right, lads!' It was their own lieutenant. They welcomed him with a joyful shout, which showed that he had won the honest affections of his men, a prize worthy of an officer's aim.

'I had a struggle for it,' he observed, as soon as he was somewhat recovered. 'No sooner was I on the rope, than some of the wretches in their madness cut it, and have so lost all means of reaching the shore in safety. Still we will do what we can to help them.'

The Englishmen kept to this resolution. With unceasing watchfulness they moved up and down along the beach, saving the lives of many who would otherwise have fallen victims to the waves.

The wearied seamen, their labours over, threw themselves on the sands to rest, scarcely allowing the thought to trouble them of what next they should do. They had not enjoyed many minutes' repose before they were roused up by a party of soldiers, who, without much ceremony, marched them all off to a tower in the neighbourhood, which Ronald recollected observing before the ship struck. Here, in spite of all Mr Calder's expostulations, they were locked up in an upper chamber without food or water, and left to their own devices.

It is not surprising if their remarks and reflections were not very complimentary to the people on whose shores they had been thrown.

CHAPTER XVIII.

JOB'S PLAN FOR ESCAPING.—A HINT FROM GERARDIN.—A ROPE BROUGHT IN A BASKET.—DESCENT FROM THE TOWER.—THE GUARD MADE PRISONER.—GET ON BOARD A FISHING-BOAT.

'IF I'd my way I'd break out of this here hole, knock the mounseers down that stands guard, and cut and run,' observed Job Truefitt, as he woke up after a sound sleep on some straw, in the afternoon of the day on which he and his companions had been shut up in the tower. 'We might get hold of some fishing craft or other, and make good our escape. I've heard of such things being done afore now.'

The sentiment was warmly echoed by the speaker's shipmates.

Mr Calder and the other officers had overheard what was said. It was intended that they should. Probably the same idea was occupying the lieutenant's mind; he got up and took a survey of the interior of the tower. The upper part was of wood, and through a chink came a ray from the setting sun, and cast a bright light on the opposite wall. It showed the prisoners the direction of the ocean, and the point towards which they must make their way if they could escape from the tower.

Mr Calder, with no little exertion, climbed up to the chink to look out; the chamber was without any window; there had been one in the stone wall, but that had been blocked up. From the dome shape of the roof it appeared, too, that the chamber was the highest in the tower. Mr Calder having completed his survey of the surrounding country, as far as his position would allow him, descended to the floor. He said but little; he was pondering the means of escape. To be kept a prisoner now, almost at the commencement of what everybody said would be a long war, was more than his philosophy would enable him to bear with patience. Morton guessed what was passing in his superior's mind.

'It would, indeed, be terrible to be shut up,' he observed.

'It is only just what I ought to have expected,' said Rawson. 'My ill-luck will stick to me to the end; no fear of that going, though everything else leaves me.'

His remark produced a laugh among his companions, who, if they even believed in ill-luck, had very little compassion on him when he complained of it; indeed, it was suspected that he rather liked to be joked on the subject.

'I should like to have a look out too,' said Ronald, climbing up by the inequalities in the stone wall and the planks which formed the side of the tower.

The sun was just sinking in the ocean, and casting a rich glow over the whole western sky. The storm had completely ceased, though the waves still rolled in with a loud roar, lining the coast with a fringe of foam.

The tide was low; a few ribs on the reef, almost abreast of the tower, was the only remnant of this once beautiful frigate, with the addition of the broken timbers and planks which strewed the shore, and which the peasantry had not yet carried off. The appearance of the coast indeed in the immediate neighbourhood of the tower offered no hopes of escape to the Englishmen, even should they succeed in getting out of their prison. To the north, however, Morton observed a high reef of black rocks, running out into the sea, and circling round so as to form a secure harbour. Two or three small craft were floating on the surface of this little haven, either launched after the gale, or which had ridden it out in safety, while several boats, appearing like black dots on the yellow sand, lay drawn up on the beach.

Ronald was still employed in making his survey, when steps were heard ascending the rickety creaking stairs of the tower, and Mr Calder ordered him down, that he might not excite the suspicion of the Frenchmen that they entertained the idea of escaping.

The door opened, and two soldiers entered with a jar of wine, and some bread and cheese and fruit. Placing the provisions before the lieutenant, they made signs that he might divide them among his people. Ronald, thinking it might be politic to get into conversation with them, mustering all his knowledge of French, thanked them warmly for what they had brought.

The man answered, somewhat gruffly, that they were only obeying orders, and that they had been directed by a young officer of the marine, who had been wrecked, to bring the provisions.

'Pray thank him for us, and say how grateful we feel for his gift,' said Ronald.

'We may not see him again,' answered one of the men. 'He is ill in bed, and he will be going away into the interior, as soon as he is able to be removed.'

The men said that they did not know the young officer's name. There could be little doubt, however, that Alfonse Gerardin had sent the provisions.

Ronald in vain tried to ascertain if the soldiers knew how they, the English prisoners, were to be disposed of, but the Frenchmen only shrugged their shoulders, and replied that that was no business of theirs. It was not likely that they would be kept for ever in the tower, which, as the rats had already deserted it, was very likely to tumble about their ears.

'It is a wonder, then, that it did not come down during the late gale,' observed Ronald.

'Ah,' said one of the men with a shrug and a wink, 'it is a wonder truly, considering how rotten it is from the top to the bottom. But we must not stop here, talking with you Englishmen, or we shall be suspected of wishing to help you to escape. Adieu, adieu,—*au revoir*. You don't seem much cast down. Perhaps you would be, if you knew the fate prepared for you.'

With another wink from the chief speaker, a corporal, by his uniform, the man took his departure.

'I am certain, sir, they had meaning in what they said,' observed Ronald to Mr Calder, explaining the Frenchman's remarks. 'Gerardin is not ungrateful, and wishes to help us to escape.'

Rawson laughed at the notion of a Frenchman being grateful, and even Mr Calder seemed to doubt that he, or any one else, had the slightest idea of helping them to escape.

'People are not fond of putting their lives in jeopardy, to help those in whom they have no interest,' he remarked.

It seemed too likely that the lieutenant was right, for the night passed, and noon of the following day arrived, and no one came near them. At that time the two soldiers who had before appeared brought in their food, but left it without saying a word, and again hurried down the stairs.

Ronald was persuaded that the corporal gave a significant look at him, as he followed his companion out of the door. It was probable that the two men did not trust each other.

'It is all your fancy, Morton,' said Rawson, gloomily. 'Depend on it we shall be marched off to some horrible out of the way fortress, and be shut up for the next ten years of our lives, while our old shipmates are crowning themselves with laurels, or what is better, making no end of prize-money, and rising to the top of their profession. When we get back once more to the shores of old England, there we shall be wretched white-haired old mates and midshipmen, forgotten by our friends, and cared for by nobody. There's one consolation,—

I'll not learn a word of their beastly lingo, they may depend on that.'

Although the picture Rawson had drawn was very melancholy, and too likely to be true, his latter observation so tickled the fancies of his hearers, that they all burst into a loud laugh, in which Rawson himself could not help joining.

'Well, my lads, though we may have some difficulty in breaking out of this, and more in making our escape, there's no doubt that the alternative, as Rawson describes it, will be a very unpleasant one,' exclaimed Mr Calder. We must all go, or none; and yet I would force none to go, for the attempt may cost us our lives.'

'Never fear, Mr Calder, sir; there'll be no skulkers among us,' exclaimed Job Truefitt, from among the seamen. 'Just you give the word as if you was on the quarter-deck of our own tight little frigate, and there is not a man here who wont obey you as smartly, whatever you thinks fit to order, whether it is to jump off the top of this here tower, or to knock over every Frenchman we meet.'

'Yes, sir,—yes, sir,—that's it. Job speaks the truth,' exclaimed several of the men simultaneously.

The men required no incitement to induce them to attempt escaping, although there was but little fault to find with the provisions which had been sent them. There was excellent bread and cheese, and fruit of various sorts, and some fried fish, though certainly there was neither beef nor pork, while the *vin du pays* was of a somewhat thin and sour description. A few bottles of fiery hot *eau de vie* would have suited the taste of the honest tars much better.

This day, like the former one, passed away, and nobody came near the prisoners; they all wished that the time was come when they were to make the attempt to escape. The next day, at noon, a much larger supply of provisions was brought to them. Two men accompanied their friend, the corporal, to carry them. He also carried a good-sized basket, which he deposited in a corner of the chamber, and then nodding, without saying a word, hurried down the steps; as if their friends outside had divined their wishes, there were half-a-dozen bottles of brandy!

Morton and Rawson were examining the contents of the corporal's basket.

'I thought so,' exclaimed Ronald, joyfully; and he pulled out a long rope, amply strong enough to support the weight of a man. There was no longer any doubt that they had friends outside, anxious to assist their escape.

The weather had now become perfectly serene. A light south-easterly breeze, and smooth water, would enable them to run along the coast just out of sight of those on land, while several small vessels in the harbour would supply them with a craft suited to their purpose.

The prospect in view put them all in high spirits, and with infinite relish they discussed the viands which had been brought them. While thus engaged the door of their prison opened, and two persons in naval uniform appeared before them. One Morton at once recognized as Alfonse Gerardin, though he looked even more pale and sickly than when he had been rescued from the wreck. Ronald sprang up to greet him. His companion, on whose arm he rested, was a strongly-built middle-aged man. Alfonse gave his hand to Ronald.

'I could not bear the thought of your going away without seeing you once more,' he said. 'I could not have obtained leave had it not been for my father, Lieutenant Gerardin, of whom I told you.'

'What you told me was merely that he had been killed,' said Ronald.

'So I thought, but happily I was mistaken. He had been knocked overboard, but he was picked up by a boat, and unable to regain the ship was brought to shore, not far from this, when hearing of the shipwreck he found us out.'

'And you are the young gentleman to whom my dear boy

here is indebted for his life,' said Lieutenant Gerardin, in broken English, grasping Ronald's hand warmly. ' I am grateful to you. Though my nation is at war with yours, I love your countrymen. I would serve you gladly at the risk of my life. You are to be removed into the interior to-morrow, and a far-off fortress will be your habitation. This night you must make your escape; I have provided part of the means. There is a fishing-boat in that little harbour to the north; she pulls fast, and has oars and sails aboard, as also some water and provisions, but not sufficient. Carry all you can with you. I have bribed some of the guards, but not all; you may meet with opposition; you will know how to deal with your enemies. Do not think me a traitor to France; I owe her no allegiance, and yet I am bound to her. Now farewell!—we may never meet again, but you will at least not think that he whom you so bravely saved from death is ungrateful.'

Alfonse Gerardin said but little; he warmly shook Ronald's and Glover's hands, and then he and his father hurriedly took their departure.

The rest of the day was spent by the party in talking over their escape, and the best mode of meeting all possible contingencies, and then most of the old hands lay down to sleep, that they might be fresher when the moment of action arrived.

No sooner was it dark than Mr Calder set to work to remove some of the planks above the brickwork. It was, as the corporal had hinted, very rotten, and quickly gave way to their pulls. An aperture of size sufficient to allow a man to force himself through was soon made. Mr Calder then securing the rope, and lowering it to the ground, directing his men to stand in the order they were to descend, told Rawson to bring up the rear, went himself through the hole, and slid down noiselessly to the ground. The midshipmen followed, and then came the men; not a word was spoken, but they imitated their leader's example in picking up some large stones with which to defend themselves, should they be suddenly attacked. One after the other the men came gliding down in the rapid way none but seamen could have done; not the slightest noise was made; their feet, as they touched the ground, made no more sound than those of cats. All had descended except Rawson, when a noise was heard in the room above, as of a door opening. There was a scuffle, but no one cried out; in an instant Job Truefitt was swarming up the rope hand over hand; Morton, the most active of the party, followed him. Whatever there was to be done was to be effected quickly. With the deepest anxiety the rest of the party waited to ascertain what had happened, while two or three prepared to follow. Job crept in at the hole in the wall, and looked round the prison. At first he could see nothing. At last he fancied that he could distinguish something moving on the other side of the room. He sprang towards the spot, and so did Morton.

'Here we are, Mr Rawson; here we are, come to help you,' whispered Job. A deep groan was the response. It was soon evident that there were two people on the ground, struggling in a deadly embrace—but which was friend or foe, was the question. They had tight hold of each other's throats, and were actually throttling each other.

'You catch hold of one, Mr Morton,' whispered Job, who had recognised Ronald. 'I'll take t'other, and then we'll settle with the mounseer, whichever he may be.'

Ronald found by his jacket that he had got hold of Rawson, but it was not without digging his nails into the Frenchman's wrist that he was able to make him relax his hold of Rawson's throat. Still more difficult was it to induce the latter to take his gripe off his opponent's neck. To bind the legs and arms of the Frenchman, and to gag his mouth, was the work of a few moments. Ronald stumbled against his lantern, at which Rawson must have struck when he entered.

'It may prove of service,' thought Ronald, as he hung it round his neck.

Rawson soon recovered. Two more seamen had come in

by this time. Their first care was to barricade the door. At first they thought of leaving the Frenchman in the room, but it was agreed that, as he might make some noise, and give the alarm, it would be better to take him part of the way with them. He was speedily lowered down, much to the astonishment of those below, and to his own annoyance. Then Morton and the rest of the party followed. Who their prisoner was it was impossible to ascertain, for fear lest the moment the gag was removed he might cry out. He was a soldier, but not their friend the corporal, as he was a shorter and stouter man.

There could be little doubt that the guard was in the room below them, and when their comrade was missed, others probably would go up to look for him. No further time was to be lost. Mr Calder, therefore, ordered the men in a whisper to close up together, carrying their prisoner among them, and to move off in the direction of the harbour. As they began to advance, Morton recollected the rope which they ought to have taken with them, as should it be left behind and recognised, it might betray the friends who had supplied it to them. As the rope was long enough to allow of its being slipped round a beam, and then again to reach the ground, he was on the point of ascending once more to execute his project, hoping quickly to overtake his companions, when a noise in the room immediately above him arrested his movements. The guard was on the alert. His delay, contrary to the orders of his superior, might cause the ruin of the whole party. He let go the rope and sprang after his companions.

'It cannot much matter,' he thought; 'our friends would have warned us to carry off the rope.'

The English seamen hurried on till they came to a deep hollow in the sands. Here Mr Calder ordered them to leave their prisoner.

'Remember, mounseer, if you hallo or make any row, we'll be back and blow your brains out for you, whispered Job Truefitt, as he placed him on the ground.

A grunt was the only answer. It was doubtful whether the prisoner understood what was said, though he might have guessed the meaning of the remark.

The seamen pushed on as fast as they could move. It was no easy matter to find their way, for the night was very dark, and though the sky was clear, there was a slight mist, which concealed all objects, except those close at hand, from view. This was, however, an advantage, as well as a disadvantage, to the fugitives. Though they had, in consequence of the mist, greater difficulty in making their way towards the shore, it assisted to conceal them from any persons who might chance to cross their path. They had made their escape at an early hour, that they might have longer time to get an offing before daylight.

Mr Calder strode on ahead, Rawson brought up the rear, Ronald pushed on, and ranged up alongside his lieutenant. He had a fancy that if there was danger, it would be there, and he wished to be near him. The road lay chiefly over sand-hills, very heavy walking. Now and then they came to rocks, which still further impeded their progress, but there were bits also of hard ground, over which they passed at a run. The wind being from the south, they kept at their backs, while the gentle ripple of the sea on the beach, assisted still further to guide them. At last Mr Calder stopped.

'We ought to be up to the harbour by this time,' he observed in a low voice. 'I see no signs of it.'

All the party had now pulled up. As they did so, the sound of voices from no great distance reached their ears. The speakers were to the north of them. It was not likely that they were pursuers. Still, if they passed near, they might discover them. The seamen crouched down to the ground. The voices grew louder and louder. They seemed to be coming towards the very spot where the Englishmen were collected.

'Lads, we must master them, whether many or few,' whispered Mr Calder. 'Take care none escape.'

Morton had been attentively listening to the speakers. 'They are fishermen just landed,' he said, in a low tone. 'They are on their way to their homes. I doubt, from what they say, if they have landed their fish.'

'Be ready, lads,' said Mr Calder, expecting that the next instant they would be grappling with the Frenchmen. Each of you seize his man, bring him to the ground, and gag him. Take care none get away.'

Suddenly the voices ceased. Morton thought that they had been overheard, but once more the fishermen went on talking; their footsteps were heard, but gradually the strength of the sound decreased, their voices became less and less distinct, till they were altogether lost in the distance. The lieutenant now led the way rapidly onward.

'If we had been a minute sooner we should have been discovered, thought Morton. 'All is for the best.'

They had now reached the little harbour. Several boats were drawn up, but all at a considerable distance from the water. It would be difficult to launch one of them without making a noise. A small boat was distinguished a short distance from the shore. Ronald offered to swim off to it, and bring it in. His clothes were off in an instant.

'Stay, I may have to cut the cable,' he observed, putting his clasp knife between his teeth.

The water was somewhat cold, but he did not heed that. Excitement kept his blood in circulation. He soon reached the boat. His knife came into requisition, and though there were no oars, he found a loose bottom board, and managed to paddle in with it to the beach.

It was still necessary to be very cautious. Lights were seen in some huts not far off, and the inmates might hear them, and suspect that something was wrong.

The boat would not hold the entire party, so Mr Calder and Glover, with some of the men, embarked first, to select the craft most likely to suit them.

It was an anxious time for those on shore. The crews might be on board some of the boats, and if one of those was selected, the alarm might be given.

'We shall have to knock some of the fellows on the head if they are, that will be all,' observed Rawson, coolly.

The boat, however, returned without any disturbance, and the rest of the seamen got into her, bringing her gunwale almost flush with the water. Scarcely had they got twenty yards from the shore, when a voice hailed in French, 'Yes, you were before us; don't wait—*bon soir*,' answered Ronald, promptly, in the same language.

They pulled out as fast as they could, and got on board a a large half-decked boat, with her sails on board, and pulling eight oars.

The question was now, how to get out of the harbour. Rawson in the punt went ahead, to pilot the way, while the anchor was noiselessly weighed. The oars being got out, the little craft stood after the boat.

The mouth of the harbour was discovered, they were in the open sea. How joyously beats the hearts of all to find themselves free! As they drew off the land, the breeze freshened, the punt was cast adrift, and sail was made; just then there were lights seen on the beach; shouts were heard. There was a grating sound as of a boat being launched. They were about to be pursued, there could be no doubt about that. Still sharp eyes would be required to see them. Impelled by wind and oars the boat stood out to the westward.

The wind was fair, the sea was smooth. Of course in the darkness it was impossible to select the best boat, but they had happily hit upon one which at all events seemed a fine little craft, and they hoped she might prove the fastest. The seamen bent their backs to the oars with right good will; the water hissed and bubbled under the bows.

'The mounseers must be in a precious hurry to catch us, if they do catch us,' exclaimed Job Truefitt. 'Give way, mates: if we can't keep ahead of a crew of frog-eaters, we desarves to be caught and shut up in the darkest prison in the land, without e'er a quid o' baccy to chaw, or a glass o' grog to freshen our nip.'

The men, however, required no inducement to exert themselves to the utmost.

'Avast pulling!' exclaimed Mr Calder, after they had made good three miles or more from the harbour.

There was no sound of oars. The Frenchmen, it was supposed, had thought the pursuit useless, and had given it up. Still daylight must find them far away from the coast, and spell and spell throughout the night the undaunted seamen laboured at their oars.

CHAPTER XIX.

A SAIL IN SIGHT.—A GALE COMES ON.—REACH THE FRIGATE.—
RONALD REJOINS THE 'THISBE.'—MADE LIEUTENANT.

HEN morning dawned, and hunger reminded the escaped prisoners that it was time for breakfast, they looked about and discovered in the forepeak a supply of water and provisions, and what was of most consequence, a compass. She was evidently, then, the very craft the Gerardins had intended for their use.

'I hope they won't get into a scrape for what they have done for us,' observed Ronald. 'Though he is an odd fish in some respects, I liked that fellow, Alfonse Gerardin; and from the glimpse I got of his father, I should say he is first-rate.'

The health of their friends was therefore drunk in some very fair claret, which was found among the stores, and never has a merrier party floated in an open boat out in the Atlantic.

Two days passed, and Mr Calder calculated that they were well into the Chops of the Channel.

Several vessels had been seen, but none had been approached. Mr Calder did not care about this; he hoped to carry the boat into Falmouth or Plymouth harbour in safety.

The evening was drawing on. 'A sail on the starboard bow!' was the cry. She was a ship standing across channel; unless she or they altered their course, she could not help falling in with them. From the look of the vessel it was impossible to say whether she was a friend or an enemy.

'If them there to'sels weren't cut by an English sail-maker, I'm ready to pass for a Schiedam drinking big-breeched Dutchman for the rest of my born days,' observed Job Truefitt, in a decisive tone, as standing up on the forecastle deck, and holding on by the mast, he shaded his eyes with his hand, and took a severe scrutiny of the stranger.

'Maybe I've handed them more than once and again.'

'What do you make her out to be, Truefitt?' asked Mr Calder from aft.

'Why, sir, maybe I'm wrong, and maybe I'm right; but if I'm right, then I take it she's no other than the thirty-two pounder frigate, 'Thetis.' I served aboard her better nor twelve months, so I don't deserve to have eyes in my head if I shouldn't know her again,' answered Job.

'I think that you are very likely to be right, Job, and I'll trust that you are,' said Mr Calder. 'Take a couple of reefs in the mainsail as you hoist it, lads. The sky gives promise of a blowing night, and we shall do well if we can have a stout ship under our feet.'

As the lieutenant was speaking, a heavy squall passed over the boat, which, had her sails been set, she would have felt severely. As it was, the spray which it carried drove over her in thick masses, as she drifted before it. Dark clouds were breaking up heavily to the southward, while others drove across the sky, their outer edges glowing, like red-hot coals, with the beams of the setting sun. The squall, however, passed away, sail was made, and the boat sprang briskly over the rising seas towards the frigate. All were now as anxious to be seen by those on board her, as they were before to escape observation. It was very evident that a storm was brewing, and a pretty heavy one—such a gale as the French fishing-boat they were in could scarcely weather. Every instant the wind increased, and the seas rose higher and higher. The frigate, it was very probable, was outward bound, for as the wind got round she trimmed sails and steered to the westward. The boat was now close hauled. If not seen by the frigate, it was scarcely to be hoped that she would cut her off on the other tack. The gloom of evening was coming on also, causing the small sails of the boat to be less discernible.

'They'll not see us,' sighed Rawson. 'And as to this wretched little craft living out such a night as we are going to have, that's a sheer impossibility.'

'The craft has carried us thus far in safety, and may carry us into Penzance or Falmouth harbour, I hope, even if we do miss the frigate,' observed Morton. 'We shouldn't so mistrust Providence, I think.'

'You think, you youngster!' said Rawson, contemptuously. 'You haven't been tried as I have.'

'But Rawson, suppose we are preserved. What will you say then?'

'That we have obtained more than we deserve,' answered the old mate, as if involuntarily.

'The frigate sees us,' shouted Job Truefitt, from forward, making use of a very common nautical figure of speech. 'There's port the helm—square away the yards—she'll be down to us in a jiffy.'

'Time she was too,' observed Rawson, and he was right, for the gloom was increasing, the rising sea was tumbling and pitching the boat about, and even with two reefs down she could scarcely look up to her canvas.

The frigate, however, had not shortened sail, and on she came, looming large through the midst as she ploughed her way with irresistible force across the intervening space of tumbling foam-covered seas. Mr Calder gave the necessary orders to prepare for going alongside. It was a work of no little danger. The frigate had now got within a few hundred fathoms of the boat. Her canvas was reduced, and the helm being put down she rounded-to, and there she lay, dipping away heavily into the seas, making it appear to a landsman an utter impossibility to get near her, and even to a seaman a dangerous undertaking. The boat's sails were lowered, and, if it could have been done, the mast would have been unstepped and pitched overboard; the oars were got out, and the boat approached the side of the frigate. Numerous friendly hands were ready to heave ropes for their assistance from various parts of the sides, from the chains and ports.

'Now give way, my good lads!' shouted Mr Calder, seeing that not a moment was to be lost.

The men pulled on, but the ship at the moment plunged forward, and the boat dropped astern. Should this again occur they might lose the chance of getting alongside altogether. With renewed efforts they again pulled up. A rope was hove on board and secured to the bits, and by its assistance they at length got alongside.

'Now, lads, up with you!' shouted the lieutenant.

The men caught hold of the ropes thrown into their outstretched hands. The greater number sprang up the side like cats, but Morton, with the right feeling that it is the officer's duty to see his men in safety before seeking his own, hung back. Now the frigate rose on the side of a sea, leaving the boat in the trough far below her, then in another instant down she came striking the boat with a terrific crash. The side was crushed in, and the water rushing over her, down she went. More ropes were hove to those still on board. Morton caught hold of a rope with his left hand, but, at the same time, a spar struck his right a blow which rendered it powerless. He held on with all the energy of despair, for he knew that if he let go he should be lost. A poor fellow, one of his companions, was washed away close to him. His own was an awful position. He had received a second blow from a fragment of the boat. The sea was surging up round him. Should the ship roll over he must be submerged, and would inevitably be torn from his hold. He tried to cry out. The spray rushed into his mouth and almost choked him. Already it was so dark that he feared no one would see him. He believed that his last hour had come. The loud roar of waters was in his ears; he was losing all consciousness, and in another instant would have let go his hold, when his arm was grasped by a vice-like clutch, and he found himself lifted upwards till he was safely deposited on deck. He looked round to ascertain who had been his preserver. A tall gaunt young man was standing and shaking the water from his jacket, but just then an order was issued for all those who had been rescued from the boat to muster aft.

Lanterns were brought, and no sooner did the light of one of them fall on Mr Calder's countenance, than one of the lieutenants, who proved to be the first of the ship, stepped forward, and grasped him warmly by the hand.

'What, old ship, is it you?' he exclaimed, almost wringing his hand off, and speaking rapidly, as if unable to restrain his feelings. 'Where do you come from? What has happened to you? Tell me all about it.'

This Mr Calder briefly did, and warm and hearty was the reception he met with in the gun-room, to which Rawson was also invited, while the other midshipmen were taken care of in the berth.

The gale continued to increase in fury.

'We should have found ourselves in a bad way by this time on board the French fishing-boat,' observed Mr Calder. 'Ah, Rawson! we have reason to be grateful, man, and we should do well if we left off grumbling for the rest of our lives.'

'You would deprive all poor old mates of the only privilege they possess,' answered Rawson; 'that would be hard indeed.'

The frigate, it was found, was bound out to the North-American station. This was a great disappointment, as Mr Calder, especially, was anxious to rejoin the 'Thisbe' as soon as possible, not to lose his chance of promotion.

However, although the gale continued to increase, Captain Markham was not the man to put back into port as long as he could possibly keep the sea. He had a good deal of the Flying Dutchman spirit about him, without the profanity of that far-famed navigator, which has so justly doomed him to so unenviable a notoriety.

The frigate was rolling and pitching somewhat heavily, as Ronald and his companions found their way into the midshipmen's berth.

'Take your seats. You are welcome here, mates,' said the caterer as they entered. 'We shall have food on the table in a jiffy. There's cold beef, and salt pork, and soft tack, and here is some honest Jamaica rum. Not a bad exchange for the Frenchman's wish-wash claret, I suspect.'

The reception, altogether, given to the new comers was cordial, if unrefined, and not many minutes had elapsed before they were all perfectly at home. Ronald, less accustomed than the rest to a midshipman's berth, felt more inclined than usual to be silent. He found himself seated next to a midshipman, who differed considerably, both in manners and in many points, from his companions. His appearance was not at the first glance in his favour. He was red-haired, and tall, and thin; so tall, indeed, that when he stood up his shoulders touched the deck above, and his head and neck formed an arch over the table. He must have been eighteen or nineteen years old at least; indeed, he might have been older, though he still wore the uniform of a midshipman. Ronald thought that he was rather dogmatical, though his remarks were characterised by shrewd, good sense, not destitute of humour. It was not till he stood up that Ronald, who had been looking round the berth to discover the person who had just rendered him such essential service, felt sure that he was the one. Ronald suddenly put out his hand.

'I have to thank you for saving my life just now,' he exclaimed with genuine warmth. 'If it had not been for you I should be floating away dead astern.'

'It cost me but little to haul you up, so say no more about

it,' answered the tall midshipman. ' I happened to be looking over the side, and caught a glimpse of your head as you were hanging on like a codfish just caught by a hook. Besides, I find you come from the far north, and we Scotchmen always help each other.'

Ronald had detected a slight Scotch accent in his new friend.

' You must let me be grateful, at all events,' he answered. ' And you won't heave me overboard again when I tell you that I am not a Scotchman, but a Shetlander.'

' I knew that when you began to speak,' observed the tall midshipman; and they went on to talk about Shetland, and before long the latter had learned several particulars of Ronald's history.

' We must be friends for the future,' he observed, as the master-at-arms appeared at the door of the berth, with the announcement that it was time to douse the glim, and the various members whose watch it was below hurried off to their hammocks with as little concern as if the ship lay snug at her anchors, instead of being exposed to the full fury of a heavy gale.

The frigate was kept thrashing at it, in the hopes that she might hold her own till the storm abated. The important result of the first lieutenant's constant care and attention to the fitting of the rigging was now fully exhibited. Not a strand of a rope parted, not a spar was sprung.

Ronald soon saw that the tall midshipman was a great favourite with Mr Lawrence, the rough diamond of a first lieutenant, nor was he surprised when he found that he was a lord, and yet the most attentive to his duty, and most eager to master all the details of his profession.

Lord Claymore, the tall midshipman, and Ronald soon became fast friends. Ronald admired him especially for the good sense and judgment he displayed in conversation, and the coolness and courage he exhibited in danger.

The gale continued, and the frigate lay her course to cross the Atlantic.

'She has been making much lee-way,' Ronald heard the master observe to the captain.

'We shall weather Cape Clear for all that,' was the answer; 'once free we may run before it with a flowing sheet to the banks of Newfoundland.'

'Ay, if we are once free,' muttered the master, who was not at all of the touch-and-go school.

On stood the frigate. It was night. The midshipmen who had been rescued from the fishing-boat were allowed, after their fatigues, to remain below without doing duty for some days. Ronald could not sleep. This was very unmidshipman-like; he knew that it was Claymore's watch on deck, and he thought he would take a turn with him. He dressed and went on deck; it was not a tempting night; it was still blowing very hard, and the frigate under close-reefed topsails was heeling to the breeze till her leeports were deeply submerged, while the spray in thick showers flew over her. Ronald soon found his tall friend.

'I like this,' observed the latter with enthusiasm, rubbing his hands; 'the wind is strong enough to blow every inch of canvas out of the bolt ropes, if it wasn't all good and new, or to send the masts over the side if they were not well stayed up. We have the land under our lee, and if anything was to go we should in all probability drive on to it. Now, just consider the satisfaction of knowing that everything is as strong and good as wood, iron, and hemp can be, and of feeling that one has contributed to that end. There isn't a block, or a spar, or a rope, that Jack Lawrence or I haven't overhauled. See the advantage. He sleeps as soundly as if we were in harbour, when most other first lieutenants would have been up and down fifty times to ascertain that all was going right, and not have slept a wink. Take a leaf out of his book, Morton—it's what I am doing, and intend continuing to do.'

'Land on the lee-bow!' cried one of the looks-out forward.

Had any one been drowsy, that sound would have made

them rouse up very rapidly. All eyes were directly turned towards the quarter indicated. The clouds had broken away in that direction, and a gleam of light fell on the threatening headland. The officer of the watch sent a midshipman down to call the captain and master. They were on deck almost as soon as he was. The compass was consulted, and the bearing of the land taken. The master then went below to consult the chart. Claymore begged Morton to go and call the first lieutenant.

'We take things coolly aboard here, but he would not like to be below at this time, and would thank you for summoning him.'

Mr Lawrence sprang on deck after Morton. A consultation was held; it was the general opinion that the land seen was Mizen Head, and that if there were light sufficient, Cape Clear would be seen on their quarter. They might take shelter in Crook Haven; but under the uncertainty that the point seen was Mizen Head, the master refused to undertake the fearful responsibility. The determination to keep the sea was also more in accordance with the captain's inclinations.

'She has drifted to leeward more than I suspected; we must yet shake another reef out of the topsails,' he observed. 'What say you, master—do you think she will bear it?'

'She must bear it,' was the answer.

'She will bear it,' said Jack Lawrence, positively.

The united strength of all the crew was required to perform the operation.

'All hands on deck!' shouted the boatswain, giving emphasis to the summons with his shrill whistle.

Directly the order was given one of the first aloft was Claymore; Morton followed him on to the main-yard; it was not his duty to go aloft, but he could not resist the impulse which made him do so. It was fearful work, holding on to that yard, up in the darkness, with the fierce gale howling round their heads and the ship pitching furiously, while at the same time she heeled down over the roaring seas. The word was given to let go; but before the sail could be sheeted home it shook and struggled, almost freeing itself from the sturdy crew who were hauling away on the sheet.

Morton felt as if he should be shaken off the yard, but a hand with a firm grasp held him, nor let him go till he had reached the top. They descended on deck.

'Thank you, Lord Claymore,' said Morton, warmly; 'had you not held me I might have lost my life.'

'I don't say you would have deserved it,' said the tall midshipman; 'but why rush to a post of danger without necessity? stronger and older men are better fitted for the task you attempted. It was my duty, and I went. However, I like your spirit, Morton. If we weather this cape we shall know more of each other; if our masts go over the side, or we otherwise fail, we may none of us see another sunrise.'

He spoke as coolly and calmly as if talking on some ordinary topic.

Away the ship plunged through the seas more furiously than ever, bending down till it seemed as if her yard-arms literally touched the foaming tops of the seas as they came rolling and hissing by. Every officer was at his post: the captain, with his lips compressed and teeth clenched, stood watching, now the bending masts, now the compass, now the dark threatening land. The frigate drew nearer and nearer to it; still she flew ahead. A quartermaster and two of the best seaman in the ship were at the helm; Jack Lawrence stood near them; they were doing as well as he could desire.

'Keep your luff, lads,' he said once in a quiet tone; 'steady —that will do.'

Not another word was spoken by him, or by any one on deck; all eyes were riveted on the land. The ship seemed to be making no progress, for there it still lay on the lee-bow. Some thought they could hear the roaring of the surges, as with the whole force of a south-westerly gale they were hurled against the cliffs. Still the canvas held the fierce wind, and the well-set-up rigging supported the masts.

'Morton, the land is drawing abeam,' exclaimed Claymore suddenly; 'the ship will be saved. I did not think so at one time, though.'

He was right: gradually it seemed to rise up more broad on the lee-beam; but as the ship surged onward amid wildly-leaping waves, the water, lashed into masses of foam, was seen over the lee-quarter leaping over the cliff from which she had so narrowly escaped. Still there were other points and headlands farther to the north, from which she was not altogether clear. For another two hours or more the same press of canvas was kept on her. Few breathed freely till the order was being given to take another reef in the topsails; the order was accomplished without a casualty, and the watch below were allowed to turn in.

Some days after this the 'Thetis' fell in with a line-of-battle ship homeward bound: she took Mr Calder and his companions on board.

'We shall meet again, I hope,' said Lord Claymore, as Morton was about to go down the side.

'I should be sorry if I did not think so,' answered Morton, as the young men grasped each other's hands.

Westward steered the 'Thetis,' and eastward the huge old 'Thunderer;' the latter reached England, and the officers and men of the 'Thisbe' once more rejoined her, to the satisfaction of most of their friends, who had given them up for lost.

The 'Thisbe' finished her commission with considerable credit to her captain, officers, and crew, who had likewise not a small amount of prize-money to boast of. Ronald Morton on his being paid off joined a sloop-of-war in the West Indies; here he especially distinguished himself, and, to the great delight of his father, obtained his promotion. He returned home, and was immediately appointed second lieutenant of his old ship, the 'Thisbe,' now commanded by Captain Calder, and bound out to the East Indies.

CHAPTER XX.

RONALD SECOND LIEUTENANT OF THE 'THISBE.'—A BALL AT CALCUTTA.—RONALD'S GALLANTRY.—A CHALLENGE.—HIS REPLY.

RONALD MORTON had gone through the usual vicissitudes of a midshipman's career, during the full swing of a hot and somewhat bloody war.

He had run a good many chances of being knocked on the head, but he had done a good many things also to be proud of, though he was not overmuch so, and he had gained a fair amount of credit.

Once more he was on board his old ship, the 'Thisbe.' When he first joined he was a ship's boy; he was now her second lieutenant. The first was Rawson—he was a totally changed man. He had performed a very gallant action under the eye of the admiral, had been highly spoken of in the 'Gazette,' had in consequence at once received his promotion, and had been an active, enterprising officer ever since. He seldom or never grumbled now, or talked of his bad luck; indeed he seemed to think that the world was a very good sort of place for some men to live in, and that the British navy was not a bad profession after all for a fellow to belong to. He and Ronald Morton had not met for some years. They were glad to find themselves once again shipmates.

The 'Thisbe' was commanded by one they both loved and

respected—honest, gallant, fighting Tom Calder. Tom had won his upward way by courage and zeal, rarely surpassed. The Lords of the Admiralty could not refuse him his promotion, had they wished it. The whole navy would have cried out at the injustice. Happily, honest Tom had no one to whisper evil against him. He had not an enemy in the world—so, to be sure, it is sometimes said of a goose, but then the goose is his own enemy. Tom, on the contrary, had proved true to himself, and that, in fact, lay at the bottom of his success.

Of the old 'Thisbes,' as they were pleased to call themselves, Dicky Glover was the only officer. He was, however, still a mate. He was senior mate, though he could not help now and then just thinking that it would not be so very unfortunate—only a merciful dispensation of Providence—should they go into action, seeing that somebody must be killed, should a shot happen to knock over the third lieutenant, and give him a chance of promotion—not but what Dicky had a very kind feeling for the said third lieutenant. He was always ready to do him any service, to lend him his books or money; the latter the lieutenant was most fond of borrowing: still Dicky and he were very good friends; Dicky had plenty of money, and Peter Sims, the third lieutenant, had none. How he had got his promotion was surprising to those who knew him, till it was whispered about that he had a very near relative in a high position, who had no difficulty in obtaining it for him. Sims was, however, generally liked; he was very inoffensive, he never talked about himself or his friends, seemed to wish to be let alone, and to let others alone. He was always ready to do a good-natured action, to take a brother officer's watch, or to give up his own leave to accommodate another.

Before the mast there were several hands who had served in the 'Thisbe,' when commanded by Captain Courtney. Two had attached themselves especially to Ronald—one was Job Truefitt, and the other Bobby Doull. No men could have been more faithful or attached than they were to him—Job regarded him as his son, and constituted himself his guardian, while Bobby looked up to him as to a superior being whom it was an honour to follow and obey.

The frigate was bound out to the land so famed for tigers, and curry, palanquins, pagodas, and prize-money—the East Indies; she had a quick run down Channel, when a northerly breeze carried her almost to the tropics.

Rio was visited; the frigate touched at the Cape, and finally anchored at the mouth of the Hooghly, near the flag-ship of the admiral on the station.

The usual compliments passed, the sails were furled, and shore-boats, manned by strange-looking natives, with stranger-looking fruits and vegetables, chattering unknown tongues intended to be English, came alongside. The admiral himself was up at Calcutta, and everybody on board the 'Thisbe' was anxious to pay a visit to the city of palaces. Sims offered to stop, but Rawson bluntly told him that he could not trust the ship to his charge; so he, pocketing the compliment, accompanied the captain and Morton, with two or three more of the gun-room officers, and Glover and several of the midshipmen, up to the city. They luckily took their full-dress uniforms with them; and having lionized the city in palanquins all the day, they found themselves in the evening at a magnificent ball, given by one of the principal officers of the Company's Civil Service.

The officers of the 'Thisbe' stopped near the entrance to admire the brilliant spectacle. Superb chandeliers hung from the ceiling or projected from the walls, amid gay coloured banners, and wreaths of exquisite flowers; while below them moved the fairest of Eve's daughters to be found in the capital of the East, amid numerous military officers in various handsome uniforms; and rajahs, and nabobs, and princes, and chiefs of every description, habited in the richest and most picturesque of oriental costumes, with turbans and daggers and sword-hilts sparkling with gold and silver, and gems of fabulous value.

The gallant captain of the frigate, and most of the officers who accompanied him, were more accustomed to the quarter-deck, and the battle and the breeze, than to ball-rooms or palaces, and they stood for some time totally entranced, and scarcely able to express their surprise to each other at the gay scene.

Morton had in his boyhood learned most of the dances then in vogue, and a quick eye and perfect self-possession enabled him to appear to advantage when at rare intervals he entered a ball-room. Still, feeling himself a stranger among a crowd, he very naturally preferred remaining in a quiet spot, that he might at his leisure watch what was going forward. Captain Calder felt very much as he did, for he was even still less accustomed to ball-rooms, though his true gentlemanly feelings and innate sense of propriety prevented him from committing any solecism in good manners. Sims and Dicky Glover stood together.

'This is very slow work, sir, I think,' observed Dicky to his superior, with whom, bye-the-bye, he felt himself in a ball-room on the most perfect equality. 'I vote we shove forward, and look out for partners. There are lots of pretty girls, and I flatter myself that if they were asked they would prefer us blue-jackets to the red-coats.'

'As to that I am not quite certain,' answered the lieutenant. 'You see these soldier officers out here, at all events, are generally matrimonially inclined, while such would be a very inconvenient inclination for us to indulge in; and so not from superior merit but from the force of circumstances the soldiers are likely to carry the day.'

'That argument of yours is irresistible, but still I don't see that it should make us give up our chance of a dance,' answered Glover, pushing a little more forward.

Like riflemen they advanced, skirmishing, one supporting the other. Dicky, however, was the most adventurous; without him, probably, Sims would have remained in the background. Sims had some modesty. Glover had the allowance with which, for wise ends, midshipmen are usually gifted.

'There's a pretty girl! she hasn't footed it for a long time; there's nothing like trying it. I'll go and ask her,' exclaimed Dicky, as if suddenly seized with an irresistible impulse; and before Sims could make any remark he had crossed the intervening space to where the lady at whom he had pointed was sitting, and was bowing and scraping, and smiling with the greatest self-confidence.

The young lady looked rather astonished, and not over well pleased, but this did not in any way abash Mr Glover. While he with praiseworthy perseverance was still scraping away, requesting the hand of the lady for a cotillion, a minuette, or a country-dance, a gentleman came up and spoke to her. Glover looked at her earnestly, and spoke a few words; she put out her hand, he took it, and wrung it till she almost cried out.

'Cousin Susan!' he exclaimed. 'Well, I didn't think it was you, and yet I ought to have known you among a thousand. But you know you were but a little girl when we last met, and now you are grown up and married. Well—but I'm so very glad!—how jolly! I didn't expect to enjoy this ball; but now I shall like it very much.'

Thus Glover rattled on, and to the surprise of Morton and Sims, and his other shipmates, who had not overheard the conversation, was seen standing up to dance with an air of conscious superiority and perfect self-satisfaction. Sims was rather jealous. Morton was highly amused. Glover flew up and down the room, enjoying the dance to the full. What cared he for the heat. What mattered to him that he trod on the toes of innumerable rajahs and nabobs, who would gladly have stuck their jewel-hilted daggers into him, or given him an embrace with a tiger's claw; an instrument worthy of Asiatic invention. His cousin, however, had soon introduced Glover to a more active partner, and so engrossed was he at first that he quite forgot to come back to his friends.

While Morton was watching the dancers an officer with a young lady stood up near him to join them. His eye was attracted to her countenance, and he was struck by its excessively pleasing expression. He looked and looked again: he thought her exquisitely beautiful, and while he looked he could not help half fancying that he had seen that countenance before. Still where it had been he could not discover; he had seen so few ladies during his sea-life that he was convinced he should, before long, remember. Yet what puzzled him was, that he felt so very familiar with the countenance. Eyes have a remarkable sympathy for each other; after a time the lady knew that she was observed—not with idle, careless admiration, but especially noticed. She looked up for a moment and observed a countenance of manly beauty and intelligence not easily forgotten. There were none in that vast assemblage to be compared to it, she thought, and yet she tried not to allow herself to dwell on the thought; her partner carried her off in the rapid dance.

Morton stood watching her with greater interest than he would have allowed even to himself.

'Yes, I must have seen her—but where? In my dreams —in my fancy,' he muttered to himself as his eyes continued following the fair young girl. 'Nonsense! I am allowing my imagination to run away with me. And yet I do know that countenance, I am certain of it.'

Perhaps the young lady saw his eyes following hers. She seemed at all events to be paying but very little attention to the observations of her partner.

Morton at length noticed him; he was a young man, and had the air of a person thoroughly well satisfied with himself; but as Ronald watched him more narrowly he was convinced that he had taken more wine than his head could bear; his flushed countenance and unsteady movements after a time showed this. His partner probably had made the same discovery; and though in those days his condition would not have excited the disgust it would at the present in the mind of a well-educated girl, she was evidently anxious to obtain a seat, and to release herself from his society. Still he held her hand with a look of maudlin admiration, and insisted on forcing her once more down the dance. It was evident that she would have to struggle to escape from him, and rather than attract observation she allowed herself to be dragged once more towards the bottom of the room.

Such was the interpretation Morton put on what he witnessed, and he felt strongly inclined to rush forward to assist her. The couple had got close to him, by which time the gentleman had become still more excited and unsteady—his foot slipped—the fair girl looked up imploringly at Morton's countenance, so he thought—her partner fell to the ground, and would have dragged her with him, when Ronald sprang forward and saved her from the threatened catastrophe.

'Thank you—thank you!—oh take me to my friend!' she exclaimed, her voice trembling with nervousness.

Ronald led her through the crowd; her partner picked himself up, and uttering an exclamation would have followed them, had not some acquaintance near at hand held him back, and ultimately persuaded him quietly to retire to another room; leave the ball altogether, he would not.

'To be cut out by a sea-monster, a porpoise, a mere nautilus —that will never do!' he hicupped out. 'No, no—I must have my revenge on the fellow. I'll insult him; drill a hole in him; my honour requires it. Couldn't show my face again until I have killed my man.'

The young man did not give vent to these expressions until his more sensible acquaintance had retired; but two or three much of his own character remained, who partly from a love of mischief, utterly regardless of the consequences, persuaded him that he had received so gross an insult that it could be atoned for only by mortal combat.

'We'll settle matters for you,' said Lieutenant Bolton, a chum of Maguire's. 'Go back when you feel a little better; tread on his toe, or dig your elbow into his ribs, and tell him quietly you intended to do so. It will wonderfully facilitate our arrangements.

Meantime Morton—totally unconscious of the annoyance preparing for him, and with the fair stranger whom he had rescued resting on his arm, was looking for a vacant seat in which to place her.

'Who is your chaperone?' he asked. 'Where do you think we can find her?'

'Mrs Edmonstone,' she answered. 'Mamma was unwell, and papa could not come till late in the evening, and so she took charge of me. She is one of the few ladies we know well in Calcutta, and whom mamma liked to ask to take her place. Ah, there she comes : she will, I am sure, thank you, as I do, for saving me from so very disagreeable an accident.'

'I rejoice that you escaped it,' answered Morton before he looked up; when he did so he saw approaching them the very lady with whom Glover seemed to be so well acquainted: she now had his arm.

'That is Mrs Edmonstone,' said Morton's companion. 'There are two seats; she is going to take one. I am afraid I must sit down.

Morton led her to the seat next her friend, and would have retired, though most unwilling so to do, when Glover caught him by the arm, exclaiming, 'Mr Morton, allow me to introduce you to my cousin, Mrs Edmonstone—she wishes to make your acquaintance; she knows that if it had not been for you, I should have been food for the sharks long ago.'

Dicky had indeed been saying a number of complimentary things about Morton, which he fully deserved. Mrs Edmonstone held out her hand and said frankly, 'I am indeed glad to have an opportunity of thanking you for saving my cousin's life, and affording him the advantage of your friendship; your name, and, I may say, your many gallant deeds, have long been familiar to me: all his family are grateful to you.'

Morton bowed and felt gratified, for Mrs Edmonstone's manner was so frank and cordial that he experienced none of the oppression which a sensitive person is apt to feel when receiving compliments, however well merited, if not bestowed with tact. She, supposing naturally that he had already been introduced to her younger companion, did not think it necessary again to go through that ceremony.

Encouraged by her manner, Morton remained talking in an animated way to her and her friend, Glover standing by and occasionally indulging in amusing remarks, which savoured more of the salt ocean than of the ball-room, but had no want of refinement to shock the ears of his auditors. Morton felt himself altogether in a new world; it was not very strange, but it was very different to anything he had ever before enjoyed; he put forth powers of conversation which he had not supposed himself to possess. He also was struck with the lively and intelligent remarks of the younger lady, and at the same time enchanted with the perfect simplicity which they betokened.

'Certainly her manners and conversation do not belie her looks; she is charming, she is perfect,' he more than once said to himself.

Few men can so conceal their feelings, especially if they are not aware what those feelings are, when in conversation with a lady, without her having an idea, undefined and uncertain though it may be, of the matter. The party were so interested in each other's conversation that they might have continued talking till supper was announced, entirely regardless of what was going forward in the rest of the room, had they not been interrupted by the appearance of another person on the stage, who came up to claim the young lady's hand.

He was slight and, though not very tall, of a good figure, with handsome features, and a remarkably dark complexion; he was dressed in a rich semi-oriental military costume, and had a dashing independent air about him, which Morton thought approached very much to a swagger, but perhaps at that moment he was not a very unprejudiced judge. Ronald could not help staring at him in a somewhat marked manner.

'Extraordinary!' he exclaimed to himself, 'that I should come unexpectedly into this ball-room and meet two persons with whose countenances I am so familiar, and yet not have the slightest notion who they are. That young man's face I know perfectly well; I must have met him over and over again, in a very different dress to what he now wears, and under very different circumstances, and I must have known him intimately, of that I am certain.'

'Do you not dance, Mr Morton?' asked Mrs Edmonstone, seeing him look about the room, as he was doing, in an abstracted manner, and fancying that he wished probably to be introduced to a partner. The instant her voice recalled his scattered senses, 'Thank you,' he answered; 'I so seldom have had opportunities of doing so that I can scarcely call myself a dancer; at present I confess that I feel more amusement in looking on than I should in dancing.'

'Can you tell me,' said Morton, 'who is that young man in the handsome costume, who is dancing with your friend?'

'I can indeed say very little about him,' was the answer. 'He is a Captain Gerardo, I understand,—a foreigner, that is to say, not English; either a Frenchman, or Spaniard, or Portuguese. He has been attached to one of the native courts in the East—I do not know which—and has come here on his travels before returning home. He seems to have come with several good introductions, especially to natives of high rank, and must be wealthy, as he is lavish in his expenditure. My husband, however, is not quite satisfied about him, and is making inquiries to ascertain whether or not he is an impostor.

Numbers come to this country expecting to find a fine field for the exercise of their talents. They now and then, however, have to beat a precipitate retreat. I would not willingly have allowed my sweet friend, Edda, to dance with him, but he has been introduced to her father, who rather affects him, and I could not interfere.'

' Edda!' repeated Ronald to himself, the name conjuring up a thousand recollections of his far-distant home, for he had there heard it frequently. ' What is your friend's surname?' he asked; ' I did not hear it.'

' She is the daughter of Colonel and Mrs Armytage, who are at present in Calcutta. He is on the staff—a somewhat haughty, proud man, and not a favourite of mine, but she is a gentle, amiable woman; only yields too much to him, I think.'

' How strange!' repeated Ronald aloud.

' Do you know them, Mr Morton?' she asked.

' If Mrs Armytage is the daughter of Sir Marcus Wardhill, of Lunnasting Castle, in Shetland, I know of them, though I have not seen her since I was a child. I was born on the estate, and brought up by her elder sister, who had lost her own child. Her story is a very romantic and sad one. You probably have heard of it.'

' Something, but I do not recollect all the particulars; Edda herself knows but little. The families keep up no communication, I fancy.'

' But slight,' said Morton, not liking to enter too minutely into particulars, and yet deeply interested. ' I have news from Shetland occasionally, but I have not been there since I was a boy.'

' Shall I tell Miss Armytage that you know her family?' asked Mrs Edmonstone, with some hesitation.

Ronald considered a moment. ' I will beg you not to do so,' he answered. There can be no object gained. She knows nothing of my family, and probably takes but little interest in Shetland itself, while I have reason to know that her father has not for many years been on good terms with Sir Marcus Wardhill.'

'Probably you are right; I will do as you wish,' said the lady, and she kept her word.

Supper was over, and the guests began to take their departure. Morton and Glover saw Mrs Edmonstone and Miss Armytage to their carriage, and were going back to wait for the rest of their shipmates, when a young man in military uniform stepped up to the former, and, politely bowing, said that he had been deputed by his friend, Lieutenant Maguire, to demand the only reparation which one gentleman could afford another, for an insult he had that evening received.

'Assuredly, sir, you mistake my identity,' answered Morton, calmly. 'I am not acquainted with Lieutenant Maguire, nor have I insulted, intentionally or otherwise, any human being.'

'Some people entertain very different notions to others as to what is an insult,' said the officer, with a sneer, intended to excite Morton's anger. 'My friend Maguire is exceedingly sensitive as to his honour. Not to lose time, sir, by any circumlocution in my remarks, you are, sir, I am led to understand, Lieutenant Morton, of his Majesty's frigate 'Thisbe'?'

'I am, sir,' said Morton; 'your information on that point is correct.'

'I knew I was right, sir,' said the young officer, with a bullying air, mistaking a look of astonishment, which Morton could not suppress, for an exhibition of fear. 'Mr Maguire conceives that early this evening you purposely tripped him up, and when you had brought him to the ground, you carried off his partner and laughed at him. Any one of these acts, sir, was an insult, to be washed out only with blood, as any man with a spark of honour in his composition will allow.'

Morton, though very much inclined to laugh at this absurd

assertion, felt at the same time it was annoying. The only reply he could give was, that the young man was tipsy, and fell in consequence, and that he had nothing whatever to do with the matter. This answer would not be satisfactory to the gentleman who had brought the challenge. Still, it seemed too preposterous that he should allow himself to be drawn into a quarrel, against his will, by hair-brained young men who had lost the few wits they possessed by drinking. His own high sense of honour had never before been called in question—his gallantry had always been conspicuous.

'I cannot reply to you at once,' he answered quietly, turning to Lieutenant Maguire's second. 'Leave me your card and address, and I promise you you shall hear from me. Perhaps, in the meantime, your friend and his advisers may think better of the matter, and, at all events, you can convey him my assurance that I had no intention of insulting him, or of hurting his feelings in any way.'

'Well, sir, I must be content with your reply, though I cannot say that I conceive it to be a very satisfactory one. My name is Bolton, a brother officer of Maguire's. Here is my card and address. I shall expect your friend.' Saying this, the young man, with a pompous air, turned on his heel and walked out of the room.

'This is indeed provoking, to have a quarrel thus pertinaciously fixed on me,' said Morton, taking Glover's arm. 'I must see the captain, and put the matter into his hands.'

Morton told Captain Calder what had occurred.

He looked considerably vexed, though he laughed as he answered, 'I will act as your friend, as it is called, with all my heart, and go and see these young donkeys. If they insist on fighting, it shall be with cutlasses or boat stretchers. Do they think sailors are accustomed to handle their little pop-guns, and practise to commit murder with a steady hand? But seriously, my dear Morton, what do you wish?'

'To abide by God's laws, Captain Calder, and to set at nought those of men,' answered the lieutenant.

'Spoken like yourself, Morton, and I have no fear that discredit will be brought on the service if we all so act,' said the captain. And now let us collect our forces, and beat a retreat to our quarters.'

CHAPTER XXI.

PARTY AT MRS EDMONSTONE'S.—INTRODUCTION TO COLONEL ARMYTAGE.—VISIT TO THE 'OSTERLEY.'—THE 'THISBE' ORDERED TO BOMBAY.

ORTON had been anticipating a delightful day: he was to have called, with Glover, on Mrs Edmonstone, and he hoped to have met Miss Armytage, who was staying with her; but his first thought on waking was the disagreeable circumstance which had occurred at the conclusion of the previous evening, and the still more disagreeable events to which it would in all probability give rise.

He was well aware how much the line of conduct he intended to pursue would be criticised, how the story would be garbled and misrepresented, and how, in all probability, he would be accused of showing the white feather. Under ordinary circumstances he would have been very indifferent to what was said of him: he could well afford to allow idle tongues to prattle forth slander about him till weary of the occupation, but he could not bear to fancy that Mrs Edmonstone, or rather her friend, should hear anything to his disadvantage which he might not be present to refute; still, happily, he had not forgotten Bertha Eswick's remark, impressed on his mind in childhood—' Do what is right, lad, and never mind what men say of thee.'

The temptation of meeting Miss Armytage was at last too strong to be resisted, and with his captain and brother officers he repaired in the evening to the house of Mrs Edmonstone. Their hostess received them in the most friendly manner, and introduced them to several of her friends, so that they at once felt themselves at home. Morton's eyes ranged round the room in search of Miss Armytage; she was nowhere to be seen. He longed to ask Mrs Edmonstone where she was, but he was withheld by a feeling of bashfulness very unusual with him. Numberless fears entered his mind. Was she prevented by illness from appearing—had her father heard who he was, and kept her away that she might not meet him; or had Colonel Armytage been suddenly called away to another part of the country, and had his daughter accompanied him?

That the latter suspicion was correct he was convinced by overhearing the disjointed remarks of some people near him: 'Great loss to our society—quite unexpected—very charming woman—sweet girl, the daughter. About him—two opinions —proud——'

The speakers moved on. Morton was convinced that the sweet girl must refer to Miss Armytage—surely to no one else. But then came the thought that he was not to see her that evening—perhaps he might never again meet her. The pain and disappointment he felt opened his eyes more rapidly than anything else would have done to his own feelings. As to enjoying the evening, that was out of the question. Still it would be a satisfaction to hear something about her. He would inquire where Colonel Armytage had gone. He was looking round for Mrs Edmonstone, as he felt that he could ask her better than any one else, when his heart gave an unwonted bound, for he saw entering the room, and leaning on the arm of a fine military-looking man, whom he had no doubt was her father, Miss Armytage herself. On the other side of her, endeavouring to engage her in conversation, walked the stranger whom Glover thought so like Alfonse Gerardin. The resemblance struck Morton, as his glance fell on his countenance, as even greater than on the previous evening. Miss Armytage seemed rather annoyed than otherwise with his attentions. As Morton had been walking forward when he first saw the group he could not stop short, so he continued to advance. The young lady put out her hand frankly, though a gentle blush rose on her cheeks as she did so.

'Papa,' she said, 'I must introduce Mr Morton to you. I am sure that you wish to thank him for the service he rendered me yesterday evening.'

Colonel Armytage bowed, and assured Mr Morton that he was exceedingly obliged to him; but he said this in a stiff way, which evidently annoyed his daughter.

'I was fortunate indeed in being at hand; but I can claim no merit,' replied Morton, in a modest manner.

Mrs Edmonstone came up and welcomed her young friend.

'I am so glad you have come back,' she exclaimed, affectionately taking her hand. 'I was quite vexed at your having to run away to a dinner-party, lest you should be too tired to dance this evening.'

Edda assured her that she was not. She, on this, turned round quickly to Ronald. 'You dance, sometimes, Mr Morton, I know.'

'Yes,' he answered quickly, stepping forward and asking Miss Armytage to dance.

She smiled and promised.

The young stranger looked very much annoyed. He had fancied himself secure of her hand. Many men of rank and wealth would have been proud of the honour Ronald had obtained, though not more proud than he was. That evening was the brightest he had ever spent. But there were clouds in the horizon. He learned that Colonel Armytage had received a high appointment at Bombay, and that they were about at once to sail for that presidency, on board the 'Osterley,' a Company's ship, which was to touch there on her passage home.

'We sail in two weeks or so,' said Miss Armytage. 'I shall be truly sorry to leave Calcutta.'

'I had little expected to find it so delightful a place,' answered Ronald.

Miss Armytage slightly blushed when he said this. Why, she could scarcely tell. Perhaps it was his manner—perhaps an unconscious look he gave. Though many sought her hand, she declined dancing again, in consequence of feeling tired, from having danced so much the previous evening.

Ronald was constantly by her side; for whenever he left it, he was quickly again attracted back; nor was he ever in want of an excuse for returning. Towards the end of the evening he observed the eyes of several people glancing towards him. It struck him that he formed the subject of conversation, especially among a group of military men. It was not, however, till he happened to meet Sims that his suspicions were confirmed.

'I knew it would be so,' said his brother lieutenant. 'The fellows here, among the military, have got an idea that you refused to fight Maguire; and I believe that donkey, Bolton, has been setting the story afloat. I should like to keel-haul him.'

'Let him alone; it matters little what so insignificant a fellow says or does,' observed Morton. 'The story can hardly last out the usual nine days; and if we all behave well, we can allow these empty-headed fellows to amuse themselves for that time at our expense.'

The ball came to a conclusion without any unusual occurrence. Morton could not help feeling sure that he stood well in the opinion of Miss Armytage. He had so little conceit in his composition that it never for a moment occurred to him that he had excited any warmer sentiment.

After this he frequently met her at Mrs Edmonstone's, as well as at other houses. She invariably received him in the same friendly manner, and exhibited evident pleasure in his society.

Probably she had not dared to probe her own feelings. Colonel Armytage treated him as he would any other young officer who had proved a credit to his profession. Mrs Edmonstone always treated him with the greatest consideration.

'I have told her all about you, sir,' said Dicky Glover one day. 'That cousin of mine is a first-rate person, and she says she thinks it an honour to know you.'

'I am much obliged to her for her good opinion,' was Morton's reply.

His spirits were somewhat low; the 'Osterley' was about to sail. He had by chance become acquainted with her commander, Captain Winslow. By his invitation he was on board to receive Colonel Armytage and his family. He conducted Mrs and Miss Armytage over the ship.

'I wish that you were to accompany us in the frigate,' said Mrs Armytage. 'In war time we do not know what enemies we may have to encounter.'

'I should indeed rejoice, if my duty would allow it; but I trust that you will have no cause for alarm: the 'Osterley' is said to be a fast ship, and report speaks highly of her commander, Captain Winslow.'

Mrs Armytage had spoken without thought. She had been much pleased with Morton, and it did not occur to her that her daughter might have been so likewise, in a far greater degree, or that he might misinterpret her remark.

'Oh, of course I see that would be out of the question,' she observed; 'but perhaps the admiral would send your ship to Bombay, and then you could watch us. I do not know how it is, but I have a perfect dread of this voyage.'

Ronald Morton did his best to soothe the lady's alarm, hoping also that she would not impart it to her daughter.

Colonel Armytage, when he rejoined the party, was considerably annoyed at hearing the remarks of his wife.

Ronald could not help feeling that his manner on the present occasion was colder than ever, and somewhat supercilious into the bargain. He, by some means or other, introduced the subject of duelling, and spoke of it as the only method by which gentlemen could settle their disputes. 'Military men, of course, hold their lives in their hands, and the man who shirks a duel, or does not insist on having satisfaction for an insult offered him, should, in my opinion, leave the noble profession of arms and turn shopkeeper or shepherd. When I commanded a regiment, if any officer showed the white feather in that respect, I took good care that he should not long be one of ours.'

Morton could scarcely doubt that the colonel's remarks were aimed at him; but he thought of his gentle daughter, and refrained from making any reply. A still higher motive might also have restrained him.

A pilot vessel accompanied the Indiaman till she was clear of the river. Morton was therefore able to accept Captain Winslow's invitation to remain on board till the ship was left to pursue her voyage alone.

Had Colonel Armytage exhibited towards him, at first, the same temper that he did subsequently, he would have felt himself compelled, however much against his will, to return on shore. Fortunately the colonel was engaged for the greater part of the day in writing in his cabin, so that Ronald was able to enjoy several hours of uninterrupted intercourse with Miss Armytage; nor did he, when her father appeared, alter in the slightest degree his tone of conversation or manner towards her.

At length the huge Indiaman was fairly out at sea. The pilot announced that he must take his departure. Morton bade farewell to his friends. Mrs Armytage held out her hand frankly, and her daughter followed her example, though there was a softness and perceptible tremor in her voice which made him wish more than ever that he could take Captain Winslow's place, or even that of one of his officers. Colonel Armytage parted with him with a cold shake of the hand and a formal 'Good-bye, sir;' and he was in the boat and soon on board the pilot vessel. The Indiaman's yards were swung round, and under all sail she stood to the southward.

No sooner had Morton reached the deck of the pilot vessel than, as he stood astern watching the Indiaman, his eye fell far beyond her, in the horizon, on a sail. He saw that it was a large ship. He pointed her out to the pilot.

'Yes, sir, there's no doubt of it. She is a large ship,' was the answer. 'Maybe she's an Indiaman bound up the Hooghly. Maybe she's the "Rajah," which sailed two days ago, and has been becalmed; or a China ship looking in for orders; or one of the men-of-war on the station.'

'I care not what she is, provided she is not an enemy's cruiser,' said Morton. 'She seems to have very square yards.'

'Difficult to make that out, I should think,' muttered the pilot as he walked the deck, and then went forward to give some directions to his native crew.

Till the pilot vessel re-entered the Hooghly, and Morton lost sight of the Indiaman, his eye was seldom off her, while his thoughts were even still more constant.

Once more he was on board the 'Thisbe.' He felt no inclination to revisit Calcutta, and he only went up there once to pay his respects to Mrs Edmonstone. She very naturally talked of Miss Armytage, and spoke warmly in her praise. It was a subject of which Morton was not likely to grow tired.

'Admiral Rainer tells me that he has ordered the 'Thisbe' to proceed to Bombay, so that you will have an opportunity of renewing your acquaintance with my young friend,' she added. 'I think that I shall charge you with a small parcel for her; some articles which were not ready before she sailed.'

This was delightful news for Morton. He had not heard that there was any chance of the frigate being sent round to that presidency. Of course it was not out of the pale of probability that Mrs Edmonstone was likely to know where the ship was to be sent before the officers belonging to her. Two or three days passed before the captain himself had the information confirmed by the admiral's secretary.

'You are right, Morton,' he said when he came on board. ' We are bound for Bombay, and if we put our best foot foremost we shall get there as soon as that old tea-chest, the "Osterley."'

Morton got his parcel from Mrs Edmonstone, and three days afterwards the 'Thisbe's' keel was ploughing the waters of the Indian Ocean. During the voyage one pair of eyes, at all events, kept a bright look out for any sail of the appearance of the 'Osterley' Indiaman. The second lieutenant was continually going aloft, spy-glass in hand, sweeping the horizon. Some of his shipmates might have suspected the cause, but he gave no reason for this practice which he had adopted. It was war time, and he might have been on the look-out for an enemy.

'We shall be much obliged to you, Morton, if you make out a rich prize some day,' observed Sims. 'A Dutchman from Java, or a Spaniard from the Manillas, would be about the thing.'

Day after day passed, but neither friend nor foe was seen.

At length, however, the 'Thisbe' touched at Ponte de Galle, when she fell in with another frigate direct from England, which had letters on board for her. Ronald got one from his father. He could not bring himself to live on shore, and having applied for employment, had been appointed boatswain of a line-of-battle ship, the 'Lion,' which, it was expected, would be sent out to the East India station.

Ronald Morton loved and honoured his father too well not to feel pleasure at the thoughts of meeting him; at the same time he wished that he could have retired and remained on shore till he could join him.

Without further adventure the frigate came off Bombay.

'The Indiaman you were on the look-out for must have

arrived before us,' observed Captain Calder, pointing to a large ship which lay in the roads.

With a beating heart Ronald watched her as they drew near; but as the 'Thisbe' dropped her anchor at a short distance off, he saw that he was mistaken. The 'Osterley' had not arrived, and considerable alarm was expressed by those who had been expecting her.

CHAPTER XXII.

'THISBE' IN SEARCH OF THE 'OSTERLEY.'—A CHASE.—THE 'OSTERLEY' OVERTAKEN.—FOUND IN POSSESSION OF THE FRENCH.—RETAKEN.—THE PASSENGERS NOT ON BOARD.—MORTON PLACED IN COMMAND OF THE 'OSTERLEY.'—THE UNKNOWN ISLAND.—OLD DOULL ACTS AS PILOT.

HE non-arrival of the 'Osterley' at Bombay created considerable anxiety in all those who had friends on board, or who were otherwise interested in her in their feelings or purses. At length the fears for her safety became so great that Captain Calder was requested to sail in search of her. No one received with more satisfaction the announcement that the ship was to put to sea than did Ronald Morton; at all events he would be doing the only thing in which he could now take an interest. His heart had been tortured with a thousand fears as to the fate of one whom he had discovered that he ardently loved. Had nothing unusual occurred it probably would have taken him much longer to ascertain the true state of his heart: misfortune has a wonderful power of testing the feelings and revealing their condition.

Neither Rawson nor Sims could make him out, they agreed.

'What can have come over the poor fellow?' said the latter. 'The climate does not agree with him; he should go home invalided.'

Glover might have suspected the true state of the case, but he kept his counsel to himself.

The 'Thisbe' overhauled every vessel she fell in with, and made inquiries at numerous places as she ran down the coast, but nothing was to be heard of the 'Osterley.' She rounded Ceylon, and stood across the Indian Ocean. Ronald Morton had kept a sharp look-out for any strange sail before, on the passage to Bombay; he kept a sharper look out now.

The frigate had got about a third of the way across the Bay of Bengal, when the second lieutenant, who, much to the surprise of his subordinates, spent many of his spare moments aloft, made out a sail to the southward steering west. She was a large ship, but whether man-of-war or merchantman, friend or foe, it was impossible to say. Ronald came on deck, and all sail was made in chase; the idea seized him that the ship in sight was the one of which they were in search.

'I am afraid you will be disappointed,' remarked Captain Calder. 'She is probably some homeward-bound Indiaman from China; this would be her track remember.

The chase did not alter her course, but all the sail she could carry was packed on her; she sailed well, but the frigate sailed better; there was a fear that she might not overtake her till nightfall. Morton walked the deck with greater impatience than he had ever before exhibited, now looking out to windward, now at the sails, now at the chase; as the frigate drew nearer the chase, the opinions were strongly in favour of her being an Indiaman.

'But if she is, why should she run away?' observed Glover, who was always inclined to side with Morton.

'An Indiaman she is,' observed Rawson. 'I hope soon we may be near enough to send a shot across her fore-foot.'

The chase sailed well, and though the frigate gained on her it was not at a rate to satisfy Morton's impatience. It was getting dusk as they drew near; his glass had scarcely ever been off the chase.

'That must be the "Osterley;" and yet it is strange,' he exclaimed. 'What can have happened to her?'

The frigate at length ranged up alongside. By this time it was dark; lights were seen glimmering through her ports. Captain Calder hailed. 'Wa, wa, wa,' was the only answer he received.

'She must be in the hands of an enemy,' he said.

Morton's heart sank within him.

'Heave-to, or we fire!' cried the captain.

In a little time the creaking of blocks was heard, and the Indiaman's courses being hauled up, she slowly came to the wind. The frigate hove-to to windward of her, a boat was lowered and manned, and Morton leaped into her, followed by Glover.

'Give way, lads!' shouted the lieutenant, eagerly.

She was soon alongside; her officers and their followers scrambled on board: little help was afforded them to do so; on the contrary, the expression of the countenances which looked down on them, seen by the glare of the lanterns, showed that if not backed by the guns of the frigate, they would have been received at the points of boarding-pikes and with the muzzles of pistols presented at their heads. The determined looks of the sturdy man-of-war's men made the crew of the Indiaman hold back. Directly Ronald stepped on board he glanced his eye anxiously around; he had no longer any doubt that she was the 'Osterley,' but with not a face that met his gaze was he acquainted.

A rough piratical-looking man, in a naval uniform, stepped forward, sword in hand, and presenting the hilt with an air which none but a Frenchman could assume, said—

'Monsieur, the fortune of war places us in your power; we yield ourselves prisoners, and claim your clemency.'

'On what ground do you claim that? Where are the passengers and crew of this ship who sailed in her from Calcutta?' exclaimed Ronald.

'The fortune of war threw them into our hands, as we have been thrown into yours,' answered the captain, drawing himself up. 'The courtesy for which our nation is famed has prompted their captors to treat them with courtesy.'

'I trust so,' exclaimed Morton, with a look which the Frenchman could not fail to understand. 'But tell me—what commission do you bear? Do you belong to the Imperial marine of France?'

Morton asked these questions with an agitation he could scarcely conceal, for from the appearance of the captain and his crew he could not help dreading that those in whom he took so deep an interest had fallen into the power of a band of pirates; all the atrocities of which such ruffians could be guilty occurred to him.

'Speak, man; tell me—what are you?' he shouted, for the man seemed to be hesitating about giving a reply.

'What we are you perceive, monsieur,' he answered. 'We are cavaliers and Frenchmen, and are at present prisoners to an honourable enemy; as such we expect to be treated.'

'How you are ultimately treated depends on your conduct towards those whom you have had in your power,' said Morton. 'Enable us to recover them, and you need have no fear on that score.'

The Frenchman shrugged his shoulders, and protested that he had had nothing to do with the capture of the Indiaman; that he had been put in charge of her by others to carry her home, and, moreover, that he knew nothing of the passengers, except that he had been assured that they were in safety.

When Morton interrogated him as to where he had last come from, he declared that he had been, with his crew, put on board at sea, from a country craft, and the captors of the ship had taken all the passengers out and carried them he knew not where.

Ronald would not believe this statement; but the man persisted in it, and seemed obstinately determined to make no other

Captain Calder directed Morton to take command of the recaptured 'Osterley,' and Glover went as his lieutenant, with a couple of midshipmen, Job Truefitt, Bob Doull, and about thirty other hands. They not being sufficient to work the Indiaman, some twenty of the prisoners were retained on board her. It now became a question what course to steer. At length, as the wind was favourable, Captain Calder resolved to return to Calcutta, and should he not hear of the missing prisoners, to get the admiral to send some other ship in search of them. This determination of the captain was the only consolation Morton could obtain. Still the fact of their having fallen in with the Indiaman was of itself considerable encouragement.

Two or three days passed by; the wind was light, and not much way was made. It would be difficult to describe the varied feelings with which Morton visited the cabins which had been occupied by the Armytage family.

To calm the agitation of his mind, he went on deck and paced up and down by himself. At length, as he turned to walk forward, he saw Bob Doull coming aft, hat in hand, to the quarter-deck. The young seaman gave the usual hitch to his waistband, with a scrape of his foot, while he swung back his hat, and then waited till his superior looked as if he was ready to listen to him.

'What is it, Doull?' asked Morton.

'Please, sir, I've found among these outlandish chaps forward, we took aboard the prize, an old man who says as how he knows something about me, sir,' said Bob, twisting his hat round and round.

'About you, my man; who can he be?' inquired the lieutenant.

'Why, sir, he says as how he's my daddy,' answered Doull, bluntly. 'He may be, cause as how my daddy went away to foreign parts many years gone by, and never came back; but if he is, he's a rum sort of one. I can't say as how I takes much to the old gentleman as yet.'

'Let me see the man, and hear his story,' said Morton. 'I had no idea that we had an Englishman among the prisoners.'

'Bring him aft at once; let him speak to no one; I must question him.'

Before long, Bob Doull was seen dragging along a tall, gaunt, grey-headed man, with a long beard and moustache, on whose head it was evident neither scissors nor razors had operated for many a year past. He was dressed like a French sailor, and except for a peculiar gait and certain movement characteristic of a British seaman, he would have been taken for a Frenchman.

'Please, sir, this old man says as how he is my father,' began Bob, handing him aft on the quarter-deck. 'Come, cheer up, and tell Lieutenant Morton all you know.'

The old man cast an inquiring, doubtful look at Morton's countenance, but seemingly satisfied with his scrutiny, he exclaimed, 'I want, sir, to make a clean breast of it. For many years of my life I haven't known what happiness is, and don't ever expect to know it again.'

'As to that,' said Morton, interrupting him, 'I'll hear you by-and-by; but first, I wish to know where you have come from, and where the passengers and crew of this ship are now to be found?'

'I was coming to all that presently,' persisted the old man. 'It's of the past I want to speak.'

'But, man, lately, what have you done?—what crimes have you committed?' exclaimed Morton.

'None that I know of,' answered the seaman. 'I was always a wild blade, from the time I first set foot on a ship's deck. There was no mischief I was not up to, no crime I feared committing. I had done many bad things, but the worst was to come. I was still a lad, and so was my chum, Archy Eagleshay, and another, an older man, and older in crime, too, but he's gone to his account, as we must all go, great and small.'

'You speak truth, my man,' exclaimed Morton, now losing all patience. 'Again I ask you to pass over your early days, and to come to the latter events of your career. How did you happen to be on board this ship, among a set of Frenchmen and ruffians of all nations?'

'That was what I was coming to tell you, sir,' giving a peculiar look at Morton, who was doubtful whether it was caused by stupidity or obstinacy. He saw, at all events, that there was no use in attempting to draw forth the information he required before the old man was ready to give it.

After a pause, seeing that Morton was not again going to speak, the old man continued: 'Well, as I was saying, sir, he who is gone came to Eagleshay and me, and says he, "Are you lads ready to gain more golden guineas than you ever set eyes on in your life?" Of course we were. "It's nothing but carrying off a slip of a baby who can do little more than talk, and just leaving him in the plantations." We didn't ask questions, but we went on board a little sloop he owned, and then we waited, cruising about, till one evening he told us to pull on shore, and there we found a nurse and child, and the woman gave us the child. Away we went with it aboard the sloop, and made sail, and never dropped anchor till we reached the port of Dublin. Then our captain sold the sloop, and we all went aboard a ship and sailed for America. We didn't reach it though. We had done a cursed deed, and God's curse was to follow us. Our ship went down, and we were left floating on a raft; we were well-nigh starved, when a ship fell in with us, and we were taken on board. The captain was a kind-hearted man, and he said he would take care of the little fellow; and as our captain—he that's gone—had got the money for the deed he'd done, he didn't try to keep him; indeed, he could not have kept him if he'd wished; and so the good captain drew up a paper from what we'd told him, and he made us put our names to it, and he went and locked it up, and after that he never talked about the matter.

We didn't know what he might do, so we ran from the ship at the first port we came to. From that day to this I never set eyes on the youngster, or heard of the good captain again. Well, one bad thing leads to another. We all then went out to the West Indies, and we shipped aboard some strange craft, and strange flags they sailed under. It was difficult to know, when you came on deck, what was flying at the peak. There were many things done which sickened me, and some of my shipmates I saw hung up at Port Royal in a way I didn't like, and at last I got away back to England. I then took a wife. Many years, you'll understand, had passed by. I thought I was going to remain on shore, and be quiet and honest. I'd one little chap born, and I began to be fonder of him than I had been of any living creature before; but I was short of money, and the old feeling came over me. When I wanted it out in the West Indies then I took it. I now did a thing or two which made me fly the country. From that day to this I have never set foot on the shores of old England.'

Morton thought that he might now venture to interrupt the old man. He had been so anxiously waiting for the account he might give of the passengers, that he paid little attention to the first part of the narrative.

The old man declared that he knew nothing particular about them. He was on the other side of the island when the Indiaman arrived. He knew that a number of people had been landed, and that huts had been built for them, and that they were living on shore; but sentries were placed in the neighbourhood of the spot, and no one was allowed to pass to communicate with them.

'But what is the character of the men who have possession of the islands? Are they men-of-war's men, privateers, or pirates?' inquired Ronald.

The answer the old man gave was not perfectly satisfactory. 'They might be pirates, for they were a rough set; but then privateers were often rough enough, and little better.

Then again some of the ships which came in wore pennants, and the officers had uniforms; but it was easy enough for a privateer or a pirate to fly a pennant, and any man could put on a uniform, as he had often seen done by villains who finished their career by being hung up in chains.'

Morton took several turns on the deck. Could nothing satisfactory be made out of the old man?

'Could you find your way back again to those islands you speak of?' he asked.

'Maybe I could tell the course we've steered; for when it has been my trick at the helm I marked it well—it has always been the same. Five days had passed since we tripped our anchor before you fell in with us. Nor'-west by west, half west; and we ran between seven and eight knots an hour—seldom less, I should say. There, sir, can you make anything out of that?'

'I hope so; and could you pilot us into the harbour from which you sailed?' asked the lieutenant.

'That I could, I am bold to say, seeing that I've been fishing over every spot of it for the last ten years, or more,' said the old man.

'That will do, Mr Doull. Stay aft here, with your son, as you say he is; and I think you are right, for there is a likeness. I will trust to you, and I will do my best, if you prove true, to get you pardoned for any offence against the laws which you have committed.'

Ronald called Glover and signalised the frigate. Both ships hove-to, and he went on board. His consultation with Captain Calder was soon over, and on his return both ships shaped a course in the direction indicated by the old man.

CHAPTER XXIII.

WHAT HAD BEFALLEN THE 'OSTERLEY.'—HAD BEEN TAKEN BY THE ENEMY AND CARRIED INTO PORT.—PASSENGERS KEPT PRISONERS ON THE ISLAND.

HEN the 'Osterley' left Calcutta she stood across the Bay of Bengal, and there appeared to be every prospect of a favourable commencement of the voyage. She had a good many passengers, but not so many as she would have had, probably, had she been going home direct. They were chiefly married ladies, accompanying their children; or civilians, or military men returning after many years' service; or invalids, hoping to regain their health in the land of their birth.

Altogether, Miss Armytage did not expect to find much to interest her among the companions of her voyage, as they, one after the other, made their appearance on the poop-deck of the Indiaman, on which she was seated. It is possible that, while the pilot vessel continued in sight, she might have taken an occasional glance to ascertain how the little vessel was performing her voyage, and afterwards it is certain that she was lost in a reverie, from which she was not aroused till her mother had several times addressed her with the inquiry whether she was not excessively hungry, and would go down and get ready for dinner. Mrs Armytage was a very good-natured woman, and not destitute of sense, but she had no romance in her composition. She was a great contrast to her unhappy sister, Hilda.

Edda aroused herself. 'Yes, mamma; if it is necessary to appear at dinner, I will go down with you.'

'Of course, dear; and here is Captain Winslow coming to offer you his arm.'

However, he offered it to Mrs Armytage herself, and with his most polite of bows, begged that they would take their seats near him at table. Captain Winslow was courteous to all his passengers, but he certainly paid more attention to the Armytage party than to all the rest.

After dinner, most of the passengers were collected on the poop, watching two vessels which appeared in the distance. One was evidently a native craft, a Dow or Pattarmar, from her high stern, curiously-projecting bow, and lofty lateen sail. She had apparently communicated with the other stranger, which was a ship of some size, and was now working in towards the land.

The ship engrossed the chief attention of the passengers. She was a flush-decked vessel or corvette—large for that class of craft, with very square yards. Miss Armytage hoped that her mother would not overhear the observations which the appearance of the strange sail called forth. She was looked upon by all as a very suspicious craft. Under what flag she sailed was a question, but it was very evident that she was a man-of-war, a privateer, or a pirate. She was an armed vessel —she was not a British man-of-war—she might be an English privateer, but she had the look of a foreigner.

By degrees the suspicions respecting the character of the stranger increased, till few had any doubt that he was an enemy. Captain Winslow, however, was not to be intimidated by the appearance of the ship. Captain Winslow had probably made up his own mind as to what he would do, but, under the circumstances of the case, he judged it necessary to call his officers and the principal passengers together, to ask their opinion as to what course should be pursued. Colonel Armytage was, of course, summoned to the consultation. The captain opened the proceedings.

'No one will doubt that, should the sail in sight prove an enemy—for that has not yet been ascertained—we should run for it,' he observed. 'There is no disgrace in that; our business is to carry passengers and cargo, and we shall do wisely to stick to our business as long as we can; but the question, gentlemen, which I have to submit to your consideration is, shall we fight and defend our ship, the passengers and property confided to our care, or shall we yield to what may prove superior force?'

'Superior force or not, I say, sir, by the powers! let us fight it out to the last, and drive off the enemy,' exclaimed the first mate. He spoke out of order, but his opinion was echoed by his brother officers, and by most of the passengers, Colonel Armytage was in favour of fighting to the last.

'Should she prove a privateer, and we take her, we should do well to hang every one of her crew up to the yard-arm as pirates, for they are in no degree better,' he exclaimed, in a tone which showed his annoyance at the prospect of so disagreeable an interruption to their voyage.'

'We shall do well to take the enemy before we decide what is to be done with him,' observed the captain.

Some few of the passengers were for temporizing measures; they proposed hoisting a flag of truce, and endeavouring to come to terms with the enemy.

'Not very likely, gentlemen, that if the enemy think they have the power to take the ship, and everything on board her, they will be content with a portion,' answered the captain. 'The majority are decidedly for fighting; we will prepare the ship for action.'

The Indiaman was kept on her course, but all the sail she could possibly carry was set on her. The stranger was at this time to the south-east, her hull just rising above the horizon.

The Indiaman was before the wind, so was the stranger, but her courses were brailed up, and she was evidently waiting for some purpose or other; she certainly, at present, did not look like an object to be dreaded.

The alarm of the ladies gradually subsided, till they began to wonder why it should be thought necessary to make such preparations for fighting; why the shot was got up, the powder-tubs filled, and the guns loaded, and boarding nettings made ready for rigging.

For some time the stranger did not appear to alter her position. When, however, at length the Indiaman, under all sail, began to put forth her speed, giving evidence that she might be many leagues to the southward by nightfall, the ship in the distance let fall her courses, and her head coming round, she was seen to be steering a course which would intersect that of the 'Osterley.'

'It will come to a fight, sir, I suspect,' observed the captain to Colonel Armytage.

'So much the better, for I suppose that there is but little doubt that we shall beat off the enemy,' answered the colonel. 'We have plenty of men, and some serviceable guns, and I trust your fellows will do their duty like men.'

'I trust so, too, sir; but probably that ship out there has more men and longer guns than we have,' said the captain, gravely. 'We should not conceal from ourselves that the contest will be a severe one, at all events, and the termination doubtful. I would not say this to the crew, or to the passengers generally, but in the event of disaster, how are we to protect the helpless beings committed to our charge—the ladies and children? Some of these Frenchmen, I have heard, are fiends incarnate in the moment of victory, and if we offer a stout resistance, and are conquered at last, what is to be done?'

'I should feel inclined to blow up the ship rather than run any risk of the ladies suffering violence,' exclaimed the colonel, pacing the deck in an agitated manner.

'That were scarcely right in the sight of God, or wise in that of men,' said the captain, calmly: 'I had to propose that at a signal which the chief officer who survives shall give they all assemble in the main cabin, and that then we rally round them, and refuse to yield till the enemy agree to terms.'

'Your plan is good, but you look at the dark side of things,' remarked Colonel Armytage.

'I look at both sides, sir,' was the answer. 'The "Osterley" is a fast ship, and we may run away from our pursuer; if we are overtaken, we may beat her off, or after all she may prove to be no enemy at all. You see, sir, I turn the state of the case right round; I like to settle beforehand how, under all circumstances, I shall act.'

'I see, Captain Winslow, you are a man of forethought— a useful quality in your profession,' said Colonel Armytage, though he did not make the remark with the best possible grace. In truth, he was inclined to look down on the sea captain as a person of a very inferior grade to himself, though compelled under peculiar circumstances to associate with him. With one of his formal bows he said that he must go below to make the ladies understand the arrangements contemplated for them.

Edda heard of the expected combat with perfect calmness.

'How I pity the poor men who may be wounded in the battle!' she remarked.

Her father sneered.

'May we go on deck and help them?' she asked suddenly. 'I am sure that we can be of use.'

'Certainly not,' he answered, sternly. 'We shall have enough to do without being interrupted by the interference of women.'

'Oh, father! do not say that,' said Edda. 'We would be of all the use in our power; we would tend the wounded; we would take food to those who were weary; we would carry up powder and shot if required. I have read of women doing such things. Why should not we?'

'Because there are men enough to fight, and it is considered that you will be safer down below,' said Colonel Armytage, casting a look of involuntary admiration at his daughter. 'Round shots are no respecters of persons, and one might destroy you or your mother or the other women as readily as the roughest man on board. In Heaven's name, child, keep out of danger.'

A part of the hold was quickly arranged for the accommodation of the ladies during the expected action. Two lanterns were hung up in it below the beams, but notwithstanding all that was done, it was a very dreary, dark abode. Edda entreated that she and her mother might remain on deck till they were within range of the enemy's guns. Most of the other ladies followed her example, and the deck once more resumed its usual orderly appearance, though there were signs of the expected strife in the warlike costumes of the gentlemen, who walked up and down with swords buckled to their sides, pistols in their belts, or muskets on their shoulders.

The captain had not vainly boasted of the sped of the ship, and, as he now hauled up a little to the westward there appeared to be a considerable chance of her running the stranger out of sight during the night. Darkness was now coming on. The stranger was seen on the lee-quarter continuing the pursuit under all sail. Some of the more timid suggested that part of the cargo should be thrown overboard to lighten the ship, so as to afford them a better chance of escaping, but to this the captain would not consent. He was responsible for the property. He hoped to defend it and every part of it, and even if hove away it could do little to aid their escape. His calmness and determination infused courage into all around him. Night came on. The stranger was still far beyond gunshot. Not a light was allowed to be shown on board the Indiaman. The ladies were induced to retire to their cabins, many under the happy belief that all danger had passed, and that they might look forward to a pleasant continuance of the voyage. None of the officers or crew, however, went below.

Many of the passengers also remained on deck. As night closed in, far off was still to be seen the dark outline of the stranger ship. Was she gaining on the 'Osterley?' Captain Winslow and his officers looked and looked again. There seemed to be little doubt about that. No more canvas could be clapped on the Indiaman. Everything had been done that could be thought of to make her sail fast. A hurricane just then would have been welcome. Clouds were gathering in the sky, and, as the night drew on, the darkness increased. At length the stranger was hid from sight. Some declared that they could still see her, but Captain Winslow was of opinion that they were mistaken. Still even he, as he walked the deck, continued to cast many an anxious glance astern. He called his first officer to him, and they held an earnest consultation together.

'We'll try it,' he observed; and the yards were squared away, and the Indiaman was once more steering to the southward dead before the wind; it was her best point of sailing. It was hoped that the stranger, believing that she was bound for Madras, would continue the chase in that direction. The darkness continued.

'Well, sir, I trust that we have given that suspicious-looking gentleman the go-by,' observed the captain to Colonel Armytage. 'Perhaps it might be better to inform the ladies of this, to tranquillize any alarm they may still feel.'

'Have no anxiety on that score. I do not allow my wife and daughter to indulge in idle apprehensions,' answered the colonel in the supercilious tone in which he frequently spoke.

'This man may be a very important personage, but he is a very disagreeable one,' thought Captain Winslow, as he turned away.

The worthy captain was well-nigh wearied out, so, summoning his first officer to take charge of the deck, he returned to his cabin to endeavour to snatch a short rest, leaving directions to be summoned should any change occur in the present state of things.

The first officer had been one of the most anxious to fight. He believed that they might not only beat off the enemy, but take her also, and he now kept a bright look-out, hoping that she might again appear. He was a young man, and thought more of the honour and glory to be gained than of the risk to be run. Over and over again his night-glass swept round in the direction of the eastern horizon. The range of his vision was limited. After taking a long gaze he suddenly exclaimed, 'There she is though!' He called an old quartermaster and bade him take the glass.

'Yes, sir, she's the ship, there's no doubt about it. She has been keeping way easily with us,' observed the seaman. 'I'd sooner that craft, Mr Lloyd, were a hundred miles away, or a thousand, for that matter, than where she is: we none of us likes her looks, and she'll prove a rummish customer if she gets alongside of us.'

'Oh, never fear, Davis; you'll all fight like Britons, and beat her off; or take her, maybe. But call the captain, and let him know our friend is in sight, away on the larboard beam.'

Captain Winslow was on deck in an instant. He had been dreaming of the stranger. There she moved like a dark phantom, silently stalking over the waters.

There was something peculiarly ominous in her appearance. The very silence with which she glided on through the darkness was threatening. She soon came up within range, but not a shot was fired. There she remained gliding on, with her courses brailed up, keeping pace with the Indiaman. It was very evident that she might have come down upon her long before had she chosen.

The approach of the stranger quickly became known in the

cabin, and the gentlemen passengers were soon congregating on deck, many of them buckling on their swords and examining the locks of their pistols by the light of the binnacle lamp. Various opinions were offered. Some thought that Captain Winslow ought to begin the battle by firing a broadside into the stranger; but he declined the proposal, and suggested that it would be better to ascertain first whether she was inimically disposed.

'She can scarcely be a friend, or she would not frighten people so horribly,' observed some one, but the speaker was not discovered.

The remark produced a laugh, and the spirits of the more timid began to rise.

'Perhaps the gentleman intends to wait till daylight to commence sport,' observed the previous speaker.

Another hour passed by; Captain Winslow could not help feeling that his ship was completely in the power of the stranger. She evidently sailed two feet to his one; could shoot ahead and rake him, or could stand off and cannonade him with her long guns, without his being able to return a shot. A sturdy Briton as he was, he almost wished, for the sake of all on board, especially of the females, that it had been determined to yield at once.

'No, no, that would never do,' he muttered soon after to himself; 'we'll fight, and defend them like men.'

The stranger had been edging in nearer and nearer to the Indiaman. The ladies had been assembled and sent to their apartment in the hold. They were told it was only as a precautionary measure in case of an action. They endeavoured to keep up each other's spirits, hoping for the best. Miss Armytage sat by her mother, calm and resigned, endeavouring to read, but her mind often left the page and wandered far away.

Some few tried to talk, but they found the effort vain. A few young girls laughed and joked, and tried to persuade themselves that there was nothing to dread, but they too soon became silent, and the whole party sat patiently waiting for the event they dreaded, yet hoped might be avoided. They had no means of ascertaining what was taking place; Edda offered to go up and learn, but her mother entreated her to remain where she was, reminding her of her father's commands. The time passed slowly by; many thought that it must be soon day. All hoped that it would be, for they fancied that with the light the stranger would be discovered to be a friend. Not a sound from the deck above reached them. The silence itself was painful. It was suddenly broken by the deep-toned voice of the captain speaking through a trumpet. Then came the concussion and fierce roar of the guns overhead, followed by the thunder of those of their opponent, and the crash of the shot as they tore their way through the sides of the ship. Many of the ladies shrieked loudly, with wild fright, and clung trembling to each other. Yes, the bloody fight had really begun; how would it terminate? Next there was a crashing sound as if the ship had struck on a rock, and she trembled in all her timbers, and there was still the roar of the great guns, but added to it the rattle of musketry; and now followed wild shouts and shrieks, and the clashing of steel as cutlass met cutlass, and men strove desperately for life, and there was the sharp report of pistol shots, and the cries increased; and there was the tramping of feet, every moment becoming louder, and the clashing of swords, and the shouts and cries growing nearer. And now one of the officers rushed down the ladder. His face was pale; there was blood on his arm.

'Ladies, we will defend you to the last,' he exclaimed. 'But come up on the main-deck, and keep together. We have been boarded and overpowered. We have rallied on the after-part of the deck, and hold it still; but there is no time to be lost.'

Miss Armytage and her mother were the first to lead the way. When they reached the main-deck they saw the gallant band of the defenders struggling with overwhelming numbers of the enemy. In the front rank was Colonel Armytage. A huge seaman, a negro, had attacked him, and was pressing him hard. He seemed to be already wounded; others were rushing on. His foot slipped and he fell. His opponent's cutlass was uplifted to give him a blow, which must have proved fatal, when a young officer sprang forward, interposed his own sword, and turned aside the weapon of his enemy.

'Yield, sir,' he exclaimed in French. 'You are a prisoner, and your life shall be respected.' As he spoke, aided by the others, he dragged the colonel, no longer able to resist, out from the *mêlée*, and at that moment Edda recognized him as the young stranger whom she had met so frequently at Calcutta.

'All who yield shall have quarter,' cried a voice from among the assailants of the British. 'We are honourable enemies, and seek the lives of none who no longer resist. The ladies shall be protected.'

'It's Hobson's choice,' said one of the passengers: 'let us make terms while we can.'

Several others expressed the same opinion. Indeed, it was evident that further resistance was useless. The ship was already in possession of the enemy. The captain was not with them. Where he was, no one knew. Too probably he was wounded; perhaps killed. Colonel Armytage was a prisoner. The first officer lay desperately wounded in the front rank of the little band, who had so gallantly held out to the last.

'Drop your swords, brave enemies, and the Frenchman who makes another stroke at your head, dies,' said the voice.

Although many had but little faith in the promise, they yielded to necessity. The captors, however, kept their word.

The captain, a stout middle-aged man, came forward, and taking the swords of the officers, bowed to the group of ladies, and assured them that everything in his power would be done for their accommodation.

'Oh, bring my father, then!' exclaimed Miss Armytage. 'Let us attend to him, should he be hurt.'

'The officer, my lieutenant, took prisoner?—certainly. He shall be placed under your charge, madam,' answered the captain, with a bow.

As soon as it was daylight, the English part of the Indiaman's crew, with the officers, as well as the military men among the passengers, were removed on board her captor, which proved to be 'La Sybille,' a French privateer corvette. Her name had lately become known for the havoc she had committed among the British merchantmen, many of which had been carried off, but what had afterwards become of them it had not been hitherto ascertained.

It was a great relief to Edda to receive a visit from Captain Winslow. He was wounded, and having been knocked down and stunned when the Frenchman boarded, he had not recovered till the ship was completely in their power.

Several of the Indiaman's officers and crew had been killed or wounded, but the bloody signs of the conflict had been removed when the ladies once more appeared on deck. Strangers navigated the ship, and Edda observed that her Calcutta acquaintance had the command. He approached, however, but seldom, and always with the signs of the most profound respect. Edda sometimes observed him standing at a distance, watching her, with his arms folded on his bosom, and a melancholy expression in his countenance. Still, she did not altogether like his look, though it would have been difficult for her to determine why. One thing certainly was against him. He had been acting the part of a spy at Calcutta, and it at once occurred to her, that it was probably owing to the information he had obtained that the 'Osterley' had been watched for, and fallen into the hands of the enemy. Senor Gerardo, as he had called himself, at the same time paid the greatest attention to Colonel Armytage, and seemed to anticipate all his wants; indeed, no captors could have behaved with more attention to their prisoners than did the officers of 'La Sybille' to the passengers of the 'Osterley.'

The two ships were now sailing together, to the eastward of south, but where they were going, no one could ascertain. A sentry was stationed at the compass, and though they were allowed to range anywhere else about the ship, when any one drew near that, they were civilly ordered to move away. Ten or more days passed, and the two ships lay at anchor in a beautiful bay, among a group of islands, some of considerable elevation, and covered with all the varied productions of the tropics. There were few signs of cultivation, but there were numerous huts and tents scattered about, and it was evident that the island had been taken possession of by the French as a rendezvous for their cruisers. Another Indiaman lay at anchor with her masts and spars in a shattered condition, as if she had met with a gale on her passage there, and had not been in a fit condition to send away. On a near inspection a battery was discovered thrown up on each side of the bay, while a strong fort in the centre commanded the anchorage, and sentries were seen pacing the beach to prevent the possibility of any prisoners escaping.

The passengers remained on board two days, while workmen were seen on shore, erecting fresh huts. During this time, Lieutenant Gerardo was constant in his attentions to Edda, but they were so delicately offered, and his manners were so gentlemanly and refined, that she was almost angry with herself for not feeling more grateful. At last the whole party were directed by the French captain who came on board, to prepare for going on shore, and informed that they were at liberty to take every part of their private property with them.

'We do not war with individuals, and we feel deeply the necessity we are under of placing a restraint on your actions.'

The young lieutenant expressed his great regret at no longer being allowed to have charge of them. 'Still I trust, Miss Armytage, that you will allow me occasionally to come and inquire after your health. "La Sybille" requires repairs, and will be detained here some time.'

At first Colonel Armytage received him with great coldness, naturally looking on him with contempt, as having played the dishonourable part of a spy during his visit to Calcutta; but the lieutenant explained the cause of his appearance there so much to the colonel's satisfaction, and his attentions were so unremitting and delicate, that he completely won his way into the good graces of the English officer.

Gerardo was too acute an observer not to have discovered the authority Colonel Armytage exercised over his family, and he fancied that the most certain way of winning the daughter was first to gain over the father. By degrees also he obtained the good opinion of Mrs Armytage. He never obtruded his services, but he offered them to her in so delicate a manner, and showed so much pleasure in being employed, that it was scarcely possible for her to refuse them. All the fruits and flowers which the islands produced were collected and brought to her and her daughter, often not obtained without difficulty, while numberless objects of interest, evidently taken out of prizes, were offered for their acceptance.

Very few of the other officers came near them; indeed, they appeared generally to be of a different stamp to the captain and his first lieutenant.

'We really might be very happy here if we did not wish to be elsewhere,' observed Mrs Armytage to her daughter.

'Yes, certainly,' remarked another lady. 'But what shall we do when our clothes wear out? It will be shocking not to be able to get any of the new fashions. I am afraid our polite captain and Monsieur Gerardo will not think half as much about us then.'

'You don't suppose that we are to be kept here for ever!' exclaimed another lady, in a great state of agitation.'

'Perhaps till the war is over—such things are done,' remarked Mrs Armytage, who, having her husband and daughter with her, was more inclined to be contented with her lot than were most of the party.

With most of the captives, however, the days in that delightful climate passed pleasantly and rapidly by. Had Ronald Morton wished Edda to be placed in a position where her thoughts would most probably be occupied with him, he could scarcely have selected one more favourable for the purpose than that in which she now found herself.

What might have been the effect of the young French lieutenant's devoted attention, it is impossible to say; but though he was present, the absent Morton ever stepped in to prevent him from making the slightest impression on her affections. The more she thought of Morton, the more vividly did she realize his noble qualities, his manly appearance; and thinking of him, she naturally taught herself to believe that, in some way or the other, she and her friends would be rescued from their present trying and anxious position. All the time they could not but feel that they were in the hands of enemies, who, though they behaved well at present, might at any moment change their conduct.

Both the French ship and the Indiaman had suffered considerably in the action; and since their arrival they had been undergoing repairs. These were now completed. The privateer's men were also refreshed, and eager to go in search of fresh spoil.

With heavy hearts the late officers and passengers of the 'Osterley' saw her under all sail, standing out of the bay. It appeared as if their home—the only means of escaping from their bondage—was leaving them. Many gave way to tears at the sight, and few looked on unmoved. Two days afterwards the corvette herself put to sea, both her captain and first lieutenant going in her. A small garrison was left in each of the forts, and the seamen remained in prison on board the dismasted prize, under a strong guard. As there were only a few small canoes on the beach, used for fishing, and none of the prisoners had arms of any description, there was very little chance of their attacking the garrison, or attempting to make their escape. An old French military officer, who acted as governor, was a very strict disciplinarian, and was continually going from fort to fort and inspecting his troops, so that neither he nor they were likely to be caught asleep. Indeed, it appeared that nothing was likely to occur to disturb the perfect tranquillity of the island.

CHAPTER XXIV.

THE 'THISBE' APPROACHES THE ISLAND.—OLD DOULL'S REVELATIONS AS TO THE 'OSTERLEY'S' PASSENGERS.—THE FRIGATE PUT UNDER FRENCH COLOURS.—EXPEDITION IN THE BOATS.—ATTACK ON THE FORTS.—'OSTERLEY'S' PASSENGERS CARRIED OFF.

O return again to the 'Thisbe' and rescued 'Osterley.' The frigate and Indiaman were once more hove-to, at a short distance from each other. In the far distance appeared a group of islands like blue hillocks rising out of the shining ocean. Volunteers from the frigate eagerly crowded on board the 'Osterley,' armed to the teeth. Morton had gained sufficient information from the old man to enable him to form a plan for rescuing the prisoners, should they be, as he trusted, still on the island. He had had frequent conversations with the elder Doull. One day the old man again referred to the abduction transaction in which he had been engaged in his youth. The similarity of the account to that Morton had heard of his father's history, struck him.

'Where was it? from what part of the coast did you take the child?' he asked, eagerly.

'Did I not say from Shetland?' replied the old man. 'And what is strange, Lieutenant Morton, the boy's name was the same as yours; but maybe you know nothing of Shetland;

it's a fine land anyhow, and you are too young to be the child I was speaking of.'

'You are mistaken in one point, Mr Doull,' said Morton. 'I belong to Shetland; I was born and bred there; and I feel almost sure that the boy you carried off was my father. He was picked up at sea by a Captain Scarsdale, who brought him up as his son.'

'Scarsdale!—now you speak it, that's the name of the master of the vessel who took us off the raft, and from whose ship we ran. For many a long year I have not thought of it. Yes, Andrew Scarsdale; and the boy was called Rolf Morton—the names come back to me as if I heard them but yesterday. There are not many other names I can remember which I knew at that time.'

'But do you believe that that was the real name of the child?' asked Morton, for he had heard his father express his belief that the name he bore was not his true one.

'That I do not know,' answered old Doull. 'If it was not, the only one of us who knew the truth was our leader—the man who led us to commit the crime—that villain, Rolf Yell. It's many a year since I have spoken his name. Now I remember, he gave me a paper to Captain Scarsdale, and put his name to it, and we saw him do it; and we—that is, Archy Eagleshay and I did; and the captain put his name, and we put ours after that, though we didn't read the paper, but the captain said that it was all right, and that it was what he wanted, and he took it below; and so I supposed that it would make everything square for the poor boy.'

This circumstantial account agreed so exactly with that which Captain Scarsdale had given his father, that Ronald had no doubt that he had found a clue which might lead to the solution of the mystery hanging over his early history.

What had become of the important document? Why had not Captain Scarsdale produced it? Yell, at all events, knew his father's real name, and he must have communicated it to

Captain Scarsdale. He longed to meet his father, that he might give him the information he had received, and consult with him as to what steps it would be best for them to pursue.

Formerly he perhaps would have been very indifferent as to the result; now he could not help feeling that if it could be proved that he was of gentle blood, it might enable him the better to succeed in realising the bright visions in which he had of late been indulging. There might be a thousand obstacles in his path, but he felt that he could clear them all away by courage and perseverance, as he would a host of enemies with the strokes of his cutlass.

Such were the feelings with which Ronald Morton prepared for the attempt to rescue the passengers and crew of the 'Osterley' from the hands of the Frenchmen. Old Doull had warned him of the difficulties to be encountered. He had described the dangers of the approach to the bay, the strength of the forts, and the number of the garrison. This of course only increased the anxiety of Morton and his followers to commence the work in hand.

While Morton was still forming his plan, old Doull, hat in hand, came aft.

'Captain Morton,' he said, 'my son Bob has been telling me how you have been kind to him, and stood by him ever since he came to sea, and I want to show you that my old heart, though it's pretty well scorched and dried up with the hard life I've led, can still feel thankful for favours done. At first I couldn't make Bob believe that I was his father, and no wonder, for an unnatural one I had been to him all his life; but I told him so many things about when he was a baby that he knows it now, and has taken to call me father, and that warms my heart and gives it such a pleasure I can't describe. After having had no one to care for me for better than twenty years, except old Archy Eagleshay—and I couldn't trust him over-much, 'specially if a cask of rum was in his way—it is a happiness to be called father—that it is, sir. I hope as how some day you will feel it. Well, sir, as I was saying, I was turning in my mind how I might serve you best. Now, I've been thinking that if we were to sail in with the ships, and attempt to take the forts by force, though we might and should succeed in the end, we might hurt some of the English people on shore, and that's what you wouldn't wish to do.'

'No, indeed,' said Ronald, shuddering. 'That I would not, of course. But what do you propose?'

Ronald had discovered the uselessness of attempting to hurry the old man, so he waited patiently for his reply.

'Why, sir, I think if the ship was to run in just before dark under the French flag, the people on shore would fancy that she had been brought back for some reason or other, and very likely wouldn't board her that night. When it is dark I will go on shore and find my way to the huts of the prisoners. I will tell them that you have arrived to bring them off, and I think that I could manage to conduct them down by a path to the shore, so that the French sentries shall not see them. In that way, sir, they may be got on board without danger.

Morton was not satisfied with the whole of Doull's plan.

'You forget the risk the prisoners would run of being fired on by the French sentries, if found escaping; while, before the ship could leave the bay, the forts would open fire on her, and very probably injure some of them. However, I will think over your proposal, and I thank you for your anxiety to serve me.'

Morton would rather have run in with both ships, reduced the forts, and carried off the prisoners in triumph, but caution as well as boldness, he knew well, were necessary to insure success. Captain Calder highly approved of the plan he ultimately laid before him.

All was ready on board the 'Osterley.' The boats were hoisted in; and while she ran on towards the land the frigate hauled her wind and stood off again.

The Indiaman rapidly approached the land. As she drew

in with it the French ensign was hoisted at the peak. Job Truefitt looked up at it.

'It's the first time that I minds that I ever sailed under that buntin', and I would be sorry to see it often hoisted over my head,' he observed to the elder Doull, pointing at it with his thumb half over his shoulder, and a contemptuous sneer on his lips. I never loved them mounseers, and hopes I never may. They are to my mind the nat'ral born enemies, so to speak, of Englishmen, and it's my belief that they'll remain the same to the end of the world.'

Doull was now summoned aft to pilot the ship among the reefs which surrounded the group of islands she was approaching. The wind had been faithful, and Morton managed so well that it was close upon sunset before the 'Osterley' got inside the reefs. It would have been anxious work to carry a ship, in the uncertain light which still remained, among those numerous rocks and shoals, even with a friendly port in which to drop her anchor. Ronald, with the old man by his side, stood conning the ship, while two seamen with sharp eyes were placed at the end of the jib-boom, and others at the fore yard-arms, to give notice of any danger they might discover.

'There'll be no use keeping the lead going, sir,' said Old Doull. 'You may get a cast of twenty fathom, and the next moment have the ship's bows hard and fast.'

Ronald knew that this was the case, nor did it decrease his anxiety. Steady hands were at the helm. The seamen were at their stations to trim or shorten sail. The Indiaman glided onward. She was already inside the reefs, and the heaving motion of the ocean was no longer felt. Hills clothed with verdure rose close before them, the shore on either side, fringed with cocoa-nut trees, seen here and there over the yellow beach rising against the deep blue sky. The forts, too, could be made out, though thrown into shade in the centre of the landscape, as the ship, boldly guided by the old seaman to a berth, dropped her anchor. The carpenter had been busily employed all day in constructing a canoe. It was forthwith lowered noiselessly into the water, and Doull and his son stepping into it, paddled away to the shore, keeping, however, as far off as possible from the forts.

'That man can be trusted,' observed Ronald to Glover, though the words implied a doubt of the fact.

'At all events we must trust him, sir,' answered the midshipman; 'that is very clear.'

After waiting for some time, and no one appearing from the shore, the boats were lowered without noise into the water, and at once manned. By this time the dim outline of the shores of the bay could alone be seen. Morton took command of one, Glover of another, and the boatswain of the frigate of a third. Sims remained on board in charge of the ship. The Indiaman's boats followed with a midshipman in each, so that there were six altogether.

There were three forts, and it was arranged that two boats' crews should simultaneously attack each of them. The oars were muffled, and away the flotilla glided from the side of the big ship, as Glover observed to the midshipman with him, like a brood of new-born serpents sallying from their parents' side intent on mischief. Not a sound was heard on shore, not a sound either did the boats make as they glided over the smooth surface of the bay. Morton's mind misgave him. It seemed strange that no people from the shore had come off to the ship.

'Surely they must have seen her even through the gloom,' he said to himself. 'Can the Frenchman have left the place, and carried off the prisoners?'

The question was soon to be solved, but his impatience would scarcely brook the necessary delay. He had ascertained from Doull the direction of the huts where the English prisoners were located. Doull had also described the best landing-places under the forts. The boats, in three divisions, proceeded on their separate courses. The centre fort was the strongest. Ronald selected that for himself. His heart beat quick as he approached it. Who when going into action does not discover that his pulse beats more rapidly, even under ordinary circumstances? Ronald felt that the safety of one now dearer to him than life was involved in the success of his undertaking.

As the boats drew closer to the shore it was necessary to proceed more carefully, for fear of running on the rocks, which jutted out in certain parts of the bay. Though the surface of the bay was smooth, there was a slight surf on the shore, the noise of which, as it broke, tended to overpower any sound which the oars made as they dipped into the water.

Could the French garrisons be asleep? No sentry's challenge was heard on the walls. Perhaps, believing that it was unlikely an enemy should discover them, and impossible for one to approach at night, they had all, in fancied security, gone to rest; but then they must have seen the approach of the ship.

Ronald had promised to send up a rocket the instant the parapet was gained and the enemy aroused. A few more strokes, and the boats would reach the landing-place. Just then a loud hail came from the walls of the fort. Ronald answered, in French, 'People from the captured Indiaman.'

'Stay there,' said the sentry, who had, it seemed, either been asleep or just come up to his post. This, however, was an order the English were not very likely to obey, so on they dashed as fast as possible, knowing that in another minute their purpose would be discovered. Leaping on shore, several carrying ladders, they rushed to the walls. At the same moment a rocket flew into the night air high above the heads of the combatants, to give notice to their comrades that the attack was begun. The ladders were placed in position, and up they climbed, in a way British seamen only can climb, each eager to be first, and yet one helping on the other in the noble race of honour. In vain the sentries and a few men left on guard rushed out to oppose the assailants, and shouted and bawled to their comrades to hurry to their assistance. A pistol bullet or the stroke of a cutlass silenced the voice of many a boasting Frenchman for ever.

The English had made good their footing in the fort, but before they had time to advance, they found themselves opposed by the whole garrison, who, though just awakened from sleep, surprised and bewildered, fought with the fury of desperation. They had, however, seized in the hurry and darkness the weapons which first came to hand, and many were but imperfectly armed. Now they were driven back—now more of the officers coming among them, they again rallied and stood bravely for a few minutes, but every foot of ground Morton and his followers gained they kept, and onward they fought their way. The pistol shots, and shouts, and cries from the other forts, and high above all, the true hearty English cheers to which the seamen gave vent, showed the enemy that they were attacked by no insignificant force. By whom they were attacked they probably could not tell, till those well-known cheers reached their ears. Still they bravely stood their ground.

'On, lads, on!' shouted Morton, laying about him with his cutlass more furiously than ever. He began to be afraid, from the pertinacity of the Frenchmen, that they expected reinforcements. Again the British seamen made a fierce charge; those of the enemy in the front rank were cut down or driven back upon their companions in the rear. They in their turn gave way, and the whole body of Frenchmen took a hurried flight across the fort, with the intention of escaping through the gate on the land side. This was what Morton was especially anxious they should not do. He dashed after them like a dog endeavouring to turn a flock of sheep. He and several of his followers reached the gate almost at the same moment, but not in time to stop them. Out dashed the Frenchmen, driving each other forward. The British seamen followed close upon their heels, cutting down those they could overtake, but they in their fall somewhat impeded the pursuers. Morton marked well the way they took. It was towards, he believed, the huts of the prisoners. He guessed what their purpose would be—on he went in hot haste. Once some of the fugitives, finding so few of their enemies close at their heels, stopped, and stood at bay. They had cause to repent their temerity. Three were brought to the ground by the edge of Ronald's cutlass, somewhat blunted as it was, while others, with severe wounds, again took to flight.

In the dark many of the pursuers and pursued were scattered, but Morton followed what he believed to be the main body. Suddenly cries and shrieks arose in front, and men's voices were heard shouting, and he thought he recognised that of old Doull and—yes, he was certain—that of Colonel Armytage. Among the female voices was one which thrilled through every nerve. Ronald rushing on, shouted to his men to collect them round him; in another instant he found the two Doulls and Colonel Armytage fiercely engaged with a party of the fugitives. His cutlass soon put the latter to flight.

'Where are the ladies?' he exclaimed; but he scarcely waited for an answer. He divined too well what had occurred.

'There! there! the scoundrels have carried them off towards the woods,' cried Colonel Armytage.

In another instant Ronald was among the Frenchmen. Some of the men finding that with their burdens escape was impossible, let them go free, but others continued their flight. The cries of children and the shrieks of women resounded through the woods. Edda Armytage was still in the hands of the enemy. On rushed Morton; young Doull was by his side.

'There's some people with a lady, sir,' he exclaimed, making a dash towards a path which led down a dell on one side. There were several men, and Ronald at that moment caught sight of a female dress among them. Morton's quick ear recognised Edda's voice.

'Oh, save me! save me!' she cried out.

The man who held her boldly came to the front, while his comrades retreated. Ronald's cutlass was upraised to strike, when the Frenchman placed his captive before him as a shield. The rest rallied round him, and Morton, with Doull alone by his side, found himself opposed to a dozen or more desperadoes, while he felt almost unnerved by seeing Miss Armytage in their power. His dread was that some stray shot or the careless stroke of a cutlass might injure her. All he could do was to keep at bay the rest of the Frenchmen, while he continued to summon his followers. They, however, it appeared, were skirmishing on either side, or rather following the retreating enemy in every direction. Ronald made the most desperate efforts to cut down some of his opponents, but each time that he appeared to be gaining a success the big Frenchman thrust himself before him. He had received one or two severe cuts, and was beginning to despair that help would come in time to prevent the Frenchman from escaping.

Edda had from the first recognised his voice, yet she dared not trust herself to address him by name. Still not for a moment did Ronald relax in his exertions. The Frenchmen had the advantage of knowing the ground, and they were evidently, Ronald conjectured, aiming at some particular spot, where they might hold out successfully. The path was steep, and numerous creepers of a tropical vegetation crossed it. In one of these the big Frenchman must have caught his foot; he stumbled, and before he could recover himself young Doull sprung like a tiger on his throat, and held him tight. The ruffian still attempted to retain his hold on Miss Armytage.

'You look after the others, sir—I can settle with this fellow,' sung out the young seaman; but his officer thought more just then of saving the lady than of beating the enemy.

While the Frenchman was still paralyzed with the vice-like clutch which Doull had taken of his throat, Ronald cast his arm round Edda, and forced her from his grasp.

'Hurra!' shouted Bob Doull, 'I'll soon finish off the villain now.'

He was as good as his word, for never for a moment relaxing his hold of the man's throat, he threw himself on him with such force, that he brought him to the ground; with his knee he kept down one of the man's arms, and with his left hand the other.

'I shall have done for him soon, sir,' he shouted; 'he's giving in, no fear.'

What cared Ronald now for wounds, or for the enemies who were attacking him! Supporting Edda with one arm, he kept them back, and prevented them from rescuing their companion. Suddenly Bob Doull sprang to his feet, and laying about him with his cutlass, quickly put the rest of the Frenchmen to flight.

'Oh, Ronald, what happiness to be saved by you!' murmured Edda, scarcely conscious of what she was saying, as Morton, followed by Bob Doull, who kept a cautious look-out on every side, returned to the huts.

Those words revealed to him what he had scarcely dared to hope. He found old Doull severely hurt, while Colonel Armytage had been unable to follow, in consequence of his former wounds. He did not recognise Morton, but he expressed himself full of gratitude to the gallant officer who had been the means of rescuing his daughter. Mrs Armytage was soon afterwards conducted back to the huts; she, with the other ladies and children who had been carried off, having been rescued by another party of seamen. The remainder who had escaped, and hid themselves, now made their appearance; husbands and wives looking for each other, and mothers and nurses hunting for their children.

Glover and the boatswain now sent two midshipmen from the forts, to announce their capture, and to state that they had secured the garrisons. It was thought advisable, however, to get the ladies on board without delay.

Captain Winslow and the officers and the crew of the 'Osterley,' who had been hutted at a distance from the rest, on hearing the firing, had broken through the sentries, and hurried to the spot. Arms were put into their hands, and they were directed to hold the centre fort, while the passengers were once more conveyed on board.

Ronald would not entrust Edda to the care of any one, but had supported her on his arm till the boats were ready to embark the passengers; he now carefully placed her in one of them, with her mother, and other ladies, under charge of Colonel Armytage.

'I would that I could accompany you on board, but my duty keeps me on shore. I know not what number of the enemy may be on the island; they may rally and attack the forts: it is of the utmost consequence that they should be held by us till the ship is clear of the harbour: you and your companions will be safer on board than even within one of the forts. I trust by dawn to be on board, and to carry you off in safety from the scene of your captivity.'

These words, which might have been spoken to any ordinary person, were heard by all, but the tone of voice and the gentle pressure of the hand were understood by her to whom they were addressed, and she whispered, that she was sure whatever he did was for the best.

As soon as the boats shoved off, Ronald went round to visit the forts. He found Glover and his party standing guard over the prisoners they had captured—a ragamuffin crew composed of natives of nearly every country in the world, and from their appearance Ronald had strong suspicions that they might deservedly be looked upon as pirates. In the other fort Mr Tarbot, the boatswain, had charge of a similar crew. They were very sulky, and as the light of the lanterns fell on their scowling countenances, Morton thought that they looked capable of committing any atrocity, and he felt grateful that Edda and her friends had been rescued from their power.

The sound which gave him the most satisfaction through the hours of darkness was the regular striking of the bell on board the Indiaman. It assured him that her people were on the alert, and that all was going on well. It was nearly dawn when, hearing a sentry hail, he hastened to the spot. 'A friend,' was the answer, and he recognized the voice of old Doull; he directed him to come into the fort, and he soon appeared with a companion, whom he introduced as Archy Eagleshay. The latter was a man very similar in age and appearance to Doull, though his countenance betokened far less acuteness and intelligence. Ronald was much relieved at the return of Doull. On many accounts he was anxious not to lose sight of him, and for the present it was specially important to have him on board the 'Osterley,' to take her out of the harbour through the intricate passages by which he had piloted her in.

At early dawn every one was astir. The former crew of the 'Osterley' were employed in collecting all the property of the passengers, and in carrying it on board the ship, greatly to the satisfaction of its owners. Four seamen had fallen in the attack, and nearly twenty of the enemy. They were all hurriedly interred, friends and foes sleeping side by side on the shores of that lovely bay. The prisoners were next divided among the boats, and carried on board. Their company would gladly have been dispensed with, but Morton judged that it was the only safe way to break up this nest of hornets. The last thing that was done was to spike all the guns; some were simply dismounted, and others were tumbled over the parapet among the rocks. There was not time to do more, for Morton was anxious to get to sea and rejoin the frigate.

Once more the anchor of the 'Osterley' was weighed, and with the wind off the land she stood out of the bay.

CHAPTER XXV.

DIFFICULTY OF NAVIGATION.—AN OLD ENEMY APPEARS.— ENEMY CHASES THE 'OSTERLEY.'—THE 'THISBE' APPEARS.

HE Indiaman, under the skilful pilotage of old Doull and his companion Eagleshay, wound her devious way among the shoals and reefs which guarded the entrance to the bay. Many of the ladies were collected on deck—Edda was one of them; she eagerly watched every movement of the young commander of the ship, as he stood in the weather rigging, or sprang on to the hammock nettings that he might obtain a clearer view of objects ahead. What she thought and felt it would be difficult to describe, but other ladies who were watching him too, agreed that he was a noble specimen of a true sailor. Not for a moment, however, did he turn to look at them : now by hand, now by voice, did he direct the men at the helm the course to steer. Rich and deep were the tones in which the words—starboard—steady—hard a-starboard—port—port—hard a-port, and similar orders were issued. Colonel Armytage was assisted on deck. He overheard some of the remarks which were made, and seemed perfectly ready to acknowledge their justice.

'Certainly I have seldom seen a finer young man,' he observed with a warmth unusual to him. 'We owe him a debt of gratitude, too, for the gallant way in which he rescued us from our disagreeable captivity. By-the-by, to what family of

Mortons does he belong? It never before occurred to me to inquire.'

Edda heard the question; it showed her that her father had begun to think of Morton in another light than that of a common acquaintance. He was no longer either disposed to treat him with the supercilious air in which he did on their first acquaintance. She could have replied, because Ronald had told her that he belonged to Shetland, but she could not bring herself to speak. Those the colonel addressed hazarded various opinions, but all were agreed that from his manner and appearance he must belong to a noble family. Colonel Armytage seemed to have the same impressions.

'Yes, certainly I mistook him at first,' he remarked. 'There were some reports to his disparagement about a foolish duel, but from what I have since seen of him, I have little doubt he was in the right. Such a man would certainly never refuse to fight unless the man with whom he had quarrelled was palpably in the wrong.'

This was, for Colonel Armytage, saying a great deal. His companions agreed with him. It did not occur to them that a man might refuse to fight a duel from a higher motive than knowing that he was so clearly right that the world could not help taking his part.

The observations she overheard made Edda's heart glow and beat quicker than wont. To every word of praise it warmly responded.

'Yet they know not one-tenth part of his worth; his nobleness of mind, his generosity, his tenderness,' she said to herself.

Edda Armytage might, perhaps, have been inclined to over-estimate his various good qualities, gallant fellow as he undoubtedly was.

The conversation to which she was listening was cut short by a cry from the mast-head of 'A sail in sight.'

'Where away?' inquired Sims, who had charge of the deck.

'To the southward,' was the answer.

That was not the direction the frigate was expected to appear. The ship was not yet clear of the reefs. Sims went aloft, and came down with an anxious look. He told Glover that he did not like the look of the stranger. 'She is a big ship, with square yards and white canvas: an enemy, I am certain,' he observed. 'If she was to catch us jammed up among these reefs she might handle us in a way which would make us look foolish.'

'We shall be clear, sir, before she can get near us,' answered Glover. Besides, we have some bull-dogs as well as she has.'

'Mere pop-guns to hers, depend on that,' observed Sims. 'What do you say to her being a heavy frigate, capable of blowing this old tea-chest out of the water?'

Morton was informed of the sail in sight, but he was too much occupied in guiding the ship out of the labyrinth of reefs to make any other reply than the simple one, 'If she is like an enemy get the ship ready for action.'

What he felt his countenance did not show.

The 'Osterley' continued to thread the narrow passage; the slightest inattention would have brought her upon the reefs. Those who could employ their eyes kept looking now at the approaching stranger—now at the direction where they hoped the frigate would appear. At length old Doull's deep voice was heard exclaiming, 'We are free now, sir, of all dangers; we may stand away to northward.

Ronald sprang down on deck, and the deep sigh which escaped his bosom showed the anxiety he had felt.

'Brace up the yards on the starboard tack!' he cried out, as he stepped aft, and, calling for his telescope, took a steady examination of the stranger. He expressed no opinion as to what she was, but ordered all the sail the ship could carry to be set on her. As she had now a large crew this was rapidly done. The stranger must have seen, by the way the 'Osterley' made sail, that she was strongly manned. Captain Winslow and his officers, after a long look at the former, pronounced her to be the very ship which had captured them. Ronald longed to try and turn the tables, and to take her, but a glance at the passengers made him feel that his duty was in this case to do his utmost to escape. A bright look-out was kept for the frigate.

'If the mounseers catches sight of she, they'll be inclined to put the helm down pretty sharp, and go about on t'other tack,' observed Job Truefitt.

As the stranger approached all doubt as to what she was vanished. She had before proved herself a good sailer. She maintained her character, and with a regret almost amounting to anguish, Ronald saw that there was little probability of avoiding a fight. He had brave men under him, but the Indiaman was badly armed, and the enemy had before found her an easy prey.

'We must, I fear, Winslow, place the ladies and children below, as you did before,' he observed, with a sigh. 'I pray heaven the frigate may heave in sight, for the honest truth is, I never felt so little inclined to fight; yet, if fight we must, I should never fight more fiercely.'

'Spoke like a brave man, Morton,' answered his friend. 'When I have helpless women and children under my charge, though I would fight to the last gasp to protect them, I would always rather run than fight.'

'Sail ho! ho—o!' shouted the man at the mast-head, with a prolonged cadence.

'Where away?' asked Morton.

'To the north-west,' was the reply.

His heart gave a bound; it was the quarter in which the frigate was likely to appear. He kept away a little towards her. The 'Thisbe' showed her number. The 'Osterley' signalized, 'We have all safe on board. An enemy to the south-east.'

There was no time for further greeting. The frigate made all sail and stood on. The tables were now fairly turned. The Frenchman made her out, and going about, stood away to the southward.

'We shall have Captain Gerardin and his sentimental lieutenant among us again before long,' observed Captain Winslow, rubbing his hands.

The corvette showed that she had a remarkably fast pair of heels, and night coming on hid the pursuer, as distance had already hid the pursued, from the sight of those on board the 'Osterley.' Sail was taken off the 'Osterley,' and she was hove-to, that she might wait for the return of the frigate.

A very important question now arose as to what port they should steer for. The passengers very naturally begged that they might be carried to Bombay, but Morton conceived that they ought to return to Calcutta. However, that was a point Captain Calder could alone decide. Poor Captain Winslow, on his part, wanted to get back the command of his ship; but that of course, Morton had no power to bestow on him. All were eager for the morning, but never did a night appear to pass by more slowly. Dawn broke at last, and a sail was seen to the southward. She proved to be the 'Thisbe'—the corvette had escaped.

'We'll catch the fellow one of these days, though,' exclaimed Captain Calder. 'And if he proves to be a pirate, and I believe he is very little better, we'll hang him without compunction at his own yard-arm.'

His captain highly commended Morton for his conduct, and decided that the 'Osterley' should return under his charge to Calcutta, where Admiral Rainier still was, that he might decide how she should be disposed of.'

'She's worth some thousand pounds to us Morton,' he observed. 'It will help you to furnish house whenever you set up in that way ashore.'

Ronald hoped that it would not be long before he should

employ his well-gained prize money in the manner his captain suggested. He cared little to which port the 'Osterley' might be sent, except that he would have preferred the one at the greatest distance, which might have prolonged the voyage.

Never had Ronald Morton been so happy. He was in the constant enjoyment of the society of Edda Armytage. She no longer concealed her love for him, and his attentions appeared to meet the approval of both her parents. The days thus glided swiftly by. It was with anything but satisfaction to him that the 'Osterley' at length made the mouth of the Hooghly. A line-of-battle ship was at the anchorage. As the 'Thisbe' brought up, the two men-of-war exchanged numbers, and Morton discovered with infinite satisfaction that she was the old 'Lion,' on board of which his father was boatswain.

Ronald was unwilling to leave the 'Osterley' even for a short time, so he despatched a boat with a note to his father, to inquire after his health, at the same time giving an account of what had occurred, and promising to visit him as soon as he was at liberty. No reply was sent, but in a short time a boat from the 'Lion' came alongside the 'Osterley,' and Rolf Morton himself stepped on board. Ronald welcomed his father with the affection of a son. He thought not of the subordinate rank he held in the service, nor of the fine lady and gentlemen passengers who might be making inquiries as to who he was.

After a short conversation on the quarter-deck, they retired to Ronald's cabin, where a considerable time was spent in giving and listening to accounts of each other's proceedings.

'And let me hear again this strange story you tell me of these old men,' said Rolf. 'I must talk to them, and listen to what they have to say, though I scarcely expect that any good will result to us from it.'

Rolf Morton had never been of a sanguine temperament; he had become still less so as he advanced in life. Ronald, on the contrary, was accustomed to look on the bright side of objects. He believed that he had obtained a clue which would lead to the discovery of a matter now he felt of so much importance to his future happiness.

The two old men were sent for. They looked at Ronald, and then at his father; but neither seemed willing to speak. Archie Eagleshay, especially, put on a stupid expression of countenance, as if he had lost all recollection of past events. After a time, however, Doull repeated the account he had already given to Ronald, and the other old man nodded his head to confirm the correctness of the statement.

'Would you swear to all this my friends, in a court of law in England?' asked Ronald.

Even Doull hesitated. The idea of a court of law, in consequence of his early transgressions, had terrors for him which he could not overcome. As pale a hue as his sunburnt skin would allow came over old Archy's face as he heard the words, and Ronald soon discovered that he had made a mistake by putting the question.

'Well, my friends, we will not ask you to do what you do not like,' he remarked. 'But do not you think that if it was to serve my father and me, and that we would take care that you suffered no injury, you could swear to the truth of the story you have told us? It is my belief that you see before you the very man you assisted to carry off when a child from his family and his country. He bears you no ill-will in consequence. Surely you would wish to do your best to repair the injury you have done him?'

'I would do anything to serve you, Captain Morton, that I would, sir, or swear anything you please: and for that matter, so would Archy.'

'No, no, my friends,' exclaimed Ronald, somewhat inclined to laugh; 'I only wish you to swear the truth, nothing else can serve me. However, the time for doing so has not yet arrived. We must get home first.'

'The truth!' muttered Rolf Morton. 'Where is that to be found? I doubt that it will serve us anyhow.'

'Well, dear father, all is in God's hands,' said Ronald, after he had dismissed the old men; 'I have always been content and proud to be your son, and to me, therefore, as far as my own feelings are concerned it matters little who was your father, or to what family he belonged, except—ah—I for an instant forgot—others may value family more than I do.' And Ronald told his father of his love for Edda Armytage, and of his belief that his love was returned.

Rolf Morton listened earnestly. He had more knowledge of the world than his son, and he was less accustomed to look on the bright side of things.

He shook his head.

'I doubt not she is all you say, and I am grateful to her mother's sister for instructing you in your boyhood, but I have little cause to love her race. The old Sir Marcus worked me all the ill he could, and from what I have heard of this son-in-law of his, he is a proud and vain man, not likely to have much regard for the feelings of young lovers' hearts. But cheer up, Ronald. You have a noble profession, and the way to its highest rank is open to you.'

'But Edda has promised to be mine, and her father could scarcely wish to make her break her word,' answered Ronald, with a simplicity which would have made a man of the world smile.

'I would not damp your spirits, lad; but if you would escape having your hopes stranded, don't trust too much to promises.'

Ronald thought that his father was taking too desponding a view of matters.

'We'll hope, father, that in this instance you are mistaken as to Colonel Armytage,' he answered, in a cheerful tone. 'I am sure that you would like both his wife and daughter.'

'Ronald, my boy, you forget that I am a bo'sun,' said Rolf, rising from his seat. 'Let us go on deck.'

They there met Glover, who welcomed Mr Morton with the greatest cordiality.

'I first went to sea with you, Mr Morton, you remember,' he observed. You taught me more of seamanship than I ever learnt from anybody else. Besides, you know if it hadn't been for your son I should long ago have been food for the fish.'

It was now time for Rolf to return on board the 'Lion.' His son and Glover attended him down the side with as much attention as they would have paid to an admiral.

A number of the passengers were collected on the poop-deck, waiting for the boats to convey them up to Calcutta.

'Who is that man to whom Mr Morton and Mr Glover are paying so much attention?' asked Colonel Armytage, who happened just then to look up from his book.

No one could tell him. After he had seen his father off, Ronald joined the party on the poop. He certainly would not have gone, had Edda not been there. The feeling came forcibly on him that he ought to tell her about his father. It had never occurred to him before. As he was going up to address her, some ladies stopped him, and asked, 'Who is that fine looking, officer-like man who just now left the ship?'

'He is my father,' said Ronald, firmly. Edda looked up at him with a surprised expression.

'Why, Mr Morton, if I mistake not, he wears the dress of a boatswain,' said Colonel Armytage, in a cool, deliberate manner.

'Yes, sir—he is boatswain of his Majesty's ship the 'Lion.'

'Your father a boatswain!' said the colonel in the same slow manner. 'You should have informed me of this before, sir.'

'The question was not asked me,' answered Ronald. 'I was wrong, I feel, in not mentioning it.'

At that moment his eye caught Edda's, casting on him a look of such sorrow and pain that he was about to spring to her side, when she suddenly sunk on her seat, and would have fallen on the deck had not Mrs Armytage and another lady at hand caught her in their arms.

'It is of no consequence,' exclaimed Colonel Armytage, in

a peremptory manner; you have undoubtedly duties to perform about the ship. We will not detain you from them.'

Ronald felt that his only dignified course was to retire. With a heart bursting with indignation, he walked forward. Not long after this the boats arrived to carry the passengers back to Calcutta, where they purposed remaining till the arrangements respecting the ship were concluded. Ronald had been directed to retain the command till it could be legally restored to Captain Winslow.

Miss Armytage had gone below, and was kept out of his sight till she was ready to leave the ship. He came to assist her down the side. She gave him a look full of sorrow, but which he interpreted to mean, ' Do not think that what I have heard can diminish my affection for you; it were worth little if it did.' But she had scarcely time to falter out a few words before her father stepped up and effectually stopped any further communication.

The manner of Colonel Armytage, indeed, was so rude, that Ronald had to recollect who he was, to assist him in commanding his temper.

The passengers in the boats were concealed by the awnings which covered them, but Ronald could not help standing on the deck, watching them with a heavy heart as they took their way up the broad stream of the Hooghly.

The next day he received three letters; two were official, one of them was from his captain, expressing the warm approbation of Admiral Rainier for his conduct in the attack on the enemy's forts; the other was from the officials of the Honourable East India Company, promising him some substantial proof of their sense of his merit. The third letter was private. He opened it with some misgiving.

' It is as I expected,' he exclaimed bitterly; my father was right.'

The letter was from Colonel Armytage, and was couched in almost offensive terms.

'Sir,—You took unwarrantable advantage of the opportunities afforded you of paying attention to Miss Armytage during our late voyage; and in case you should misunderstand my behaviour towards you while you had command of the 'Osterley,' I feel it necessary to state that, considering your true position in society, I consider your conduct most reprehensible, and desire that from henceforth all communication between you and any member of my family shall cease. My daughter is too obedient, and has too high a sense of propriety to differ in opinion with me on this subject.—I am, sir, your obedient servant,

'A. ARMYTAGE.'

When Ronald told his father what had occurred, Rolf replied—

'You will serve your country the more devotedly, and depend on it she has need of you.'

CHAPTER XXVI.

RONALD JOINS LORD CLAYMORE'S SHIP.—THE 'PALLAS' AT SEA.—A CHASE.—ENEMY'S FLEET IN SIGHT.—'PALLAS' CHASED BY ENEMY.—LORD CLAYMORE'S MANŒUVRE.—ESCAPE OF 'PALLAS.'

NO part of the British coast presents a harbour of beauty equal to that of Plymouth Sound, with its lofty banks covered with trees from the summit to the water's edge, its rocks and headlands, its numerous bays, inlets, and other indentations, the towers and glittering white buildings of the picturesque town at the northern end, and the lordly castle and waving woods of Mount Edgcombe on the west.

On a bright summer morning a frigate was seen gliding slowly up the Sound, and making her way towards Hamoaze. The French flag under that of England proclaimed her to be a prize. She was quickly boarded by boats from the shore, every one in them eager to be on board, for a prize crew are supposed to have their pockets well lined with coin, and to be ready to spend it. She was soon known to be 'La Forte,' captured by the 'Thisbe' in the East Indies. She at once went into dock, her crew was paid off, and Rawson got confirmed in his rank of commander; but Ronald Morton received no further acknowledgment of his services. He had been paid some prize-money, and he might have remained on shore to

enjoy some relaxation after the number of years he had been employed; but he had few even of the acquaintance young naval men usually make, and idleness was the very last thing in which he wished just then to indulge. Action, excitement, was what he wanted. He longed once more for the battle and the tempest. In this mood, when the ship was paid off, he went on shore. A tall thin young man, in a post-captain's uniform, met him before he had walked a hundred paces, and after looking at him hard, held out his hand, exclaiming—
'Morton, old shipmate, I'm glad to meet you.'

'So am I, you, Lord Claymore,' returned Ronald, happy to encounter one he had known and liked so much.

'Well, you see, Morton, that I have got the two swabs on my shoulders,' said the young lord, laughing. 'I've worked hard for them, let me tell you; my lords of the Admiralty don't give promotion for nothing to those who don't happen to be born with silver spoons in their mouths; and I was not, I know. Mine was of wood or iron. I hope that you will get your's soon—you deserve it. I met Rawson just now, and he was speaking of you. But, in the meantime, what do you say to taking a berth as my first lieutenant? I've interest enough to obtain that for you. Come along with me for a few yards. You can see the ship I have just commissioned. She is not long off the stocks. I cannot say much for her at present. She is small and cramped, but she carries thirty-eight guns, and I'll make her do something one of these days.'

Ronald at once accepted Lord Claymore's offer. They shortly after fell in with Glover. Lord Claymore told him that he should apply for him as his junior lieutenant.

In a week the two old shipmates found themselves appointed to the 'Pallas' frigate, nominally of thirty-two guns, though in reality mounting thirty-eight. Of course Job Truefitt and Bob Doull followed them. Ronald had been puzzled to know how to dispose of the elder Doull and Archy Eagleshay, when the two old men applied to enter. At first he was inclined to laugh at the notion, but when the captain saw them he desired that they might not be refused.

'There is stuff in them yet—they will be useful.'

They proved that Lord Claymore was right, and he soon rated them as quarter-masters.

'We must be sharp in manning the frigate, Morton,' said his captain. 'Promise largely. We'll redeem our word, depend on that.'

Bills soon appeared, posted all over Plymouth:—'The ' Pallas,' fitting for sea, in want of a few prime hands. The fastest frigate in the service—sure to come back in a few weeks with a full cargo of Spanish pewter and cobs. Plenty of liberty at the end of each trip. Engaged to make more prize-money in three weeks than any other ship in three years.'

Lord Claymore was not unknown to fame. Many men joined in consequence of the deeds he had already done, and some, after reading the placards or hearing them read, though they had no great faith in the promises. Still, the ship could not be manned entirely without sending out press-gangs.

At length the 'Pallas' was ready for sea.

'I hope we may fulfil all our pledges,' observed Ronald one day, after the frigate had left the shores of England far astern.

'I am determined to do so,' exclaimed the captain. 'Morton, I have lived long enough to know that a man can do nothing without money. That is irresistible, in politics, war, or love—rather marriage; it conquers all opposition. There is but one way by which seamen can make it. We are on that course. We'll take good care that the opportunity does not escape us.'

Morton thought awhile. For the first time in his life, perhaps, the idea occurred to him that money would aid his cause. 'It may serve to elucidate the mystery of my father's birth; or why can I not win my way up to fame and fortune? I will show Colonel Armytage that the boatswain's son may become his superior in rank, and surpass him in wealth, just as much as the boatswain does in all the qualities which make a man truly noble.'

Ronald did not allow himself generally to give way to such feelings, but they would arise in spite of him, when he thought of the ungrateful conduct of Colonel Armytage towards him. Lord Claymore, who took an interest in all serving with him, observed Morton's depressed spirits. He did not, however, inquire directly into the cause.

'By-the-by, Morton, you are a Shetlander, if I recollect rightly,' he exclaimed. 'I have been lately among your people, and a kind-hearted, hospitable race they are. Among other places I visited was Lunnasting Castle, where I made the acquaintance of Sir Marcus Wardhill and his daughter, a handsome person, though no longer young. He is a hale old man, but somewhat eccentric, and rather morose, I suspect; has a bee in his bonnet—that is the case with many of his family. There is a cousin who lives there; not quite as old as Sir Marcus—a very odd fellow; indeed, I should say decidedly mad. You may probably know something of them?'

Ronald told him that he had been brought up in the castle.

'A relative of the family?' said the captain.

'I can scarcely be called so,' said Morton humbly. 'A distant one only, on my mother's side. My father was about to take command of a merchantman when he was pressed into the navy. He has remained in the service ever since. He is now but a boatswain, but he is a man of whom any son may be proud.'

Ronald then told the captain all he knew of his father's early history, and of the discovery of the two men who had carried him off.

'I understand the whole affair,' exclaimed Lord Claymore, warmly. 'With all my heart I'll help you to clear it up. You will have plenty of employment for your prize-money: the lawyers will take good care of that; but never mind, we'll have enough for their maws, and to spare. Sharks must be fed as well as other fish, you know. As to that Sir Marcus Wardhill, I like him not. I should have little compunction about sending him on his travels; but I was interested in his daughter, a stately lady, still bearing the marks of great beauty; the Lady Hilda, they call her.'

'Yes, I used, as a boy, to think her very lovely,' said Ronald, warmly.

'I may say she is so still,' returned his captain. 'But do you know, Morton, there is something very strange about her; she talked to me in the oddest way; inquired if I understood astrology, and would favour her by working out her horoscope, and would inform her when the lost one would return.'

'She has been sorely tried,' observed Ronald. 'Her father and Lawrence Brindister are but sorry companions for one so gifted; and the death of her husband and loss of her child were blows she has never recovered.'

Lord Claymore had not heard the circumstances of the case, and so Ronald gave him the whole story as he had heard it. His captain was much interested.

'What a delightful thread to unravel!' he exclaimed. 'I should like to aid in it; but unless you have a clue, it is not likely that her son will be discovered.

'She lives on in hopes that he may,' answered Ronald. I pray that she may not be disappointed. I owe her a debt of gratitude I can never repay for all the instruction she gave me.'

'Perhaps you may be able to serve her,' remarked Lord Claymore. 'Though it strikes me, from what I can make out, that she was but repaying the debt she owes you.'

Ronald did not inquire what his captain meant, for they were both summoned on deck with the pleasant information that a sail was in sight. The frigate was at this time off the Azores.

'What does she look like?' was the question hurriedly

put, as the captain himself was buckling his telescope over his shoulder preparatory to mounting the rigging to take a look at the stranger should the answer be promising.

'A ship, and a big one,' was the reply.

In a few seconds Lord Claymore had joined the look-out man aloft. When the captain was thus active it was not likely that the officers and crew would neglect their duty. Lord Claymore took a long steady look at the stranger through his telescope, and returning on deck ordered the ship's course to be altered a couple of points, and all sail to be made in chase.

'Morton, I have a wonderful presentiment that yonder craft is loaded with the pewter and cobs we have been promising our fellows,' he exclaimed, walking the deck with a quick step. 'Her top-gallant-sails and royals have a foreign cut, and the blanched hue of cotton cloth such as the rich galleons of Spain usually carry. They are heavy sailers, too, and the 'Pallas,' as I thought she would, has shown herself light of heel. We shall get up with the chase before any third party steps in to snap up our prey.'

Not only Ronald, but every man and boy in the ship entered fully into the captain's eagerness. All longed for prize-money; the greater number, probably, that they might spend it as sailors in those days got rid of their hard-earned gains, in wild extravagance and debauchery; a few might have thought of their old fathers, mothers, and sisters, whose comforts they hoped to increase; or some one, more romantic than his shipmates, might have had in view some quiet woodbine-covered cottage, on the sunny slope of a hill, with green fields and a sparkling stream below, a seaman's paradise, with an Eve as a companion.

Ronald Morton, in spite of his resolution to the contrary, could not help thinking of Edda Armytage, and the possibility of yet winning her; still, again and again he tried to overcome aspirations which appeared so utterly hopeless. Indeed, why should he ever wish to make her his? Had she ever attempted to assure him that she did not share her father's feelings? Had she not, from what he had heard, been willingly receiving the attentions of Alfonse Gerardin, a mere adventurer, at best, who must have been guilty of the most barefaced falsehoods to have gained so completely, as he appeared to have done, the good opinion of a person generally so acute as Colonel Armytage? No, he did not want money for himself; it was to place his father in the position in life to which he was born, should it be, as he had every reason to hope, superior to that he now occupied; still, as he thought all this, and much more, his captain's remark, 'With money you can do everything,' rang in his ear.

Not a man or boy on board that ship who was not thinking at that moment of the same thing—money; most of them were talking of it too. With eager eyes they watched the chase as a wild beast does its prey, longing to get possession.

The stranger at first did not seem to have understood the character of the frigate. Her people were not keeping so good a look-out as were Lord Claymore's crew; when they did, all sail was crowded in flight. Away she went before the wind. A stern chase is proverbially a long one; a tub can sail with the wind aft.

Many hours of the day had passed: evening was approaching: should the night prove a dark one, she after all might escape. The captain was becoming anxious, so was every one on board. The nearer they had got to the chase the more like a Spaniard she appeared. All was done that could be thought of to make the frigate sail; every inch of canvas she could carry was set on her; studding-sails on either side hanging down to the very surface of the water, which they swept as she glided proudly on, while other light sails were placed even above the royals, till she looked like a lofty pyramid of snow gliding over the deep. Faster she glided— the breeze was increasing; now she rushed through the water; the officers looked over her sides and watched with satisfaction the foam which rose on either side and formed a long sparkling frothy line astern.

'We shall do now, Morton,' exclaimed the captain, in high glee. 'Don't you hear the dollars chinking away in her hold?'

Lord Claymore wanted the money—not that he was avaricious—far from that; but he had numberless schemes in view, and he knew full well that without the gold they could not be carried out.

As the chase was neared, the Spanish colours were seen flying at the peak. Not a shot did she fire. From the squareness of her yards and the whiteness of her canvas, as seen in the dusk of evening, as the 'Pallas' got her within range of her guns, it was not altogether certain that she might not prove a man-of-war.

'So much the better,' answered the captain, when Glover and the master gave it as their opinion that she was so. 'We shall have more honour, though less gold. We must look out for the gold another time.'

The men were sent to their quarters, and the ship was prepared for action. The chances that the chase would escape were small indeed.

'There's many a slip between the cup and the lip,' observed Mr Hardman, the second lieutenant, who had experienced the truth of the saying in his own person so often that he seldom failed to give expression to it on every opportunity. Though he numbered many more years than either the captain or first lieutenant, he had not been promoted till some time after them. Sometimes when he foretold a slip, he was mistaken.

'Ready with a gun forward!' exclaimed the captain.

The chase was well within range.

'We don't want to injure her more than we can help,' he added. 'Send a shot past her first. Fire!'

The gloom prevented the shot being seen as it flew on over the surface just free of the chase.

The Spaniards thought that the next might come in

through the stern-windows. Down went her helm; studding-sail booms were cracking away on either side; royal and top-gallant sheets were let fly; top-sails and courses were clewed or brailed up, and the Spaniard yielded himself to the mercy of his captors.

The frigate brought to in a more deliberate way, taking care to be to windward of the prize; boats were instantly lowered and manned, and Hardman and Glover hurried off to take possession. Perhaps the captain would have liked to have gone, but it would have been undignified. Glover soon returned with the satisfactory information that she was the 'Carolina,' a large Spanish ship, richly laden from the Havanah to Cadiz. A prize crew was immediately put on board, and the prisoners were removed to the 'Pallas.' They pulled their moustaches, lit their cigars, and resigned themselves to their lot. By dawn the next morning the 'Carolina,' in charge of her new masters, with Glover as commander, was on her way to Plymouth.

Lord Claymore's satisfaction was not small when he discovered that the 'Carolina' formed one of a large convoy, and that it was believed the other ships were astern. Sharper than ever was the look-out kept for a strange sail. Day after day passed, however, and no merchantman or other ships appeared. Hardman began to crow, though the loss was his as well as that of the rest: it was an odd amusement, though some men will suffer anything to prove that they are true prophets.

A week had passed.

'I told you so, Morton,' he observed. 'There's many a slip between the cup and the lip. The convoy probably stole by us during the night when some of our volunteers, who had been keeping so sharp a look-out during the day, were nodding.'

'Sail ho!' was sung out at that moment in a loud cheerful tone from the mast-head.

'Who'll prove right now?' exclaimed Morton, as he sprang aloft with his glass at his back.

Others were looking-out likewise. All sail was instantly made in chase. It was some time, however, before it could be made out whether the stranger was friend or foe, man-of-war or merchantman. At last Hardman condescended to take a look at her.

'Those sails have a decided English cut about them,' he observed, in a tone of satisfaction. 'Depend on it she's not got a dollar on board that will ever enter our pockets.'

'To my mind,' observed Job Truefitt, who with Bob Doull was standing on the fore-top-gallant cross-trees, 'that craft out there looks as if she was come from the land where the gold and silver grows. He looks like a Don, every inch of him. Mark my words, mate, we shall line our pockets with the rhino, and have a pretty handsome sum to take home to our old mothers or sweethearts.'

'Well for those who have them, but I have neither one nor t'other,' answered Bob. 'I've made up my mind to have a jolly spree on shore, and live like a lord till it's all gone.'

'That won't be long, I suspect,' said Job.

The conversation was cut short by a summons on deck. The frigate was nearing the chase. The whole of her hull could now be seen clearly from the deck. As to her character there was little doubt. She was a merchantman of considerable tonnage. However, as yet she showed no ensign at her peak by which her nation might be known. She was pronounced to be Dutch, French, Danish, and Spanish in turn. At last the captain thought of sending for some of the prisoners to give their opinion on the subject. The Spaniards did not take long before they declared their belief that she was one of the convoy to which they belonged, and if they were not mistaken she was very richly laden.

A scarcely suppressed shout ran round the decks as the fact became known.

'Ay, but we've not got her yet,' observed Hardman.

Both captain and crew looked as if they wished they could

urge on the frigate by means more potent than the light breeze then blowing. What plans and projects might not even then have been working in that fertile brain! Still the chase did her best to escape.

'She has something to run for, or she would have given in before this,' observed the captain, rapidly walking up and down the deck, and eyeing his anticipated prize. 'Her violent efforts to escape is a good sign, at all events.'

There was now no longer any doubt as to the character of the chase, for she hoisted the Spanish flag, though she still held on. That she could escape seemed impossible, and Lord Claymore was unwilling to fire, for fear of damaging her, not in consequence of tenderness towards her, but because he hoped in a short time that she would become his property.

'Perhaps she has some notion that she will haul aft her sheets and escape to windward of us,' observed the master.

'Not at all likely that she will make so hopeless an attempt,' answered Morton.

'No; but what do you say to the fellows blowing themselves up,' put in Hardman. 'There's many a slip between the cup and the lip; it is the only way by which they can disappoint us, unless they heave their cargo overboard, which they may have done already, by-the-by.'

His brother officers, as usual, laughed at Hardman's prognostications. At length the frigate got the chase directly under her guns, when, instead of making the slightest attempt to escape, she hauled down her flag, and heaving-to, waited to be taken possession of. This was done as soon as a boat could be lowered from the frigate; Morton went in her, and Evans the mate, who spoke Spanish, accompanied him. He stepped on board the prize. She was a handsome ship, and from her very appearance Morton hoped that she would have a rich cargo. The captain received his captors very politely, and at once produced his invoice.

'That is what you want, gentlemen,' he observed, with a deep sigh; 'your gain is my loss, I am a ruined man.'

'There are all sorts of valuable things here, sir,' observed Morton's subordinate. 'I only hope they are not all shams.'

'We'll go below and examine,' was the wise reply.

The ship was undoubtedly laden with all sorts of West India produce. Then some chests were come to; they were full of bars of silver.

'Pretty pickings, these,' observed Evans.

Some smaller boxes were next examined.

'As I am a gentleman and a Welshman, if I ever cast my eyes on diamonds before, these are diamonds!' he exclaimed, holding up a rough-looking but shining stone beween his fingers. They might have been pieces of glass for what Morton could tell.

'These little boxes are worth some thousands, Morton, I can tell you,' exclaimed Hardman, half beside himself with delight. 'A magnificent haul!' Suddenly he recollected himself,—'That is to say, if they ever reach England in safety. But, you know, there's many a slip between the cup and the lip.'

Morton was too busy to laugh just then. He had discovered some larger chests, containing some large gold candlesticks, which the captain informed them, were to ornament the church of our Lady of the Conception, in Madrid. There were just three of them, enormous and massive articles, not less than five feet high, besides, a quantity of rich plate of gold and silver. Morton sent back Evans to make a report to the captain. Lord Claymore heard the account with unrestrained delight.

'We'll have it all safe on board, without delay,' he exclaimed. 'It will not do to let it fall again into the enemy's hands; in the frigate, at all events, we shall be able to fight for it.'

The men cheered as they saw the chests hoisted up the side. It was bringing back the good old buccaneering days;

such a prize had not been made by any cruiser for a long time. A mate was sent home in charge of her.

'Take care you don't get caught, and clapped into a French prison,' said Hardman, as he shoved off.

Scarcely were the chests of treasure stowed below, and the prize out of sight, than another sail was descried from the mast-head—chase was made—the prisoners confessed that she was one of their convoy, and as the 'Pallas' came up with her, they stated that she was even more richly laden than the last. She saw that flight was useless. She was speedily boarded, and found to contain more dollars, bars of gold and silver, and other treasure. It took no long time to transfer the whole to the 'Pallas.'

'If we go on at this rate, Morton, we shall have enough of the needful to satisfy all the land sharks in the kingdom, and to establish your rights, whatever they may be, against all opposition.'

Morton's hopes began to rise high. The wealth they were collecting seemed almost fabulous; though he knew that but a small share would come to him, he thought that it would be ample to carry out his objects.

The treasure had not long been stowed away, when the wind got up with a heavy sea, and the ship laboured considerably. Hardman, when sitting over his wine with his messmates in the gun-room, began to talk of planks starting, and rich argosies going suddenly to the bottom. No one, however, paid much attention to his prognostications of evil. By dawn the next day another sail hove in sight. Chase was made, but the stranger showed that she had a fast pair of heels; the 'Pallas,' however, had a faster pair, and by noon had gained upon her so much that she was seen to be an armed ship of considerable size. No sooner however did the 'Pallas' get her under her guns, than she hauled down her flag and hove-to. Though a heavy sea was running, she was immediately boarded and found to be a richly laden Letter of Marque. She also had a chest of dollars; but as there would have been great danger of losing them in transferring them to the 'Pallas,' they were allowed to remain on board; Evans was sent in charge of her.

'Take care that you do not slip into a lion's mouth,' said Morton, as his brother officer took his departure.

'If I do, I hope that I shall slip out again before he has time to shut it,' was Evans's reply.

Fortune was smiling, it seemed, on the 'Pallas.' Four rich prizes had already been made; it was difficult to calculate their worth. The sanguine temperament of the captain might have over-estimated it.

'My share alone is little short of a hundred thousand pounds,' he exclaimed, showing Morton a sheet of paper on which he had been making a rough calculation—'a splendid fortune for a man of moderate wishes. I wish that you had a larger share. We captains get the lion's part certainly; but perhaps it is as well as it is. What a stimulus it is to an officer to exert himself to obtain command in time of war.'

'Yes,' thought Morton; 'but let men exert themselves to the utmost, how many fail to obtain the desired rank, or if they get that, the coveted wealth!'

'Remember, however, Morton,' continued Lord Claymore, 'I have promised to assist you in establishing your claims, or your father's rather, whatever they are. He may be the son of a peasant, or noble. No one cares less for what is called gentle blood than I do; but it is not the estimate which we set on an article, but at which the world at large holds it, which is its true value. I don't feel happier because I am the possessor of a hundred thousand pounds than I did ten years ago when I was a beggar; but depend on it, the world will esteem me much more highly than it did.'

Morton always listened with pleasure to the remarks which dropped from his captain's lips, always full of shrewdness and good sense.

It was now time for the 'Pallas' to return home. Four prizes had been despatched to England. All were anxious to ascertain that they had arrived there safely.

'Little chance of that,' observed Hardman; 'plenty of the enemy's cruisers about, to snap them up.'

Though homeward bound, as bright a look-out as ever was kept, in the hopes that another prize might be taken.

When off the coast of Portugal, at dawn one morning, a light silvery fog lay on the water, bright but sufficiently opaque to conceal all objects even close at hand. The wind at dawn was light, but as the sun rose, so did the breeze, and the royals and top-gallant sails, which had at first been set, were, one after the other, taken off the frigate.

'This fog is, indeed, provoking. We may run by a whole convoy of the enemy's merchantmen without seeing them,' observed Morton, who had become as eager as the most avaricious of his shipmates in the pursuit of wealth, by the royal road opened up before them.

'Of course,' answered Hardman; 'very likely at this moment we are passing within hail of some Spanish galleons, whose cargoes would make every man on board independent for life.'

The looker-out at the mast-head hailed the deck.

'A ship, sir, close to—I see her mast-heads over the fog.'

'What does she look like?' asked Morton. 'A large ship, sir, line-of-battle ship, I should say.'

The officers were alert in an instant. Hardman flew aloft. Scarcely had he got there, than he shouted, 'There's another! another!—three of them—line-of-battle ships and enemies.'

The last words had an electric effect. From the movements of the line-of-battle ships, as they were seen over the fog, there was no doubt that their look-outs had discovered the 'Pallas.' In an instant the captain was on deck; Morton had already ordered the ship to be kept away, and was again setting top-gallant sails and royals; he thought the royal masts would scarcely stand.

'Never mind, we must do everything to preserve our booty and our liberty,' answered Lord Claymore.

The breeze increased almost to a gale. The wind soon dispersed the mist, and the three huge line-of-battles ships were seen rushing on towards the frigate. A broadside from one of them would have sunk her. Her top-gallant masts bent like willow wands. Every moment it appeared that they must go. Lord Claymore stood watching them, and now and then taking a glance at his enemies, and though cool and collected, seeming positively to revel in the excitement of the scene. The wind was abeam; and the frigate, which proved herself but a crank ship, heeled over till her hammock-nettings dipped in the seething, foaming waters, which bubbled and hissed up through the lee scuppers.

On tore the 'Pallas.' It was a race for liberty and the preservation of the wealth in which they had been rejoicing.

'What will you take for your prize-money in prospect now, Morton?' asked the pertinacious Hardman. 'I told you so, old boy—there's many a slip between the cup and the lip. It's the great truth I've learned in my life—I shall always stick to it.'

'It may apply equally to our enemies astern, though,' observed the captain, who had overheard the remark, 'we will see if we cannot make it so.'

The line-of-battle ships were by this time beginning to feel the fury of the gale, which was well nigh carrying her masts out of the frigate, or sending her over on her beam-ends. The more, however, the Spaniards saw her pressed, the less willing they were to shorten sail. She now kept edging more and more away to bring the wind further astern, squaring her yards as she did so, the Spaniards having to do the same. They did not seem to think it worth while to spend much powder and shot on her, as they, of course, felt sure of capturing her in the end. It was a grand sight to see the little English frigate dauntlessly doing her utmost to escape from her huge pursuers, the foam in dense masses flying over her, while, with bending masts, and lee-shrouds bulging out, she dashed through the frantic waves, her side, as she heeled over, half buried beneath them. What hope was there of her escaping?

One huge Spaniard was on her weather, another on her lee-beam, while the other was coming up fast astern on her weather quarter. Still Lord Claymore did not despair. He stepped down among the crew and spoke to them.

'My lads, never say die while there's life. Let every man and boy of you do your best, and we'll yet give the Dons the slip. Be smart, as if your lives depended on it. To your stations now.'

Every man stood ready, watching the captain's eye. He had explained his plan to his officers. All was ready. There was a dead silence—the gale roared louder than ever—the frigate tore through the waves. The Spaniards were close upon her; angry at her still holding out, they began to fire; the shots came fast and thick, flying over and on each side of the frigate, but hitherto none had struck her. At length the Spaniards saw again that firing was of no use—they should only be knocking their destined prize to pieces—like vast mountains of snow they came rushing on. It appeared as if they were about to crush the little frigate with their united weight.

'Ready, lads!' shouted the captain of the 'Pallas.' 'Clew up! Haul down!'

Those magic words put every human being on board the frigate in motion. Tacks and sheets were let go. Some hauled away at the brails. Topsails were clewed up, top-gallant sheets were let fly, stay-sails hauled down, and the frigate, which an instant before was under a cloud of canvas, was now reduced to her bare poles.

The Spaniards, totally unprepared for such a manœuvre, at first scarcely comprehended what had happened. On the huge ships sailed in their headlong course. It did not occur to their captains to attempt instantly to shorten sail, but one and all turned their eyes aft to see what their expected prize was about.

Lord Claymore watched them for a short time, but only to assure himself that they were well to leeward of him. The frigate had not lost her way through the water.

'Down with the helm!' cried the captain, in a cheerful tone, which gave encouragement to all. 'Hoist away! Flatten aft the sheets!'

Not an officer, or man, or boy, but put his hand to halliards sheets, braces, or bowlines; and if the way in which she had been stripped of her canvas had appeared like magic to her pursuers, much more must the style in which sail was again made. Off she flew on a bowline on the other tack, while the three line-of-battle ships were hurrying headlong miles away to leeward.

A loud, hearty cheer burst from the throats of the British seamen as they saw the success of their captain's skilful manœuvre.

'What do you say now, Mr Hardman?' he said, laughing. 'There's many a slip between the cup and the lip.'

'Yes, my lord; the Spaniards must confess to the truth of the saying just now,' he answered. 'But we are not altogether clear of them yet.'

'No, by Jove! the fellows are after us!' exclaimed the captain, pointing to leeward, where the three ships were seen under shortened sail, slowly coming up on a wind. 'We must trust to our heels and the shades of night. That trick won't answer twice.'

Though not over-well managed, the Spanish ships sailed well, and were once more in hot pursuit of the 'Pallas.' The wind had decreased a little, which was somewhat in her favour, but still, with the pressure of sail upon her, she heeled over as much as before. In smooth water she might have had the advantage, but, with the heavy sea then running, the Spaniards were evidently coming up with her. They were seen also to be steering different courses for the purpose of cutting her off. Lord Claymore, however retained his usual composure.

'Night will be down upon us soon, and then we will give the Dons the slip,' he observed calmly, and gave the order to have a lantern fixed on a ballasted cask prepared.

This was for some time carried over the stern and then lowered into the water. When this was done, the ship's course was altered, and she stood to the north-east leaving the enemy to follow the false light. After a little time one watch was sent below, and except that the sharpest eyes in the ship were kept on the look-out, everything returned to its usual routine, and many a weary form lay stretched in the hammocks.

Dawn came at last. As the first bright streaks appeared in the sky, look-outs were aloft, and as the darkness rolled away towards the far west, they shouted, 'No sail in sight!'

The captain breathed more freely—so did Morton. He had begun to fear that his prospects so lately brightening were again to be blighted. By keeping a constant look-out the 'Pallas' once more made the Eddystone Lighthouse.

'Now, my lads, we'll show our friends on the shore that we have redeemed our pledges,' cried the captain. 'Have on deck those chests with the golden candlesticks, Mr Nibs,' he added, turning to the purser. The chests were got up, and tackles being made ready to each mast-head, a golden candlestick was sent up and fixed above the truck. It was no easy work, but sailors can do anything that is possible. Thus with bags of dollars at the yard-arms, and rich brocades pendant from the stays, the frigate sailed up Plymouth Sound. Great was the excitement she caused, though she had already been looked for, as her four prizes, in spite of Hardman's prognostications, had arrived in safety before her.

All her crew who wished it got leave on shore; there was no fear of any running from her; their places would instantly have been filled by hundreds of eager applicants for a berth on board. Fully did Bob Doull carry out his intentions; and strange, though not very unusual, were the scenes witnessed in Plymouth and its neighbourhood for several days after the arrival of the ' Pallas.'

Coaches-and-four and coaches-and-six were seen driving about Plymouth, laden inside and out with seamen and their sweethearts, decked out in costumes of the most gaudy colours and extravagant fashion. Suppers and dancing closed the day. There was no great variety, perhaps, in the style of their amusements. The great object seemed to be to get rid of their money as rapidly as possible.

Ronald Morton, for the first time in his life, found himself possessed of what appeared to him a very large sum of money.

'It will be enough to sift this affair of my father's to the bottom, and if claims he has, to establish them thoroughly,' he observed to his captain.

Lord Claymore laughed heartily.

'My dear fellow, you know not what amount a lawyer's maw is capable of swallowing,' he answered. 'It will prove a mere soppit if the matter is contested, as undoubtedly it will be. However, we will see about it when we return from our next cruise. Till your father returns home, you can do nothing.'

Once more, her officers and crew having spent all their superfluous cash, the ' Golden Pallas,' as she was now called, put to sea.

CHAPTER XXVII.

LORD CLAYMORE AND THE FIRE SHIPS.—'PALLAS' ENGAGES BLACK FRIGATE.—COLONEL ARMYTAGE IN THE PENINSULA.

'MORTON, we ought to be content with the prizes we have made; we must now do something in the fighting way, or we shall be looked upon as mere buccaneers, who think of nothing but making money.'

This remark was made by Lord Claymore, after the frigate had been for some time in commission—had been to America and back, and being now on the French coast, had sent home a few more captures, though not of any very great value.

'That may be very well for a captain who has made the best part of eighty thousand pounds,' thought Morton, 'but for a poor lieutenant, who has made not a twentieth part of that, yet wants it as much, it is a very different affair.'

Ronald had begun to find the value of money, and also that it has wings with which to betake itself away. He acquiesced, however, in the propriety of fighting. An opportunity was not long wanting.

Before many days had passed the frigate was off the Isle d'Aix, on the French coast. She stood in; the captain and most of the officers with glasses at their eyes watching for the appearance of a French fleet. At length the masts and spars of several line-of-battle ships came in view. Still the frigate stood on till a three-decker—an eighty-gun ship—three seventy-fours, four frigates, and three brigs were counted. The little English frigate paraded up and down before the roadstead, but none ventured out to attack her. It was the French squadron under Admiral Allemand.

'I have been thinking over a plan which may sound terrible to the ears of some, but it is both feasible and right, I fully believe,' said the captain, after taking several turns on deck, and addressing his first lieutenant. 'We might set fire to or blow up into the air, one and all of those ships. I only wish that there were more together. You see they are deep in the water. They have stores on board, and are evidently intended for some expedition or other; an attack on our West India Islands, or to attack us in some other vulnerable part. They must or should be got rid of: other plans might be adopted; but I hold to that of THE FIRE-SHIPS. I should delight in conducting the enterprise. With a few brave men under me, on whose coolness and judgment I could rely, it would be certain to succeed. Morton, I would select you. Would it not be a glorious work?'

'If you selected me, my lord, I would certainly follow you, and do my utmost to carry out your directions,' answered Morton; 'but the idea of employing fire-ships has never been congenial to my taste. I would rather meet the enemy and destroy him in a general engagement.'

'That sounds very right and chivalric,' replied Lord Claymore, smiling; 'but observe the true state of the case. The object of going to war with an enemy is to sink, burn, and destroy his ships at sea, and to do him all the injury in our power on shore. In a general engagement you attack his fleet with yours, at the cost of some of your ships, perhaps, and the loss of many hundreds of your men. If a great victory is gained, a tenth, or at all events a twentieth, part of the enemy are killed and wounded. Now, by my plan the lives of very few of our own people are risked; perhaps no one may be lost; while the ships of the enemy are entirely destroyed; and though, of course, some of their people are sacrificed, probably not more are lost than in a general engagement, while the chances are that the war in consequence is more speedily brought to a conclusion, and the lives of thousands saved, and people able to return to their peaceful and useful occupations. Morton, I look upon war as a terrible curse. The sooner it can be put an end to the better, but I am very certain that in this instance it can only be by humbling our proud foes to the very dust. Napoleon will bite till every tooth in his head is drawn.'

Although Morton's reason was convinced by the reasoning of his enthusiastic captain, his feelings were not entirely satisfied. He, however, promised to aid him as far as he had the power in carrying out any project of that description which he might conceive.

The subject was again and again reverted to during the time the frigate was on the coast, and while he was engaged in the most stirring and often hazardous operations—such as cutting out vessels, armed and unarmed, landing and destroying telegraph stations, and storming and blowing up forts.

Once more the 'Pallas' returned to L'Isle d'Aix. The French squadron was still there.

'We must be at those fellows,' exclaimed Lord Claymore, as he walked the deck, looking towards the enemy with a greedy eye. 'We must get them out somehow or other, if we can. It would have a grand moral effect to carry off a prize from before their very noses.'

Morton was as eager as his chief. There was a soldier's wind, so that the frigate could stand in or off shore at pleasure.

'This is an opportunity many would rejoice to have; don't let us throw it away,' continued the captain, watching the French ships through his telescope. They lay at their anchors, seemingly determined not to move in spite of the bold enemy proudly cruising before their eyes.

'Give them a shot or two, Morton,' said the captain; 'we'll try if that does not excite them to bestir themselves.'

In advance of the rest of the squadron was a large frigate, painted black and heavily armed, and near her were three brigs. Still they were all under shelter of the batteries on the island.

With a shout of satisfaction the British crew observed the topsails of the black frigate and her three consorts let fall. It was a sign that they were coming out. The sails were sheeted home. Out they all four stood. The canvas of the 'Pallas' was reduced, and she was hove-to, in the most gallant way, to wait for them.

'We must have him, I am determined,' exclaimed the captain, as the enemy's frigate drew near. Everybody was as eager and sanguine as the captain, except Lieutenant Hardman.

'We have had all the luck hitherto—we must not expect to keep it,' he remarked to Glover. 'Remember what I often have said: There's many a ——'

A shot from the enemy, which came whizzing close over his head, and the loud shouts of 'Fire!' from the captain, cut short his remarks.

The crew gave a hearty cheer, and obeyed the order by delivering a rattling broadside at the advancing enemy.

More sail was now made on the frigate, so that she might be kept completely under command. The brigs coming up also commenced firing, as did the batteries on the island, but, boldly standing on, the English frigate gallantly engaged them all. The crew required no words of encouragement. Most of the men stood at their guns stripped to the waist, with their handkerchiefs bound round their heads, labouring with that determined energy which was the sure promise of victory. Now, as they could bring their guns to bear, they aimed at the brigs, now again at their larger opponent, the black frigate. As she drew near it was seen that she was greatly superior to the 'Pallas,' both in size and as to the number of her guns, while probably also her crew were much more numerous, but that in no way daunted Lord Claymore. On the contrary, he seemed the more eager not to part with her, but to carry her off as his prize.

In spite, however, of this superiority, the black frigate, as well as the brigs, showed a disposition to keep at a respectful distance. Several times the 'Pallas' had to tack to avoid the shoals surrounding the island. Besides this, her captain's aim was, by manœuvring, to get to windward of the black frigate, and also between her and the batteries, so that their shot would be likely to damage friends as well as foes. The brigs, which showed signs of being much cut up in their rigging, seemed inclined to keep at a respectful distance. The shots of the 'Pallas' were, however, aimed chiefly at her more worthy antagonist. The guns were admirably served. Again the men cheered. The first step towards victory had been gained. The mizen-mast of the black frigate had been shot away, and over the side it went, with its yards and sails.

The 'Pallas' ceased firing—so did the batteries, for they would have hit the French ship had they continued to do so. Once more the British frigate tacked. She had gained a position directly to windward of her opponents. Once more she opened her fire; it was with dreadful effect. She, however, was suffering much, both in spars and hull.

'This must be cut short,' observed the captain, calmly. 'Now, master, up with the helm, and carry us alongside the enemy. My men, be ready to board, the cutlass must decide the day.'

In gallant style the small English frigate bore down upon an opponent nearly twice her size. The 'Pallas' poured a well-directed broadside into the black frigate, and the instant afterwards there was a fearful concussion. The main-deck guns were driven in by the sides of the French ship, and at the same moment the maintopsail-yard was torn from the mast, and much other damage was done aloft, while the bumpkin, chain plates, cat heads, and bower anchor were carried away. In vain the captain called to his men to aid in lashing the two frigates together. Before they could assemble they had separated. Ronald, with a boarding party, was about to spring on to the deck of the French frigate, but he was too late to make the attempt.

Once more Lord Claymore was about to bear down on the French frigate, when Hardman pointed out to him two more French frigates coming out under all sail to the rescue of their friend. To have remained longer would have been madness. Lord Claymore was not a man to do a foolish rash thing. Waving his hat to the brave captain of the black frigate, who kept his post on a gun watching their proceedings, he ordered the tacks to be hauled aboard, and, without further injuring his opponent, stood out to sea. The guns were run in and secured, and the crew were sent aloft to repair damages. So severe, however, were they, that the 'Pallas' could scarcely have escaped from her pursuers, had not a sloop of war hove in sight and taken her in tow. The enemy's frigates, disappointed of their expected prey, returned to their anchorage.

'We must be back there some day, Morton, for if life and strength is allowed me, I will not rest till I have carried out my plan for the destruction of this remainder of the Frenchman's fleet.' Lord Claymore spoke, and faithfully he kept his word.

When the frigate rejoined the admiral she was found to be in so shattered a condition from her engagement with the Frenchman, that he sent her home to undergo repairs.

Morton was once more in England. He found a letter from his father, saying that the 'Lion' had not yet received orders to return home, but he hoped that she soon would. He added, that this trip had satisfied him; that if he was allowed once more to set foot on British ground he had determined to take up his abode on shore, and that what with the prize-money he had made, and the produce of his farm in Shetland, he should be able to live on shore in a style suited to the rank his son had gained, so that he should have a home to offer him whenever he was not employed. This was satisfactory news to Ronald. Curiously enough, his father did not once allude to Doull or Eagleshay. He seemed to have forgotten all about the mystery of his birth, and that it might possibly by their means be cleared up. The truth was, that he had always been contented with his lot. He saw his son in the fair way of rising in his profession, and he fancied that no advantage would be gained by ascertaining the truth, even if it were possible to do so.

Soon after the letters had been brought on board, Glover came into Ronald's cabin.

'Here, Morton, is news which will interest you!' he said, showing an open letter. It is from my cousin, Mrs Edmonstone—she and her husband are in England; they arrived some time ago. She tells me that they made the voyage with the Armytage family; Miss Armytage still unmarried, her mamma as amiable as ever, and the colonel as much the reverse as before; he is supposed to have gained very little advantage by his visit to India; his extravagance and love of play have ruined him: however, he has interest in high quarters, and soon after his return home, he got an appointment in the army in the Peninsula, and he has gone out there with his wife and daughter. In what part of Portugal or Spain they are, she does not tell me, but I will write and ascertain. There is a bare possibility of our being some day in the neighbourhood; and, judging of your wishes by mine own, I am sure that you would like to meet Mrs and Miss Armytage again, though you may wish to stand clear of the colonel.'

There is a happy familiarity among messmates which seldom exists between other people.

Morton thanked Glover, and acknowledged, after a moment's thought, that he should be delighted again to meet Miss Armytage.

'Am I bound to obey her father, who discards me simply because he believes me to be of inferior birth to his daughter?

I feel convinced that I am her equal. I have at all events gained the rank of a gentleman; I may some day obtain the fortune to support it, and to maintain her as well as her father can do. No; I feel that I am bound by no laws, divine or human, to yield to his unjust demands. If she loves me still, and I can win her, I will.'

Glover, who was fully acquainted with his friend's feelings, and to whom part of these remarks were addressed, highly applauded his resolution, and promised to afford him all the aid in his power.

The 'Pallas' was found to have received so much injury that her repairs would take a long time. Lord Claymore and his officers and crew were accordingly turned over to another frigate, the 'Imperious,' and ordered to proceed forthwith to the Mediterranean.

CHAPTER XXVIII.

RONALD JOINS THE 'IMPERIOUS.'—CHASE OF A FELUCCA.—THE MARQUIS DE MEDEA.—THE SPANISH PRIEST.—RONALD ASTONISHES THE PRIEST.

HE 'Imperious' had been some time in the Mediterranean. She had not been idle, nor had her crew; that was not likely under such a captain as Lord Claymore. She had been up the Levant, and cruising among the Ionian Islands, and then back to Gibraltar, and had returned to Malta; and her blue-jackets and marines had landed on the Spanish and French coasts, and, as they had done before on the Biscay shores, had captured forts, destroyed barracks, and other public buildings, and burnt a town or two, and cut out merchant-men and armed vessels of all sorts; indeed, had done as much mischief as they possibly could. In all these proceedings Ronald Morton had greatly distinguished himself, and his captain promised him that he would not rest till he had obtained for him his rank as a commander.

Morton was in better spirits than he had been for a long time. He was as ready as ever for any daring exploit, but he had no desire to throw his life away if he could help it; he had a fancy that there was something worth living for. The good Lord Collingwood so highly approved of the proceedings of the 'Imperious,' that he sent her back, after her return to Malta, to continue the same sort of employment.

On the passage, when not far off Minorca, a large felucca was sighted, which, from her manœuvres, was evidently anxious to avoid the frigate. Lord Claymore had received directions from the admiral to look out for a craft of this description, which was known to be a pirate, and to have committed innumerable atrocities. Chase was instantly made. The felucca on seeing this, and apprehending danger, rigged out her tall tapering lateen sails, wing-a-wing, as it is called, one on each side. She appeared like a graceful sea-bird, and did her utmost to escape. She sailed so well that there seemed a great possibility that she might effect this. The 'Imperious,' like some hugh bird of prey, followed in her wake, resolved on her destruction. As yet the felucca was beyond the range of the frigate's bow-chasers. One shot from those long guns striking her masts or slender spars, would effectually have stopped her flight. Over the blue waters she flew; the officers and crew of the frigate were watching her.

'She has an evil conscience, or she would not fly so fast,' observed Glover.

'Very likely; but like other rogues, she will escape the punishment she deserves,' answered Hardman. 'The wind is falling, that is in her favour.'

'Not if it fall altogether; we may take her with the boats,' remarked Morton. 'There is every sign of a calm.'

She has sweeps, and it is extraordinary the rate at which these craft can pull,' observed the pertinacious Hardman. 'She has every chance of getting away from us.'

'Hardman is a wise fellow. He is always expecting blanks that he may enjoy the prizes the more when they turn up,' said the surgeon.

'He loses the pleasure of anticipation, though,' said Morton. 'That is too often greater than the reality.'

'Ah, but I am saved the disappointment of the reverse,' answered the second-lieutenant. 'See our courses are hanging against the mast, and the felucca has lost the wind altogether. She has got out her sweeps, and off she goes like a shot.'

Just then the captain called Morton. 'We must take that fellow in the boats. Call away the crews of the pinnace and first and second cutters. Do not lose a moment. He will show fight, and it may save bloodshed to overawe him.'

The boats were instantly made ready, and in two minutes were pulling away full of armed men, and led by Morton to the attack of the felucca.

The crew of that vessel did not for some time discover them, and continued as before urging her on at a rapid rate with their long sweeps, evidently hoping to escape. The boats, however, gained on them fast, and in a short time they were seen to lay in their long sweeps, finding, probably, that escape was hopeless, and to prepare for the attack. As the boats drew near, Ronald ordered them to separate so as to board at different parts of the vessel. Her deck was soon crowded with men, who, from their varied costumes, had a very suspicious appearance. Some were at their guns, others held cutlasses or pistols in their hands, threatening to make a stout resistance. One tall old man in a Spanish dress, with a huge white moustache and a long thin beard, stood on the companion hatch waving his sword, and with loud vociferations calling on his men to fight. As the boats got within hail, Morton rose and ordered the crew of the felucca to throw overboard their weapons and yield, for they showed no flag which could be hauled down as a sign of surrender. The answer was a round of grape and langrage from three guns, and a volley of musketry. The missels flew, whizzing and whistling close to his head. Happily he was unhurt; but two of his boat's crew were hit, and the side of the boat riddled in several places. The British seamen dashed on, and in another instant were clambering over the low bulwarks of the felucca.

'What! are we, who have been fighting with honest Frenchmen all our lives, to be dared by a set of cut-throats like you?' Take that,' exclaimed Job Truefitt, as he dealt a blow which nearly severed a pirate's head from his shoulder.

The man fell dead, and Job and the rest springing on, the ruffians gave way, and many were driven overboard right across the deck, as a flock of sheep are swept away by a torrent. The old captain defended himself with all the fierceness of despair. He fought with the feeling that a rope was about his neck. Ronald at last reached him, and by a dexterous turn sent his sword flying over the side. The old man drew a pistol, but before he could fire it, Bob Doull, had sprung up at him, and, wrenching it from his hand, pulled him down to the deck. In vain he struggled, other seamen surrounded him, and he was secured. Several men of the pirate crew were driven overboard, and the rest leaped down below to avoid the cutlasses of the British. Some in the madness of their rage began to fire up at their captors. Fortunately, none of the latter were killed, or it would have fared ill with the pirates. Truefitt and others on finding this, leaped down among them, and singling out the culprits, bound them hand and foot, and bringing them on deck, threw them down with a kick in their sides, and an order to behave themselves.

Soon after the din of battle was over, some cries were heard proceeding from a cabin in the after part of the vessel. Morton at once, knocking off the companion-hatch, followed by a midshipman and several more, leaped below. As the skylight hatch was on, the cabin was very dark, but there was light sufficient to enable him to distinguish two old men and a young lady struggling in the power of some of the pirate crew, who had apparently forced their way into the cabin from forward. The ruffians were soon hauled off from their intended victims, and secured, with a double allowance of kicks, on deck, while Morton busied himself with rendering what assistance he could to the young lady and her companions. They were Spanish he found by their dress and language. One was habited in the costume of an ecclesiastic.

He was a thin, small old man, in whose sallow cheeks it seemed as if the blood could never have mantled, while from his calm exterior it could not have been supposed that he had just been rescued from imminent danger. The young lady, before Morton could reach her, had sunk down on a locker half-fainting.

'Air, air!' she murmured out, 'Oh, my father! see to him.'

The old man had sunk on the deck of the cabin. The priest stooped down to raise him up, while Ronald helped to knock off the skylight, and then went to the assistance of the young lady. The stream of fresh air which came from above helped to restore both daughter and father. They were then got upon deck, and the pure atmosphere, with a sight of the British flag, and their late masters bound hand and foot, soon completely restored them. The old gentleman was a fine looking Don of the ancient régime; the daughter, a perfect Spanish beauty, with raven hair and flashing eyes, and dark clear complexion. The old Don was profuse in his expressions of gratitude towards those who had rescued him from the hands of the pirates. He and his daughter, with his father confessor, the priest now present, had been travelling in France, when they heard that Spain was about to throw off the yoke of Bonaparte; and fearing that they should be detained, they got on board a small vessel to return to their own country. On their passage they had been attacked and captured by the felucca.

'That we have escaped with our lives is a mercy, when we reflect what atrocious villains are those into whose hands we fell, and from whom you have so nobly rescued us. That captain—the sooner you hang him at your yard-arm the better. He cumbers the earth. It is a disgrace to humanity to allow him to live.'

'We do not execute people in England without a trial; if the captain of the felucca is found guilty, he will probably be hung,' answered Morton, to whom this remark was made in French, a language the old Don spoke very well. Ronald did not altogether like his manner, or the expression of his countenance.

The sweeps of the felucca had been got out, and the boats had also taken her in tow, and she was now rapidly approaching the frigate.

During the time, Morton endeavoured to ascertain what he could about his new companions. Thinking that he might very possibly gain the information he wished for most easily from the priest, he took the opportunity of addressing him when out of hearing of the rest.

'You and your friends must have suffered much while in the power of those ruffians,' he remarked. 'That old gentleman has not yet recovered; he seems from his manner to be a man of rank.'

'Yes; he is one of the old grandees of Spain,' answered the priest.

'May I ask his name? for I wish to address him properly,' said Ronald.

'Certainly,' returned the priest. 'He is known as the Marquis de Medea.'

'How strange!' exclaimed Morton, involuntarily, for he had heard that name frequently repeated at Lunnasting, and had been taught to consider the possessor of the title certainly not in a favourable light.

The priest, as Ronald said this, gave him a glance as if he would look through him to his inmost soul, and yet he spoke softly and blandly as he asked, 'Why so? Why strange, sir?'

'It is a name I frequently heard in my boyhood,' answered Ronald, not supposing that there was the slightest necessity for being on his guard with the mild-looking priest.

'That is strange,' repeated the priest. 'Where was your boyhood passed, may I ask?' said the priest.

Ronald told him, 'Chiefly in the castle of Lunnasting, in Shetland.'

Again the priest gave a piercing glance at him.

'May I inquire your name?'

'I am called Ronald Morton.'

'You say you are called so. Will it appear impertinent if I ask if you believe that you have the right to bear another?' said the priest.

'Why do you put the question?' was Ronald's very natural demand.

'You said that you were called Morton. I fancied, from your tone, that you insinuated that you have a right to some other name,' said the priest.

'I may have some such idea; but at the same time I am perfectly contented with the one I bear.'

The priest appeared lost in thought.

'Do you remember your father?' he asked, abruptly.

'Certainly; he is, I trust, alive still. I hope to meet him shortly;' surprised at the way in which the priest continued to cross-question him. Some men would have been much annoyed, and refused to reply; but Ronald saw that his interrogator had some good reasons for putting the questions, and felt no inclination to disappoint him.

'May I ask if you were ever considered like the lady of Lunnasting Castle? Donna Hilda, I think you called her,' inquired the priest.

'I have not, that I am aware of, mentioned her name,' answered Morton, looking in his turn hard at the priest. 'I will reply to your question, though, before I ask one in return. I have heard that I was like her, and that is not surprising; my mother was very like her—they were cousins. Now I must inquire how comes it that you know anything of the family of Lunnasting? Were you ever in Shetland?'

'There are few parts of the world where I have not been. The members of my order go everywhere, and should know everything that takes place on its surface,' answered the priest, evasively.

'I do not recollect you in Shetland,' said Ronald, 'May I ask your name?'

'I am called Father John,' replied the priest, humbly. 'I would yet further ask you, what you know respecting the Marquis de Medea?'

Ronald considered whether he should reply.

'There can be no harm in speaking the truth, surely,' he said to himself. 'I will tell you,' he answered frankly. 'The marquis is believed, at Lunnasting, at all events, to have inherited the estates which should rightly have belonged to the son of Don Hernan Escalante, the husband of the Lady Hilda of Lunnasting, as she is called in Shetland, the daughter of Sir Marcus Wardhill. Moreover, it is believed that, instigated by the present marquis, a pirate crew attacked the castle, and carried off the son of Donna Hilda, of whom I speak, the rightful heir to the title and estates of Medea.'

Never, probably, had the countenance of the priest exhibited so much astonishment, or indeed, any sentiment, as it did at present.

'By what wonderful means have you become acquainted with what you have told me?' he asked.

'By the simplest of all; by having been told by those who were acquainted with the facts,' answered Ronald.

'But how were they informed of those facts?' asked the priest, with increased interest.

'They learned them from a Spanish naval officer, Pedro Alvarez by name, who was the lieutenant of Don Hernan. He had promised to assist his captain's widow and her infant son to the utmost of his power. He returned to Shetland for that purpose, and when he heard that the boy had been carried off, he sailed away in search of the pirate; he, however, never returned to Shetland, and it is believed that he perished before he accomplished his purpose. The young Escalante has never been discovered, though the poor Lady Hilda lives on in expectation of recovering her son.'

'No wonder that sacrilegious wretch, Pedro Alvarez, never returned to you. He was guilty of murdering one of the familiars of our most holy Inquisition. Had he ever caught the pirate he could not have returned to Spain, but must have been a wanderer on the face of the earth, with the mark of Cain on his brow.'

'I was a mere infant when he last came to Shetland, so that I have no personal recollection of him, but from what I have heard, he was very much liked by all with whom he associated,' said Ronald.

'Your heretical countrymen would probably think that killing an officer of the Inquisition was a very venial offence, and not look upon him with any horror on that account; but depend on it, an avenging Nemesis followed him to his grave, or will follow him, if he still lives,' remarked the priest. 'But we are now close to your ship. I would advise you not to let the marquis know that you are acquainted with that part of his history, which he would desire to keep secret. At first I thought that you were the son of Don Hernan, but I see that I was mistaken.'

As soon as the felucca was towed alongside the frigate, the prisoners, as well as the marquis and his daughter, and the priest, were removed on board.

After inspecting the felucca, the captain resolved to keep her as a tender to the frigate, believing that she might be made very useful in capturing the enemy's merchantmen, as, from her rig, she might get close to them without being suspected.

Lord Claymore highly commended Morton for the gallant way in which he had taken the vessel.

'I scarcely know what to do with the prisoners,' he observed. 'We must not cut their throats, or hang them at the yard-arms, but that would be the simplest way of disposing of them, and they probably will not come to any better end.'

Ronald also told his captain all he had heard of the Marquis of Medea.

'The old scoundrel!' was the answer. 'However, he is our guest, and he has a lovely daughter; we must treat him politely.'

The most important information, however, was the statement made by the marquis, that Spain had at length declared herself independent of France, and formed a league with England.

'It may be true, but we must not trust to it till we have more certain information,' remarked Lord Claymore.

The calm lasted long enough to have the felucca over-hauled, somewhat cleansed, and put in order. Glover was placed in command of her, with two midshipmen and twenty men. The prisoners were secured below on board the frigate, and sentries put over them, while Lord Claymore gave up a cabin to the young lady, and accommodated the marquis and the priest with cots in his own. It was very difficult to please the old marquis, who, notwithstanding the trouble taken to attend to his comfort, grumbled at everything—so much so, that Lord Claymore would have sent him on board the felucca to shift for himself, had it not been for his daughter, who showed herself contented and thankful for the kindness she and her father were receiving, while her brilliant smiles and joyous laughter proved that she was sincere in her expressions.

The breeze came at last, and the frigate, followed by the little felucca, stood on towards the Spanish coast.

In the course of his duty, Morton was going the round of the decks, when he heard a voice from among the prisoners calling to him in French: 'A poor dying wretch would speak to you. Have pity, brave Englishman, and hear what he has to say!'

'Who are you?' asked Morton.

'I was captain of the felucca. I am now a criminal, expecting speedy death,' returned the speaker.

DON TACON'S CONFESSION.

The master at arms held up the lantern he carried, and as its light fell on the countenance of the person who had addressed him, Morton recognised the old white-bearded captain who had made so desperate a resistance when his vessel was attacked. He had been lying at his length on some straw on the deck. He was now supporting himself on one arm that he might have a better look at the lieutenant as he passed.

'What would you say to me?' asked Morton.

Many things, if you will listen to me,' answered the old pirate. 'I overheard part of your conversation with the priest. I know more about you than you suppose.'

'What can you know about me?' asked Morton, very much surprised. 'Here are two persons I fall in with unexpectedly and both assert they know more about me than I do myself,' he thought.

'If you will have me removed out of earshot of my comrades, I will tell you,' replied the old pirate. 'We cannot speak in a language which some of them do not understand.'

Morton ordered the old man to be unshackled, and to be conducted to another part of the deck. After he had gone his rounds, he returned and took a seat on a bucket by his side.

'Thanks, sir, for this kindness,' said the old pirate; though as he spoke Ronald rather doubted his sincerity. 'It is not thrown away. You see before you a victim to circumstances. I have done many evil deeds—many things of which I repent —but necessity drove me to commit them; poverty, that stern task-master, urged me on—not inclination, believe me. I say this that you may not look at me with the disgust that you might otherwise do. However, I am not now going to give an account of my life—I may some day, if you desire it; simply I will tell you who I am. You know already who the old man is whom I took prisoner.'

'I should like to know who you are,' said Ronald.

'I am, then, the celebrated Don Annibal Tacon,' said the

old man, in a tone of no little conceit. 'I have made my name famous in most parts of the world. For some reason or other, however, my enterprises have not been as successful as they ought, and I have continued in the same state of poverty in which I began life. I say this as an excuse for myself, and to excite your compassion. It is not the matter on which I wish to speak to you. I have, since my early days, been acquainted with the Marquis de Medea. He, too, led a wild life in his youth; and there are many things he did which he would not like mentioned. Many years ago, when you were but a child, he encountered me in Cadiz. Promising me a large reward, and giving me a handsome sum as an earnest of his intentions, he engaged me on a hazardous and daring enterprize. It was no less than to sail to the North of England—to the islands of Shetland—and to carry off from a castle, situated on the shores of one of them, a child, the son of a certain Captain Don Hernan Escalante. I see you are interested in my account; you may well be so. I heard you speaking of that castle. I accomplished my errand. I attacked the castle, bore away the child, and purposed to return to Cadiz to receive my reward, and to learn what the noble marquis wished as to the disposal of the boy. I had some idea, indeed, of concealing him, and employing him to wring from the marquis the gold which I might require. My plans were, however, frustrated. I was driven by a gale nearly across the Atlantic, and so many British cruisers swarmed in all directions, that I was continually driven back whenever I attempted to approach the Spanish coast. At length a Spanish vessel hove in sight. As she drew nearer, I recognized her as a corvette commanded by an officer I knew, Pedro Alvarez by name. I at first thought she was a friend, but, by the way she approached, I suspected she had hostile intentions. I endeavoured to make my escape, for I have always held that men should never fight if they can help it. That is to say, if an enemy has a rich cargo on board, a wise man may fight to capture it; but if he himself has anything of value on board, he will fly to preserve it, and only fight when he cannot preserve it by any other means.

'The corvette bore down upon us, and so well did she sail, that I found escape impossible. She ran me aboard; and Pedro Alvarez and half his crew, leaping down on my decks, drove my people before them; he fought his way into the cabin—there was the infant, on the possession of whom I rested the hopes of my future support. He seized it, and hurrying back to his own vessel, called his people to follow him, and then, casting my craft free, he stood away to the eastward, without firing a shot at my vessel, seeming content with the mischief he had already done me. Believing that he would at once go back to Spain, denounce the marquis, and proclaim me as his tool, I dared not return to Cadiz. I therefore sailed for the West Indies, and employed myself in an occupation which I found tolerably lucrative, seeing that all the transactions were for ready money, though it must be owned that it was somewhat hazardous. Some people might call it piracy. It was not till long afterwards, when I was paying a visit to Cadiz, that I learned that Pedro Alvarez was himself an outlaw, that he had not returned to Cadiz, and that neither he nor his ship had ever again been heard of.

'From the words which reached my ears while you were talking to that wily priest, I have an idea that you are no other than the son of Don Hernan and the lady of that northern castle. By whatever means you got back there, my evidence will be of value to prove that you are the child I carried off. I have no doubt about it; I would swear to the fact. Let us be friends, then. You assist to preserve my life; I will help you to obtain your rights as the Marquis de Medea, and to become the master of the immense estates belonging to the family.'

The old villain looked up into the young officer's face, expecting a favourable reply. Ronald was almost inclined to laugh at his outrageous audacity and cunning. 'You are entirely mistaken as to whom I am,' he answered. 'The child you carried off from Lunnasting was never brought back. I cannot even tell you if he is still alive; but whether or not, I have no power to make any bargain with you. You must abide by the consequences of your misdeeds.'

'I have always done that,' answered the pirate, with an humble look. 'From my youth up till now I have been an unfortunate man. I hope some day the tide will turn; but there is not much time left for that.'

Ronald made no reply. He resolved to tell the captain all he had heard; and on going aft he left directions that the old prisoner should be strictly watched, and not allowed to communicate with any one.

As Ronald could not speak to Lord Claymore in the cabin lest he should be overheard, he waited till he came on deck.

'A pretty set of scoundrels!' was Lord Claymore's remark. 'That cunning priest, too, depend on it, has a finger in the pie. A curious coincidence there is, too, in your own history, and in that of the story you have just told me. You want to find out to what family you belong, and here is a title, estates, and fortune, waiting to be filled by the rightful heir, if he can be found.'

Though the captain entertained a considerable amount of contempt for the marquis, for the sake of his daughter he treated him with his usual courtesy. He felt that he should be very glad to get him out of the ship; still, by keeping him on board, he might possibly gain some information which might prove useful in establishing the claims of Hilda Wardhill's son to the property of his father. The most important object was to discover if that son was alive, and where he was, and what had become of Pedro Alvarez.

Lord Claymore and Ronald talked the subject over with such intense eagerness, that the latter almost forgot his own interests in the desire he felt to be of service to one whom he justly looked on as his patroness and the protectress of his youth. The homicide of the familiar of the Inquisition fully accounted for Pedro's not returning to Spain; while as that country had been for so many years at war with England, he might have found it impossible to send him back to Shetland. He might have written, to be sure, but the letters might have miscarried. Nothing was more probable. It was too likely, however, that both he and the boy were lost. Still Lord Claymore hoped the contrary, and, perhaps, his anxiety was not a little increased by the satisfaction he anticipated in ousting the rascally old marquis from his estates and rank.

The coast of Spain was soon after made, and the active operations in which the ship was engaged allowed the captain or Morton very little time to think of that or any other subject.

CHAPTER XXIX.

RONALD MEETS HIS FATHER.—OLD DOULL RECOGNISES ROLF MORTON.—MORTON RECOGNISES FATHER MENDEZ.—ROLF MORTON'S DIPLOMACY.—A FORT ATTACKED.—BLUE JACKETS ON SHORE.

 FEW days after the 'Imperious' reached the coast, a brig of war hove in sight. The frigate stood towards her, and when the two vessels had hove-to, the commander of the brig came on board, and confirmed the statement made by the marquis and the priest, that Spain had made peace with England, and had determined to throw off the French yoke.

'Much good may our allies do us,' remarked Lord Claymore who had a profound contempt for the Spaniards. 'A cowardly braggadocio set. I would place no dependence on their support in case of need.'

The commander of the brig bowed; he was not likely to dispute the matter with his lordship.

'By-the-by, I have brought a passenger—an old shipmate of mine, whom Mr Morton will at all events be glad to see.'

'And so shall I,' said Lord Claymore, glancing at the gangway, at which a fine, stout, elderly-looking man appeared, dressed in plain clothes. Ronald sprang aft, and grasped his hand.

'Father, I little expected to see you. Where have you come from?'

'From Malta last,' answered Rolf Morton. 'I went out there to look for you. When I arrived home in the old "Lion," and was paid off, I applied for and obtained my discharge from the service. I found that I had made a mistake in going to sea the last time. It did not suit me. I felt, too, that for your sake as well as my own, it would be better for me to live in a private capacity on shore. You are a lieutenant, and may soon be a commander. It would stand in your way in society to have it said that your father was a boatswain; not that you would be ashamed of me, I am sure, but we cannot make people wiser, we must take them as they are. Besides, I am more at liberty to attend to the subject you wrote to me about. I am not very sanguine of success, but still it would be satisfactory, for your sake, to discover after all that I was of good family, and to find some relations for you.'

After Rolf Morton had talked for some time with his son, Lord Claymore sent for him. He had heard from the commander of the brig that he had retired from the service. He shook him warmly by the hand.

'It will be pleasant for you to be together, and as the brig has to return immediately, I shall be glad if you like to remain on board. Your son, I doubt not, can put you up.'

Rolf Morton thanked the captain for his kindness. It was the very thing he wished. He wanted to be for some time with Ronald, and to talk to old Doull and Eagleshay, to ascertain what they knew about his early days.

Most of the prisoners taken in the felucca were sent to Malta, but Captain Tacon was kept on board the frigate, as Lord Claymore considered that he might assist in clearing up the matter in which he was so much interested, and be made useful in other ways, from his knowledge of the coast and of the towns and villages near it.

Rolf was naturally eager to see Doull and Eagleshay. The

two old men were sent for. Their astonishment was very great when they were told that he was the boy they had carried off from Shetland nearly fifty years before. He assured them that he clearly recollected the circumstance, and that two of the men were tall, like them, and that there was one much older and shorter. They both looked at him very earnestly for some time. At last Doull exclaimed—

'I remember well a mark on the laddie's hand; a spike or a nail had run through it just between the bones of the fore and second finger... It was a curious mark to be in the hand of so small a child, and I mind well thinking that mark will never wear out, and I shall know the boy whenever I meet him again.'

While the old man was speaking, Rolf was examining his hand. He held it out with the back up; there, sure enough, was visible, through the brown, hairy skin, a deep mark, evidently produced as Doull had described.

'Father,' there can be no longer any doubt about the matter,' exclaimed Ronald with more excitement than he usually exhibited.

'I am afraid that the evidence will not be considered very strong in a court of law,' observed Rolf. 'However, it leaves no doubt on my mind that these two men assisted to carry me off. But that is all! they cannot say, more than I can, to what family I belong; and as for this paper which they say they signed, that of course is irretrievably lost. Ronald, I have made up my mind what I will do—I will go back to Whalsey and take possession of my farm. I no longer fear Sir Marcus Wardhill—he can do me no harm, and I will try to live at peace with the old man. I will take these two men, Doull and Eagleshay, with me. Lord Claymore will give them their discharge. They are no longer fit for duty. They shall be well looked after, for I bear them no ill-will for the injury they did me. All has been for the best, I doubt not: we can but do our duty and trust in Providence.

Ronald heartily entered into his father's plans, though he felt much more sanguine than he did as to the result. He said that he had little doubt but that Lord Claymore would grant a superannuated discharge to the two old men.

'All will be right,' said Rolf, cheerfully. 'I must, however, take a cruise with you first, my lad. It will be time enough to think of going home when we fall in with a ship bound that way.'

Rolf had gone into the gun-room soon after his arrival on board, and did not return on deck till the evening. When he made his appearance, the marquis and his daughter and the priest were assembled there. All the officers, and especially Glover, welcomed him cordially, and Lord Claymore came up and spoke to him in the kindest way. Rolf looked across the deck at the Spanish party, and could not help fixing his eyes on the priest.

'I am sure it is him,' he exclaimed. 'I never saw a stronger likeness; years have only dried him up a little.' And without another word he walked up to the old man, and said—

'What, Father Mendez! it is long since we met; but don't you know me?'

The priest cast a calm glance at him, totally free from astonishment, as he answered—'Time changes all people. If it is long since we met, you must excuse me if I do not recollect you.'

'I forgot that,' said Rolf, frankly. 'My name is Morton —we met in Shetland. Were you not then called Father Mendez?'

'I am called Father John,' said the priest in the same calm tone as before.

This reply would have irritated many men, but Rolf looked at him, and said quietly—'That may be your present name, but unless my recollection strangely deceives me, you were called Mendez.'

The priest bowed and replied—'I have seen many people in the course of my life. It is possible we have met, but you will understand that the memory of a man, as he advances in life, is not as good as it was in his youth.'

'I have the advantage of you in that respect, certainly,' persisted Rolf, in a manner very different to his usual custom.

'Come, come, Father Mendez! we were too much together in days gone by for you to have forgotten me any more than I have forgotten you,' continued Morton. 'I do not wish to annoy you, but I wish you to do an act of justice. The son of your former patron and friend, Don Hernan Escalante, was carried off from his mother's house by the crew of a schooner which suddenly appeared before the place. He has never since been heard of: what has become of him? I ask. His mother has friends in this ship who will insist on knowing the truth. It will be wiser for you to speak it at once.'

The priest was more thrown off his guard by this appeal than he probably had ever been before.

'I know nothing of Don Hernan's child,' he answered quickly. 'I did not carry him off, nor was I privy to it. I could not be guilty of such a deed; the members of my order never employ violence to bring about what they desire. That alone ought to convince you that I am guiltless of the charge you make against me.'

Morton was not in the slightest degree more convinced than at first by what the father said.

'Then, at all events, you do not deny that you were in Shetland, and that I knew you as Father Mendez?' said Rolf.

The marquis and his daughter were all this time watching the speaker with looks of astonishment.

'There would be no object in denying that such was the case,' answered the priest. 'I was in Shetland rather more than twenty years ago, and I was then known as Father Mendez. I am at present called Father John.'

'I thought so,' observed Rolf, bluntly. 'You'll understand me, sir—I am but a rough seaman, and all I want is fair play. You and I were present at the marriage of that unhappy lady of Lunnasting Castle. We are the only surviving witnesses, besides Pedro Alvarez, and where he is to be found no one knows. What I ask you is, to help me to see her righted, and to find her lost son. Now that England and Spain are friends again, her son may be discovered with less difficulty than before; when discovered, assist in enabling him to regain his father's property in Spain, which was, if I remember rightly, at once taken possession of by his relative, who, from the accounts received in Shetland, was a very great rogue; the Marquis of Medea he was called. I am not wrong, I fancy.'

Father Mendez rapidly thought over the state of the case. The marquis had certainly supported him during the misfortunes which their country had suffered by the French invasion, but he had been anything but a generous patron, and it occurred to him that he might make a far better bargain with the rightful heir, if he could be found; and he believed that Rolf Morton, notwithstanding what he said, had the clue to his discovery, if he did not already know where to place his hand on him. When therefore, Rolf, feeling that he might have been too abrupt and uncourteous in the way he had addressed him, apologised for his roughness, the priest answered blandly—

'Do not concern yourself, my friend, on that account. We are old acquaintance. I have good reason to remember your sterling qualities, which far outweigh all others, and I own that it would be with great satisfaction that I found you looked upon me as a friend. I love justice as much as you do, and most anxious I am to attain it for the son of my old and esteemed friend, Don Hernan. Tell me how I can assist you, and I promise you all the aid I can afford.'

Rolf Morton was not so completely deceived by this speech as the priest might have supposed. He, however, thanked him, and rejoined Ronald in his quarter-deck walk, which they had to themselves, as the captain and most of the officers had gone below.

Very great was Rolf's surprise when he found that the dignified old gentleman on the other side of the deck was the Marquis de Medea, and still more so on hearing that the very man who had carried off the young Hernan Escalante was in irons below.

Ronald reported to Lord Claymore the fresh discoveries that had been made. 'All will go right, Morton, in the end, depend on that,' he answered. 'I am very sanguine that the young Hernan, if he is forthcoming, will obtain his rights, and so will your father his; those two old men were not fallen in with by you in so unlikely a way, except for some object. "Never despair!" has always been my motto, adopt it, there is no safer one.'

Lord Claymore would very gladly have landed the disagreeable marquis and the priest on the first part of the coast of Spain they made; but as the French still held numerous ports and towns to the west, they would have found it impossible to travel towards Cadiz, to which they expressed their wishes to proceed, and as there was a lady of the party, he could not, without great want of courtesy, have put them on shore. For the sake indeed of Don Josef's daughter, Donna Julia, the captain would very gladly have borne with his haughty and morose manners. The young lady, indeed, contrived to enchant every one on board; and those who knew the character of her father, and entertained hopes of dispossessing him of his property, could not help feeling compassion for one so young and lovely, who would, should they succeed, be in reality the principal sufferer.

The frigate was not to be idle; numberless were the dashing exploits performed by her gallant crew. In most of them Ronald took an active part, and several times his father insisted on accompanying him, as he observed, just to make him feel young again. Numerous vessels were also captured—one was a French privateer; some Spaniards taken in a prize were on board her. From these men Lord Claymore learned that within a day's sail there was a strong and important castle, garrisoned by French troops. This castle commanded a pass on the road by which the chief communication was kept open between the borders of France and the French army on the Ebro. A Spanish force, it was said, had already assembled, and commenced the siege of the place, but with little success. The frigate made a long tack off the coast; when she again stood in the fort was made out, situated on a commanding elevation, overlooking the road which wound along the shore. The frigate had her guns run out, and the crew stood at their quarters, ready for action. The officers, with their glasses, were examining the coast. The sun shone brightly; the water was blue, still more blue was the sky, shedding a brilliancy over the sand, the rocks, the hill-sides clothed with verdure, showing here and there the darker tints of orange or olive groves, with lighter shades where vineyards clothed the ground. Had it not been for that ominous-looking little fort, with its extended outworks, the landscape would have exhibited a picture of perfect rest and peace.

Nearer and nearer approached the frigate, gliding majestically over the smooth sea. Suddenly, emerging from a ravine, appeared a long line moving slowly on. Then dots which might have been mistaken for minute insects separated from it, and here and there puffs of smoke were seen, which were replied to by the fort with other puffs, and the faint thunder of cannon was heard on board the frigate.

'Those must be Spaniards attacking the fort,' exclaimed the captain, mechanically whistling for a breeze to urge on the ship with the rapidity that might satisfy his impatience.

In a short time the whole line was enveloped in smoke, and every gun on the south side of the fortifications commenced firing, forming so dense a cloud that the operations of the assailants could no longer be distinguished.

'The Spaniards will have completed the work, and gained all the glory, before we can get there to help them,' cried Glover. 'I wish we had more wind!'

'So do the Spaniards, but depend on it they will wait for us. There will be nothing desperate done till we get up to their assistance,' observed Hardman.

The marines were now ordered to prepare for landing. The captain had made up his mind to storm the place under cover of the frigate's guns. Morton volunteered to lead the party. The captain was doubtful about letting him go. Rolf declared that if his son went, he would go also as a volunteer. At last the wished-for breeze came, and the frigate rapidly approached the scene of action.

The breeze lifted the canopy of smoke which hung over it, and the combatants could now be seen, the Spaniards pushing on in great force and clambering over an out-work, from which the French, still fighting bravely, were retreating.

'Ay, those Spaniards have many an act of outrage and cruelty to avenge,' observed the captain. 'Their blood is up now; I never saw them fight so bravely.'

The spectacle greatly increased the eagerness of all on board the frigate to take part in the work. The crews of the boats, and those who were to go on the expedition, stood in readiness, with pistols in their belts, and cutlasses at their sides; the marines drawn up, stiff and prim, ready to step into the boats, offering a strong contrast to the blue-jackets, with their rolling, somewhat swaggering movements, while several not told off to go were stealing round in the hopes of being able to slip unnoticed into the boats.

The Spaniards, apparently encouraged by the approach of the British ship, and knowing that those they had some reason to suspect were witnesses of their conduct, charged with greater vigour.

A FORT STORMED.

At length the wished-for moment arrived. The 'Imperious' reached in as close as the depth of water would allow. A spring had been got ready on her cable. The moment the anchor was dropped she opened her broadside on the fort, while the boats collecting on the other, the men sprang into them, and giving way, they pulled with lusty strokes towards the shore. The forts opened fire on them, but the boats were small objects, and though the shots ploughed up the water ahead and astern of them, no one was hit. As they reached the beach some way to the southward of the castle, the marines and bluejackets sprang on shore, and instantly formed; then 'Onward!' was the word. The Spaniards welcomed them with vivas. There was little time for Morton to exchange greetings with the Spanish chief. A supply of scaling ladders had been prepared and brought on shore, and Lord Claymore had taken good care that they should be long enough. The seamen carried them, and rushed on, following Ronald and his father. Rolf kept up with the activity of a younger man. On they went; they soon distanced the Spaniards. The outworks had been secured. Through them they dashed. The scaling ladders were planted against the walls; the French made some attempt to throw them down, but some of the seamen held them fast at the foot while the others climbed up. Nothing could stop their impetuosity.

The Spaniards were now swarming up likewise. The enemy fought with the courage of despair. They well knew that, should they fall into the hands of the Spaniards, their doom would be sealed. A number of Spaniards had made good their footing, when the French charged them with such fury that many were cut down, or hurled back over the wall. Two or three were defending themselves bravely. One of the number fell. Morton, seeing what was taking place, and that they would all be killed, calling some of his men, made a dash at the enemy. Rolf was by his side, and lifting up the man who had been wounded, bore him out of the fight. More marines and seamen clambered up.

The Frenchmen gave way and fled to the citadel. Some were cut down while bravely defending the gate. The rest got in; the portal was closed, and then a white flag was hung out, as a token that the governor was ready to surrender on terms. His sole proposal was that he and his men might be conveyed on board the British ship-of-war, to save them from the certainty of being cut to pieces by the Spaniards, should they have them in their power.

The Spaniard whom Rolf had rescued was full of gratitude. He had been knocked down, but his wound was not dangerous. He was a militia-man; a brave fellow, as he had proved himself by the ardour with which he had scaled the walls. He put his house and everything he possessed at the service of those who had preserved his life. He lived, he said, some way to the south. He should now return home, having had fighting enough, and a wound to show as a proof of his patriotism.

Ronald took the offers at what he believed them worth, and parted from him on the most friendly terms. The prisoners were conveyed on board the frigate; and as they embarked, the scowling looks the Spaniards cast on them showed what would have been their fate had they remained on shore.

Part only of the work to be accomplished was performed. As the French would soon again occupy the fort if it was left without a garrison, and as the Spaniards could not be depended on, it was necessary to blow it up. A supply of powder was found in it; some more was landed from the ship. Excavations were made under the walls; the train was laid. One gig only remained. Bob Doull undertook to fire the train. The rest of the crew were in their seats, with oars in hand, ready to pull off. Ronald stood up in the stern-sheets to give the word. Bob applied the match, and stooped down as if to blow it, and was in consequence sent reeling backward, while the fire, like a snake, went hissing along the ground. Ronald shouted to him. He picked himself up, and rushed down to the boat with his hair singed and his face blackened like a negro's.

'Shove off, my lads! Give way!' cried Ronald.

Not a moment was to be lost. As it was, they could scarcely hope to get beyond the influence of the explosion. There was a hollow, rumbling sound, and then, in clouds of smoke and flame and dust, up flew the whole of the fortress into the air. The next moment down rushed huge masses of masonry; it seemed indeed as if the solid rock itself had been rent, and filled up the whole of the road. Some loud splashes astern showed that the boat had but narrowly escaped destruction.

'The French will find it difficult to pass this way again for some time to come,' observed Morton to the midshipman who accompanied him.

'Yes, sir,' observed the youngster, who was somewhat of a philosopher. 'It is wonderful how easy it is to knock a thing to pieces. It must have taken some years to have put all those stones together.'

CHAPTER XXX.

LORD CLAYMORE ON SHORE.—MORTON AGAIN MEETS EDDA.—
RONALD'S NEW FRIEND, DON JOSEF.

HE frigate continued her cruise further to the south; she touched at several places, and Lord Claymore or Morton went constantly on shore to urge the Spanish authorities and the people to take up arms, and to assist in organising their forces. From the information the captain received, he considered it important to communicate with some influential people a short way in the interior. He gave his instructions to Morton, therefore, and directed him to take two men as a body-guard, and to set off at once. Ronald selected Truefitt and Doull, the first for his steadiness and the other for his cool courage, and having procured a guide and a horse, and two wretched mules which had been too decrepit for the enemy to carry off, proceeded on his mission.

Ronald and his guide rode on ahead, the two seamen following. Neither of them were better horsemen than are sailors in general, but they were at all events able to stick on, in spite of the kicks and stumbles and flounders their animals occasionally gave; each was armed with a good thick stick, besides a cutlass by his side and a brace of pistols in his belt.

'This is a pleasanter sort of a cruise, mate, to my notion, than we've had the chance of for many a day,' observed Doull.

'Keep up on your four legs, you brute, now. The people here, though, seems to me to be an outlandish set; did you ever hear such a rum way of speaking as they've got? they all seem to have got lumps of biscuit or duff, or something of that sort, down their throats.'

'That's the way they have. Different people speak a different lingo, just as different animals make different noises,' answered Job, sententiously. 'I can't say as how I likes these Dons; they've too stuck up and stand clear a manner about them to please me.'

'That's my notion, too, Job,' said Bob. 'I like the Mounseers a precious sight better; when one is friends with them, they take to our ways a hundred-fold better than these Dons. They'll talk and laugh away, and drink too, with a fellow, just for all the world as if they were as regular born Christians as we are. That's what a Don will never do; he won't drink with you, he won't talk to you, he won't laugh or dance, and what's more, he won't fight with you; and that's what the Mounseers never refuses to do, and that's why I likes them.'

Morton enjoyed the change very much, from his usual life on board ship; he had not the same objection to the Spaniards as had his followers, and as he had now sufficiently mastered their language to converse with ease, he was never at a loss for amusement, and was able to obtain all the information he required about the country. Three days were consumed in reaching his destination; the French, he found, had lately been in that part of the country, but had retired northward. The people were anxious to drive the French out of their country, but they wanted arms, and money, and leaders.

Ronald was treated with great courtesy wherever he appeared, and he felt himself a much more important personage than he had ever before been. He had concluded the work on which he had been sent, and was about to return to his ship, when one of the Spanish officials informed him that he had received notification of the approach of a British commissioner, a military officer, to assist them in organizing their forces.

'He must be a great man, an important person,' observed the Spaniard; 'for he travels with many attendants, and his wife and family. No Spanish ladies would dream of travelling about the country at a time like this.'

Morton considered that it would be his duty to communicate with the commissioner, and hearing that he was only a day's journey off, he set out to meet him. The village at which he arrived in the afternoon, like most in Spain, consisted of neat, low, white-washed houses, with bright, red-tiled roofs, most of them having massive wooden verandahs and trellis-work in front, forming arbours, over which vines in rich profusion were taught to trail. The interior, at all events, had a neat and clean appearance, but several blackened ruins, loop-hooled walls, the upper part of which were thickly bespattered with bullet-marks, showed that it had been lately the scene of, perhaps, a brief but desperate encounter between the hostile forces. The inn where the British commissioner was said to be was pointed out to him. It was a long low building like the rest in the place; the ground floor being divided into two compartments, one serving as a kitchen and common eating-room, the other as a stable and sleeping-place for the muleteers; the upper part consisted of one large room, with dormitories roughly partitioned off round it. An English cavalry soldier was doing duty as sentry at the door. He informed Morton that the colonel had gone out with some of the authorities in the neigbourhood, but that the ladies were upstairs.

While Ronald was doubting what he should do, another man appeared and begged that he would walk up and remain till the colonel returned. Handing the bridle to his attendants with directions to them to wait for him, he threw himself off his horse, and followed the servant through the dark smoky kitchen to the stairs leading to the upper floor. His heart beat more quickly than usual, for he had a hope, though a faint one, that he was about once more to meet Edda Armytage, yet again he thought it very improbable that Colonel Armytage would bring her and her mother, accustomed as they had been to all the luxuries of life, into a part of the country in which travelling was so inconvenient and dangerous. Still they were in Spain. Of that Mrs Edmonstone had assured Glover. He sprang up the steps. The door was opened. He walked in with more than usual precipitation. At one end of the room were several persons with cloaks over their shoulders, and, hat in hand, sitting silent and solemn, evidently waiting the return of the commissioner. At the further end, in the deep window recess, sat two ladies. The back of one was turned towards him. The other was looking down at a piece of work on which she was engaged. Though jaded and looking very sad, her countenance was, he was certain, that of Mrs Armytage. His quick step roused both the ladies. They turned round. In an instant Edda's hand was placed in his. The rich blood mantled in her cheeks, her eyes sparkled with pleasure. She forgot everything but the happiness of again meeting him. Mrs Armytage received him most cordially. The Spaniards looked on at what was taking place, and twirled their moustachios. They thought the young stranger officer a very happy fellow. After the first greetings were over, and Ronald had explained how he came to be at the place, Mrs Armytage told him that Colonel Armytage had met with considerable pecuniary losses, and that when he received the appointment he now held, he wished her to accompany him, and that Edda had insisted on not being left behind.

'We knew that there were inconveniences to be encountered, though we did not suppose that there were any dangers to be feared to which we would not gladly submit for the sake of accompanying Colonel Armytage, who so much requires our care,' observed Mrs Armytage. 'The inconveniences are more ridiculous than disagreeable, and I fully believe Edda enjoys them; and as to dangers, we have found none hitherto, and rather look for them to add zest to the interest of the journey.

Mrs Armytage went on speaking in this strain for some time, when she became very grave. Ronald suspected that, although she might not have been unwilling to come, it was not only her husband's state of health which had induced her to accompany him. He knew how selfish and tyrannical Colonel Armytage always was, and he suspected that he had not given his wife the choice of remaining behind. Edda, as she watched her mother's countenance, grew silent, and a shade of melancholy also stole over her features. Mrs Armytage at last spoke.

'We are truly glad to see you again, Mr Morton, and you know how high you stand in both Edda's estimation and mine. Nothing you have ever done has forfeited our regard, but I dread that when Colonel Armytage returns he will not treat you in the way that we would desire. You know that he is irritable, and that when he has taken up a prejudice it is difficult to eradicate it. He has not got over the objections which he formerly expressed to you. Earnestly do I wish that he would. But you are generous and noble-minded; you will not think unkindly of us because one we are bound to obey treats you unjustly. I know that I describe my daughter's feelings, and I speak thus because I feel that it is due to you to say it.'

While her mother was speaking, Edda looked up imploringly at Ronald. He could not help perceiving that her countenance wore an expression of tenderness and love towards him, and it was a sore trial for him to promise compliance with the unjust demands which her father might make on him. Mrs Armytage had spoken as she felt she was bound to do. In her heart she rebelled against her husband's commands. Edda was old enough both to judge and act for herself, she considered. She had perfect confidence in her sense and discretion. Scarcely conscious of what she was doing, she rose from her seat and went

RONALD MEETS COLONEL ARMYTAGE.

to her room, leaving her daughter and Ronald together. The window recess was very deep; Edda had retired into it, and was thus concealed from the view of the people at the other end of the room. Ronald stood with his back towards them.

'Edda, I have never ceased to think of you, to ground all my expectations of earthly happiness on the hopes of making you mine,' he exclaimed in a low deep voice. 'You require no assurances of my love and my constancy; then promise me that you will not consent to become another's whatever may occur. I dare not ask you to disobey your father, and marry me against his will; but for your own sake, for mine, I do entreat you not to yield to his authority so far as to marry one you cannot love. I have hopes, great hopes that his objections to me may be removed; but till they are so, I dread lest he should compel you to give your hand to some one else. The promise I ask will give you strength to resist any unjust exercise of authority. No one holds in more respect than I do the duty of the obedience of a child to a parent; but in this case it would, I am certain, work woe to you, sorrow to your mother, and ultimate regret to your father. You will be firm, Edda? Promise me.'

'Indeed, indeed I will,' answered Miss Armytage. 'Most faithfully and unreservedly I promise you that.'

At that moment there was a commotion among the people at the other end of the room, and a scraping of their feet on the floor as they rose from their seats. They simultaneously began to bow with a formal air; the noise they had created made Ronald turn his head, and as he did so, he saw an officer in full uniform entering the room, followed by a number of persons in various costumes. A second glance told Ronald that Colonel Armytage was before him.

Ronald at once advanced to meet him, and said, 'I am an officer of his Majesty's ship 'Imperious.' I was sent by my captain to communicate with the people in this district, and hearing that you were in the neighbourhood, I considered it my duty to inform you of what I have done.'

'In that light I am perfectly ready to receive you sir,' said the colonel, with a stiff bow. 'But you will have the goodness to proceed at once with your narrative: you see that there are a number of people waiting to transact business with me, and that my time is short.'

Ronald felt a disagreeable sensation at his heart as the colonel was speaking, but he overcame his feelings, and at once entered on the business which had brought him to the place.

The manner of Colonel Armytage was stiff and ungracious in the extreme. Ronald had done everything so well, and gave so clear an account of all the arrangements he had made, that the colonel could not do otherwise than express himself satisfied. At length he rose, and said in a formal way, 'I think now, sir, our business is ended. You will, I conclude, at once return to your ship, and express to Lord Claymore my satisfaction at the arrangements which have been made. His lordship will, however, see the necessity of leaving to me the task which he has hitherto performed so efficiently.'

Edda had not dared to stir from her seat, but had continued with her head bent down over some work, only venturing at times to cast a furtive glance at her father and Ronald, to ascertain how they got on together. Mrs Armytage soon afterwards joined her, and continued equally silent, her countenance exhibiting still greater anxiety and nervousness.

The colonel ceased speaking, and looked as if he expected the young officer to make his bow and walk straight out at the door, but Ronald felt that he must risk everything rather than take his departure without exchanging another word with Edda. He therefore, as soon as he rose, observing that Colonel Armytage had beckoned to one of the Spaniards to advance, said quietly, 'I will pay my respects to Mrs and Miss Armytage before I go.'

Before the colonel could reply he had crossed the room to them.

'Mrs Armytage, whatever happens, I entreat you to think favourably of me,' he said; and then he took Edda's hand, willingly given him, and he whispered, 'Farewell, dearest; we shall meet, I trust, ere long, again, when I have hopes that some of the difficulties which now surround us may be surmounted. Your promise, though we were interrupted before the whole was given, has afforded joy and contentment to my heart.'

'Oh, but I give it entirely,' Edda exclaimed, eagerly. 'No power shall make me break it, believe me Ronald.'

'You will be benighted, sir, and brigandage is rife,' exclaimed Colonel Armytage, looking up with an angry glance, which Edda observed, but Ronald did not.

'Go, go!' she exclaimed. Heaven protect you!'

Morton shook hands with Mrs Armytage, bowed to the colonel, and walked with as much dignity as he could command out of the room.

He threw himself on his horse, and rather than remain in the place he determined to ride back to a village he had passed on his way there, where he might find refreshment and rest both for man and beast during the night.

As Ronald passed the group of Spaniards, he saw one of those who had come in with Colonel Armytage stare very hard at him. It struck him at the moment that he recollected the man's features. He had just mounted his horse, when the person in question rushed down the steps, and grasped him by the hand.

'I am ashamed, my brave friend, that I should not at once have known you!' exclaimed the Spaniard. But we both of us look to much greater advantage than we did on the day we stormed the fort, when we were covered with gunpowder and blood. But you must not go; come to my house, it is not many leagues off. You can be spared from your ship for a day or two longer.'

Ronald thanked his friend Don Josef very warmly, but assured him that it was his duty to make the best of his way to the coast, as the ship would be standing in to take him.

'How unfortunate!' said the Spaniard. 'I have to see your commissioner—he seems a very great man—or I would accompany you all the way, and we might stop at the houses of some of my friends. Still I must go a little way with you. Wait a moment; I will send for my horse: it is a poor animal —the only one those thieving French have left me. But a day of retribution is coming, and soon, I hope.'

The steed was brought out; it was a far better animal than Ronald expected to see. The Spaniard mounted, and the cavalcade moved on.

The village was soon left behind. Ronald's new friend, however, had not accompanied him more than a league when he said he must return, or he should miss his interview altogether with the commissioner. He had given Morton during that time a great deal of information as to the state of the country, and the temper of the people generally. One feeling seemed to pervade all classes—the deepest hatred of their late master, and a desire to be free.

'Better times may arrive, the country may be restored to peace, prosperity may be her lot, and then I trust that you will come and visit me at my home, and receive the thanks of my wife and children for the benefit you conferred on me.'

Saying this with the usual complimentary Spanish expressions, Don Josef turned his horse's head, and rode back towards the village from which they had started, while Ronald continued his journey.

CHAPTER XXXI.

A SPANISH INN.—THE SPANIARDS AROUSED TO ARMS.—RONALD HEADS A GUERILLA BAND.—EDDA RESCUED BY RONALD.

HE sun had set some short time when Ronald, with his companions, reached the village where the guide told him he could obtain shelter and refreshment. The village itself was small and mean, and the only house of entertainment it possessed offered but few attractions to the travellers to remain there. However, as their beasts required rest, they were compelled to dismount, and while the guide with the boys of the inn led the animals into the stables, Ronald and the two seamen walked into the common room, which served as dining-hall, kitchen, and apparently the sleeping-place of the family, as well as of a numerous family of fowls. A very unattractive dame, who presided over the culinary department of the establishment, was now engaged in preparing supper for a very mixed and somewhat suspicious-looking company, who were seated at a long table, on benches at one side of the room. None of them rose as the strangers entered, and the few who condescended to pay them any attention scowled at them from under their brows, as if resenting their appearance as an intrusion. Ronald was very little moved by the want of courtesy with which he was received, but, walking up to the presiding genius of the place, he inquired, in the best Spanish he could command, whether he

and his followers could have beds and food. The old woman looked up with a sinister expression without speaking, while she continued stirring the pot boiling on the huge wood fire. Her eyes were bleared with the smoke, and her face was wrinkled and dried, with a few white hairs straggling over her brow, while the long yellow tusks which protruded beyond her thin lips gave her a peculiarly hag-like look. Ronald repeated his question.

'Food?—yes, and good enough for any one,' she answered in a low croaking voice; 'but for beds, the enemy carried them off, and everything in the house. There is space enough and to spare, upstairs, for a taller man than you to stretch his legs. You can go and look when you have a mind; your valise will serve you as a pillow, and a sack with some straw must be your mattress. Many a better man has slept in a worse bed.'

'I do not doubt it,' answered Ronald, calmly. 'My men and I will manage well enough, but we are hungry, and shall be glad of food.'

'All in good time, said the old woman, somewhat softening her tone, and pleased at being spoken to in her own language. 'You may carry your baggage upstairs, and select any corner you like for your sleeping-place. The girl will be in and give you a light presently. See that there are no holes in the roof above you, in case it should rain. You will find it warmer too if you avoid those in the floor beneath you.'

The old woman said this evidently with serious good-will. Ronald thanked her, and directly afterwards a stout buxom girl came from the further end of the hall, with a brass oil lamp in her hand. Taking the advice of the old woman, Ronald went upstairs to select a corner where he and his party might rest a night. The apartment consisted of the entire upper floor, but as the old woman had warned him, it contained not a particle of furniture, though, from its appearance, there was little doubt that there would be a large number of inhabitants. In several places through the roof he could see the stars shining, while the faint rays of light, and odours anything but faint, which came up through the floor, showed the numerous holes and rents which time had made in the boards.

'This is a rum place for our lieutenant to sleep in,' observed Bob Doull to Job; 'and as to the gentry below there, they are as cut-throat a crew as I ever set eyes on. I'll not let his valise go out of my hands, for it would be whipped up pretty smartly by one of these fellows, and we should never see more of it. Looking at the land from aboard the frigate, I never should have thought it was such an outlandish sort of a country. Should you, Job?'

'Can't say much for their manners. May be they are better than they look,' answered the elder seaman; 'but if it came to a scrimmage, I can't say but what I wouldn't mind tackling a dozen of them.'

These remarks were made while Morton was taking a survey of the unpromising apartment. It had apparently been used as a barrack by the French when, not long ago, they occupied the village, and very little trouble had since been taken to clean it out. Morton asked the girl if his surmise was not correct.

'Yes, the demons! they have been here, and Heaven's curse go with them!' she answered, with startling fierceness. 'It was dark when you rode in, or you would have seen the number of houses burnt down, vineyards and orange-groves rooted up for firewood; but that was not all the harm they did. Woe, unutterable woe, they inflicted on thousands. I had a lover, to whom I was betrothed; they slew him, and me they rendered wretched. But I need not tell my own griefs. Thousands have suffered as much as I have. There, senor, that corner you will find the freest from inconvenience. Place your valise and saddle-bags there—they will be safe. We are honest, though our accursed foes have made us poor indeed.'

The poor girl's dark eyes flashed fire as she spoke. Ronald felt sure that he might trust her entirely. He ordered Bob and

Job, therefore, to deposit his scanty baggage in the corner indicated, and to follow him below.

'What! does the lieutenant think he'll ever see them again if we does?' observed Bob.

'Orders is orders,' answered Job; 'but just you keep a bright look out on the stair while we're below, and as soon as we've stowed away some grub, we'll take it watch and watch, and go up and sit on 'em. The Dons will find it a hard job to carry them off then, I'll allow.'

Satisfied with their arrangements, the two seamen followed their officer. He took his seat at one end of the table, and, as he did so, he fancied the other guests seemed to regard him with more friendly glances than before. Not a minute had elapsed before Maria placed before him a smoking puchero (a dish to be found from one end of Spain to the other, composed of various sorts of meats minced with spices). There was a soup also, of a reddish tinge, from being coloured with saffron, and sausages rather too strong of garlic, and very white bread, and two dishes of vegetables, one of which was of garbanzos, a sort of haricot beans. There was wine also, and brandy; indeed, the inhabitants must have managed cleverly to hide their stores from their invaders to enable them to produce so good a supply. Job and Bob did not conceal their astonishment; the viands suited their taste, and they did ample justice to them.

Though Ronald was in love, and had just cause to be anxious as to its result, and though he had only just parted from his mistress, yet he was a sailor; he had been a midshipman, and he had always a remarkably good appetite; and now, much to his surprise (for when he stopped at the door of the inn he had no thoughts of eating), he felt every inclination to do justice to the feast set before him.

'He'll do,' observed Job to Bob, as they sat at a respectful distance from their officer. 'At first I could not tell what had come over him as he got on his horse after he'd been talking to that young lady up at the window. Whenever I sees a man able to take his grub, whatever's the matter with him, I knows it's all right.'

Ronald had addressed some of the Spaniards near him. They listened respectfully. He spoke to them of the tyranny to which Spain had been so long subject; of the sufferings she had endured; of the only means of freedom—the rising of the whole nation, as a man, to throw off the yoke. 'The English will help you, but they can only help, remember. It is you who must do the work,' he added.

'True, true! the cabaliero speaks well!' resounded from all parts of the room.

'It is to urge you to rise in arms, to drive the invaders from your country that I have come among you,' said Ronald. He warmed on the subject. His hearers grew enthusiastic.

'We have arms! we have arms!' they shouted. 'We will bring them forth; we have powder and shot. The enemy are not far off. We will go and meet them. We will drive them before us like sheep.'

Ronald was satisfied with the effect of his address. He knew perfectly well that in the morning, after they had cleaned their arms and filled their pouches with powder, they would stop and consider before they advanced to meet the enemy. Altogether, he felt that the evening had not been ill-spent, and at the end of it the very people who had, when he came among them, cast on him such sinister looks, now regarded him with the greatest respect. It was late before he threw himself down on a sack of straw in a corner of the upper room, wrapped up in his cloak. Though the room was occupied by a large portion of the rest of the guests, who kept up a concert of snores all night long, he managed to sleep soundly till daylight.

The next morning after breakfast, having bid farewell to his new friends, he continued his journey. Nothing would induce his horse to go out of a walk, while the mules refused to proceed at a faster rate than their more noble companions, so that their progress was of necessity slow. As they proceeded the sad traces of warfare were everywhere visible. Whole farmsteads burnt to the ground, houses in ruins, churches unroofed, groves of orange and olive trees cut down, fences destroyed, and fields once fertile returning to a state of nature, and overrun with weeds. The guide looked at them as objects to which he was well accustomed, but now and then he ground his teeth and swore vengeance on the heads of the fell invaders of his country.

Job had been remarking where the devastating hand of war had passed, and had counted up the objects destroyed. At length he gave expression to his thoughts.

'Well, to my mind, it's a mortal pity people take to fighting on shore. Why don't they stick to their ships, and always have it out afloat? that's the sensible thing, and then the only harm's done to the ships and the men who has the fun of the thing, and gets the honour and glory, and that's all natural and right.'

Bob heartily joined in with Job's notion.

'If I was a king, I wouldn't let 'em,' he remarked. 'I'd say, just you let the farms, and the gardens, and the women and children, and the churches alone; and if you wants to fight, by all manner of means fight it out, but keep afloat, and don't come here.'

The seamen had been conversing for some time in this strain, when the clatter of a horse's hoof was heard behind them, and turning their heads they saw the same Spaniard who had accompanied them on their way the day before. They told Morton, who turned his horse's head to meet him.

'Thank heaven that my steed has carried me so well, and that I have come up to you,' exclaimed Don Josef. 'There is work for you; your aid is wanted; you will not refuse it, I know? But come, ride back with me as fast as your beast's legs will move, and I will tell you. Give him the spur! spare him not; I may supply you with a better soon. The French are at no great distance from this; secure as they fancy themselves, we have spies among them to inform us of all their movements. After daybreak this morning, one of the spies arrived, and brought me notice that the enemy were advancing, and that they having heard that a British commissioner was in the neighbourhood, had resolved to carry him off. On hearing this, I instantly set out to warn your countryman of the danger to which he was exposed, but on my way I met a person who informed me that he and his party had set forth at a very early hour, and were actually advancing in the very direction where they would encounter the enemy. I, on this, instantly sent forth a person to warn him of his danger, and galloped after you, to entreat you to head a party, of strength sufficient to meet the enemy. I directed all the men in the district to assemble in arms; they want a leader, however, in whom they may have confidence. I have told them that they would find one in you, and they believe me. You will come, will you not?'

'Indeed, I will!' answered Ronald, belabouring his horse, and digging his spurs into his flanks with an energy proportioned to his anxiety. So eager was he, that for some time he could scarcely ask questions. One thought alone occupied his mind: Edda was in danger, and there was a possibility that he might preserve her from it.

The party soon got back to the village, where, in front of the inn, a large number of men with arms in their hands were assembled. They received Morton as he rode up with loud vivas. He had won their regards the previous evening by the way he had addressed them, and Don Josef had been telling them what a gallant fellow he was. They were, therefore, now prepared to place the most implicit confidence in him, and to hail him as a leader in the enterprise Don Josef had projected. The Spaniard had been giving him an exact account of all the information he had received, and of the plans he had formed. Ronald thought them excellent; there was, however, no time to be lost. Messengers with the fiery cross—at least a message of the same import—had been sent round to all the neighbourhood, and armed men were coming in from every direction. When their numbers were counted, Morton found himself at the head of a guerilla band, mustering upwards of three hundred men, cavalry and infantry. They varied more in their arms than in their costume, and though many were somewhat ragged, when massed together and all looking fierce and eager for the fight, they had a very warlike appearance.

The great object was to overtake Colonel Armytage before he could reach the spot where the ambush was supposed to be placed; he travelled with only a small escort of a dozen troopers, merely sufficient for protection against any brigands who might be roving through the country. As to the French, he had fancied that they were at a considerable distance, and had no fear of falling in with them: he ought of course to have been better informed. The truth was, that though formal and dignified, and so far fitted to have intercourse with the Spaniards, his manners were not sufficiently conciliatory to have gained their affections, and they consequently neglected to give him the information on many points which it was most important for him to obtain.

Job and Bob exchanged a few passing remarks as they bumped along in a way to which they were not at all accustomed, and which caused their words to come out like shot from guns irregularly served in action, or the pantings of a broken-down steam-engine; only such an invention was not known in those days.

'I'd sooner be serving my gun aboard the frigate than be on the top of this here brute,' observed Bob. 'But it's no odds, I suppose; if we catches the Mounseers, and drubs them, we shall ride back on their backs—eh, Job?'

'Not so sure of that; they'll sham lame and refuse to carry us,' answered the other seaman. 'But I say, Bob, what a hurry our lieutenant's in; to my mind, it's all about that young lady at the window; mark my words, there'll be a splice some day or other, and good luck to him too; a finer-hearted fellow never stepped, for all he's a boatswain's son. There's some men born to be officers, and he's one of 'em.'

People seldom dream of the way in which they and their acts are discussed by their inferiors.

Don Josef now told Ronald that they were approaching the spot where he hoped to overtake Colonel Armytage and his party, but no traces of them could be seen. They must have proceeded faster than Don Josef had calculated. ' On, on ! ' was the cry. They met a peasant, a half-witted fellow; he had seen such a party—a carriage with ladies, a waggon and some horsemen—pass an hour before.

' We shall be too late, I fear,' exclaimed Don Josef; ' but on, my friends; we may still overtake the enemy.'

The party redoubled their speed; never had Ronald been worked up to such a pitch of anxiety and eagerness.

The sound of shots was heard; the road wound among low broken cliffs, and trees growing thickly together; it was a likely place for an assault; so frequent were the bends made by the road that seldom was there a direct view of more than a hundred yards. Horse and foot rushed on, till Ronald remembering that their impetuosity might do more harm than good, halted them; and begging Don Josef to remain with them and not to advance till summoned, rode on with the two seamen, and six other men, of the best-equipped and best-mounted of the party. Now again he pushed on as rapidly as he could. How his heart beat ! Should he be in time to rescue his friends ? If not, how would they be treated ? His eagerness prompted him to shout to his men, but he recollected caution was necessary, and restrained himself. Again the rattle of musketry was heard, and dropping shots, and even the shouts of the combatants reached his ears; he was close to them; a carriage was the first object which met his view. The mule which dragged it had drawn it against the side of the cliff, against which it lay half upset. Before it were a party of men drawn up across the pass, and bravely contending against a whole host who appeared beyond. It was evident, however, the small band would be quickly overpowered, for men were seen climbing the cliff with muskets in hand, belonging to the opposite party. By their dress, and the rapidity with which they climbed the cliffs, they seemed to be seamen. Ronald's plans were formed in a moment; he instantly despatched the most trusty of his party to direct Don Josef to send a hundred men up the cliffs, so as to gain a higher level than the French, and to advance with all rapidity with the rest. Putting spurs to his horse, Ronald, with his small body of companions, darted on, shouting in English and Spanish, 'To the rescue! to the rescue! Do not give way—a strong force is at hand!'

He had neither been heard nor seen by the commissioner's escort: at that moment they wavered and drew back. Once losing ground, the French dashed in among them; while some of the latter engaged each of them in single combat, a French officer and several others made their way to the carriage; Ronald and his band galloped on. At that moment only were they discovered. A shriek was heard. The Frenchmen were dragging the ladies from their carriage. Ronald repeated the shouts he had already uttered. Among the French were sailors as well as soldiers.

'We'll tackle them,' cried Job.

'What business has they to be here?' exclaimed Bob.

The French officer was in naval uniform, and Ronald, even at that distance, recognised Alfonse Gerardin.

Mrs Armytage and her daughter shrieked for help; they fancied they had been attacked by bandits. They had been more alarmed for the safety of Colonel Armytage than for their own; he was nowhere to be seen.

'Fear not, my beloved Edda; you and your mother are in perfect safety,' said Alfonse Gerardin, who had thrown himself from his horse. He was now endeavouring to draw her, with as little violence as possible, from the carriage. 'I have sought for you through many lands; I have found you at last, and we will never again part.'

These expressions frightened Edda far more than any threats would have done. There was a concentrated energy and determination in the way he spoke them that made her feel that he would keep his word.

'Oh, spare me! spare me!' she exclaimed. 'You are not a brigand; you do not war with women. Let us go free, and hasten to the assistance of my father. You expressed friendship for him. Prove it now.'

'I will, Edda, I swear; but you cannot remain here. Any moment you may be sacrificed. The shot are falling thickly around. It is hopeless to expect help from any one but me.'

At that moment Edda saw him change colour, and then she heard the sound of a voice which she knew full well—'To the rescue! to the rescue!' while Bob and Job shouted, 'Down with the Mounseers; down with them!'

Edda saw Ronald coming. She struggled to free herself; while Alfonse, having leapt on his horse, was attempting to lift her up on the saddle; but he was not a good horseman, and it seemed doubtful whether he would succeed.

While some of his followers were endeavouring to carry off Mrs Armytage, in obedience to his orders, the others were facing about to defend themselves against the approaching enemy. When the French saw the small body of men led by Morton, those who had faced to meet them boldly advanced. Morton dashed forward. His great object was to reach Alfonse Gerardin. He saw nothing else, he thought of nothing else but Edda Armytage in his power.

'Release her, or you die!' he shouted.

Truefitt and Doull meantime had each singled out a French seaman, and with hearty good-will were attacking them with their cutlasses. So fierce was their onslaught that they drove them back into the midst of the *mêlée*, where Colonel Armytage's troopers were still holding their own against their foes. The French were, however, pressing them very hard. Alfonse looked round and saw that the way was open to him. In another moment Ronald Morton would be at his side. He stooped down, and throwing his arms round Edda, by a violent effort lifted her off the ground and placed her on his saddle.

'Retreat, men!' he shouted, 'Let alone the other lady.'

He was galloping off, but Ronald digging his spurs into his horse's flanks, and cutting down a French soldier, who attempted to stop him, was in another instant by the side of the young lieutenant. Gerardin saw him coming with uplifted sword. He raised his own weapon to defend himself, while he still held Edda with his left arm. He knew that Ronald would not dare to fire; he doubted whether he would even venture to strike, for fear of injuring Miss Armytage. Ronald's eye was practised, his nerves were well strung.

'Release her, villain!—madman!' he shouted again. He saw what Alfonse, who had to turn his head to look at him, did not see, Truefitt and Doull springing across the road. Bob seized the horse's head; the animal reared. Gerardin, in attempting to seize the rein, loosened his hold of Edda, and she would have fallen to the ground had not Truefitt caught her. The enemy were gathering thickly around. Bob, seeing what had happened, let go the rein to defend his own head, as well as his shipmate's, from the blows showered on them. Morton, too, was attacked on all sides. He did not seek for revenge. Gerardin's horse sprang forward and saved his rider from the only blow aimed at him by Morton. All these events had passed within a few seconds of time. At that instant the Frenchmen uttered a cry of 'Retreat!—retreat! *Sauve qui peut!*' They had good reason for so doing; for the cliffs on either side appeared covered with guerillas, who began firing down upon them, while a strong band was seen advancing at full speed along the road.

'Ronald Morton, I hate you!' exclaimed Gerardin, turning

round in his saddle, and shaking his clenched fist at the English lieutenant. 'You have foiled me again and again. I know you, and who you are; you stand between me and my birthright; you shall not foil me again. I have before sought your life; the next time we meet we will not separate till one or the other dies.'

These last words were uttered as, surrounded by the survivors of his band, he was galloping off. The advantage of having sent the Spaniards to crown the height was now apparent. They drove the French riflemen down to the main body, and the enemy, not being able to ascertain the number opposed to them, gave way before a very inferior and undisciplined force. Ronald did not attempt to follow them till he had placed Edda in safety by the side of her mother, whom he found half fainting in the carriage. Then telling her that he would go in search of Colonel Armytage, he leapt on his horse and joined Don Josef and the surviving troopers who were moving on in pursuit of the enemy. He had not gone far before he fancied that he could distinguish Colonel Armytage mounted on a horse among the French, and drooping as if badly wounded.

The road sloped considerably in front. The French were descending the steep. Calling to his companions to charge, he led the way, attacking the rear-guard of the enemy with irresistible impetuosity. Down they went before the Spanish blades like corn before the sickle. Those in front endeavoured to fly. Some few turned to withstand their opponents, but they, too, gave way, and Ronald and his followers fought on till they reached the prize the French fancied they had secured: the person to capture whom the expedition had apparently been despatched. The colonel, who had been secured to his horse, was almost insensible, and seemed not at all aware by whom he had been rescued. The French, meantime, when they discovered the small number of the guerilla band opposed to them halted, and seemed about to return; but Ronald showed so bold a front that they apparently thought better of it, and on finding that they were not again attacked, formed in order, and continued their retreat.

Ronald observed, as he rode back, that although there were numbers of dead on the road, there was not a wounded man alive among them.

CHAPTER XXXII.

COLONEL ARMYTAGE WOUNDED.—CROSSING THE BAY OF BISCAY.—CHASED DURING A GALE.—THE BRIG DISMASTED.—CAPTURED.

ONALD MORTON'S heart beat high with hope when he rode back, and was able to announce to Mrs Armytage and Edda that he had recovered Colonel Armytage.

'Though wounded and faint from loss of blood, I trust that he is not seriously hurt,' he added.

He received an ample reward in the look of love and gratitude which Edda gave him.

Before the arrival of the colonel, the carriage was got up, the traces were repaired, the mules caught, and everything was in readiness to move. Don Josef, who now came up, insisted on their returning to his house.

'Even if the enemy were not in the neighbourhood,' he observed, 'it would be useless for the commissioner to proceed further, utterly unable as he is to attend to business.'

After a time Colonel Armytage yielded an unwilling consent to the arrangement. He had learned that Don Josef was Morton's friend. and he was evidently doubting in his mind how he should treat Morton himself. He had just rendered him a great service, and the very man whom he had once favoured as the suitor of his daughter, and who had promised to come and claim her when circumstances would allow him, he had seen in the ranks of the enemy, and he now learned had also attempted to carry off his daughter. These thoughts occupied his mind as the carriage moved on in the centre of the party. Ronald had too correct notions of generalship not to march in true military order. He sent forward an advanced guard, and kept a rear guard at some distance to give timely notice of the approach of an enemy, should they be pursued. He himself was everywhere, seeing that his newly-raised band of guerillas were attending to their duty, though he did not fail, whenever he passed, to make inquiries at the carriage-window as to how Colonel Armytage was bearing his journey.

It was dark when the country-house of Don Josef was reached. He literally made his house the home of the foreigners, for he made them occupy all the best rooms, and retired himself to a small chamber remote from all the rest. It was one of those glorious nights which in no part of Europe are seen to greater advantage than in the clear atmosphere of Spain. The moon, in full lustre, shone out from a sky undimmed by a single cloud, and every object on which its light fell stood out clear and defined, casting the darkest of shadows behind it.

When the guerilla band had been refreshed they assembled in the patio, or yard in front of the house, and gave vent to their satisfaction at their victory in patriotic songs. It was great enjoyment to Morton to find himself again by the side of Edda, and to feel that he had just conferred so great a benefit on her father that he could scarcely refuse his consent to their union. He little knew the unyielding nature of the man with whom he had to deal. Both Edda and Ronald referred to the threats they had heard uttered by Alfonse Gerardin.

'I cannot understand him,' she said, ' who he is, nor what he is. My father certainly favoured his suit in a way I could not fancy he would do that of a person of whom he knew nothing, while he treats you, whom he does know, with evident dislike. I cannot conceal it from myself. You know the pain it must give me. Nor can I help owning that my father is acting a cruel and wrong part.

Ronald knew how near the enemy were, and would have been anxious for the safety of his friends had not Don Josef assured him that he had sent out scouts to watch their movements, and to give the earliest notice of their approach.

The next day a surgeon arrived, who pronounced the wounds Colonel Armytage had received to be in no way dangerous, but expressed his opinion that he would be unfit for a long time to perform the duties intrusted to him. Of this the colonel himself seemed to be fully aware, and he accordingly at once wrote to beg that he might be superseded.

In the afternoon a scout arrived with the information that the French were retreating northward. This was accounted for by the rumour of the approach of a strong Spanish force.

Ronald would gladly have remained to watch over the safety of Edda and her parents, and Don Josef did not fail to employ every argument he could think of to persuade him that he would be right in so doing. He had, however, been absent from his ship much longer than had been intended; and though he could give a very good account of the way he had employed his time, and he knew that his captain would be perfectly satisfied, he felt sure that she would be employed in some work in which he would wish to take a part. Edda had too high a sense of the duty of an officer to attempt for a moment to detain him, though her sad looks showed how much she felt the parting. She talked hopefully of the future; of the happiness which might be in store for them when her father's objections were overcome.

'They must be conquered some day,' she exclaimed. 'Why should he object on the score of birth? We are cousins, though distant ones, and as for fortune, I have never been ambitious, and shall be well content to share what you may have, till—— You know some day, Ronald, Lunnasting in all probability will be mine. I am not greedy of it. I would gladly see it belong to my long-lost cousin, poor aunt Hilda's son, if he could be found; but after the lapse of so many years, that is not likely. Indeed, it is for your sake alone, Ronald, that I should prize it.'

Ronald pressed her to his heart. 'Thanks, thanks, generous one,' he whispered. 'We may yet obtain ample fortune to satisfy our wishes. Of that I have little fear.'

The tears came into Mrs Armytage's eyes when Ronald wished her farewell. It appeared to her as if the only person to whom she could look with confidence for protection and support was about to leave her, for even should Colonel Armytage recover his health, his temper was not likely to improve, while, should he grow worse, she would be left in a still more helpless condition.

Ten days more passed, and a fine brig stood into the harbour. The master came on shore, and finding out Colonel Armytage, announced himself as Captain Carlton, of the 'Helen,' bound direct for London. Nothing could be more convenient; every arrangement was soon concluded; the colonel and his family went on board; the generous Don Josef bade them farewell, and with a favourable breeze, a course was shaped for the Straits of Gibraltar.

The 'Helen' remained only a couple of days at Gibraltar. Colonel Armytage refused to go on shore, or to allow his wife or daughter to go. They were glad, therefore, once more to be at sea. The weather continued fine, and the wind favourable, and there was every promise of a prosperous voyage. The wind was from the south-east, and as the 'Helen' ran along the coast of Portugal the sea was perfectly smooth, except that a slight ripple played over its surface, on which the sun sparkled with dazzling brilliancy. An awning was spread, under which the ladies sat, and when the rock of Lisbon rose in view and the pine-crowned heights of Cintra, just then especially notorious, not for its beauty, not for its orange groves, but on account of the disgraceful treaty which had there lately been concluded, even Colonel Armytage condescended to come on deck, and to admire the beauty of the scene. Through their glasses the Cork convent could be seen perched on its lofty crags, and below them to the north the mass of odd-looking buildings known as the palace of Mafra, containing a royal residence, a monastery, barracks, and a church. Further north, little more could be seen than a long line of yellow sand, with pine-covered hills.

'Now, ladies, I think you have seen enough of Portugal,' said Captain Carlton. 'We'll haul off the shore, if you please; for, to tell you the truth, it's a treacherous coast, which I'm in no way fond of. From here, right away till we come to Vigo in Spain, there is not a single harbour into which a ship can run for shelter; I don't say that it's a disgrace to the people— they didn't make the coast; it was so formed for some good reason, I doubt not, but still I always like to give it a wide berth.'

The fine weather continued till the 'Helen' had passed Cape Ortegal, and was fairly in the Bay of Biscay. The wind then increased, and became variable, and dark clouds were seen banking up in the south-western horizon. The kind old captain became less cheerful than usual. The brig no longer glided on smoothly and sedately as before, but began to roll and pitch with the rising sea. The ladies came on deck, but were unable to read and work as they had previously done, but Edda declared that she enjoyed the change, and found amusement in looking at the dancing seas, and in watching a shoal of porpoises which went careering along, sporting and rolling and keeping way with the brig without effort.

'Ah, young lady, you are looking at those fellows, are you?' said Captain Carlton. 'Just watch how they go along. Now I have heard people on shore talk of a porpoise as a fat, heavy creature who hasn't got any spirit in him, just like a hog, for instance, wallowing in the mud. I should like to see the race-horse which could keep up with them. They would beat that gallant frigate which passed us the other day, and as to this brig you see, they swim round and round her as if she was at anchor, and we are going a good seven knots through the water. People fancy when they see their black tails when they dive that they are rolling along, but the truth is, there isn't a creature darts quicker through its native element than a porpoise.'

The captain's lecture on the much-maligned fish was suddenly brought to a close by a cry from the masthead of a sail on the larboard-quarter. In war time merchantmen keep a sharp look-out, or ought to do so, that they may have timely notice to enable them to avoid an enemy. On the present occasion all Captain Carlton could do was to make more sail and to continue the same course he had been steering. As there were threatenings of a stiff breeze, if not of a gale, the hands were ordered to stand by to take it in again, should it be necessary.

The stranger gained rapidly on the brig, and as she was pronounced to be a large ship, then a man-of-war from the squareness of her yards, and at length a frigate—

'Could she be the "Imperious?"' Edda ventured to ask.

The old captain shook his head.

'No, my dear young lady,' he answered gravely; 'it goes to my heart to alarm you, but the truth must be spoken. I am very much afraid that the stranger is an enemy.'

Edda's heart sunk within her. English prisoners, she knew, whether combatants or not, were detained in France for years, and the Emperor had shown his intention of keeping them till he had attained the objects he sought.

Mrs Armytage fainted when she heard the report, and the colonel came on deck to ascertain its truth. He evidently did not like the look of things.

'Cannot you make this craft of yours sail faster?' he asked, in an angry tone of the master.

'It is the people who built her, sir, are to blame, not me. I am doing, and will do, all a seaman can accomplish to escape the enemy; I have no wish to be taken. I have a wife and family waiting my return home, and Heaven have mercy on them! we shall be utterly ruined if the brig is taken.'

Colonel Armytage was silent; the chances of escape seemed small indeed. Still pressed as she was with a far larger amount of canvas than the master would have ventured to carry under ordinary circumstances, the brig tore through the rising seas at a greater rate than had ever before probably been got out of her.

The master stood watching the masts and spars with an anxious eye. They bent and cracked with the greatly increased strain to which they were exposed; the weather-shrouds and stays were tautened to the utmost. At length the master turned round to Edda and Mrs Armytage, who, having recovered from her first alarm, had come up on deck.

'My dear young lady, and you, ma'am, do go below, let me pray you; this is no place for you,' he said, with deep earnestness. 'Any moment we may have the masts and spars rattling down on our heads, or the enemy's shot flying along our decks. Please Heaven, while the masts stand we'll hold on. They can but take us in the end; but, dear ladies, do go below. We shall act more like men if we know that you are safe.'

Thus urged, most unwillingly Edda and her mother retired to the cabin. The colonel, however, remained on deck.

'It shall never be said that where danger was present I was absent,' he remarked.

'Maybe, but you would be of much more use looking after your wife and daughter in the cabin,' muttered the honest old captain.

Edda and Mrs Armytage went into their own cabin. They knelt down. They could not strive like men, but they could pray that the ship might be preserved from the threatened danger, or, if it was Heaven's will that it should overtake her, that they might have strength given them to bear whatever it was their lot to suffer.

The breeze was freshening rapidly, the movement of the brig increased as she plunged with a violent jerk into one sea, and then rose up the watery ridge only to sink down again into another watery valley. Still on she tore. The master was keeping his word. On a sudden there was a cry; then followed a fearful crash.

'Oh, my father! he may have been killed,' exclaimed Edda, as she rushed on deck.

Both the masts had gone by the board, and the brig lay a helpless wreck on the tossing waters. The frigate was close to them. For an instant a wild hope rose in Edda's heart. Was she after all the 'Imperious?'

The hope was soon banished. The flag of France flew out from the stranger's peak. Edda looked round for her father, trembling with fear. He had fallen, and lay on the deck unable to rise. She rushed towards him, all his unkindness, his harshness and injustice forgotten. She attempted to lift him up; but her strength was unequal to the task. He soon somewhat recovered.

'I am not materially injured, I fancy,' he said at length. 'This is a fearful accident; I was struck by a falling block, and was stunned. I shall be myself again directly. But where is the master? What has become of the crew?'

Edda gazed horror-struck at the spectacle which met her sight. Several of the men lay crushed under the masts and heavy spars which had fallen on the deck, a few who had leaped below were returning to their assistance, but Captain Carlton was nowhere to be seen. Just then a cry struck Edda's ears; she gazed out on the foam-covered sea. Among the wildly leaping waves she caught sight of the old master's countenance—it was turned towards the brig with a look of agony. He was swimming bravely, sorely buffeted as he was by the seas. The effort was beyond his strength. With a wild cry he threw up his arms, and the next sea rolled over his head.

Edda would have sunk with horror had not the call of duty supported her.

'Father! oh come below! we can do nothing to help ourselves, and shall be safe there,' she exclaimed, in an imploring tone.

'No, no, girl; I must be on deck to receive our captors. See, they are coming!'

He raised himself to his feet, and was pointing to the frigate, which, having passed to windward of the dismasted brig, was now hove-to. A boat was at that instant being lowered from her side.

'Then I will not leave you, father,' said his daughter, clinging to the bulwarks near him.

The boat from the French frigate approached; she came close to the brig, but it was both difficult and dangerous for the crew to get on board. More than once they made the attempt, and each time the boat was driven off again by the sea; at last they shouted to the English seamen to come and help them. The surviving crew of the brig had gone below, as is the practice of seamen likely to be captured, to put on their best clothing and to secure any valuables belonging to them. At last they appeared, and with their assistance and the ropes they hove-to the boat, and the Frenchmen succeeded in getting on board. Their officer was the first up the side. Edda looked at him, and almost shrieked with terror when she recognised Alfonse Gerardin.

CHAPTER XXXIII.

THE 'IMPERIOUS' HOMEWARD BOUND.—THE FIRE-SHIPS ARE PREPARED.—THE FRENCH FLEET IN BASQUE ROADS.—RONALD CONDUCTS A FIRE-SHIP.—GENERAL EXPLOSION OF FIRE-SHIPS.

HE 'Imperious,' with a fine breeze from the southward, was standing across the Bay of Biscay. She had been actively engaged all the time she had been in the Mediterranean, chiefly on the coasts of France and Spain, capturing armed ships and merchantmen, destroying telegraph stations, blowing up forts, and harassing the enemy in every possible way.

The Marquis de Medea and his daughter, with Father Mendez, had been, at their own request, put on board a Spanish vessel bound round to Cadiz, as they fancied that the unsettled state of the country would make the journey by land dangerous and disagreeable. Don Tacon had before that been sent to Malta to take his trial as a pirate, but by some means or other he had been completely, if not honourably, acquitted, and very soon afterwards disappeared from the island. He was supposed by some speedily to have taken to his old courses, and several merchantmen reported that they had been chased by a suspicious-looking lateen-rigged craft, on their passage between Gibraltar and Malta. He had latterly, when the ship was at sea, been allowed a good deal of liberty on board the frigate, and had been allowed to go about the decks at pleasure.

He was, however, again deprived of this liberty in consequence of having been found one day climbing up over the quarter, as if he had been prying into the captain's cabin. No one had seen him go; it was, therefore, supposed that he must have been concealed there for some time. When caught he at once begged to be secured.

'My life is not safe if I am left at liberty,' he exclaimed, frantically tearing his hair. 'I have looked at the past. I look at the future. I am miserable. I see nothing but wretchedness before me. I contemplated self-destruction. I purposed dropping quietly over the stern into the water. I did not wish to create confusion. If I had jumped overboard before you all, a boat would have been lowered, and I should have been picked up; but—must I own it?—my courage failed me. I—I who have been in a hundred fights, and have braved death in a thousand forms—I felt fear. I clung to the side trembling, and climbed on board again, and here I am.'

Ronald had a very just suspicion that Don Tacon was acting. He had formed, indeed, a perfectly just estimate of his consummate impudence and roguery, but still it was difficult to account for the reason of his having got there.

He might have gone there for the sake of eaves-dropping, for the captain was in the cabin at the time, but then it was not likely that he understood English enough to comprehend what was said. There was one very suspicious circumstance against the worthy Tacon.

A few days before Ronald had been with the captain in his cabin discussing a very important matter. It was no less than Lord Claymore's long-projected plan of destroying the French fleet whenever it could be found collected in one of these exposed roadsteads. Lord Claymore had become more than ever sanguine as to the success of his plan.

'It must succeed, my dear Morton,' he exclaimed vehemently. It will be of advantage to our country, equal to that of a great victory; but it will be gained without one-tenth part of the loss which a general action would entail. I must obtain my recall forthwith, and lay my plans before the Admiralty. They must listen to me; they can scarcely refuse to consider my plans. They won't do it for love; they never do love a man who has got brains in his head, unless those brains are subservient to their will and pleasure.'

Ronald remembered that such had been some of the remarks made on the occasion referred to. Lord Claymore was rather inclined to laugh at his suspicions; but notwithstanding that, took good care that Senor Tacon should not again have an opportunity of throwing himself overboard.

It was not till some time after the Don had been sent to Malta, that Lord Claymore missed a couple of sheets of paper, on which he had drawn out some of his proposed plans. He, however, thought that very likely they had been blown overboard, and troubled himself no more about the matter. After some time he obtained his recall, and the frigate was now on her way to England.

'A sail on the starboard bow!' was the cry from the masthead. The captain was anxious to get to England, and if he chased in that direction he should be led deep into the bay, and perhaps not be able to get out again; but when the stranger was made out to be a frigate, and, in all probability an enemy, the temptation to pursue her was irresistible. The helm was put up and all sail made in chase of the stranger. Away flew the gallant 'Imperious,' with the wind on her quarter, and far ahead kept the other frigate, steering directly in for the French coast. There could be now no longer any doubt that she was an enemy. An English ship could never have run in that way; but it was strongly suspected that the Emperor had ordered his naval officers to avoid fighting unless sure of success.

Once having commenced a pursuit Lord Claymore was not the man to give it up until he had caught the chase, or run her to earth. Every means that could be thought of was tried to increase the speed of the frigate, but it was soon evident that the enemy was very fast and could easily keep ahead. Still Lord Claymore hoped that some chance might enable him to come up with her and bring her to action. The weather, however continued fine, which was so far in favour of the Frenchman, that there was little chance of his carrying away any masts or spars, by which the 'Imperious' might have gained an advantage. Night drew on; but the moon rose and her beams fell on the chase exactly in the position she had so long held. It was now very evident that she was steering for Basque Roads.

'She may get there but we'll bring her out for all that,' exclaimed the captain, as he walked the deck, with his night-glass in hand, watching the chase.

Hour after hour passed without the slightest alteration in the relative position of the two frigates. Day came and the chase continued.

The officers each snatched a few hours' rest; the captain probably took less than any one. The land was made out ahead and then on the starboard bow. It was the island of Oleron, forming the south side of Basque Roads. There was no longer any hope of bringing the enemy to action, still the 'Imperious' stood on. The chase was seen to bring up under a strong fort, below which several line-of-battle ships and two frigates were at anchor.

'The fellow has shown us his den, at all events,' observed Lord Claymore, examining the enemy's squadron, while the frigate continued standing in towards the anchorage. The crew were at their stations, eyeing the French squadron and forts with the most perfect unconcern, though it was possible for them, had they made the attempt, to blow the English frigate out of the water; but so perfect was the confidence of the seamen in the captain, that they felt as if there was no more danger than in Portsmouth Harbour.

'Morton!' exclaimed the captain, 'look at that fleet of Frenchmen. Think of the havoc and devastation they will commit among our merchantmen and colonies if they get free away from this. Every one of them we could destroy with our fire-ships and explosion vessels. It must be done. I shall never forgive myself if I do not stir every nerve to get the Admiralty to undertake it. We will stand further in. I delight in thus bearding them in their very harbours.'

A shot, however, from the fort, which flew between the masts, showed him that he had stood close enough in. The frigate wore round, and did what Job Truefitt observed she wasn't often apt to do—showed her stern to the enemy. It was surprising that she was not pursued. This made Lord Claymore suspect that the line-of-battle ships were not yet completely ready for sea.

Away sailed the 'Imperious' with all the haste she could make. The wind held fair; England was soon reached. A powerful squadron, under Lord Gambier, was despatched to watch the enemy's fleet, and the captain of the 'Imperious' used every exertion to obtain leave to carry out his plans.

While the captain was absent in London, Morton had charge of the ship. He seldom or never went on shore. As soon as the frigate reached Spithead he got Glover to write to his cousin, Mrs Edmonstone, to inquire for the Armytages. Her answer was unsatisfactory; she had heard nothing of them for several months. She, indeed, knew no more of their movements than did Ronald himself. His mind was racked with the most painful doubts and fears. He could not even conjecture where they were. He had expected to have heard that they had long ago arrived in England. He missed the counsel and support of his father at the present juncture. Rolf had some time before returned to England with old Doull and Eagleshay. He had from thence, accompanied by them, gone to Shetland, where he had re-occupied his farm. Ronald received a letter from him. He had abundance of occupation in repairing the house and improving the property, which was in a sadly neglected state. He had not seen Sir Marcus Wardhill, but he understood that he was failing. The Lady Hilda seldom left the castle. She was said to spend most of the hours of the day and night in her turret chamber, occupying herself with her books, though, as the country people observed, she got very little good out of them. 'But you know, my dear Ronald,' he added, 'I am not the man to interfere with my neighbours' doings. I wish that the poor Lady Hilda's lot had been happier, and as for Sir Marcus, whatever may be his feelings towards me, I never bore him any ill-will.' In a P.S. he added, 'I have just had a visit from Lawrence Brindister; he looks wonderfully little changed. It is thought wears out a man, they say, and he, poor man, does not do much in that way. He shook me warmly by the hand and shuffled about the room, examining everything, and talking of old times, while he made his comments on everything he saw. He is madder, in my opinion, than ever, for he talked in the strangest way of events of which he was cognizant; but when I questioned him, said he should say nothing till you made your appearance. I hope, therefore, Ronald, that you will come as soon as you can get leave, and induce our eccentric cousin to give us the information he possesses, though I confess that I shall not be surprised if after all it turns out he knows nothing of importance. I received a visit from my old friend Captain Maitland. He came over in his boat from North Mavin. He bears his eighty winters wonderfully well. I used to think him an oldish man nearly thirty years ago. How time flies. Though I say come when you can, I would not for a moment draw you away from your duty. You know that so well that I need not have said so. I shall be looking soon for your promotion. I met Captain Courtney while I was in Portsmouth; he told me that you were sure to get it, and that he would see that you were not passed by. Again, my dear boy, good-bye. No more at present from your affectionate father, 'R. M.'

His father's letter cheered Ronald for a time. He was

glad to find that he was contented with the lot he had selected, and he determined not to tell him of his own anxieties and unhappiness. Glover, at his request, again made inquiries of Mrs Edmonstone, but her reply was as before—she could gain no information about the Armytages. The duties of the ship, however, gave Ronald ample occupation, so that he had very little time to think about himself.

Lord Claymore now returned on board in high spirits. He had obtained his object, and was at once to set to work to prepare the explosion vessels and fire-ships according to his proposed plan.

'We must, however, part, Morton, I am on many accounts sorry to say,' he observed.

'Indeed, so am I, my lord, to hear you say so,' answered Ronald. 'I had hoped to continue with you in the "Imperious" till she was paid off.'

'Why, the fact is, my dear Captain Morton, I have got your commission in my pocket, and appointment to a sixteen-gun sloop-of-war, the "Scorpion." I met Courtney at the Admiralty, and he insisted on my bringing it down to you, it having just been put into his hands by the first lord. I sincerely congratulate you, though I must say you have only obtained what you deserve.'

Morton's heart bounded. What officer's does not on receiving unexpectedly his promotion! He thanked Lord Claymore most cordially.

'Come on shore then with me in an hour, and go on board your ship and take command,' said Lord Claymore. 'Get her ready for sea as rapidly as possible. You will accompany me, and I hope before our return we shall have managed to destroy the whole French fleet.'

Ronald begged that Truefitt and Doull might accompany him, a request that was at once granted; and then he put in a word for Glover, and asked if he might have him as a first lieutenant.

'Yes, I esteem him; he is a good officer, but I can get a man to fill his place, who will suit me better,' was the answer.

So it was arranged. Ronald went on board and read his commission. Glover and his two constant followers joined in a few days, and the 'Scorpion' was rapidly got ready for sea.

Two explosion vessels were, in the meantime, being prepared under Lord Claymore's directions, and ten or a dozen fire-ships. The first were terrific engines of destruction. Ronald accompanied him on board one of them. She in the first place contained one thousand five hundred barrels of gunpowder, in casks, placed on end, and bound tightly together by stout ropes; the intervening spaces were filled with wet sand, rammed down with great force, so that the whole formed one solid mass. On the top of it were placed an immense number of hand grenades and rockets, and no less than four hundred live shells with short fusees, so that they might explode soon after the fire reached them.

'What do you think of that?' asked Lord Claymore. 'Woe betide the unfortunate ship she comes in contact with,' he answered. 'Not a man of her crew can escape, I should think.'

The 'Imperious,' with the two explosion vessels, the 'Scorpion,' and such of the fire-ships as were ready, sailed for the Bay of Biscay. They reached the English blockading squadron under Lord Gambier. Many of the captains were highly indignant at finding one junior to themselves appointed to so important a charge.

'I hate to see gallant men yield to feelings so contemptible,' observed Lord Claymore. 'But let them rail on. He laughs who wins.'

If the deed was to be done, no time was to be lost. The time for the terrific experiment arrived. The French ships lay at their anchors across the harbour with springs on their cables, in two lines, so placed that the broadsides of the inner line could be fired clear of the outer one. The island of Aix, with powerful batteries, guarded them on one side, that of Oleron, also with strong forts, on the other. To make their position still more secure, a boom of half a mile in length, composed of numerous spars, and formed in the shape of an obtuse angle, was placed in front of them, and secured by anchors and cables of immense thickness.

The French fleet consisted of twelve line-of-battle ships, a store-ship of fifty guns, and three frigates, amounting altogether to a number of guns perfectly capable of sinking the whole British fleet, had they attempted to force an entrance.

Besides the line-of-battle ships, the French had three frigates placed as an advanced guard in front of the other lines, and close to the boom. This boom was, as has been said, composed of a great number of spars lashed together and floated by large buoys, and was secured in its position by huge anchors and cables of great thickness. The boom was in the shape of an obtuse angle, the apex facing out, so that a vessel striking it would glance off either on one side or the other.

The object to be attained was, first to force the boom with the explosion vessels, so as to allow an entrance for the fireships. By means of these fire-ships it was believed that the whole French squadron might be destroyed.

The 'Scorpion' lay near the 'Imperious,' and Lord Claymore invited Ronald to accompany him one night to reconnoitre the enemy's position.

Ronald had been dining with Lord Claymore. Soon after it was dark they left the frigate in the captain's gig, and pulled with muffled oars towards the boom. The night was very dark, but the lights on board the enemy's ships could be clearly made out. They enabled Morton, who had taken the helm, to steer a right course. The object to be guarded against was falling in with any of the French boats which would be very likely rowing guard. A midshipman with a sharp pair of eyes was placed in the bows to give instant notice of the appearance of any other boat. It was supposed that, to a certainty, the French would have guard-boats on the watch near their boom, and the danger to be apprehended was coming suddenly upon them. However, the gig was a remarkably fast boat, and Morton hoped that they might easily escape if pursued. Of course his companion had no doubt about it, or he would not have run the risk, seeing that so much depended on his superintendence of the undertaking in hand. Except the rush of the tide as it swept by, a perfect silence reigned on the waters.

'How calm and solemn is the night?' thought Ronald. 'How different will be to-morrow, when all this space will be full of burning ships, and the roar of guns and shrieks of dismay and agony will rend the air!'

At length the boom was reached: they now spoke in low whispers. Lord Claymore pointed out a frigate close to on the other side of it.

'This must be our point of attack,' he observed; 'we'll break the boom and then set fire to that frigate. She will cut her cables to escape her doom, and will carry consternation and confusion among the ships astern.'

'The plan must succeed if all hands do their duty,' answered Ronald.

'That is the point,' said Lord Claymore somewhat bitterly. 'Many of those to be employed are untried. I wish that I could trust all as I do you. We'll pull along by the boom a little further, and then make the best of our way on board.'

The gig had not proceeded fifty fathoms when a voice hailed, 'Qui va là?'

'Round with the boat, Morton. Pull up your larboard oars, lads,' whispered the captain.

Again a Frenchman hailed, and immediately afterwards a bullet came whizzing close to them. The gig's crew required no urging to bend to their oars. They must have been seen, for a whole volley followed them. They were not at first pursued, and it was evident that the French boats were at the inner side of the boom.

The shot continued to fall thickly round them, but no one was hit. At last they got beyond the range of fire.

'Avast pulling!' cried Lord Claymore.

The sound of oars was heard on either hand. It would be impossible to fight the enemy with any hope of success. Flight was their only resource. Morton steered for the frigate. The enemy's boats continued to come after them. Morton kept a look-out for the frigate's light. The Frenchmen saw at length that the pursuit was useless, and gave it up. No sooner was this ascertained than Lord Claymore began to talk on various subjects with as much composure as if they had not just narrowly escaped losing their lives or liberty.

A strong leading wind was required to execute the project. It came at last. In the afternoon the boats assembled round the various vessels destined for the undertaking, which then proceeded towards the stations allotted to them in readiness for the night, when their operations were to commence.

It was a solemn time even for the thoughtless, and highly exciting to the most phlegmatic. To many the undertaking appeared desperate in the extreme. Ronald had unbounded confidence in the judgment and bravery of their leader. He had himself volunteered to conduct one of the fire-ships. Lord Claymore was to lead in the largest explosion vessel.

Two gun-brigs were stationed at each end of the enemy's line, and within the distance of two miles. They had lights hoisted to guide their friends, but screened from the enemy. In the centre space between these two vessels the fire-ships were to be conducted. The 'Imperious' and three other frigates anchored about a gun-shot and a half from the boom to support the boats accompanying the fire-ships. Five or six sloops-of-war and brigs were placed near the east end of the island to make a diversion, while a bomb-vessel and several small craft, supplied with rockets, took up their stations near the Boyart shoal.

Under the veil of night the vessels took up their stations. The wind, which was increasing, blew directly into the harbour. In the centre of the space formed by the two light-vessels, the frigates, and the boom, were collected the fleet of fire-ships and the explosion vessels.

The awful moment had arrived. The terrific work of destruction was to begin. The darkness was intense. The two lights on either hand were the only guides on which those piloting the vessels had to depend. The explosion vessels led the way, under all sail. Morton stood at the helm of his fireship to guide her course, his heart beating as it had seldom beat before. He was calm and collected, but fully impressed with the awful nature of the work in which he was engaged. The darkness rendered the moment still more solemn. He could not help feeling also that at any instant he and those with him might be launched into eternity.

The train was laid, all was ready; a spark from one of the explosion vessels might ignite it suddenly. He could not see five yards from where he stood. The darkness was oppressive. A single star in the sky above would have been a relief. His ship proceeded under easy sail, to give time for the explosion vessels to produce the intended effect. The eyes of all on board were on the watch for the awful event. They could hear the people of the vessels on either side of them, but could not catch even an outline of their forms. Thus the fleet of fire-ships glided on to their work of destruction.

'The leading explosion vessel must be near the boom,' observed Job Truefitt, who had accompanied him. 'Nothing can have gone amiss, I hope.'

'Not where he is, sir,' answered Bob, confidently. 'See—there! there!'

A terrific roar was heard. Bright flames darted forth, seeming to reach the very sky, and illuminating the whole surrounding space hitherto shrouded in darkness. In the centre the light fell on the fire-ships on either side, on the two light vessels with the high land and the forts behind them, while right ahead was the French fleet riding calmly at anchor. Like some ocean volcano, the explosion vessel continued for a few moments sending upwards its sheets of flame, while missiles of every description were flying in showers around.

Ronald trembled for the fate of his gallant friend. Could he have had time to escape?

Ronald's own turn was to come soon. The fire which had been raging so furiously, ceased as rapidly as it had commenced, and all was again dark. Not a minute had passed when a second volcano burst forth, and burnt like the first.

'Now, lads, make sail!' shouted Ronald.

The topsails were on the caps; they were hoisted and sheeted home; the courses were let fall, and Ronald steered his fire-ship directly for the spot where the first explosion had taken place. He hoped the boom had been broken, but if not, he expected to be able to force a passage with his ship. He fancied that he heard Lord Claymore hail as he passed. He hoped that it was his voice. The wind blew stronger and stronger. On flew the fire-ship. The boom was reached. With a crash she forced her way through it. She was bearing directly down for the French fleet.

'To the boats!' shouted Ronald.

The cry was repeated by the other officers with him.

'Wait till I give the word to shove off, so that no one may be left behind. To your stations, and fire the trains,' he added. He looked to ascertain that the helm was properly placed, and that the vessel was standing the right way. The instant after small snake-like lines of fire was seen stealing along the decks. Ronald sprang to the side, the deck, as he did so, seemed to lift beneath his feet. He threw himself over the bulwarks, and slid down by a rope left there for the purpose, into the boat.

'Shove off! shove off!' he shouted.

The other officers were leaping into their respective boats. He hoped that he was, as he intended to be, the last to leave the ship. Flames were bursting forth on every side of the ship, and climbing up the masts; rockets were going off, and fiery missiles of all sorts were rising from the hold, and falling around in every direction. Thus amply capable of fulfilling her mission of death and destruction, she bore down on the French ships.

The boats shoved off, but one poor fellow was blown up before he reached the one to which he belonged, and his mangled form fell close to the captain's gig.

The rockets, too, were flying in every direction, as many directing their course towards the retreating boats as towards the ships of the enemy. No sooner, too, did the French perceive the nature of their approaching foe than they opened their fire on her, for the purpose of knocking away her masts, and altering the direction in which she was coming. Their shot also fell thickly round the boats.

The lights from his fire-ship showed Morton several others approaching the spot; and now the flames burst forth rapidly from one after the other; the distance at which they were ignited showing in a certain degree the amount of courage and judgment possessed by those who commanded them. Some were close to the boom, others were a mile, and others nearly two miles further off. On drove the fiery masses, like huge monsters of destruction, independent of human control.

Every object, far and near, was now lighted up by their flames. On, on they went, carrying havoc, terror, and confusion wherever they went; their loud explosions, added to the roar of the guns, which opened on them from the whole French squadron, increasing the awfulness of the scene. The enemy soon saw that their firing was in vain: even their boats failed to tow aside the fiery masses borne down on them by the gale. One after the other they cut their cables, and attempted to run up the harbour; but in the darkness and confusion, aided by terror at their approaching foes, they ran on shore, some on one side, some on the other; some were already grappled by the flaming ships, which literally covered them with showers of fire, while all the time the roar of the guns sounded as if a general action was taking place. Most of the fire-ships had got inside the boom, but Morton saw that one only just beginning to burn would miss it.

'Now, my lads, we'll get hold of her, and tow her down on the Frenchmen!' he exclaimed.

'Ay, ay, sir! we're all ready,' was the answer.

On they dashed towards the flaming mass. They got hold of the burning vessel, and towed her up towards the now retreating French ships.

Ronald saw Lord Claymore similarly engaged with another fire-ship. While they were pulling on one of the French frigates made sail, and passed to windward of them. As she did so she discharged her broadside into the two fire-ships, but the boats escaped without damage.

They were, however, compelled to let go, and allow the fire-ships to proceed on their course alone.

'Well done, Morton, those craft are performing their duty admirably!' he shouted. 'It is time, however, to be out of this; we can do no more at present, I fear.'

Morton's own boats and others had joined with Lord Claymore's. There was no difficulty now in seeing their way; the fire-ships gave them light enough. The explosions and the cannonading had much lulled the wind; the boats which had ventured inside the boom had again nearly reached it, when one of the enemy, which had driven on shore, was seen to be grappled by a fire-ship. In vain the Frenchmen strove to free themselves; their burning enemy held them in her deadly embrace till their ship was set on fire in several places; not till then did the fire-ship drift on, leaving them to their fate. They were lowering some of their boats, but most of them had been destroyed. It was too clear that numbers of the hapless crew must fall victims to the flames.

'They are no longer enemies—we'll try and save them,' shouted Morton.

His proposal met with a ready response from the officers and crews of the other boats, and in spite of the shot from the heated guns of the burning ship, away they dashed to the rescue of the Frenchmen.

CHAPTER XXXIV.

EDDA IN GERARDIN'S POWER. — THE FRIGATE STEERS FOR ROCHELLE.—CAPTAIN TACON.—PEDRO ALVAREZ AND FATHER MENDEZ.—TACON BETRAYS LORD CLAYMORE'S PLANS.

WHEN Edda Armytage discovered by whom the brig had been captured, her dread of the consequences, added to the grief and terror she had been experiencing, overcame her, and she fainted. When she returned to consciousness she found herself on a sofa in a handsome well-furnished cabin; her mother was tenderly watching by her side, and her father was walking up and down making observations partly to himself and partly to his wife.

'Yes, it is provoking to be captured just as we were reaching England, I own that,' he observed. 'How long we may be detained it is impossible to say. Yet things might be much worse. For the first lieutenant of the ship I have a great regard. You never appreciated him properly, Edda. Is that poor daughter of ours likely to come round soon? I must beg the surgeon of the ship to see her. Oh, well, if you think there is no danger perhaps she is better as she is. Now, with regard to this young officer, I take a deep interest in him. His history is, I confess, a mystery, but I hope to have the means of clearing it up. You, of all people, ought to take an interest in him. How constant and devoted he is to our daughter: from the first time he met her at Calcutta he admired her: nothing could be more tender or delicate than were his attentions to her when we were in his power. She has since made him the most ungrateful return. Her coldness, and the scornful way in which she treated him, was enough to drive any man away unless he was truly and sincerely attached. You tell me she does not and cannot love him. All nonsense. It is a daughter's duty to set her affections where her father desires. I have my reasons. That is sufficient. You speak of that young English lieutenant. He is a fine-looking fellow —granted. But what else is he? The son of a boatswain— not holding the rank of a gentleman. He has himself risen from before the mast. He is said to be held in estimation in his own service—granted; but he certainly, according to my idea, showed the white feather in that duel affair with young Maguire.'

'But, Colonel Armytage, surely you do not forget that this M. Gerardin was among those who made that dreadful attack on us in Spain—that he certainly attempted to carry off Edda, and would have succeeded had it not been for Mr Morton's gallantry.'

Mrs Armytage had seldom ventured to differ so strongly with her husband.

'I have always doubted whether it was Gerardin who figured on that occasion,' he answered. 'Morton, of course, is ready to suppose so, and you and Edda were too frightened, I suspect, to know what happened. Appearances are deceptive; I did not recognise him, and depend on it he will be able to assure us that he was not there.'

The lady after this dared not reply.

Colonel Armytage was in an excessively amiable mood. He was altogether not so much displeased at having been taken prisoner, for he anticipated very little satisfaction on his arrival in England. He had left it with an accumulation of debts, and he felt very sure that his creditors would give him no rest when they heard of his return. On the other hand he could live cheaply in France; the climate suited him; and he concluded that though he might be detained as a prisoner, he should be able to select his residence. But what pleased him most was the having fallen into the hands of his old acquaintance, Captain Gerardin, and his son, who, from his previous acquaintance with them, he was certain would do all in their power to make his position as agreeable as they could.

Edda had overheard the latter remarks made by her father. They did not contribute to afford her comfort, although they had the effect of arousing her attention. She kept her eyes shut, however, that she might have time to collect her thoughts. She soon comprehended very clearly what had happened, and remembering the counsel given her by Mrs Edmonstone, she resolved to treat the young foreigner with the same coldness which she had exhibited towards him at Calcutta. She forgot one very important point—their positions had been changed. He was then a prisoner—she was one now. At length, when her mother bent fondly over her with an expression of deep anxiety at her protracted fit, she could no longer resist opening her eyes to assure her that she was recovering.

A short time after this, a knock was heard at the door of the cabin, and the captain of the frigate entered. He said that he came to take the commands of his passengers as to the hour they would prefer having their meals. He was most anxious that they should enjoy every accommodation his ship could afford. He had not forgotten their kindness; and if they were destined to be made prisoners he was too happy to be their captor that he might prove to them his gratitude.

Though Captain Gerardin's countenance was sufficiently battered and weather-worn, there was an honest, good-natured expression about it which made Mrs Armytage feel far more confidence in his expressions than in those of his son.

It was not till the next day that Edda could be persuaded to go on deck; the sea was smooth, and the air soft and balmy, and she could not help looking out on the blue ocean which she had learned to love so much. Alfonse Gerardin only occasionally approached her. When he did so his manner was so gentle and courteous that she could not help acknowledging to herself that she had no reason to complain of him. Captain Gerardin was good-natured and hearty, and laughed and talked with her and her father and mother with well-bred ease and freedom.

The frigate, he told them, was attached to a squadron now at anchor near Rochelle, and that she was now on her way back to rejoin it.

The next morning land was seen ahead, and soon afterwards the frigate came up with a small lateen-rigged craft standing the same way. Captain Gerardin hailed, and asked where she was bound? In return, a person who said he was the captain, replied that he was in search of a French squadron which would soon be ready to sail, and that he had very important information to communicate.

'We will heave-to, and you can come on board,' answered the captain of the French frigate.

In a short time a boat was launched from the deck of the little felucca, and pulled towards the frigate. She was soon alongside, and a tall thin old man made his appearance on deck. Captain Gerardin scrutinized him severely, and he stared at the captain in return.

'We have met before, my friend, if I mistake not,' exclaimed the former. 'I see before me Don Annibal Tacon.'

'The same, though changed, I suspect, since we last parted,' said Captain Tacon. 'And I may venture to say that I behold one with whom I have exchanged some hard knocks, but love not the worse, and whom I once knew as Pedro Alvarez; though from the flag under which you serve I presume you have changed your name as well as your nation.'

'You are right, friend Tacon,' answered the captain. 'What is more, you are the very man for whom I have been long searching; but let me have your information first, and then I will tell you the reason why I have been anxious to find you.'

'It will take some time,' answered the old pirate. 'If you like to make sail, I will order the felucca to stand on in your wake.'

'No; but direct her to stand on under our lee,' said the captain. Your people may be very honest and faithful, but they may take it into their heads to run away, and leave you with us. It is well to be cautious with such gentry.'

Captain Tacon was profuse in his thanks. 'Certainly, rogues like mine do require to be watched,' he remarked. 'Ah, as I have always thought, honesty is the best policy, but somehow or other I never could manage to adhere to it. But before you make sail I may as well bring some passengers I have on board here. They are rather unwilling passengers, I own; I might call them prisoners, for they are Spaniards, enemies to France—an old man, a marquis and his daughter, and a priest. I took them out of a vessel bound for Cadiz; and as I did not know how to dispose of her, after removing every thing of value, I scuttled her.'

'But what did you do with her crew?' asked the captain of the frigate. 'Let them go down in her,' answered Tacon coolly. 'I thought it would show my other prisoners that I was not a man to be trifled with.'

'By all means let them come on board here,' said the captain of the frigate, anxious to get the prisoners out of the power of such a ruffian. 'I will send an officer and a boat to conduct them.'

A boat was lowered; one of the lieutenants jumped into it, and soon returned from the felucca with the persons Tacon had described. They were helped up the frigate's side, and the old man advanced, with his daughter leaning on his arm, and followed by the priest, who, though concealed by those in front, was, by peering out on one side, able to take a steady survey of the officers on the quarter-deck.

The captain received the marquis and his daughter with great politeness.

'We have already ladies on board, and I hope mademoiselle will have no cause to complain of her treatment while on board the ship, though our accommodation is somewhat limited.'

Mrs Armytage and Edda signed to the young lady to come to them, and she advanced at once, glad to find herself in the society of some of her own sex, whose countenances showed that they were worthy of her confidence.

The marquis stood alone, and the old priest was seen behind him.

No sooner did the eyes of the captain fall on him than he exclaimed, 'What! Father Mendez is it you still on this side the grave? I meet you very opportunely, for of all people you were the one I desired to see. What! do you not recollect your old shipmate?'

'Perfectly,' answered the priest in a low tone; 'but I should have thought, Pedro Alvarez, that I was the person of all others you would have been most desirous of avoiding—I, who am cognizant of your crimes, of the sacrilege you have committed, of your traitorous conduct—you, an outcast from the bosom of our Holy Mother Church—even now I find you in command of a ship belonging to the enemies of our country. If I speak, it must be to pronounce the curse of our Holy Church and of Heaven on your head.'

'Hold, father! you are going ahead too fast,' exclaimed the old seaman, bluntly; 'I have braved the curses of your Church too long to care for them; those of Heaven—Heaven alone can pronounce or inflict; but call not one a traitor who was unjustly driven from his country, and has never ceased to love her. However, you are an ancient comrade, and as such have the privilege of speaking freely. I wish to be on friendly terms with you and every human being. I am never happier with the feeling that I have made an enemy. But, as I was saying, I rejoice to meet you, for you can render me a service which will enable me to accomplish an object which has been nearer my heart than any other in the world.'

The English prisoners, as well as the marquis and his daughter, were near.

'Yes, I will confess to you, my friends,' he added, addressing them: 'I am not a Frenchman by birth, but a Spaniard— Pedro Alvarez by name, as Father Mendez called me. With your wife's family, as I told you, Colonel Armytage, I am well acquainted. For many months I have resided in Shetland.'

The marquis started, and cast an inquiring look at the captain's countenance.

'Circumstances occurred there of which Father Mendez is cognizant. We will speak of them by-and-by. My ship was wrecked, and my captain and all his crew perished. I was the only officer saved. On my return to Spain I was accused of heresy, and an officer of the Inquisition was sent to apprehend me. Perhaps the Marquis de Medea may know something about that. In self-defence I was compelled to slay the alguizal. I knew that the vengeance of the Inquisitors would follow me, and I escaped on board a ship-of-war which I had been appointed to command. I at length left her, and so managed that my officers believed me to be dead, and on their return home reported accordingly that such was the case. I wandered about in many parts of the world till the French Republic was established, and then I entered the naval service of France, and for convenience' sake changed my name. For long I continued in it and served France faithfully, but an event occurred which compelled me for a time to quit it. I went to India, and for several years I remained in the eastern seas in command of a privateer, and having made some money in her, I returned to Europe, when I received the command of this frigate. Such has been my career. There is no great mystery in it, but it was necessary that I should give an account of it, lest any present should consider me a monster in human shape, and guilty of all the crimes of which the father accuses me.'

The marquis, who had been anxiously watching the captain's countenance, breathed more freely when he ceased speaking. 'Certainly, my friend, I think that you have every excuse for your conduct,' he exclaimed, offering his hand to the captain, who did not seem very anxious to accept it. 'I for one shall be happy to welcome you back to Spain when peace is restored, and as the Inquisition has been abolished you need have no fear on that account. My friend, Father Mendez, will, I am sure, also retract his disparaging expressions he has applied to you. He must acknowledge that they are unjust—not such as you deserve. Come, father, say that you regret having spoken so harshly of the worthy officer.'

But the father shook his head without speaking.

'It matters little,' said the captain. 'He laughs who wins. Perhaps when all the details are filled up, some of my very worthy friends may not be so well pleased.'

He looked significantly at the marquis. At that moment Alfonse Gerardin crossed the quarter-deck. The marquis looked at him and started.

'Who is that young man?' he asked, in an agitated tone

'One of the officers of my ship, as you see by his uniform, answered the captain, carelessly.

'A sail on the larboard beam!' sung out a man from the mast-head. Soon afterwards the cry was heard that there were three, four, five sail—a whole fleet of ships in sight. The captain went aloft, and so did several of the officers, to examine the strangers with their glasses. On their return on deck, they pronounced them to be English, but the greater number of the ships were well on the frigate's quarter.

'As soon as we are seen they will give chase, but we must do our utmost to get under the batteries of Aix before they reach us. We have a good excuse for running away.'

More sail was set on the frigate. It was a question, however, whether she could reach the shelter which was sought for, in time. Several of the English ships were seen making sail in chase.

Edda Armytage looked out eagerly towards them. She at all events had no wish to remain a prisoner. Some wild hopes, too, rose in her heart as she understood that the pursuing ships were frigates.

'They will not overtake us, young lady,' said the captain, who observed the nature of her thoughts. 'I would rather, too, that you did not indulge in the wish, for I cannot bear to see you disappointed.'

'Thank you for your kindness, but it is but natural that I should wish to be free,' she answered, endeavouring to smile.

She fancied, by the countenances of some of the other officers, that they had not the same confidence as the captain. She observed the point for which the French frigate was steering, and it appeared to her that the English ships were just as near. This gave her hopes. Still she was afraid that the French would fight, and that there would be a desperate struggle before they allowed their ship to be captured. She was not aware that the French frigate was to windward of Rochelle, and that the English were some way to leeward, which gave the advantage to the former. The ships were, however, rapidly approaching each other. She saw, indeed, that even the captain thought that there might possibly be a fight, for the guns were being cast loose, and powder and shot were brought up on deck.

So much engaged had everybody been in observing the movements of the English fleet on the larboard beam, that no one had been watching the proceedings of the little felucca which had been on the other side. A loud oath from the lips of Don Tacon gave them notice that something was wrong, and looking out over the starboard bulwarks she was seen close hauled under all sail, standing away to the southward. The old man walked up and down the deck, throwing furious glances at her, while he stamped and swore, and tore his hair.

'The rogues, the villains, the scoundrels, to desert me thus!' he exclaimed. 'To take advantage of me when they saw that I could not pursue them. Who is one to trust in this world? My curses go with you, you knaves!' he shouted, shaking his fist at the far-distant vessel. 'Ha! it is some satisfaction to know that none of you know anything of navigation, and that you will cast yourselves away to a certainty. May every one of you be food for the fish before many days are over!'

No one pitied the old pirate, and he was allowed to rave on without interference.

The frigate tore through the water—the breeze was freshening. This was all in her favour. Still the British ships were coming up fast; the leading frigate began to fire her bow chasers, but the shot fell short. She waited for some time. One fortunate shot, and the Frenchman would be her prize. The forts on the island of Oleron could now be seen clearly with the naked eye. The English frigate drew still nearer. Captain Gerardin judged that she was nearly within gunshot.

'Ladies, this quarter-deck is no longer a place for you,' he said, addressing Edda and her mother, and the Spanish young lady. 'I regret to drive you from it, but I must use the authority of a captain, and order you below.'

Mrs Armytage and her daughter saw that he was in earnest, and prepared to obey. A shot which whistled close over the quarter showed the wisdom of his order.

'Oh, but my father—my father! will he not come?' exclaimed the daughter of the marquis in the most bitter anguish.

'Your father will do as he thinks fit, Donna Julia,' said the captain. 'I only exert my influence where ladies are concerned. Spain is at present united to England. He cannot be called on to fight.'

'And you, Captain Alvarez, you are a Spaniard. Why unite with the enemies of Spain?'

'Spain disinherited me,' he answered, turning away. 'But, ladies, hasten below, there is no time to be lost.'

Another shot came whistling by, and cut short all further conversation.

The captain now ordered a couple of long brass guns to be run out aft to return the compliment the English were paying him. They were served well, and the nearer the enemy approached, the more effective they became. At length a shot struck the taffrail, and glancing along the bulwarks, sent the splinters flying about the deck. The marquis turned pale.

'It is my duty to go and look after the safety of my daughter,' he observed, diving rapidly below.

'I am not a belligerent, and if I am wounded I cannot attend to the spiritual affairs of the dying,' said Father Mendez, following his patron.

'It matters little what becomes of me, since all my worldly possessions are on board the craft those scoundrels are carrying off,' remarked Don Tacon, as he sulkily walked the deck.

Colonel Armytage kept his post on the deck, eyeing the English ships.

'It would be wiser for you, sir, to go below,' said the captain. 'We shall be hotly engaged soon, and there is no reason why you should expose your life.'

'I have never avoided danger in whatever form it has presented itself,' answered the colonel, haughtily. 'I do not feel disposed to show on the present occasion that I have a faint heart.'

'As you like, colonel,' said the captain, shrugging his shoulders. 'It is an odd fancy some men have for making targets of their heads.'

The shots now came with greater rapidity on board the frigate. Her sails had several holes in them, and some of her standing as well as of her running rigging had been cut away. Still, only one of the chasing ships was near enough to fire, but the other two were coming up fast. The brave captain looked at his foes, and then at the friendly forts.

'We shall soon escape from them,' he observed to his

lieutenant. 'But one of these shots may any moment cut short my career. Should I fall, fight the ship to the last. And, Alfonse, remember—Colonel Armytage and Father Mendez know all.'

The French frigate was drawing in closer and closer to the fort. Suddenly one of the guns from it sent a shot flying past her towards her enemy. Several followed. The French garrison had got the range. Still, the Englishman did not give up the pursuit. A fortunate shot might enable him to bring the enemy to closer action. At length, however, a shot from the fort carried away his foretop-gallant-mast, another might do still further damage; and as it would have been extreme rashness to continue the pursuit further, he hauled his wind and made the best of his way out of the range of the guns of the forts, while the French frigate came to an anchor safe under their shelter near several line-of-battle ships and frigates.

No sooner had the sails been furled than Captain Tacon came aft, and begged at once to be taken to the admiral.

'I told you that I was coming to give important information,' he said coolly. 'I prefer giving it to the admiral, who has the power to reward me as I deserve.'

The captain had nothing whatever to say against this, and accordingly conducted him on board the flag-ship. The old pirate then gave the information that the English had resolved to attempt the destruction of the French fleet by fire-ships; and, as a proof, exhibited the plan which he had abstracted from Lord Claymore's cabin.

'I will consider the information you have brought me, and judge of the probability of its correctness,' answered the admiral. 'You shall, according as it is found to be correct, receive your reward. Take him on board again, Captain Gerardin, and see that he does not escape. He will probably be equally ready to inform the British government, if he has the opportunity, of what we are about.'

Tacon looked not over well pleased; he well knew that expostulation would be useless.

'The fates are against me, and I am truly an unfortunate and much-to-be-pitied man,' he muttered, as he was led away.

Captain Gerardin took him back on board the frigate, and, to prevent the possibility of his escaping, put him into irons. 'A hard necessity, friend Tacon,' he remarked; 'but necessity often compels us to perform unpleasant acts.'

'Ah, yes, it is my unfortunate fate! I am truly much to be commiserated,' answered the old pirate. 'Now there is the marquis, up there, in your cabin. He is a much greater scoundrel than I am, and yet rank and wealth are his lot.'

'Oh, we have a bonne-bouche prepared for him, which he may not relish much more than you do those mancles on your legs,' remarked the captain, as he left the worthy Tacon to his solitary reflections.

The French admiral, meantime, paid much more attention to the information he had received than he was willing to acknowledge he should do. It corroborated what he had received from other quarters, and he instantly issued orders to prepare for the expected attack. Lord Gambier's squadron had for some time been cruising off the coast, and it was considered a wonder that Captain Gerardin's frigate had got safe into harbour.

Meantime the prisoners, for so they were, though treated more as friends and passengers, were detained on board. The preparations for the attack were concluded, and the French were convinced that it could not succeed. It was now the common subject of conversation; and Edda heard that Lord Claymore was about to take an active part in the operation, and, of course, supposing that Ronald Morton was still with him, she felt sure that he would likewise be engaged, and would be foremost wherever danger was to be encountered. Never had she passed a time of suspense so painful. It was shared, however, in a great degree, by her mother and by Donna Julia.

She was becoming much interested in the young Spanish girl, though she could not entirely make out her character. At all events she was warm-hearted and enthusiastic, but though gentle in her manners, she seemed more inclined to resent an injury than to forgive it. Still she was very different to her father, for whom Edda had conceived a great dislike. No one, indeed, liked him. Her father kept studiously aloof from his society, and even Father Mendez rarely or never spoke to him. Edda's chief annoyance arose from the attentions paid her by Alfonse Gerardin; they had become more frequent, and he was far more confident in his manner than he had ever before been. How to treat him under the present circumstances she could not tell. The cabin was no sanctuary to her. He entered it at all times with perfect freedom, and evidently with the captain's sanction.

One day, believing that he was on duty on deck, where the rest of the party were assembled, she remained in the cabin to read. She was seated on a sofa, and had succeeded in fixing her attention on the book, when the door opened, and on looking up she saw Lieutenant Gerardin approaching her. She let her eyes again drop on the page before her, but not a word could she read. He sat down by her side, and before she was aware of it had grasped her hand.

'Hear me, Edda!' he exclaimed with vehemence. 'I can exist no longer in the state of uncertainty I have endured for so many years. From the first moment I saw you, I loved you. You know it. My love was sincere, faithful, disinterested. I am not a mere adventurer, as you may suppose. My birth is equal, if not superior, to yours. Rank and wealth will be mine. All I offer to lay at your feet. You doubt my words. The means of proving my claims have only lately, in the most wonderful way, been placed in the power of my guardian and protector, Pedro Alvarez, whom you know as Pierre Gerardin, the captain of the ship. Let me have the satisfaction of telling you, dear Edda, that I am your cousin. the long-lost son of Donna Hilda Escalante.'

Edda looked incredulously in his face, and endeavoured to withdraw her hand; she suspected that he had by some means become acquainted with her family history, and having concocted a story, was practising on her simplicity.

'I tell you the solemn truth. Why do you doubt me,' he exclaimed, almost fiercely. 'You have surely often heard how a child was carried away by pirates from Lunnasting, and that no tidings had ever been gained of him. I was that child. The chief of the band, Tacon, is a prisoner on board this ship. For the sake of obtaining his liberty, he will be ready to acknowledge his part in the transaction. I was rescued from his power by my father's faithful lieutenant, and my constant friend and guardian, Pedro Alvarez. He had no means of getting to Shetland, nor could he return to Spain. After wandering about in many parts of the world, taking me with him, he repaired to France, then at war with England. He sent to Shetland, and from the answer he received, he believed that my mother was dead. He fancied that, even should he be able to get there, my claims would not be acknowledged, and he determined, therefore, till peace was restored, not to make the attempt. My father, as you may have heard, would have succeeded to the title of the Marquis de Medea and to a magnificent estate. On his death the inheritance became mine; but without proofs of my birth, Pedro Alvarez himself being unable to return to Spain, how could he hope to succeed in obtaining for me my rights? He had carefully abstained from telling me the secret of my birth, and I fully believed that I was his son. I have been brought up as a Frenchman, and as a Frenchman I have always felt and acted. To support the honour and glory of our great emperor has always been my ambition and aim; though he may meet with reverses, he must succeed in the end—I am sure of that as I am of my own existence. Spain, which has foolishly abandoned him, will again be brought under his power, and through his means I feel sure that I shall some day obtain my father's inheritance.

ALFONSE DECLARES HIS LOVE.

You look incredulous, lady. Proud England, too, will be humbled, and France, and all who adhere to her, will be triumphant. Those glorious days, when France will rule the world, will soon arrive, sweet Edda; and I ask you to share with one who loves you with devotion and tenderness unsurpassed, the wealth and rank which will then be his.'

'I thank you, Monsieur Gerardin, from my heart, I do, for your sentiments towards me,' she answered, in a gentle tone. 'But be assured that I cannot return them. To be frank with you, my heart is given to another. To you I can only be a cousin, a friend, and well-wisher. You will, I feel sure, find many girls whose hearts are disengaged, who will love you for yourself, and not for the wealth and rank which I hope may be yours.'

'My friend and well-wisher!' he exclaimed, starting up and walking about the cabin. 'Those are cold words to address to one who loves you as I have done. You tell me that you love another. He shall pay the penalty of interfering with me. I knew that he was my rival. He has escaped me often, but the next time we meet we will not part till one has fallen.'

He continued pacing up and down before her; and stamping furiously on the deck, he exclaimed—'Thus will I trample all my enemies under my feet! Ay, little does that usurping kinsman of mine dream what I prepared for him. I have him in my power, and I will take good care to exercise that power. He lives on under the belief that he is the owner of broad lands and wealth unbounded, and it is a pleasure to watch him as he paces the deck, and to know that I, all the time, am the true marquis, and that he is the impostor. Ah, cousin Edda! you supposed me a quiet, gentlemanly young lieutenant of marine. You now know who I am and what I am. I am one not to be trifled with—not to be opposed with impunity. You would have thought me a person of importance if I were simply the inheritor of the castle and the estates of

Lunnasting—those estates which would have been yours had I not appeared. Without them, remember, you will be reduced to poverty—the most complete poverty—your father confesses as much. Let that weigh with you. Your love I shall gain ere long. I fear not on that point. Come, cousin, be mine—be mine. Neither heaven nor earth shall keep you from me!'

He rushed towards her and endeavoured to grasp her hand. She shrunk from him with dread, for there was a glare in his eye, and a wildness in his look which suggested the horrible idea that he was attacked with insanity. She looked round with the intention of escaping from the cabin, when the door opened and Donna Julia entered. Hernan was calm in an instant, and bowing to the Spanish lady, he said in English—'Cousin, soothe that poor girl. The blow that I have to strike will be terrible indeed to her.'

He disappeared as he spoke. He hurried on deck. His great anxiety was now to bring the marquis, Tacon, Father Mendez, and Pedro Alvarez together before Colonel Armytage, that the whole chain of evidence might be clearly exhibited to him. He was about to propose this to the captain, when a gun was fired from the flag-ship, and the signal was seen flying for the first lieutenants and four boats from every ship to come alongside.

Hernan hurried off in obedience to orders. When he got on board the flag-ship he found that a number of vessels which had been seen joining the English fleet, then at anchor about six miles off, were supposed to be fire-ships, and that an immediate attack from them was apprehended.

The fleet of boats was to be on the watch near the boom, to attack any English boats which might approach, or to tow the fire-ships clear of the men-of-war.

The night was of pitchy darkness when the flotilla of French boats started on their perilous expedition. Long they watched, every moment expecting to see the flames from the fire-ships bursting forth close to them, or to be engaged in a deadly conflict with the English boats.

'Hark!' said Hernan to the midshipman by his side; 'I hear the sound of oars. Ah, there is a boat! What boat is that?' he asked, in a loud voice.

Little did he dream who was in that boat, that his hated rival was almost within his power. The French boats gave chase. There could be but little doubt that the English boat had been in the midst of them. Many a loud oath was sent after her, but she flew faster than they or their oaths, and the flotilla returned discomfited to their stations at the boom. Thus the night passed away. The general opinion was, that after all they had little to fear from the threatened fire-ships.

CHAPTER XXXV.

THE FRIGATE ATTEMPTS TO ESCAPE FROM THE FIRE-SHIP.—THE BURNING FRIGATE.—DANGER OF THE PASSENGERS.—ESCAPE FROM THE BURNING SHIP.—ON BOARD THE 'SCORPION.'—LORD CLAYMORE ILL SUPPORTED.—THE 'SCORPION' SENT TO THE NORTH SEA.

HE night passed off without any attack on the French fleet from the British fire-ships. Pedro Alvarez, or rather Captain Gerardin, offered to land Colonel Armytage on his parole with his family and Donna Julia, so that they might remain in a place of safety in case of threatened danger; but the colonel, with his characteristic obstinacy, declined the favour, saying that he felt himself in perfect safety on board the frigate. It must be said that the general opinion among the French officers was, that the English would not attack them, while he, accustomed to hold the navy somewhat in contempt, persuaded himself that they would not dare to make the attempt.

The evening had passed much as others had done. Edda enjoyed it the more that Hernan was absent. The captain, as he had been accustomed, brought his guitar into the cabin, and played and sang a number of Spanish airs, and persuaded Donna Julia to do the same. Father Mendez, as he well could when he had the will, made himself very agreeable by describing many places he had visited, and narrating a number of anecdotes. Even Colonel Armytage entered freely into conversation, and he and Father Mendez soon became on very friendly terms. The marquis was the only person who was in ill temper. He sat aloof from the rest of the party, and refused all invitations to join in the conversation. The truth was, he had begun to suspect that Pedro Alvarez and Father Mendez were plotting against him. He felt himself in the power of Tacon, whom he knew would give them all the information they required, while he looked with a suspicious eye on the young lieutenant, whose likeness to Don Hernan Escalante had forcibly struck him. His daughter only fancied that he was unhappy at being a prisoner; but as she was in very pleasant society, and was treated with all courtesy and kindness, she had no cause to complain.

Some of the other officers of the ship came in, cards were introduced, and the marquis was tempted to play. Colonel Armytage joined him. It was a somewhat incongruous collection of people. With music and conversation the evening passed rapidly away, and the party continued together till a much later hour than usual.

The captain handed his guitar to Donna Julia with a gallant bow.

'One more song, sweet lady,' he said. 'It is seldom we seamen enjoy the delightful harmony you have afforded us this evening.

Donna Julia took the instrument, and running her fingers over the cords commenced a low and plaintive air. Her voice was sweet, but not strong, though it was sufficient to fill the cabin, and to rivet the attention of all present. The air was sad and plaintive, and from the pathos with which she sung, it showed too clearly her own feelings. It is wonderful how music unlocks the heart, and melts the long pent-up stream. Not a sound but that sweet voice was heard. The seamen on their watch overhead stopped in their walk to listen to strains so unusual. Suddenly a roar, more terrific than the bursting of a volcano, was heard, followed by shrieks, and groans, and cries; a bright light was seen glancing over the water through the stern ports; the ship shook from her keel. The guitar fell from Donna Julia's hands. Mrs Armytage grasped her daughter's arm, expecting something more dreadful to follow, and believing that the ship was about to blow up. The gentlemen started to their feet; the officers rushed out of the cabin. The scene which met their view was sufficient to inspire the stoutest heart with fear. Directly ahead, and rushing towards them, was a vast fiery mass, furiously darting forth flames, sufficient, should it reach her, to wrap the frigate in a destructive embrace. At the same time, from out of this floating volcano, shot forth red-hot missiles, which fell in destructive showers on her decks. The crew, in dismay, were running for shelter below, till their captain's voice was heard high above the din, calling on them to act like men, and to endeavour to save the ship by throwing overboard their dangerous visitors.

The remaining boats were then ordered to be lowered to tow aside the burning mass now close at hand. But who would venture to approach it?

'Alfonse would have attempted it!' exclaimed the captain, but not an officer moved. Certain destruction would be their doom.

'I then must go myself; who will follow me?' cried the captain.

Numbers of the crew sprang towards the boats. There was ample light to see what was to be done. At that instant the flames and sparks darted up higher than ever, and then, as if it were the work of magic, there was total darkness; the explosion vessel had sunk: the frigate was saved.

'We must get under weigh,' cried the captain. 'The boom has been shattered. Another vessel may strike the same spot with more success, and we may not escape her so easily.'

The crew flew aloft to loosen sails. They were eager to avoid a similar danger to that which had almost paralyzed them. Before they were again off the yards another fearful explosion took place close to them, but though numerous fiery fragments fell on board, few were hurt. Had they not been aloft many more would have suffered. The cable was slipped, and the frigate now began to move through the water.

On hearing the second explosion, the remaining occupants of the cabin rushed up on deck. Colonel Armytage was the least agitated, but even he did not attempt to quiet the alarm of his wife and daughter. Father Mendez trembled like an aspen leaf. The usual calmness of his exterior had disappeared. The danger which threatened was strange, incomprehensible. So occupied were the officers and crew, that none of the party were observed. The spectacle which soon after met their sight was not calculated to allay their terror.

For a few minutes all was again darkness, and then rapidly, one after the other, masses of flame burst forth from the surface of the ocean, hurrying towards them. As they approached, the sails and rigging of large vessels were seen amid the flames. No human beings could have stood on those decks; but yet onward came, rushing impetuously, the burning fleet. They were the much dreaded fire-ships. On they came. The boom had been forced. By what power could they be resisted?

The French ships opened their fire on them, and shot were flying about among friends and foes, increasing the confusion and dismay. Still the fire-ships sailed on, intent on their mission of destruction. Now a line-of-battle ship was grappled. For long her gallant crew in vain sacrificed their lives in the attempt to free her from the fire-ship's deadly embrace. The cables were cut, and both together drifted away to leeward. And now dismay seized nearly all the French officers and crews. Simultaneously the cables were slipped, and they endeavoured to avoid the threatened danger by flight. Some effected their escape, but others were overtaken by the fire-ships, and were seen surrounded by flames. The frigate had been kept under weigh, firing sometimes at the fire-ships as they sailed by, and at others at boats which were supposed to be English. As the fire reached the guns of the burning ships they were discharged right and left, and a whole broadside was poured into the frigate. It was blowing strong—a shot struck her foremast, and with all its top hamper away it went over the side, carrying the maintopmast with it. The frigate luffed up into the wind and became unmanageable. A fire-ship was approaching. On it came. It got entangled in the wreck of the mast, and soon the frigate herself was wrapped in flames.

Edda saw and comprehended the danger. 'Oh, mother, we will die together!' she exclaimed, for she saw no hope of escape.

The crew, led by their captain, made many gallant attempts to cut clear the wreck and the fire-ships, but each time the fierce heat of the flames drove them back again. Still they persevered. They all saw that, with the few boats they had remaining, unless the flames were subdued they must be destroyed. From the rest of the squadron they could expect no help; some of the ships were seeking safety in flight, others were in a like predicament as themselves. The French officers exerted themselves heroically. Again and again they led their men up among the flames, where many, as with axes in hand they cut away at the spars or ropes, lost their hold and fell headlong into the burning mass, or were suffocated by the smoke. Many were precipitated into the water; and their shrieks were heard as they struggled vainly in their endeavour to reach the burning frigate driving away before them. Even at that moment the brave Pedro Alvarez did not forget his passengers. He had done all that a man could do to save the ship, but he believed that his efforts would prove fruitless. He now thought of the means of saving his friends. He was hurrying to the cabin when he perceived them grouped together on the deck. The three ladies stood, not shrieking nor giving way to fear, but calm and collected, waiting till they received directions what to do. Colonel Armytage, with the marquis and Father

Mendez were endeavouring to shield them from the sparks, which flew thickly around, and threatened to ignite their dresses. The colonel looked up and saw that the flames were rapidly gaining on the ship. He was not altogether so stubborn and selfish as not to wish to preserve the lives of his wife and daughter. The awful scene made him also more kind and gentle than usual.

'Edda—wife, daughter, we must get you into the boats,' he said. 'Donna Julia, and her father, and the priest will accompany us. I must obtain assistance from some of the crew.'

'The boats—the boats!' shouted the captain, rushing now to one side of the ship—now to the other; they were gone!

Some of the dastards among the crew, in selfish haste to save themselves, had leaped into them and pulled away.

Where all this time was the first-lieutenant of the ship? He with his boats had not returned; what had become of him no one could tell. He might have missed the frigate, and gone in another direction, or might have been captured by the English. Secretly, Pedro Alvarez hoped that this might be the case, for whatever his adopted son, who had always been brought up as a Frenchman, might think on the subject, he had begun to wish that he could be engaged in fighting the battles of his native country, instead of those of her enemies and oppressors.

Thinking of Hernan reminded him of his prisoner, and the old pirate Tacon. To his adopted son the old man's life was of the greatest importance. Should he be destroyed one chief witness of his identity would be lost. He hurried below to release him. He was only just in time to save him from suffocation, for the smoke was already finding its way along the decks. He had found the armourer on his way, and ordering him to knock off the prisoner's fetters, he dragged him up, and placed him close to Colonel Armytage.

'Much depends on his safety : keep your eye on him, sir,' he said.

A terrible idea occurred to him. The magazine had not been drowned. Should it not be done, all on board might be blown to destruction. It was a work of awful danger, for a spark might fly in before the powder was destroyed, and produce the dreaded catastrophe. He gave the necessary orders, and then devoted himself to other endeavours to save the lives of some of those on board. That all could be saved, he knew was impossible.

For some time longer, efforts were made to clear the fireship, and while some of the crew were thus employed, others, under the captain's superintendence, were endeavouring to form a raft, but at length the flames seemed resolved to claim their victim. And now a scene of the wildest confusion ensued. Many who had hitherto been exerting themselves manfully abandoned all hope; some threw themselves overboard, others rushed below to the spirit-store, hoping to reach it before the fire had gained possession of the hold. Some rushed aft, imploring the captain to save them, and shouting loudly for boats to come to their assistance. No one among that multitude of rough men stood so calm and resigned as Mrs Armytage and her daughter. Donna Julia was scarcely less so; but her hands were clasped firmly, and every now and then she moved a few paces with rapid steps up and down the deck, regardless of the sparks which fell around her. Edda stood motionless, with her head turned away from the flames, and her eye ranging with undefined hope seaward, over the water.

'There are boats coming!—boats! boats!' was the cry.

A shout was raised by the remainder of the crew clustered on the quarter-deck.

'Lieutenant Gerardin and our comrades have arrived.'

The crew began to rush to the sides to throw themselves into the boats, but a warning cry was raised in English, 'Keep back, or we pull away!' One boat, however, dashed alongside. Ropes were hove to the people in her by the captain and others, and an officer climbed up on board, and instead of Alfonse Gerardin, whom she expected, Edda beheld, to her unspeakable joy, Ronald Morton. The bright glare revealed her to him. He did not look to see who else was there. He knew her in a moment. He asked not how she came there, but clasping her in his arms, he carried her to the side of the vessel.

'Oh, Ronald, my mother!' she exclaimed.

Several persons had followed him.

'I'll look after her, miss,' said Job Truefitt, taking up Mrs Armytage, with as much ease as if she had been a child, and accompanying his chief. An officer—it was Glover—who had got on board from one of the other boats, seeing Donna Julia, without a word, lifting her in his arms, carried her to the ship's side. With the assistance of Pedro Alvarez they were lowered safely into the boats. Many of the seamen were then about to leap in, but the captain drove them back with his sword.

'Shame on you! there are old men and a priest to be first placed in safety,' he shouted. 'Help them first, and then think about yourselves.'

Even at that awful moment the men obeyed. The marquis and the priest were lowered down, and Colonel Armytage followed. As Pedro Alvarez was helping him down the side he said in a low voice, 'Keep an eye on old Tacon, he is even now meditating how he may escape. I will lower him down to you.'

The captain then caught hold of Tacon, and without much ceremony sent him down after the rest.

Ronald's boat was now full enough, and he ordered the men to shove off and lie on their oars, while the other boats took off the remainder of the crew.

A considerable number of the Frenchmen had been taken off the burning ship, when Ronald saw the brave captain standing by himself, he having refused to quit her till his men were in safety.

'It were a pity so brave a fellow should be lost,' said Ronald.

'Oh, do – do save him!' cried Edda, who heard the remark. 'He is kind and good as well as brave.'

This was enough; he once more steered the boat towards the burning ship. Just then a burning spar fell from aloft. It appeared to strike him, for he disappeared. A groan escaped all who saw the accident.

'He may not be killed though, sir,' said Job Truefitt. 'If I may, I'll look for him.'

Ronald gave him leave. There were numbers of ropes hanging over the frigate's quarter. Job swarmed up by one of them, and directly after appeared with the captain, about whose body he had secured a rope. He lowered him down into the boat, and followed immediately. Still numbers of the crew remained. Many who had gone below hearing that there were boats alongside, came up with the hopes of escaping. When the already overloaded boats pulled away their rage and despair knew no bounds. They were seen standing on the hammock-nettings, or in the mizzen rigging, shaking their fists and uttering the most dreadful imprecations on the heads of those whom they considered were deserting them. As it was, the boats were so full that not another person could have been received on board with safety.

Morton gave the orders for the boats to pull back to the 'Scorpion.' It was heavy work, for there was a strong wind and a heavy sea; but the crews encouraging each other cheerfully pulled on.

What joy filled Morton's heart at having been the means of preserving Edda's life and that of her father and mother! He did not press her to say much; but a few words explained how they came to be on board the French frigate.

Her feelings were not dissimilar to his. She was with him again, and she had no fear for the future.

Pedro Alvarez, too, was perfectly satisfied with having

been taken prisoner, when he found from Colonel Armytage who was his captor. 'The very man I wished to meet,' he said to himself. 'He will tell me where his father is to be found, and Rolf Morton is an important witness in proving the claim of my poor Hernan. Where can he be though? Probably he had gone with the boats to the assistance of some of the other ships, and was not aware of our danger.'

Just before daylight the boats reached the 'Scorpion.' The ladies were carried below to obtain that rest they so much required, and Ronald accommodated the rest of the party as well as he could.

Pedro Alvarez at once went up to him and claimed his acquaintance. 'I wish to tell you of circumstances with which it is important you should be acquainted without delay,' he said. 'I know that you have every reason to be interested in Donna Hilda Escalante, known as the Lady of Lunnasting.'

Ronald was all attention. He knew how really interested Mrs Armytage was in all concerning her unhappy sister, while he was most anxious to show his gratitude by serving her.

Pedro Alvarez then explained who he himself was, and told his astonished hearer that the pirate Tacon, whom he had on board, was the very man who had carried off Hilda's child, which child had been rescued and brought up by him.

'Then the young officer whom I have so often and so unexpectedly met, and who appears to have such bitter animosity towards me, is no other than Hernan Escalante, the long-lost son of my kind patroness Donna Hilda?' exclaimed Ronald.

'Such is the case,' said Pedro Alvarez. 'He has fallen in love with his fair cousin, and he believes that you are his rival. He has another reason for disliking you, but of that by-and-by. I believe that I can do you a service, and certainly you can do me a considerable one. You owe me a good turn, let me tell you; for in consequence of having assisted you to escape, I was obliged to take command of a privateer, bound for the East Indies, and to make my escape from France. I was wandering about in those seas for many years; but at length, having some friends in power, I was reinstated in the French navy. However, my heart has never been estranged from Spain. She is at peace with England; and as I now hope to see the great object of my existence accomplished—the son of my old captain established in his rights—I purpose throwing off my allegiance to France, and becoming once more a Spaniard. I have told you all this, at a moment so unfitting, because I am anxious that you should endeavour to prevent any of the persons who were on board my frigate from escaping. Tacon will certainly make the attempt. He does not know of what crimes he may be found guilty, and instinctively will do what he can to be at liberty.'

In a few words the worthy Pedro also told Ronald who the marquis and the old priest were, and he undertook to do his best to keep a watch on them till they had given the evidence required to establish young Hernan in his rights.

'Believe me,' he added, 'I wish him no ill, and I would gladly make any sacrifice to see him restored to his mother and the possessor of his paternal inheritance. As to the marquis, I am not surprised at what you tell me; I never liked him when we had him on board the "Imperious," while the priest always puzzled me. Tacon showed himself to be a most perfect rogue, and I suspect will give us no little trouble before we can get the required truth out of him. However, as it can be proved that he committed an act of piracy in attacking a Spanish vessel, I shall take the liberty of putting him into irons, to prevent the chance of his escaping.'

Pedro Alvarez was well satisfied with the arrangements made by Morton, while the miserable Tacon complained bitterly of the hard fate to which he was doomed.

'Oh, the malice and cruelty of this world!' he exclaimed. 'I no sooner get my legs out of one pair of irons than I find them clapped into another—wretched—ill-used man that I am! What have I done to deserve such a lot?'

When daylight returned, the effect produced by the fire-ships became apparent. The whole French fleet lay scattered about in every direction. Some had disappeared altogether. They had either sunk or effected their escape up the harbour, but the greater number lay hard and fast on shore, some so much on the heel that a few shots from the British ships would have knocked holes in their bottoms, and when the tide rose have effectually prevented their again floating.

Soon after daybreak the gallant Lord Claymore, the soul and moving spirit of the enterprise, signalized to the Admiral that the whole might be destroyed. For a long time no notice of his signals was taken. At length some vessels were sent to his assistance, but much valuable time was lost, and several of the French ships, by throwing overboard their stores and guns, floated, and got higher up the harbour.

When the British squadron did get into action, they performed their work effectually, and four line-of-battle ships and a fifty-gun ship were taken, two of which were at once destroyed. The other two were not set on fire till night, when a panic seized the French crews, who believed them to be more fire-ships, and then some again cut their cables, and endeavoured to escape up the harbour, while one captain and his ship's company abandoned their ship altogether. One man only was left on board, who, by his bravery and presence of mind, prevented her from becoming a prize to an English midshipman and his boat's crew. When the boat pulled up, he hailed in a loud voice, ordering her to keep off, and having a number of marines' muskets ready, he fired them one after the other with such rapidity, that the midshipman of course fully believed that a considerable part of the crew were still on board.

The next day some fresh fire-ships were fitted for the purpose of destroying the enemy's ships on shore, which could not otherwise be got at. The wind was, however, unfavourable, and the enterprise was ultimately abandoned.

Ronald's own ship was not engaged in these operations, and he perhaps was secretly not sorry to avoid the risk his passengers would have run had she been so. He, however, accompanied Lord Claymore, and assisted in capturing the line-of-battle ships and in removing the prisoners. He made all the inquiries he could from the prisoners for Alfonse Gerardin, but not a word could he hear of him, and he began to fear that he must have been killed.

'Poor Hernan!' he said to himself; 'it will be sad if such is your fate at the very moment that there is a prospect of your being restored to your name and station.'

Directly after this Lord Claymore returned to England, and the 'Scorpion' was also ordered home.

Although most of the prisoners taken from the burning frigate were removed, on Morton's application Pedro Alvarez was allowed to remain on board the corvette. He kept likewise that worthy, Tacon, as he felt sure that if he did not he should never seen him again. Colonel Armytage behaved much more courteously to Ronald than he had formerly done, but still there was more stiffness in his manner than was pleasant; and in his presence his wife and daughter appeared restrained and uneasy, as if he had laid injunctions on them which they would gladly have broken through.

The day after the marquis got on board he was seized with a severe illness, brought on by the anxiety and alarm which he had experienced. The surgeon pronounced it to be very dangerous. Glover had given up his cabin to him, and now assisted poor Donna Julia in tending him, which he did with the greatest devotion.

The 'Scorpion' had a quick passage to Plymouth, where Colonel Armytage and his family went on shore.

Edda's last words to Ronald were, 'We must live in hope. My father may compel me to remain single, as I will not marry in opposition to his wishes; but at the same time I will marry no one but you.'

What more could a lover wisely desire?

'Hope has borne me up hitherto. It will, I trust, continue to sustain me,' answered Ronald, as, having escorted her and her parents on shore, he was compelled to return on board.

The marquis continued too ill to be moved, and Father Mendez claimed the right, as his confessor, of remaining with him. To this Morton had no objection, especially as the priest interfered with no one, and made himself a very agreeable companion. Ronald was doubting how to dispose of Pedro Alvarez, for whom he had begun to feel much regard. He was very unwilling to send him on shore, where he would have been committed to prison. While he was thus uncertain how to act, he received orders to fill up with provisions and stores, and proceed to the north seas for a summer cruise. For this he was not sorry, for though he would have preferred being more actively engaged in the Channel, it gave him the prospect of visiting Shetland. He had written to his father as soon as he reached England, and told him everything that occurred. It would now be impossible for him to know what steps he might think fit to take till he could meet him in Shetland. He thought over the matter with regard to Pedro Alvarez, and thinking it probable that he would not be inquired for, he offered to allow him to remain on board as his guest, on receiving his parole that he would not escape. This he of course at once gave, as he was himself very anxious to visit Shetland, that he might communicate with Sir Marcus Wardhill and Hilda, in order to arrange the proofs necessary for Hernan to establish his claims.

The marquis, as he lay on his sick bed, little dreamed of the probable result of his plots and contrivances, and of the reverse of fortune preparing for him.

Pedro Alvarez had clearly explained all his plans to Ronald.

'I will, my friend, help you to the utmost to do justice to the wronged; and scarcely any event will give me greater satisfaction than seeing Donna Hilda Escalante recover her son,' said Morton; 'but I fear that by so doing I shall make a mortal enemy of Colonel Armytage, who would otherwise succeed to the Lunnasting property; and I shall deprive his daughter of the fortune which would fall to her.'

Pedro Alvarez looked at him hard.

'Should Hernan Escalante ever succeed to the Lunnasting property, I can answer for it that Miss Armytage will not be the sufferer,' he answered.

The remark shot a pang through Ronald's heart. 'Should Hernan become owner of Lunnasting, and a Spanish marquis, what pressure will Colonel Armytage bring to bear to compel Edda to break her promises to me, and to unite herself to him. It was of that the Spaniard was thinking. But no; I have heard and read of the falsehood and faithlessness of women, but I will not believe that Edda Armytage could by any possibility be guilty of such treachery: the very thought is dishonouring to her. Did I think that such a union would tend to her happiness, I would release her from her promise; but I feel sure it would not. No, no! wealth and rank would not bribe her. She loves me. What pride and happiness to know that I am loved for myself, and myself alone! Should I be deceived, life in future will indeed be a blank.'

CHAPTER XXXVI.

LUNNASTING CASTLE. — LAWRENCE BRINDISTER. — LAWRENCE'S MYSTERIOUS SAYINGS. — UNPLEASANT ANNOUNCEMENT TO SIR MARCUS. — ARRIVAL OF THE 'SCORPION.' — THE PRIEST'S VISIT TO HILDA.

ILDA WARDHILL, or rather Donna Hilda Escalante, was to be seen in her turret chamber in the same spot, and almost in the same position, as when first in her youth and glorious beauty she was introduced to the reader. Years had dimmed and changed that beauty, but had not altogether destroyed it; and as she now sat habited in black, her complexion pure as alabaster, and her light hair braided over her forehead, which was bowed down over a volume of huge dimensions, she presented a subject which a painter would have delighted to portray.

She leaned back in her chair, and pressing her hand on her brow, exclaimed, 'In vain have I studied to ascertain how, or in what guise he will return. I demand an answer, but the oracles cruelly refuse to reply. O that I had the potent secret by which I could compel an answer, and that the dark veil which hides the future might be torn aside to disclose the view I long to see! Yet of one thing I am certain—the time cannot be far distant; of this many significant events have warned me. The return of Rolf Morton after so long an absence is strange; my father's illness, and his strong desire to see my sister Edda once more, and her daughter, who they tell me is as lovely as she was. The old man's illness will, I doubt not, induce that stern English colonel to come down, that he may secure some share of his wealth. He dreams not that my Hernan will return some day to claim his own, and prevent poor Edda's daughter from becoming the Lady of Lunnasting, as they now believe she will be.'

Her hand slowly dropped from her brow, and she gazed forth on the ocean.

'What—what is yonder object? Is it a phantom of the brain or a reality?' she exclaimed, rising from her seat, and pointing towards the south-west. 'See, there—there at the very spot where that beautiful ship first appeared, which the cruel ocean dashed to fragments on these rocks of Shetland, floats her counterpart. Can it be her—the 'St Cecilia' herself? Is all that has passed for these long years a dream? No, no; it has been too real, too palpable, too full of pain, and sorrow, and hope deferred, to be a dream. Yet, what is that?—a ship, come to mock me, as others have done; first to raise my hopes that my long-lost son is on board, and again as bitterly to disappoint them.'

'Yes, cousin; that is a ship, and a very fine ship, too; a British man-of-war, I judge, by the ensign which floats proudly at her peak,' said a voice behind her.

Hilda turned quickly round, and an angry frown rose on her brow as she saw Lawrence Brindister, who had entered just as she had discovered the strange ship. He shuffled up to the window, with a peculiar gait partly caused by the size of his shoes. His appearance, as he advanced in age, had become more grotesque. He wore a gay-flowered waistcoat, with knee breeches, and huge silver buckles on his shoes. His coat, which was much too large for his now shrunken figure, was trimmed with gold lace in a style already long gone out of fashion. His grey eyes looked larger and rounder than ever, while his hair, which had become perfectly white, was cropped short, and stood on end like the quills of an irritated porcupine.

'Why comes she here, I wonder?' he continued. 'Once upon a time, I would have gone to ascertain, but my old arms can now scarcely paddle a boat across the voe, and were I to attempt to go, and the tide catch me, I might be swept helplessly out to sea. It might not be a bad ending for the puir auld daft bodie, you'll be saying, cousin, and a wonder it had never happened before. But I've some work to do before that time, Hilda. "The prince will hae his ain again! The prince will hae his ain again!" and before long too, let me tell you, cousin.'

'Lawrence, what is the import of those words?' exclaimed Hilda, vehemently, grasping his arm as she spoke; 'for years past you have uttered them. I adjure you, tell me what you mean.'

'Cousin, I am but a puir fule,' answered Lawrence, looking calmly into her face; 'fules speak mony things without meaning, ye ken.'

Hilda looked stedfastly in his face, and he returned her gaze with an expression so unmoved and idiotic, that she saw it was hopeless to expect a satisfactory reply.

They were standing close to the window as she turned from him; her glance once more ranged over the ocean. Again she stopped and gazed; Lawrence watched the direction of her eyes.

'Ha, ha, cousin! you have discovered the other craft, have you? Who comes in her, think you? Guests are expected at the castle, I understand, and some at the cottage, if so you choose to designate my friend Rolf Morton's abode; sages learned in the law coming to investigate a knotty subject, to unravel a long-continued mystery.'

'I understand you not,' answered Hilda, still continuing to watch the two vessels. The latter-mentioned one was a cutter or smack, such as was employed in the summer months to keep up the communication between the islands and the ports of Aberdeen and Leith. She had come apparently from Lerwick, and was now observed to be steering directly for Lunnasting, while the corvette kept in the offing, and was, as far as could be seen, about to enter Eastling Sound from the east, or to pass it by altogether. The smack had got a favourable slant of wind, and rapidly approached.

Hilda stood watching her with trembling anxiety. Lawrence was also watching her narrowly, and taking apparently a strange pleasure in so doing. At length an idea seemed to strike him.

'I'll be off, and tell Sir Marcus of his coming guests,' he exclaimed, shuffling out of the room. 'He little wots how near at hand they are, and what strange tidings some of them may chance to bring. Ho, ho, ho! you shall reap as you sow; there's truth in that saying. Ho, ho, ho! "The prince will hae his ain again!"'

With these words on his lips he approached the door of Sir Marcus's chamber. The old man was seated in a large armchair, propped up with cushions, before a blazing fire. His long white hair drawn back, and fastened in a queue behind, exposed his high thin forehead, while his lustreless eyes and fallen jaw showed that the hand of time was pressing heavily on him, and summoning him to conclude his career on earth.

'They're coming, cousin! they're coming!' exclaimed Lawrence.

'Who—who?' asked the old man, rousing up, but trembling violently. 'Who do you mean, Lawrence?'

'Colonel Armytage and his wife and daughter, whom you sent for, and some gentlemen learned in the law, whom you didn't send for, I ween. There'll be strange doings at Lunnasting before long, Sir Marcus. Ho, ho, ho! "The prince will hae his ain again, his ain again!"' And Lawrence, shouting and laughing, shuffled out of the room.

Meantime, Hilda had been watching the corvette and the smack. What the former was about to do still remained doubtful, but the latter continued her course till she came to an anchor close in with the mouth of the voe. A boat which Hilda recognised as belonging to Rolf Morton went out to meet her. The smack's own boat was also lowered, and several people among whom were two ladies, embarked in her.

A tall thin man stepped into Rolf's boat with the air of a sailor, and having shaken him warmly by the hand, assisted in two other gentlemen in black dresses, who showed by their movements that they were far from well accustomed to nautical adventure.

While Rolf's boat proceeded up the voe, the other pulled towards the Lunnasting landing-place. Hilda would fain have watched the proceedings of the corvette, but believing that her sister had arrived she hurried down to meet her. At first she was about to go down to the landing-place, but her courage failed, and she waited in the great hall to receive her guests. At last they entered, ushered in by Lawrence, who kept bowing and flourishing his three-cornered hat before them in a way which seemed more like mockery than respect.

Colonel Armytage approached Hilda with formal respect, but the sisters threw themselves into each other's arms, and the younger found vent for her feelings in a torrent of tears; but not a drop fell from Hilda's eye. Edda stood hesitating for a moment, and then threw her arms round her aunt's neck, and kissed her affectionately.

'Oh, may you be more happy than either of us!' was all Hilda said, as she looked at the sweet face beaming up at her.

A gentleman followed Colonel Armytage into the room. Hilda looked towards him as if to inquire who he was.

'He is Mr Boland, my legal adviser,' said the colonel. 'I thought it wiser to bring him, in case any difficulties should arise about the succession to this property.'

'What difficulties can arise?—what doubts are there?' inquired Hilda, in an agitated tone.

'Matters will be explained to you, madam, shortly,' answered Colonel Armytage, suspecting that Hilda had not heard of the discovery of her son.

He was not a man who would have attempted to prevent him from obtaining his rights, but he had not virtue enough to resist the wish that he might, after all, never appear to claim them.

The meeting between Sir Marcus Wardhill and his once favourite daughter was very painful. He scarcely aroused himself to greet her.

'You have come a long distance, daughter, and have been a long time coming,' he said, putting out his hand, and looking up coldly in her face. 'I suppose you feared the old man might die and leave his wealth elsewhere; it was that made you come, Edda?'

Mrs Armytage, with her eyes full of tears, stooped down and kissed the old man's forehead. 'Father, no—do not be so cruel as to speak thus,' she sobbed out. 'Money I have never coveted. You sent for Colonel Armytage; you desired us to accompany him, and most gladly we came; but it was to see you, and you only, dear father.'

'Ah, so I did—now I recollect,' said Sir Marcus. 'I never loved him and he never loved me, but he is a man—he has sense; he knows the world; he can rule a disorderly household. Go out, all of you. Let him come in; we have matters to arrange, and no time is to be lost. Go, go quickly!'

Colonel Armytage and Mr Boland, when summoned, hurried up to the old man's room with due alacrity. They were closeted an hour or more with Sir Marcus, and when they came out there was a look of satisfaction in the colonel's countenance which showed that he believed he had attained the object he had in view incoming to see his father-in-law. When he soon afterwards met his wife, he appeared to be in far better humour than she had long known him.

'Your father, my good wife, is a far more reasonable man than I expected to find him,' he said, taking her hand with an unusually affectionate air. 'I had few or no difficulties with him. He told me, what I have long suspected, that your sister Hilda is the victim at times of strange hallucinations, that she is eccentric always—in fact, that she is totally unable to manage this property. He has therefore, in the most sensible way, left it entirely to us, with the proviso that we make a certain allowance for your sister's maintenance. Our daughter, therefore, becomes the heiress of Lunnasting, and as such I feel has a right to make as good a match as any girl in the kingdom.

'Poor Hilda!' was all Mrs Armytage said; she was going to add, 'Poor Edda!' for she foresaw the grief and trouble prepared for her daughter.

'Why, madam, you do not look pleased at this announcement of our good fortune,' said Colonel Armytage.

'How can I, when I know that my poor sister, who has so long been mistress here, will ere long find herself almost disinherited?'

'Nonsensical idea!' said Colonel Armytage, scornfully. 'Your sister will be as happy as her nature will allow her, with her books and abstruse studies, which, by all accounts, have turned her brain, and unfitted her for every-day life. However, we will not discuss the subject. It is settled to my satisfaction, at all events. I am no longer the miserable beggar I was two hours ago. By-the-by, what has become of our tall friend who accompanied us from Aberdeen? I expected to have seen him here. He seemed to be perfectly well acquainted with the state of things here, and intimate with those two black-coated gentlemen who professed to be ministers. From the tone of their conversation, and the merry twinkle in their eyes, I rather suspected them, to say the truth.'

'A fine-looking old gentlemen came off to receive them,' said Mrs Armytage. 'He is a resident of the island. I know no more.'

'It matters not; I only hope that we shall not have to encounter that tall, red-haired young man again,' observed the colonel. 'His manner to me was most offensive; he is a sailor, I feel sure, by the way he walked the deck. He recognized the sloop-of-war we saw in the offing; but when I asked her name he pretended not to hear my question; and the look he gave me, as he turned round, prevented me from again asking it. I wonder, though, what has become of her! Some of the people on board the smack seemed to think that she might anchor in the Sound near here. What is the name given to it?'

'Eastling Sound,' answered Mrs Armytage; 'we can have a perfect view of it from the eastern tower, if you like to go there.'

When Colonel and Mrs Armytage reached the tower, they found their daughter already there, attended by Lawrence Brindister, who had placed himself before her, that she might rest a telescope on his shoulder to look at the corvette, which was gliding gracefully down Eastling Sound, and shortening sail preparatory to coming to an anchor. Edda had not heard her parents' approach.

'Yonder seems truly a brave and gallant ship, sweet cousin mine,' said Lawrence. Can you guess her name, or whence she comes?'

'Yes, yes—it is the "Scorpion!"' she exclaimed.

'And what is there wonderful in the "Scorpion," fair coz?' asked Lawrence.

'Do not you know, cousin Lawrence, that she is commanded by a very brave officer, Captain Ronald Morton?' said Edda.

'That is fortunate, indeed,' exclaimed Lawrence, turning round suddenly, and encountering Colonel Armytage's gaze fixed on him.

'Why is it fortunate?' asked the colonel.

'Because he is, I opine, a very brave officer, as your daughter says, good sir,' answered Lawrence. And away he shuffled down the steps.

There was a pause of some duration.

'Remember, Edda,' said her father, at last, 'if your conjecture is right, and yonder vessel is commanded by Captain Morton, should he venture here, I command you to have no communication with him. He is a mere adventurer; you are heiress of Lunnasting, and the lands appertaining to it. Listen, girl! you will drive me mad if you look so melancholy, instead of rejoicing at your good fortune.'

Hilda had been watching the corvette from her own tower,

and seeing a boat leave the ship and approach the landing-place, she descended to the hall to learn who the strangers were, and to receive them, should they visit the castle. A note was soon afterwards put into her hands, informing her that two old acquaintances had arrived, and craved leave to see her.

She desired that they might be admitted, and in a short time the stout, well-knit figure of Pedro Alvarez was seen entering the hall, while by his side glided the attenuated form of the priest, Father Mendez.

Changed as they were by years, Hilda knew them at once. She trembled violently, and it was with difficulty she could rise to receive them.

'You are welcome, old friends,' she exclaimed; 'but speak —tell me by what wonderful means have you reached Lunnasting once more? What event do you come to announce?'

'The father, lady, is a more fitting person than I am to tell you,' answered Pedro Alvarez. 'He has more command of the language necessary to convey to you the information we possess.'

Hilda again started from the chair into which she had sunk, and seizing the priest's arm, she exclaimed, 'Speak without delay! You come to tell me of my son: yes, is it not so? He is found! Speak—speak! where is he? Why did you not bring him? Oh! do not mock me!'

'Lady, we come not to mock you,' said the priest, quietly. 'You speak of your son; he is, we believe, alive, and more, that he can be found.'

Hilda clasped her hands in speechless eagerness, fixing her eyes intently on the countenance of the priest.

'He can be found, I say; but at once to save you from disappointment, I must tell you that he is not here. By a wonderful chain of circumstances, not only has his life been preserved, but we can, without doubt, prove his identity to satisfy the most rigid demands of a court of law.'

The priest's slow mode of speaking did not at all satisfy poor Hilda's eagerness. She turned to his companion,

'Tell, Pedro Alvarez, where is he?' she exclaimed. 'I care not now for the means by which he has been preserved. Where can I find him? When can I see him? You swore to search for him. Did you fulfil your promise? Oh! bring him to me, if you have found him.'

'Lady, I did fulfil my promise most faithfully, and to the service of your son I have devoted my life. It may be weeks or months before you can see him, but I have every reason to hope that he is safe at this moment in France. But the means were afforded me of coming here, and, moreover, of producing all the existing witnesses necessary to prove the legality of his birth in the first place, his identity in the second, and his right, if not to the castle and estates of Lunnasting, to the rank which his father would have held of Marquis de Medea, and the valuable property attached to it.'

The hapless mother heaved a deep sigh.

'All that I doubt not; but could you not have brought him to me?' she gasped out, as she sunk once more back in her seat.

It was some time before either she or her visitors again spoke. At last Father Mendez saw that it would be advantageous to her to break the silence.

'Donna Hilda, I crave your pardon,' he said, 'but I have been charged with a request from the captain of yonder ship, one who owns himself to be deeply indebted to you in his youth, Ronald Morton. It is, that you will give shelter to an old man, who has long been ill, and his daughter, who has accompanied him. I will not tell you the old man's name; but he feels that he has much to ask you to forgive, ere he can die in peace. He has not many days to live, so you will not have long to exercise your mercy.'

Hilda scarcely appeared to comprehend the last remarks.

'Yes, yes; whatever you desire, most readily do I grant,' she answered. 'An old man, you say? If he thinks that he can die in peace on shore, let him come here and finish his remaining days.'

It was some time before Hilda was sufficiently tranquillized to listen to the details which Pedro Alvarez had to give her of the recapture of her son from the pirate Tacon, the causes of his flight from Europe, which prevented him from bringing Hernan back to Shetland, and his ultimate meeting with Tacon and Father Mendez, and of the aid which Ronald Morton had promised towards the accomplishment of his object.

'He was always a noble, generous boy!' she exclaimed, warmly; but she was little aware of the sacrifice Ronald was prepared to make to assist his rival, and one who had shown such bitter animosity towards him in obtaining his rights.

By this time the 'Scorpion's' boat returned under charge of Lieutenant Glover, with the Marquis de Medea, as Don Josef de Villavicencio had hitherto been called, and his daughter Julia. She, poor girl, had at first been astounded with the information that another person intervened between the title and estates her father had held, and that he had no right to them; but latterly, in consequence of the delicate endeavours of Glover to console her, she had become much more reconciled to her lot.

Whatever were the motives which influenced him, Father Mendez, armed with the information he had gained from Tacon, so worked either on the fears or better feelings of the dying marquis, that he professed himself ready to confess his crime, and to do his utmost to right the wronged.

Hilda, still ignorant of who he was, had him conveyed to one of the best chambers in the castle, and directed that all his wants should be attended to, while another room near his was prepared for Donna Julia.

Ronald Morton was of course not aware of the arrival of Edda Armytage and her parents; and feeling that it might be an intrusion, under the circumstances, to present himself before Hilda on that day, he directed Glover to say that he hoped to pay his respects in person on the following morning, and then hastened on towards his father's house.

CHAPTER XXXVII.

RONALD VISITS LUNNASTING CASTLE.—LEGAL VISITORS ARRIVE AT LUNNASTING.—THE RIGHTFUL HEIR DISCOVERED.—THE PRINCE HAS GOT HIS AIN AGAIN.

ITH a heart agitated by a variety of conflicting feelings, Ronald Morton, the day after the 'Scorpion' reached Eastling Sound, approached Lunnasting Castle. He was followed at a distance by his father and the three gentlemen who had arrived by the smack from Aberdeen. His great wish was that he might first meet Edda, and break to her the discoveries which had been made, and which it was now necessary to disclose. 'Should I be unable to meet her, I will endeavour to see the Lady Hilda by herself, and it will soften the blow, when I am able to remind her that her son will undoubtedly succeed in establishing his claim to his father's inheritance.' This thought was uppermost in Ronald's mind, as he opened the well-known wicket and was crossing the court-yard to enter the hall.

At that moment Colonel Armytage was sallying out to inspect the domain which he hoped soon would be his own. He stopped, and looking with an angry frown on his frown at Ronald, said, 'Captain Morton, it will prevent mistakes in future, if I at once tell you that I cannot allow your visits to this house, especially if paid, as I have reason to suppose, for the sake of seeing my daughter. While on service I was always ready to treat you as an equal in rank, but you must remember that your birth does not entitle you to associate on the same terms with the owners of Lunnasting; and as, at the express wish of Sir Marcus Wardhill, I am henceforth to be master here, I must at once, to save unpleasantness for the future, forbid you the castle.'

Morton bowed; though he bit his lip at the insult offered him, there was a smile in his eye which showed that he was not very much moved by the colonel's behaviour.

'I will not dispute the matter with you now, sir,' he answered, calmly. 'But I have a matter of importance on which to speak with the Lady Hilda, and unless she refuses to see me, I feel myself bound to communicate with her.'

Colonel Armytage, notwithstanding all Morton could say, was determined that he should not enter. He was still holding out against what Ronald was urging, when Rolf Morton and his friends entered the court-yard.

'Colonel Armytage, these gentlemen have come expressly to see Sir Marcus Wardhill and his daughter, the Lady Hilda,' said Ronald firmly. 'I must introduce them. My former captain and friend, Lord Claymore; Mr Frazer and Mr Scott, two eminent lawyers from Scotland; and my father, whom you have heard of as Mr Rolf Morton.'

Colonel Armytage looked confused.

'Of course, my lord and gentlemen, if you desire to see Sir Marcus Wardhill, I cannot prevent you. I will lead the way and prepare him for your visit.'

Scarcely had Colonel Armytage disappeared than another party entered the court-yard. In the centre walked the worthy Captain Tacon, who was examining the building with much curiosity, and looking about him with a swaggering air of independence. He was guarded on either side by Job Truefitt and young Doull, who showed by their looks that they were not at all likely to allow him to escape from want of watchfulness. Directly after them came the elder Doull and Archy

Eagleshay. Ronald directed them to wait in the hall while he went to look for Pedro Alvarez and Father Mendez. During his absence another person arrived, who was warmly greeted by Lord Claymore and the two lawyers as Mr Cameron, the Sheriff-Substitute for Shetland.

In a few minutes Colonel Armytage returned, and announced that Sir Marcus Wardhill was prepared to receive them.

He seemed very much astonished at the appearance of so many strangers, and probably had a presentiment of what was preparing for him.

He was, however, a man of the world; he was also an honourable man, according to his own code; he knew that nothing was to be gained by contending against authority, and much by yielding gracefully; and he also did not desire to oppose an act of justice, even though he might be the sufferer. With a proud resolution to do all that the strictest justice could require of him, he led the way to Sir Marcus's room.

Here also his daughters and granddaughter, accompanied by Pedro Alvarez and Father Mendez, were assembled, and and before they sat down two servants wheeled in, on a sofa, the old Spanish marquis, who was followed by his weeping daughter. Edda invited her to come and sit by her, but she declined, and stood holding her father's hand, while the priest stood on the other side of the sofa, every now and then stooping down to whisper into his ear.

The old man looked up and inquired why so many people were assembled; but when he saw Mr Cameron and the two lawyers he bowed his head, whispering slowly—'Some criminal to be tried, I see: let the case go on.'

'Not exactly that, Sir Marcus,' said the sheriff. 'I have been requested to attend here to investigate two important cases, in both of which Lord Claymore, who is known to you, has taken much interest. At his request, my two learned friends, Mr Scott and Mr Frazer, have come from Edinburgh to assist us in our investigations; but it depends on circumstances whether the cases are or are not carried into a court of law, and thus made public. With which shall we proceed first, my lord?'

'By all means with that relating to the son of a lady present—the wife of a Spanish officer, Don Hernan Escalante,' said Lord Claymore. 'We all must feel how anxious she must be to know that the interests of her child have been secured.'

It is not necessary to describe all the examinations which took place. Hilda's marriage with Don Hernan was proved by three surviving witnesses—Father Mendez, Pedro Alvarez, and Rolf Morton, though the loss of the certificate, one of the lawyers was of opinion, might prove a difficulty in a Spanish court.

'It is one a few hundred dollars may get over,' observed Pedro Alvarez, with a shrug of his shoulders.

The birth of the child, and its abduction by strangers, was proved with equal ease. And now Captain Tacon was led forward, and in pure Castilian, which Pedro Alvarez translated, confessed that he was the person who carried off the young Hernan.

'But there, there is the man who instigated me to commit the deed!' he exclaimed, pointing to the marquis, who lay on the sofa with his eyes half closed.

'Yes, I confess my crime,' said the old man, slowly raising himself up. 'I have enjoyed but little happiness since. My palaces have been burnt down, and my plate and jewels carried off by the French. May the rightful owner enjoy what remains. I have done what my father confessor directed. I am prepared for the grave which yawns to receive me, and a few hundred dollars which my daughter possesses will enable her to enter a convent, and there forget my sorrow and shame.'

Pedro Alvarez then described his recovery of young Hernan, and his career up to the moment he parted from him.

'I can without difficulty communicate with friends in France, who will inform him of what has occurred, and enable him to come here without delay,' he added 'Thence he can go to Spain, and take possession of his estates.'

What the marquis had said was translated to Sir Marcus. The number of people collected, and the discussions taking place, had had the effect of rousing him up, and his intellect seemed as bright and acute as ever.

'Then, Colonel Armytage, since a male heir is found for Lunnasting, I fear that I must alter the will which I lately made in your favour.'

'You may save yourself that trouble, Sir Marcus,' said the sheriff, somewhat sternly. 'There is another claimant to the Lunnasting property. I would save your daughters from the pain of listening to the investigation of the case which must now be held. They will, however, perhaps wish to see that justice is done to all parties, and they may be assured that it is with the greatest unwillingness that I shall say anything which may wound their feelings.'

Mrs Armytage thanked the sheriff, and expressed her wish to remain; but Hilda did not speak. She had sat like a statue with her hands clasped during the examination of the witnesses, once only casting a look of reproach at the marquis, when he confessed that he had instigated Tacon to carry off her son. Still she sat in the same position, lost in thought, and utterly regardless of everything around.

'Sir Marcus Wardhill,' said the sheriff, 'as you well know, the heir to these estates was Bertram Brindister. He was first in succession before your wife, but unaccountably disappeared, and was supposed to have been washed away by the sea. Two witnesses have now appeared, who can prove that he was designedly carried off by a noted smuggler and outlaw, Halled Yell by name, and by themselves. They are both present. All three men and the child were rescued from a wreck by Captain Andrew Scarsdale, who brought up the boy under the name of Rolf Morton. You knew his father. There stands the present Bertram Brindister, the real Lord of Lunnasting; is he not like his father?'

Sir Marcus looked up furtively at Rolf Morton, who stood with a calm countenance, expressive of more pain than triumph, directly in front of him.

'Yes, yes, he is very like,' he answered, and then conquering any fear he might have felt, he added—' But gentlemen, assertions are not proofs. This latter tale is too clumsy an imitation of the first we have just heard not to make a man of sense discredit it. Let us hear what the men have to say.'

On this the two old men, Doull and Eagleshay, stepped forward and described their having carried off a child from Whalsey at the very time the boy, Bertram Brindister, was missed, and all the events which followed, but they could neither of them tell the exact date of the occurrence.

'I thought so,' said Sir Marcus, calmly. 'The man I see before me may be Bertram Brindister, but it cannot be proved; nor can, as far as I can see, the instigator of the crime be discovered, if, as I say, there is truth in the story, which I am inclined to doubt. An important link is missing, and your case, gentlemen, falls to the ground.'

'But the link is found, and truth is triumphant. "The prince will hae his ain again! The prince will hae his ain again!"' exclaimed Lawrence Brindister, starting up and flourishing two papers in his hands, while he skipped about the room, in doubt to whom he should deliver them. This is your marriage certificate, cousin Hilda, and I have been a faithful guardian of it; and this, Mr Sheriff, is the link you require to prove that honest Rolf Morton is really Bertram Brindister, and rightful Lord of Lunnasting, and that yonder old man, who has tyrannized over me, and insulted me and wronged me in every way, is an impostor; and that he instigated the villain Yell to abduct the heir that the inheritance might be his. See, it is the paper signed by Yell, and those other two men, and delivered to honest Andrew Scarsdale. Many a long year have I kept it. You all have heard that it was locked up in Captain Scarsdale's chest, which, guided by a hand more potent than that of man, came floating by the northern end of Whalsey, and was drawn on shore by me and my old dog, Surly Grind. In a cave I had hard by, I kept the chest and its contents, but months passed away before I examined them. When I did, I saw well that nothing would be gained by publishing them. The rightful heir was away, and with his means how could he hope to contend with the wily and astute Sir Marcus Wardhill? So I did what many a wiser man might not have done, I bided my time. Maybe, Sir Marcus, you have thought me at times a greater fool than I was; but which is the greatest fool of the two—the man who obeys, or he who sets Heaven at defiance? Once, who could compete with me at school or college? and what might I not have been had you not, when I was struck down by illness, taken advantage of my weakness, and by sending me to a madhouse, confirmed my malady; but fool as you called me, I can see that Heaven's retributive justice has chastised you through life. Me you got into your power on the ground that I was insane, and the mind of the daughter, in whom you took such pride, often totters on its throne; her son was carried off, as was the rightful heir, and for long weary years has she waited his return, while the daughter you loved has been a stranger to your sight; and now deprived of fortune, dishonoured, and disgraced, you are sinking unregretted into the grave.'

'Oh spare him! spare him!' cried Edda, gliding forward and taking the old man's hand, for neither her mother nor Hilda could speak. 'Let his grey hairs, cousin Lawrence, be his protection.'

The old man's head had fallen on his bosom. He was breathing with difficulty, but she did not perceive it.

Ronald sprang to her side. 'For your sake Edda, no one belonging to you shall suffer; my generous father promised me this. Be mine. The only objection Colonel Armytage urged against me no longer exists. Let us afford a home to those whom it will be our duty to cherish and console.'

Colonel Armytage, who had through all the proceedings maintained as calm and dignified a deportment as he could command, overheard the words, and stepping forward said, 'Captain Morton, or I should rather say, Captain Brindister— for I fully believe that name is yours—you have acted nobly and generously; you have taught me to think better of the world than I was inclined to do. My daughter's hand is your's as her heart is already, and may she prove as good a wife to you as her mother has to me, and may her lot be far happier. I will use all my influence to persuade Sir Marcus not to oppose your father's claims, and I trust that the act he so long ago committed may not be bruited abroad to bring discredit on the family.'

'After all, colonel, you are a wiser man than I took you for,' said Lawrence, resuming again his former and usual extravagant manner. 'Blow the wind as it may, you always sail before it, and you keep your hat ready to bow to the rising star. That's the way of the world, and what can a poor fool like me do but approve it. But what care I now how the world wags! —'The prince has got his ain again—his ain again!' Said I not the truth when I sang that song!'

CHAPTER XXXVIII.

THE PRIEST GOES IN SEARCH OF HERNAN.—THE 'SCORPION' ENGAGES A FRENCH SHIP.—THE VICTOR'S RETURN.

A S the 'Scorpion' required her rigging set up, Ronald had a good excuse for remaining in Eastling Sound longer than he might otherwise have done. He came on shore every day; and his first lieutenant, Mr Glover, was wonderfully fertile in excuses for coming also, as soon as the duties of the ship would allow him. It was remarked that when he came Donna Julia took the opportunity of leaving her father's room, except when he went in to visit the old man. At last Ronald taxed him with the singularity of his proceedings.

'The fact is, Captain Morton, that she is a sweetly pretty, good girl,' he answered; 'and as, instead of being an heiress and a marchioness, she is likely to be penniless, I've made up my mind to splice her, if she will have me, as I couldn't otherwise look after her properly when her old father slips his cable, which he may do any day.'

Ronald advised him to make his offer forthwith, which he did, and was without hesitation accepted. The next day the old marquis died, and was buried, with due ceremony, within the walls of the old Roman Catholic chapel in which Hilda's unfortunate marriage took place.

Lord Claymore was so much interested in Hilda that he did not immediately take his departure from Whalsey.

Pedro Alvarez had at once written to France, enclosing a letter to Hernan, telling him of the wonderful change in his fortunes. It was evident, however, that he was more likely to be discovered if some one could go over to look for him. Father Mendez volunteered to go.

Lord Claymore and Rolf supplied the father with ample funds, and he forthwith started on his journey.

It was thought prudent to keep the worthy Tacon a prisoner, in case he might be required as a witness, should other claimants arise to oppose Hernan; but as he was well fed and amply supplied with whisky, he did not complain of his fate.

At length the 'Scorpion' was ready for sea. The sails were loosed, and all was in readiness to weigh. Ronald was still on shore, and had accompanied Edda to the summit of the eastern tower, the upper room in which she had appropriated to herself. As they stood together on the summit, his glance, as he looked seaward, fell on a sail just rising above the horizon. He watched her narrowly, and pronounced that she was drawing nearer.

'Edda, farewell, dearest!' he exclaimed. 'I must hasten on board, and sail in chase of yonder vessel. I received notice this morning from Lerwick that several merchantmen have been chased by a sloop-of-war, and some expected have not made their appearance, which it is supposed she may have captured. I must not delay a moment. Who knows but what I may bring her back in triumph!'

He hastened down to his boat, and as fast the crew could bend their backs to the oars, pulled on board the corvette. The anchor was tripped, and under all sail she stood away in chase of the stranger.

Edda remained on the top of the tower watching the receding ship. She was soon joined by Donna Julia. Poor girl! her lover too had gone away, and she was equally anxious with Edda.

They were not long in private, for they were soon joined by Lord Claymore and Rolf Morton; Pedro Alvarez and other inmates of the castle followed.

The stranger, a corvette, was standing in towards Whalsey close hauled on the starboard tack, and when the 'Scorpion' rounded the island and showed herself, she continued on the same course.

'That fellow by the cut of his canvas is a Frenchman,' observed Lord Claymore; 'what think you, Captain Alvarez?'

'No doubt about it,' answered Pedro Alvarez. 'But I know of no French ship in these seas.'

'See—see! there goes up the French flag!' exclaimed Lord Claymore; 'she is going about to, as she does not wish to commence the fight while the "Scorpion" has the weather-gauge. A brave fellow commands that craft; he has no intention, at all events, of avoiding an engagement.'

Both vessels were now seen standing away from the land, the 'Scorpion' steering both so as most speedily to come up with the enemy, and at the same time to keep the advantage of the wind which she possessed, while the other was manœuvring to avoid a close engagement till she had gained the weather-gauge.

'Ronald will not let him do that,' cried Rolf. 'See, the "Scorpion" is gaining on her. She has got her within range of her guns. There goes the first shot.'

As he spoke, a puff of smoke was seen to proceed from the bows of the English ship, and the sound of the gun struck faintly on their ears. Another and another followed as soon as they could be brought to bear.

As the 'Scorpion' was coming up on the quarter of the French ship, the latter could not at first discharge her broadside guns with any effect, but as her enemy got more abeam of her she too opened fire, and shot after shot was exchanged in rapid succession.

The interest of all the spectators became intense, though exhibited in different ways. Lord Claymore was all excitement and animation, evidently wishing himself on board the 'Scorpion.'

Rolf now waved his hand—now addressed his son—now cheered as the 'Scorpion' delivered an effective broadside.

The colonel stood as if snuffing up the smoke of battle, and coolly criticizing the manœuvres of the combatants.

The interests of Pedro Alvarez seemed now to side with the flag of France, under which he had so long fought, now with the 'Scorpion,' commanded by his friend. Lawrence kept moving about the platform rubbing his hands and cheering loudly every time a broadside was delivered.

'Well done, 'Scorpion'!' 'Bravo, my boy!' shouted Lord Claymore and Rolf, in concert, as the Frenchman's foretop-mast went over the side.

This caused him to luff up, and the 'Scropion,' shooting ahead, poured a raking broadside into his bows. On this, the Frenchman's helm was put to starboard, by which he was able to fire his hitherto disengaged starboard broadside. It had, however, the effect of bringing his head round, and now once more he stood towards the land, while the 'Scorpion' ran on in an opposite direction. It was but for a minute, she also quickly came about and ranged up on the enemy's weather beam, pouring in the whole of her larboard broadside.

As the smoke cleared away, the Frenchman was seen with her foremast and main-top-mast gone, while the 'Scorpion' did not appear to have lost a spar.

'Hurrah, my brave Ronald! the day is yours,' shouted Rolf. 'It is but a matter of time.'

Still the Frenchman fired on, but the wreck of his masts seemed to impede the working of his foremost guns. It appeared as if the 'Scorpion' was about again to pass ahead, when the two ships met, and lay locked together in a deadly embrace. The guns continued to roar as before, and clouds of smoke enveloped the combatants. It was a period of awful suspense —no one on the platform spoke. The firing ceased; the canopy of smoke disappeared. The two flags of England and France flew out as before from the peaks of the two ships.

'Morton has boarded the Frenchman,' cried Lord Claymore at length. 'No doubt now as to the result. The Frenchmen fight bravely though. At them again, my boys! Hurrah!—hurrah! hurrah! hurrah!' shouted Rolf. 'Down comes the Frenchmen's flag.'

The fight was over, the 'Scorpion' was the victor.

The two ships rapidly approached, steering for the west end of Eastling Island, and when at the entrance of the sound, and not far from the castle, they both came to an anchor. A boat was seen to be lowered from the 'Scorpion,' and with rapid strokes to approach the castle. With what eagerness did Edda watch her till she could distinguish the people on board. She uttered a cry of joy as she saw Ronald himself steering the boat. At the same time she perceived a person stretched at his length in the stern sheets. Poor Donna Julia almost fainted with alarm lest Glover should be the wounded man. Together they hurried down to the landing-place, where the rest of the party had already gone.

Where all this time was Hilda? She, too, had witnessed the fight. She had seen the desperate struggle, the flag of France hauled down, the ships brought to an anchor, and a wounded officer lowered into the boat. A vague, yet overpowering dread had seized her. She attempted to go down that she might meet the boat at the landing-place, but her strength failed, and she sunk back in her chair near the window, whence she could watch the boat as it glided rapidly by.

Her sister found her thus.

'Hilda, nerve yourself for a great trial,' she said, as she took her hand to lead her to the door, where Rolf Morton stood ready to conduct her down the steps.

A group was collected round a couch in the great hall. As Hilda entered, they opened out, and a young man in the naval uniform of France was seen extended upon it. Pedro Alvarez stood by him, holding one hand, while the surgeon of the 'Scorpion' was feeling the wrist of the other, and administering a restorative. Hilda tottered forward.

'Who is that?' she asked in a hollow voice, as she gazed eagerly at the countenance of the wounded man.

'Madam,' said Pedro Alvarez, looking up, 'that is Hernan Escalante, your son.'

'Mother!' whispered the young officer, and the light returned to his eyes, which had appeared so lustreless.

'My son, my son, have I indeed found you, and thus sorely wounded!' cried Hilda, kneeling down to impress a kiss on his brow, while she cast her arms around him.

'I shall soon recover now that I know I have you to live for,' he answered, in a faint voice.

'Oh, will he live! Can you cure him?' she exclaimed, turning to the surgeon. 'Gold, any amount you can name, shall be your reward if he recovers.'

'I will do my best, madam,' said the surgeon, bowing; 'he is young and strong, and I have seen those who have received worse hurts survive.'

Young Hernan was by Hilda's directions carried to her room. Day and night she watched over him, jealous of the interference of all others.

Though he long hung between life and death, her constant care was rewarded, and the surgeon pronounced him at length out of danger. He remained, however, too weak to be moved.

The only person besides the surgeon whom Hilda would allow to come near him was the faithful pastor of Lunnasting. He knew well how to minister to a soul diseased; and Hilda herself, while listening to the words of Truth which were addressed to her son, had her own mind enlightened, and was brought to trust to the loving mercy of Him who had restored to her her long-lost child. Hernan, too, awakened to a sense of the sinfulness of the designs which his own evil passions had induced him to entertain, sought for pardon through the only means by which pardon can be obtained.

When at length he rose from his sick bed he was truly an altered man, and Pedro Alvarez acknowledged that he loved him better than ever, although a Protestant minister had been the means of his reformation.

Sir Marcus Wardhill died shortly after, in a state of utter imbecility, without recognising his grandson.

On her father's death Hilda accompanied her son to Spain, where Hernan succeeded in establishing his rights to his paternal estates. He had, however, never entirely recovered from his wounds, and in two years Hilda had to endure the grief of seeing him die in her arms; but she bore it with fortitude, and, invited by her loving relatives at Lunnasting, returned to spend the evening of her days in Shetland.

Glover having married Donna Julia, inherited Hernan's estates in Spain. Their children, brought up partly in the Protestant faith, became the ancestors of those who have since fought the battle for the truth in that long-benighted land.

Pedro Alvarez not being perfectly satisfied that the officers of the Inquisition, though itself abolished, might not by some means get hold of him, continued a welcome inmate to the end of his days at Lunnasting Castle, the constant companion of Lawrence Brindister, who, on the death of Sir Marcus recovered his intellect so far that he was looked upon by Ronald's large family of young cousins as a most agreeable and amusing old gentleman, the chief promoter of every sort of pastime and amusement in which they were indulged.

For several years a gaunt old beggar might be seen at the corner of one of the streets of Cadiz, surpassing his mendicant brethren in the loudness of his complaints and the squalor of the rags which covered him; and one day Glover, passing by, recognized in him his quondam acquaintance, the ex-pirate, Tacon.

Father Mendez was never again heard of, nor was any surmise offered as to what had become of him.

As Admiral Sir Ronald Brindister might object to have more of his private history brought to light, we must bring our tale to a conclusion.

THE END.

www.ingramcontent.com/pod-product-compliance
Lightning Source LLC
Chambersburg PA
CBHW022134300426
44115CB00006B/185